Reading Development and Difficulties

D1329412

David A. Kilpatrick · R. Malatesha Joshi ·
Richard K. Wagner
Editors

Reading Development and Difficulties

Bridging the Gap Between Research and Practice

 Springer

Editors
David A. Kilpatrick
State University of New York
College at Cortland
Cortland, NY, USA

R. Malatesha Joshi
College of Education
and Human Development
Texas A&M University
College Station, TX, USA

Richard K. Wagner
Department of Psychology
Florida State University
Florida Center for Reading Research
Tallahassee, FL, USA

ISBN 978-3-030-26552-6   ISBN 978-3-030-26550-2   (eBook)
https://doi.org/10.1007/978-3-030-26550-2

This Springer imprint is published by the registered company Springer Nature Switzerland AG
The registered company address is: Gewerbestrasse 11, 6330 Cham, Switzerland

Foreword by Sir Jim Rose

Reconciling the realities of the classroom with sound evidence from research to achieve a high-quality curriculum, one that is coherent from the standpoint of the learner and manageable by knowledgeable practitioners, is no small challenge. This volume rises to that challenge admirably.

All of its authors are reading researchers and long-time members of an international organization called the Society for the Scientific Study of Reading. That organization represents dozens of countries and cuts across multiple disciplines such as education, special education, experimental psychology, linguistics, speech pathology, literacy, neuroscience, and medicine.

The chapters in this volume cover findings from a wide range of the many subdisciplines within the scientific enterprise of reading research. Educational professionals who read this volume will encounter a broad sweep of important topics relevant to their work. These chapters will enhance the knowledge base of those in our schools who are charged, on one level or another, with the lofty task of assuring that children have the best possible opportunities to acquire the skill of reading.

Robust evidence in this domain has continued to grow apace; hence, we are far better informed than ever before as to what it takes to achieve a strong command of the spoken and written word—that is to say—to become 'literate.' All of which is good news.

Arguably, however, we know far less about how much of this hard-won, often costly, research gets through the classroom door and contributes effectively to raising standards of literacy. Moreover, we have little convincing evidence of its impact on the quality of teacher training and on the decisions of those who make and unmake educational policy for designing the curriculum.

For schools, research evidence has to face the harsh realities of a time-bound curriculum. As the much-lamented Zig Engelmann observed: 'The most precious commodity' in managing the demands of the curriculum is time. 'We must treat time,' he said, 'with desperate efficiency.' Research is not immune to these realities.

It is hoped that this volume will offer an opportunity not to be missed in linking research to practice with 'desperate efficiency'.

Haslemere, England   Sir Jim Rose, CBE, FRSA, Doctor of Laws
June 2019   Formerly Her Majesty's Inspector and Director
                      of Inspection for the Office for Standards in Education, UK

                      Chair and Author of 'Independent Review of the Teaching
                                      of Early Reading: Final Report' (2006)

Foreword by Brett Miller and Peggy McCardle[1]

Reading Is Foundational—Now More than Ever

Reading is foundational, now more than ever. Learning to read opens the door to exciting new worlds, both real and imaginary, and provides the necessary skills to advance one's knowledge and skills in the literate arts, math, social studies, science, and other domains in primary and secondary school and continued educational and training opportunities as an adult. Literacy, particularly reading skills, also provides access to and facilitates meaningful and sustained engagement with critical societal systems and infrastructures such as health care, education for individuals and their dependents, and broader civic engagement (Kutner, Greenberg, Jin, & Paulsen, 2006; OECD, 2016; US Department of Education, National Center for Education Statistics, 2013). In our technology-infused environments, reading enables a critical means of staying in touch with friends and family via texting and social media, access to virtually unlimited content on the Internet, and the ability to accomplish simple everyday tasks such as navigating through space via GPS-enabled maps. Reading and access to print-related media is a necessity in today's society.

Despite the critical importance of reading as a vehicle for learning in literate societies, too many children and adults do not possess basic reading skills necessary to function fully in today's society (e.g., NCES, 2018; OECD, 2016). The corresponding challenge is particularly salient for individuals from historically under-represented and underserved groups (e.g., NCES, 2018). Such individuals may lack adequate oral language skills in English or their home language at school entry (Fernald, Marchman, & Weisleder, 2013; Garcia, 2015; Hart & Risley, 2003), experience higher rates of poverty, and have reduced access to high quality, evidence-based reading instruction in primary or secondary grades. Addressing the needs of individuals with learning disabilities as well as those who display similar

---

[1] The opinions and assertions presented in the introduction are those of the authors and do not purport to represent those of the Eunice Kennedy Shriver National Institute of Child Health and Human Development, US National Institutes of Health, US Department of Health and Human Services.

difficulties, who are found across the full range of social and ethnic strata, necessitates incorporating system-wide approaches such as universal screening for oral language and reading difficulties. For example, screening tools are needed that are sensitive to the needs of an increasingly diverse student population with varying degrees of oral and reading proficiency in their home language and the language of instruction, and for those who speak non-standard dialects (Gilbert, Compton, & Fuchs, 2012; Jenkins, Hudson, & Johnson, 2007; Washington & Craig, 2004; Washington & Lee James, 2019). The value of access to evidence-based early intervention services of appropriate intensity and duration is paramount, especially for English learners, language minority students, and dialect speakers (Hall, Steinle, & Vaughn, 2019; Washington, Branum-Martin, Lee-James, & Sun, 2019).

Although the origins of challenges with literacy are diverse, the resulting limitations can have profound current and future impacts on health, economic, and social well-being for those affected and their families (e.g., Kutner et al., 2006; National Research Council, 2012; OECD, 2016). To address these limitations, higher literacy performance will be needed both for individuals and at population levels, to lift the overall health and wellness of all. Potential lifelong challenges with reading and their sequelae make even more crucial the need to translate what is known from research into effective practice. We must enable both systemic and systematic incorporation of prevention-based approaches to reading development, and broader literacy instruction at all levels—prekindergarten through grade 12 systems in the USA and in equivalent primary and secondary systems internationally. Correspondingly, we must broker enhanced connections between the research and practice communities, enhancing feedback loops from practitioners on existing and anticipated needs. That is, we must develop and sustain meaningful partnerships between researchers and educators.

This volume, through its various chapters, takes a step forward in building this partnership by sharing information, some of which is an important background to the deeper understanding of the development of reading (such as the chapter on neurobiology) and its possible etiologies (e.g., the chapter on behavior genetics). Several chapters have direct practical applications. The chapters on the nature of reading development provide solid up-to-date information on the nuts and bolts of reading development that all practitioners need to know, and other chapters take this further with its application through assessment and intervention. To understand the combined information provided in these chapters is to understand why reading instruction must be systematic and explicit. The partnership we seek has begun to be developed, but must be strengthened and broadened—it must expand. In this volume, the authors take a major step toward doing exactly this.

Brett Miller, Ph.D.
Eunice Kennedy Shriver National Institute
of Child Health and Human Development
Bethesda, MD, USA

Peggy McCardle, Ph.D., MPH
Peggy McCardle Consulting, LLC; Haskins
Laboratories, Tarpon Springs, FL, USA

References

Fernald, A., Marchman, V., Weisleder, A. (2013). SES differences in language processing skill and vocabulary are evident at 18 months. *Developmental Science, 16*(2), 234–248.

Garcia, E. (2015). *Inequalities at the starting gate. Cognitive and noncognitive skills gap between 2010 and 2011 kindergarten classmates.* Washington, DC: Economic Policy Institute.

Gilbert, J., Compton, D., Fuchs, D. (2012). Early screening for risk of reading disabilities: Recommendations for a four-step screening process. *Assessment for Effective Intervention, 38*(1), 6–14.

Hall, C., Steinle, P., Vaughn, S. (2019). Reading instruction for English learners with learning disabilities: What do we already know and what do we need to learn? *New Directions for Child and Adolescent Development, 166,* 145–189.

Hart, B., & Risley, T. R. (2003). The early catastrophe: The 30 million word gap by age 3. *American Educator, Spring*, 4–9.

Jenkins, J. R., Hudson, R. F., Johnson, E. S. (2007). Screening for at-risk readers in a response to intervention framework. *School Psychology Review, 36*, 582–600.

Kutner, M., Greenberg, E., Jin, Y., Paulsen, C. (2006). *The health literacy of America's adults: Results from the 2003 National Assessment of Adult Literacy (NCES 2006–483).* U.S. Department of Education. Washington, DC: National Center for Education Statistics.

National Center for Education Statistics (NCES). (2018). *NAEP Reading Report Card.* Washington, DC: Institute of Education Sciences, U.S. Department of Education. Retrieved from https://www.nationsreportcard.gov/reading_2017?grade=4

National Research Council. (2012). Improving adult literacy instruction: Options for practice and research. Washington, DC: The National Academies Press. https://doi.org/10.17226/13242

OECD. (2016). *Skills matter: Further results from the survey of adult skills.* OECD Skills Studies, Paris: OECD Publishing. https://doi.org/10.1787/9789264258051-en

U.S. Department of Education, National Center for Education Statistics. (2013). *Literacy, numeracy, and problem solving in technology-rich environments among U.S. adults.* Washington, DC.

Washington, J. A. & Lee James, R. (2019). Intersection of race, poverty, and diagnostic accuracy: Identifying reading disabilities in African American children. In J. A. Washington, D. Compton, P. McCardle (Eds.), *Dyslexia: revisiting etiology, diagnosis, treatment, and policy.* Baltimore, MD: Paul Brookes Publishing, Inc.

Washington, J. A., Branum-Martin, L., Lee-James, R., Sun, C. (2019). Reading and language performance of low-income, African American boys in grades 1–5. *Reading and Writing Quarterly, 35*(1), 42–64.

Washington, J. A., & Craig, H. K. (2004). A language screening protocol for use with young African American children in urban settings. *American Journal of Speech-Language Pathology, 13*(4), 329–340.

Contents

Editors and Contributors

About the Editors

David A. Kilpatrick, Ph.D. is Professor of Psychology at the State University of New York College at Cortland. He has been teaching courses on learning disabilities for more than 20 years. Dr. Kilpatrick is also a New York State certified school psychologist and has conducted hundreds of evaluations of students with learning disabilities. He received his doctorate in psychology from Syracuse University. Dr. Kilpatrick is the author of *Essentials of Assessing, Preventing, and Overcoming Reading Difficulties* (Wiley & Sons, 2015) and *Equipped for Reading Success* (Casey & Kirsch, 2016).

R. Malatesha Joshi, Ph.D. is Professor of Reading/Language Arts Education, ESL, and Educational Psychology at Texas A&M. He is the Editor of *Reading and Writing: An Interdisciplinary Journal*, co-author with P. G. Aaron and D. Quatroche of *Becoming a Professional Reading Teacher* (Brookes, 2008), and the Series Editor of Springer's *Literacy Studies: Perspectives from Cognitive Neurosciences, Linguistics, Psychology, and Education*.

Richard K. Wagner, Ph.D. is Robert O. Lawton Distinguished Professor of Psychology and W. Russell and Eugenia Morcom Chair, Department of Psychology, Florida State University and the Associate Director, Florida Center for Reading Research. He is the author or co-author of more than 100 scientific research articles on reading and author or editor of several books. Dr. Wagner's research is focused on the normal acquisition of reading and dyslexia. His body of work has furthered the understanding of the nature of phonological processing in relation to both learning to read and to the development of reading disability or dyslexia. His public service in the field of literacy has included appointment as Chair of the National Institute for the Literacy Advisory Board, member of the study section for reading and writing of the US Department of Education's Institute of Education Sciences, and principal investigator of the Learning Disability Research Center. Dr. Wagner is a co-author of the *Comprehensive Test of Phonological Processing—Second Edition* (CTOPP-2) and the *Test of Word Reading Efficiency—Second Edition* (TOWRE-2). In 2012, Dr. Wagner and his colleague Joseph Torgesen, Ph.D., were co-recipients of the Distinguished Scientific Contributions Award from the Society for the Scientific Study of Reading.

Contributors

Donald J. Bolger, Ph.D. is an Associate Professor at the University of Maryland in the Department of Human Development and Quantitative Methodology where he directs the Laboratory for the Neurodevelopment of Reading and Langauge. For over 20 years, Dr. Bolger has studied reading and language achievement with typically developing children as well as those with learning disabilities including dyslexia and autism spectrum disorder using behavioral and functional neuroimaging methods. Dr. Bolger has a Ph.D. in Cognitive Neuroscience from the University of Pittsburgh's Learning Research and Development Center.

Brian Byrne, Ph.D. is Emeritus Professor of Psychology, University of New England, Armidale, Australia. His Ph.D. is from McMaster University, Canada. His research has focused on literacy and language development, most recently as part of an international group that has recruited school-aged twins in four countries to identify genetic and environmental influences on growth in literacy and numeracy. He is a member of the Australian Research Council Centre of Excellence in Cognition and its Disorders and of the National Health and Medical Research Council Centre of Excellence in Twin Research.

Kate Cain, Ph.D. is Professor of Language and Literacy in the Department of Psychology at Lancaster University, UK. Her research focuses on how language skills and cognitive resources influence reading and listening comprehension development, and how weaknesses in these contribute to comprehension problems. Her books include a handbook for teachers: *Understanding and teaching reading comprehension: A Handbook* (Routledge), which is co-authored with Jane Oakhill and Carsten Elbro, and *Reading development and difficulties* (Wiley Blackwell), designed for undergraduate and masters students of literacy.

Linnea C. Ehri, Ph.D. received her doctorate in Educational Psychology from the University of California, Berkeley. She was a Professor at the University of California, Davis, before joining the Ph.D. Program in Educational Psychology at the CUNY Graduate Center as a Distinguished Professor. She has received research awards from the American Educational Research Association, the National Reading Conference, the Society for the Scientific Study of Reading, and the International Reading Association and has held elective offices in the first three of those organizations. She is a member of the Reading Hall of Fame. She served on the National

Reading Panel, which was commissioned by the US Congress to report on research-based methods of effective reading instruction, chairing the sections on phonemic awareness and phonics. She has received federal research grants from NICHD and the Office of Education. She has published over 150 papers. Her research has focused on how children learn to read and spell words, the course of development, and effective methods of instruction.

Carsten Elbro, Ph.D. is Professor of Applied Linguistics and Head of the Centre for Reading Research at the University of Copenhagen, Denmark. His research is concerned with the linguistic foundations of all aspects of reading acquisition and reading difficulties. Areas of special interest are morphological processing, aspects of word knowledge, and literacy development as a kind of verbal learning. Among his publications is a handbook for teachers: *Understanding and teaching reading comprehension: A Handbook* (Routledge), which is co-authored with Jane Oakhill and Kate Cain.

Jack M. Fletcher, Ph.D. is a Hugh Roy and Lillie Cranz Cullen Distinguished Professor and Chair, Department of Psychology at the University of Houston. For the past 40 years, Dr. Fletcher, a board-certified child neuropsychologist, has completed research on many issues related to learning disabilities and dyslexia, including definition and classification, neurobiological correlates, and intervention. Dr. Fletcher directs an NICHD-funded national learning disability research center. He was the 2003 recipient of the Samuel T. Orton award from the International Dyslexia Association, a co-recipient of the Albert J. Harris award from the International Reading Association in 2006, and a past president of the International Neuropsychological Society in 2009.

Esther Geva, Ph.D. is Professor of School and Child Clinical Psychology in the Department of Applied Psychology and Human Development at the Ontario Institute for Studies in Education (OISE), University of Toronto. Esther's research, publications, and teaching focus on typical and atypical development of L1 and L2 language and literacy skills in students coming from various bilingual, immigrant and minority backgrounds, and on cross-cultural perspectives on children's psychological problems. Esther has published numerous scholarly articles and chapters in these areas, presented her work internationally, and served on numerous advisory, policy, and review committees in Canada, USA, and Europe, concerned with literacy development in minority/L2 students, including the National Literacy Panel. Esther supervises graduate students who work with culturally and linguistically diverse children and their families in the OISE Psychology clinic. Esther's research and teaching led to the publication of a book targeting primary school and clinical psychologists: *Psychological Assessment of Culturally and Linguistically Diverse Children and Adolescents: A Practitioner's Guide* (2014; Springer; Judith Wiener, co-author), and another book targeting teachers who have L2 students in their classroom: *Key Concepts for the Language Classroom: Focus on Reading* (2015; Oxford University Press; Gloria Ramirez, co-author).

Rachel Joyner is a graduate student in the Developmental Psychology program at Florida State University under the mentorship of Dr. Rick Wagner. Her research interests include phonological processing and reading comprehension. Additionally, she has a keen interest in assessment methodology for reading-related constructs.

Poh Wee Koh, Ph.D. is an assistant professor in the Department of Teaching, Learning, and Culture at Texas A&M University. She received her doctoral degree in Developmental Psychology and Education from the University of Toronto in 2016. Her research is focused on using quantitative research methods to examine the cognitive, linguistic, and sociocultural constructs associated with the language and literacy development of majority and minority learners in different orthographies.

Joyce Y. Mak is a Ph.D. Candidate in the School and Clinical Child Psychology program at the Ontario Institute for Studies in Education (OISE), University of Toronto. Joyce has received ample training on research, assessment, and culturally sensitive intervention with children and youth coming from culturally and linguistically diverse backgrounds. Joyce's doctoral research investigates the psychosocial adjustment and acculturation of international secondary students in Canada, and how supporting intentional friendships with Canadian students can improve the adjustment and acculturation processes.

Antje Malkowski serves at the Research Coordinator in the WagnerLab. Her work includes preparing of all materials needed for testing in the schools, tester training, working closely with testers and teachers, scoring, analyzing, and data entry. Recently, Ms. Malkowski has been active in the meta-analysis of reading and listening comprehension as well as novel approaches to understanding dyslexia.

Angela Massey-Garrison is a fourth-year Ph.D. student in School and Clinical Child Psychology at the Ontario Institute for Studies in Education/University of Toronto. Her research interests include literacy development in children with a special focus on English language learners. In particular, she is interested in investigating the cognitive and linguistic factors involved in literacy acquisition in typically developing and struggling learners.

Jeremy Miciak, Ph.D. is an Assistant Research Professor in the Department of Psychology at the University of Houston and affiliated faculty with the Texas Institute for Measurement, Evaluation, and Statistics (TIMES). He conducts research around learning disabilities and learning risk, with a special emphasis on issues of identification and intervention, particularly in diverse cultural and linguistic settings. Dr. Miciak earned a doctorate in Special Education from the University of Texas at Austin. He has served as Principal Investigator and/or Co-Investigator on multiple grants funded by the National Institutes of Health and the Institute of Education Sciences.

Katharine Pace Miles, Ph.D. is an Assistant Professor in Early Childhood Education at Brooklyn College, CUNY. Dr. Miles's research interests include orthographic facilitation, sight word learning, literacy assessment of students with special needs, and literacy instruction for young children that is both developmentally appropriate and grounded in the science of reading. Dr. Miles has published several articles in peer-reviewed journals, and she has presented at national and international conferences. She proudly serves as the Academic Advisor for Reading Rescue, an intervention based on the science of reading and provided to thousands of first-grade students across New York City. She also works closely with New York City's Department of Education to support literacy initiatives and research that impact the city's most vulnerable students.

Louisa Moats, Ed.D. is President of Moats Associates Consulting. She has been a teacher, psychologist, researcher, and graduate school faculty member. In addition to many journal articles and book chapters, her publications include *Speech to Print: Language Essentials for Teachers*, LETRS (*Language Essentials for Teachers of Reading*), and LANGUAGE! Live, a blended program for teaching adolescents how to read and write. She has received major awards from the International Dyslexia Association, the Australian Association for Learning Difficulties, and The Reading League for her contributions to the field.

Shawn O'Brien, Ph.D. is a Nationally Certified School Psychologist who worked in public schools for over 20 years and also private practice. She became interested in reading problems while employed at a facility for criminally adjudicated adolescents, where she observed that most teens entered with a second- to fourth-grade reading level.

Jane Oakhill, Ph.D. is Professor of Experimental Psychology at the University of Sussex, UK. She has worked on various research projects in cognitive psychology, but has always maintained a research interest in children's reading comprehension (in particular, individual differences). Jane Oakhill has published widely (including about 100 refereed journal articles and has co-authored or edited nine books). Her books in the area of reading and comprehension include *Understanding and teaching reading comprehension: A Handbook* (Routledge), which is co-authored with Kate Cain and Carsten Elbro.

Richard K. Olson, Ph.D. is Emeritus Professor of Psychology and Neuroscience, University of Colorado, and a Fellow of the Institute for Behavioral Genetics where he continues to serve as Associate Director of the Colorado Learning Disabilities Research Center (CLDRC). His research on the genetic and environmental etiology of individual differences and deficits in reading and related skills has benefitted from his collaboration with many wonderful co-investigators, graduate students, and postdocs supported through the CLDRC and from his collaboration with Brian Byrne and Stefan Samuelsson in their International Longitudinal Twin Study.

Stefan Samuelsson, Ph.D. is a Professor in special education at Linköping University in Sweden. He received his Ph.D. in education from Linköping University in 1994. Besides his interest in behavior genetics, Samuelsson has focused on reading difficulties among children, adolescents, as well as adults. In his research, Samuelsson has also addressed aspects reading difficulties in particular demographic samples, such as children with very low birth weight, prison inmates, and single cases with brain lesions.

Lesley A. Sand, Ph.D. received her doctorate in Human Development from the University of Maryland where she continued as a postdoctoral fellow and currently serves as research faculty. Prior to joining the University of Maryland, Dr. Sand worked as a learning specialist and academic tutor in the greater Washington D.C. area. She holds masters degrees from American University in Special Education and Georgetown University in Liberal Studies and has both worked with and researched extensively with individuals with dyslexia and autism spectrum disorders.

Sunaina Shenoy, Ph.D. is an Assistant Professor in the Department of Special Education at the University of New Mexico. She earned a Ph.D. in Special Education from the University of California Berkeley and completed her post-doctoral work at the Florida Center for Reading Research at Florida State University. Her research interests are in assessment, early identification of reading disabilities in bilingual and multilingual populations and international special education.

Sarah G. Wood is currently a doctoral candidate in the Developmental Psychology graduate program at Florida State University after receiving a master's degree in 2016 in Developmental Psychology. Dr. Richard K. Wagner is her doctoral advisor and is supervising her dissertation. Her dissertation, underway now, compares alternative models of reading disability by their ability to predict reading gains utilizing assistive technology (i.e., text-to-speech/read-aloud tools).

Yueming Xi is a Doctoral Candidate at the Ontario Institute for Studies in Education (OISE), University of Toronto. She received her BA in Japanese from Dalian University of Foreign Languages in China and an MEd in Curriculum and Instruction from Boston College. Yueming is a former adjunct faculty member of Japanese language and literature at Simmons College and Northeastern University in Boston. She has published a chapter comparing policies about dyslexia in different countries, and her current research examines the mechanisms underlying reading development among first and second language learners from the perspective of syntactic structure building.

Chong Zhang, Ph.D. is the assistant director of the Research Center for Psychology and Special Education at the China National Institute for Education Sciences. She received her Ph.D. in Psychology from Beijing Normal University and was a postdoctoral fellow and visiting scholar in the Department of Psychology at Florida State University and the University of Bristol, respectively. Her research is focused on issues surrounding psychological well-being, emotional intelligence, and learning difficulties among Chinese adolescents.

Fotena Zirps, Ph.D. is Senior Research Associate and Lab Manager of the WagnerLab, part of the Florida Center for Reading Research at Florida State University. She has served in this role since 2014, coordinating work on a multi-side NIHCD grant regarding reading, writing and math acquisition, and dyslexia. She has recently been involved in a meta-analysis of reading and listening comprehension as well as novel approaches to understanding dyslexia.

Part I
Reading Development and Difficulties

Chapter 1
The Componential Model of Reading (CMR): Implications for Assessment and Instruction of Literacy Problems

R. Malatesha Joshi

Abstract Literacy skills—defined as reading, writing, and spelling—are fundamental for academic achievement as well as being a productive citizen in society. However, despite spending trillions of dollars over the decades, literacy skills in the USA have not improved. In this chapter, a model, called the Componential Model of Reading (CMR) is described and how it can help in the assessment and intervention of reading problems. Some of the common assessment and intervention techniques are also outlined to help the teachers and administrators to solve the reading problems at school.

According to the most recent Nation's Report Card (National Assessment of Educational Progress; NAEP, 2017), about one-third of fourth-grade students in the USA have difficulty with literacy skills and cannot comprehend fourth-grade-level materials. There are serious consequences of poor reading at all levels—individual, societal, and national. At the individual level, about 75% of students who drop out of high school have reading problems and about 85% of individuals in the juvenile court system are functionally illiterate (Sweet, 2004). An important aspect of the value of literacy skills has been highlighted by the fact that when these juvenile delinquents are equipped with literacy skills, there is only a 16% chance that they will return to the prison system. However, when they are not equipped with literacy skills, there is a 70% chance that they will return to prison, which costs taxpayers approximately $25,000 per year per inmate. Further, more than 50% of individuals on government sponsored welfare assistance and about the same percentage with substance abuse problems have difficulty with reading. At the societal level, many states can predict the number of prison cells needed after about ten years based on the number of poor readers in fourth grade (Lyon, 2001). At the national level, it costs about $11,000 in health care for those with less than a fourth-grade reading level, but costs less than $3,000 for individuals with a fourth-grade reading level and above. Overall, illiteracy costs more than a trillion dollars in the USA. These facts have led the National Institute of Health (NIH) to declare literacy a "public health issue" (Sweet, 2004).

R. M. Joshi (✉)
College of Education & Human Development, Texas A&M University, College Station, TX, USA
e-mail: mjoshi@tamu.edu

© Springer Nature Switzerland AG 2019
D. A. Kilpatrick et al. (eds.), *Reading Development and Difficulties*,
https://doi.org/10.1007/978-3-030-26550-2_1

3

Through the National Institute of Child Health and Development, the US Department of Education's Institute for Educational Sciences, and the National Science Foundation, the federal government in the USA spends tens of millions of dollars each year on reading the research. Many of these funds are intended to help find suitable identification and intervention techniques to overcome literacy problems. Despite the amount of money spent both on research and actual remediation, the reading performance has stayed about the same for almost 40 years in the USA (see below and also Moats Chap. 3, this volume, on the gap between research findings and classroom practice). In this chapter, after providing a brief historical introduction about reading problems, I provide the rationale for the Componential Model of Reading (CMR) and how it can be applied to solve the national crisis of illiteracy. Some assessment techniques and instructional recommendations are also provided.

1.1 A Brief History of Reading Problems

During the late nineteenth century, Hinshelwood (1895) and Morgan (1896) independently published reports of individuals who, despite adequate intelligence, exhibited reading difficulties. After many decades, when a better understanding of the causes of reading disabilities was understood, the term learning disabilities (LD) was used to include children who have difficulty acquiring reading skills despite normal intelligence and exposed to literacy environment including formal instruction. Even though other types of learning difficulties such as math were included in the category of LD, the term LD was primarily used with reading disabilities given that close to 80% of the children classified as LD had reading-related problems (Aaron, Joshi, & Quotroche, 2008). With the passage of the Specific Learning Disabilities Act in 1969 and the Education for All Handicapped Children Act in 1975, the field of learning disabilities had an official status. Since the definition included the discrepancy between intelligence and achievement, the administration of IQ tests was the primary test instrument along with an achievement test. However, identifying LD through intelligence has not been found to be successful for various reasons. First of all, the relationship between reading and intelligence is bidirectional in the sense that IQ scores can improve for good readers and can go down among poor readers (Stanovich, 1993). Further, intelligence does not explain much of the statistical variance in reading; IQ explains only about 25% of the variance seen in the reading scores of all students (Stanovich, Cunningham, & Feeman, 1984). Further, the IQ-achievement discrepancy definition does not provide recommendations for appropriate instruction. Because of these and other problems with the discrepancy definition, many researchers called for disbanding the practice of identifying children as having learning disabilities based on IQ scores (Aaron, 1997; Fletcher, Denton, & Francis, 2005; Fuchs & Fuchs, 2006; Joshi, Williams, & Wood, 1998; Miciak & Fletcher, Chap. 7, this volume).

In 2004, the Individuals with Disabilities Education Improvement Act was reauthorized to include Response to Intervention (RtI) to identify children with LD. RtI generally includes three tiers with Tier 1 addressing whole class instruction; Tier 2 includes small group instruction and Tier 3 is aimed at even more intensive instruction. Despite its appeal, RtI has been criticized (see Carreker & Joshi, 2010, for a review) and it has not been as successful as it was hoped for. "Although identifi cation models based on Response to Intervention appear potentially promising, the notion that they represent real progress for identification and intervention for children with dyslexia should be considered a *popular myth* until evidence from the rigorous evaluation is available" (Wagner, 2008, p. 188; emphasis added). These sentiments are further supported by Berkeley, Bender, Peaster, and Saunders (2009), who, after reviewing the RtI implementation in the 50 states, concluded that RtI "holds a similar *trajectory* as the discrepancy model" (p. 94). Similarly, based on a meta-analysis of 13 studies, Tran, Sanchez, Arellano, and Swanson (2011) summarized that "Overall … regardless of the type of treatment and identification criteria, RtI conditions *were not effective* in mitigating learner characteristics to pretest conditions" (p. 283; emphasis added). Considering some of the shortcomings of RtI and the fact that the model addresses mostly academic problems, a new broader concept called Multi-tiered Systems of Support (MTSS) has been introduced that encompasses both RtI and Positive Behavioral Interventions and Supports (PBIS) (McIntosh & Goodman, 2016). Even though many states are testing the success of MTSS, we do not yet have clear research support for the utility of MTSS.

1.2   Componential Model of Reading (CMR)

An alternate model that has been useful in identifying and remediating reading difficulties is the Simple View of Reading (SVR) proposed by Gough and his colleagues (Gough & Tunmer, 1986; Hoover & Gough; 1990). According to SVR, reading consists of two broad components: decoding and comprehension and is expressed by the formula $RC = D \times LC$, where RC refers to reading comprehension; D is decoding, and LC refers to linguistic comprehension. According to SVR, both decoding and comprehension are needed for reading comprehension and if $D =$ zero, then RC will be zero; similarly, if LC is zero, then also RC is zero. It should be understood that decoding and linguistic comprehension are two major components and there may be subcomponents within a component. For example, phonological awareness appears to be a subcomponent of decoding and vocabulary a subcomponent of linguistic comprehension. Recently, researchers have debated whether to include other factors such as fluency (Adlof, Catts, & Little, 2006; Joshi & Aaron, 2000) and vocabulary as separate components (Braze, Tabor, Shankweiler, & Mencl, 2007; Protopapas, Simos, Sideridis, & Mouzaki, 2012; Tunmer & Chapman, 2012). However, just the two components of SVR can explain 40–80% of the variance in RC, depending on the grade level and the transparency of orthography. By contrast, it was mentioned that IQ can explain only about 25% of the variance in RC without providing information on the type of remedial instruction needed such as decoding, vocabulary, or comprehension, information that the SVR provides. Further, SVR has been found to be applicable in other orthographies (i.e., written languages) as well as for students for whom English as second language (ESL) and English as foreign language (EFL) (see Joshi, 2018; Joshi, Ji, Breznitz, Amiel, & Yulia, 2015; Joshi, Tao, Aaron, & Quiroz, 2012).

The advantages of the SVR is that it identifies the weak component so that appropriate intervention can be provided. For instance, Aaron, Joshi, and Williams (1999) administered decoding, listening comprehension, and reading comprehension measures to approximately 200 students in grades 3, 4, and 6 and found that approximately 7% of the students had good decoding skills but poor comprehension—both listening comprehension and reading comprehension. These children could be considered as exhibiting the hyperlexia-type reading difficulty (Gough & Tunmer, 1986). About 8% of the children performed poorly on decoding tasks but adequately on linguistic comprehension skills. Thus, their reading comprehension problem was due to poor decoding and not due to poor linguistic comprehension skills. These children could be considered as exhibiting dyslexia-type reading difficulty (Gough & Tunmer, 1986). Further, another 8% of the students had both decoding and linguistic comprehension problems and could be classified as low-ability readers or "garden-variety poor readers," as they have been called (Gough & Tunmer, 1986).

The SVR has also been found to be helpful in suggesting the use of appropriate instructional procedures. For instance, contrary to using only one type of reading instruction for all poor readers, Aaron, Joshi, Boulware-Gooden, and Bentum (2008) first identified the weak component of reading, whether it was decoding or linguistic comprehension, and then provided systematic decoding and comprehension instruction to both groups for 12 weeks. They were compared to another group of poor readers who were receiving the business-as-usual instruction in their schools. After 12 weeks, those with decoding problems showed significant gains in reading with decoding instruction but did not improve when provided with systematic comprehension instruction. Similarly, comprehension instruction was more helpful for those with linguistic comprehension problems. Poor readers who did not receive differentiated instruction did not make any significant gains in reading comprehension. This demonstrates that when a student has decoding skills, no matter what kind of good comprehension instruction is provided, decoding skills did not improve. An analogy may be helpful here. An automobile may not start if the battery is dead or the alternator is broken. If the alternator is broken, no matter what kind of a good battery we put in, the car will not run because the battery was not the problem. Hence, in order to improve reading among poor readers, first the poor component based on SVR should be identified and then be provided with systematic and evidence-based instruction. Thus, SVR is a simple yet valuable model to identify and improve reading problems. Unfortunately, many state-level reading tests, and even some of the universal screeners, provide a singular, overall reading comprehension score. Such a singular score does not allow teachers to know the source(s) of a student's reading comprehension difficulty.

Based on the recent findings relating to the influence of home environment, school practices, and teacher knowledge, Joshi and colleagues (e.g., Aaron, Joshi, Boulware-Gooden et al. 2008; Aaron, Joshi, & Quatroche, 2008; Joshi et al., 2012) expanded the SVR into the Componental Model of Reading. The Componental Model of Reading (CMR) consists of three domains: cognitive domain, psychological domain, and ecological domain. The cognitive domain consists of two components relating to reading, word recognition and comprehension, heavily influenced by the SVR. The psychological domain consists of factors such as motivation, teacher knowledge, and teacher expectations. The ecological domain consists of factors such as home environment, classroom environment, parental involvement, peer influence, dialectical differences, and orthography (i.e., the nature of the written language). Each one of these factors appears to contribute to the development of fluent reading. A special issue of the *Journal of Learning Disabilities* (Volume 45, 2012) provides empirical support for CMR.

It has been fairly well established that the factors involved in the ecological domain such as home environment, socioeconomic status (SES), and exposure to an enriched literacy environment can influence literacy development. Chiu and McBride-Chang (2006) examined many of the ecological factors such as home environment, number of books available at home, enjoyment of reading, and SES among close to 200,000 Grade 5 students from 43 countries and found that these factors influenced performance on a reading comprehension measure in almost every country. Further, Labov (1995), Charity, Scarborough, and Griffin (2004), and Seidenberg (2017) have suggested that the linguistic features of African-American English (AAE), which some African-American children speak, may be a source of some of African-American children's literacy problems given that there is more often a gap between phonology and orthography than typically found in Standard American English. Further, Treiman (2004) and Washington and Craig (2002) have found that AAE affects spelling performance among African-American children. Orthography is defined as the visual representation of a language as conditioned by phonological, syntactic, morphological, and semantic features of the language. Examples of orthographies are Chinese orthography and English orthography (Joshi & Aaron, 2006). In transparent orthographies, the sound and the symbol map onto each other closely compared to opaque orthographies where the correspondences between sound and symbol are not straightforward. Generally, Spanish and Finnish are considered to be highly transparent orthographies, while English is considered to be an opaque orthography. However, there are various degrees of transparencies depending on where the orthography falls on the continuum of the one-to-one match to one-to-many match between sounds and symbols. In a seminal study by Seymour, Aro, and Erskine (2003), it was shown that it might take about two years of formal instruction to develop decoding skills in English orthography compared to only one year of formal instruction in transparent orthographies like German, Spanish, and Finnish. Additionally, it has also been reported that while both speed and accuracy of reading words might have been affected among children with reading difficulties in English-speaking children, only speed of word recognition, but not the accuracy of reading words, might be affected in German- and Spanish-speaking children with reading difficulties (Joshi & Aaron, 2006). This has important implications for assessing and teaching children with reading difficulties.

Factors in the psychological domain, such as motivation and teacher knowledge, can also affect literacy development. Motivation can include aspects such as perceived autonomy, self-efficacy, and valuing reading, and all these factors have been found to affect reading performance (Wigfield, Gladstone, & Turci, 2016). Teacher knowledge, especially relating to language constructs, can also affect literacy development in school children. Beginning with the seminal study of Moats (1994), a series of studies by Joshi and colleagues and McCutchen and her colleagues have reported the importance of teacher knowledge relating to literacy and how a workshop during summer can improve teacher knowledge and in turn can improve students' academic performance (Binks-Cantrell, Washburn, Joshi, & Hougen, 2012; Joshi et al. 2009; McCutchen et al., 2002).

1.3   Assessment Techniques Based on CMR

Below is a brief outline of the common assessment techniques as well as remedial recommendations based on the CMR. Practitioners must also familiarize themselves with the current tests and publications by well-known test developers such as Psychological Corporation and Pro-Ed publishers.

1.3.1   Ecological Domain

Factors relating to the ecological domain should be part of an assessment in the evaluation of students suspected of having literacy difficulties. Many of the aspects of the ecological domain, such as home environment, can be assessed by surveys and questionnaires. These types of surveys should include information about parent/caregiver education, parent/caregiver occupation, languages spoken at home, literacy activities at home, frequency of visits to the library, access to computers and technology, extracurricular activities, and sibling information. The Texas English Language Proficiency Assessment System (TELPAS, Texas Education Agency, 2012) is a criterion-referenced measure to assess speaking, listening, reading, and writing of limited-English language speakers from Grades K-12. Oral and Written Language Scales (OWLS-II, Carrow-Woolfolk, 2011) is another standardized measure that could be used to assess language difficulties from ages 3–22 and has four scales: Listening Comprehension, Oral Expression, Reading Comprehension, and Written Expression. Dialectical differences can be measured through the standardized instrument of Diagnostic Evaluation of Language Variation (DELV; Seymour, Roeper, & de Villiers, 2009). This is a criterion-referenced test which has been used by many researchers.

1.3.2   Psychological Domain

Most of the instruments to measure motivation are self-report questionnaires and may involve Likert-type scoring. Perhaps, one of the better-known instruments to measure motivation is Motivations for Reading Questionnaire (MRQ), developed by Wigfield and Guthrie in 1997. The instrument consists of 53 items and measures 11 constructs such as reading efficacy, social reasons for reading, and compliance. Teacher knowledge relating to literacy/language constructs can be measured by the standardized instrument developed by Binks-Cantrell, Joshi, and Washburn (2012). This survey measures both the content knowledge as well as pedagogical knowledge and has been used by many researchers.

1.3.3   Cognitive Domain

Even though only two major components of reading were identified (i.e., word recognition and linguistic comprehension), there are several subcomponents that make up the two components. For instance, phonological awareness is foundational for decoding, and vocabulary is a subcomponent of linguistic comprehension, even though they are not given a separate status.

Decoding. Phonological awareness (PA) is defined as the knowledge that the spoken language consists of smaller units such as rhymes, syllables, and sounds. The smallest unit of sound is called a phoneme. Phonemic awareness, which is a type of phonological awareness, involves identifying the individual sounds/phonemes in the spoken word (Liberman, 1987). In virtually every alphabetic written language, it has been demonstrated that PA, and especially phonemic awareness, is a prerequisite for becoming a good decoder. Further, teaching phonemic awareness skills systematically and explicitly also improve decoding skills (Goldenberg, Tolar, Reese, Francis, & Mejia-Arauz, 2014). Some of the standardized measures to measure PA skills are the Lindamood Auditory Conceptualization Test (LAC, Lindamood & Lindamood, 2004); the Test of Phonological Awareness—Second Edition: PLUS (TOPA-2+, Torgesen & Bryant, 2004), and the Comprehensive Test of Phonological Processing—Second Edition (CTOPP-2, Wagner, Torgesen, Rashotte, & Pearson, 2013).

A word of caution about administering phonological awareness tasks: It is a good idea to ask the student why they answered in a particular way. For instance, some of the tasks, like rhyming tasks, have only two or three choices and so the chances of getting it correct by guessing are high. So, for an item like, "Does *bat* rhyme with *cat*?" it is a good idea to ask why the student thinks they rhyme.

In addition to PA tasks, naming of both uppercase and lowercase letters of the alphabet arranged in random order, and the common sounds of the letters should be explored. Juel (1995) found that students who knew the names of letters and their common sounds at the end of Grade 1 had a very high probability (about 0.90) that they would be good readers at the end of Grade 4. By contrast, those who did not know the names of the letters and the common sounds by the end of Grade 1 had a high probability (about 0.88) that they would be poor readers by the end of Grade 4. Thus, it is very important that the students know the names and the common sounds of letters to become a good reader and speller.

Decoding skill is generally measured through a nonword (also referred to as nonsense word or pseudoword) reading task. These are pronounceable, made-up words used to test the student's knowledge of letter-sound correspondences. Reading real words, in some instances, may be due to repeated exposure to a word (e.g., reading *Pine* if the student has lived on *Pine Street*). Decoding skill, sometimes also referred to as word-attack skill, is generally measured by the Woodcock Reading Mastery Test-III (Woodcock, 2011). Other major academic assessment batteries now have nonsense word reading subtests. We also strongly recommend administering a spelling task for its various advantages. First of all, it can be administered in a group setting, so many students can be tested at the same time. Further, as Shankweiler, Lundquist, Dreyer, and Dickinson (1996) noted "… although spelling is … not a component of reading, it provides a valuable indicator of the level of orthographic skill on which all literacy activities ultimately depend. Word recognition and all subsequent higher level processes that take place in reading are constrained by the ability to fluently transcode print into language" (p. 287). Further, there is a high degree of relationship between reading and spelling in the order of about +0.8 (Ehri, 1997). Additionally, we also recommend that spelling errors of students be scored both quantitatively as right or wrong and also qualitatively taking into consideration factors such as sound substitutions based on place and manner of articulation. The Spelling subtest from the Wide Range Achievement Test—5 (WRAT-5, Wilkinson & Robertson, 2017) and Test of Written Spelling—5 (TWS-5, Larsen, Hammill, & Moats, 2013) are two of the commonly administered standardized measures of spelling.

Rapid Automatized Naming and Rapid Alternating Stimulus Tests (RAN/RAS; Wolf & Denckla, 2005) measure speed of processing that has been found to be helpful in identifying children with literacy problems and have been widely used. They are quick, easy to administer and also can be administered in a non-threatening manner. Decoding skill and speed of processing can be measured simultaneously through the Test of Word Reading Efficiency—Second Edition (TOWRE-2; Torgesen, Wagner, & Rashotte, 2012).

Linguistic Comprehension. The second component in the cognitive domain is linguistic comprehension. It is strongly recommended that both listening comprehension and reading comprehension measures be administered. In the listening comprehension measure, the experimenter reads the passage and asks comprehension questions and in reading comprehension, the student has to read and answer the comprehension questions. In typically developing readers, all three skills—decoding, listening comprehension, and reading comprehension should be within the normal range. If there is a problem in one of the skills, reading will be affected. If there is a problem only in decoding, then it might affect reading comprehension but not listening comprehension. This is generally the case with students with the dyslexia-type problem. Among students with both listening and reading comprehension problems, their performance in decoding may be within the average range, which is generally seen among students with the hyperlexia-type reading difficulty. If the student has problems in both decoding and comprehension, generally the student is classified as either a low-ability reader or a garden-variety poor reader (Stanovich, 1988). This method of assessing reading problems bypasses administering intelligence tests and also pinpoints the weak component so that appropriate instructional procedures can be implemented.

The Woodcock Reading Mastery Tests (Woodcock, 2011) have both listening and reading comprehension measures. Further, we recommend administering two different types of comprehension measures as Joshi as well as Keenan and their colleagues have shown that reading comprehension scores can differ depending on the tests used (Joshi, Williams, & Wood, 1998; Keenan, Betjemann, & Olson, 2008; Keenan & Meenan, 2014). The Woodcock Reading Mastery Tests measure reading comprehension through the cloze procedure while the Gates-MacGinitie Reading Tests (MacGinitie, MacGinitie, Katherine Maria, & Dreyer, 2000) measure silent reading and follows the multiple-choice format for responses. The Gray Oral Reading Tests (GORT-5, Wiederholt & Bryant, 2012) measures oral reading fluency and reading comprehension. It is important to measure both literal comprehension (comprehension is assessed based on the information directly stated in the text) and inferential comprehension (comprehension is assessed based on information not explicitly stated and the student has to infer). Studies by Oakhill, Berenhaus, and Cain (2015) have shown that some students can perform well on literal comprehension but not on inferential comprehension materials.

For a general battery of tests, Woodcock–Johnson Tests of Achievement—IV (WJIV-ACH) (Schrank, McGrew, Mather, & Woodcock, 2014) is a useful tool to use for speakers of the English language. It has been recently updated and gives profiles for reading and writing performance. By measuring decoding, listening comprehension, and reading comprehension, WJIV-ACH can highlight the strengths and weaknesses of various components of reading. The Spanish equivalent of the Woodcock tests is the Woodcock–Muñoz Batería III (Woodcock, Schrank, Muñoz-Sandoval, McGrew, & Mather, 2005) and is widely used to assess the reading difficulties of Spanish-speaking children in the USA.

WJIV-ACH also measures writing skills. The Test of Written Language (TOWL-IV; Hammill & Larsen, 2009) is a norm-referenced measure for ages 9–18 and measures skills such as vocabulary, spelling, punctuation, sentence combining, and story composition.

The instruments discussed above are just a sample of different instruments that could be applied to assess literacy problems based on the CMR. However, it is useful to follow some of the well-known publishers such as Pro-Ed, Psychological Corporation/Pearson, and Riverside for updates and new publications.

1.4   Intervention Based on the CMR

As mentioned earlier, the ecological domain of the CMR consists of factors such as home environment, classroom environment, parent/caregiver involvement, peer influence, dialect differences, and the specific written language/orthography. Some of the factors in the ecological domain such as home environment cannot be altered to any great degree by classroom teachers, yet an awareness of the home environment can help the teachers to interact with students with understanding and compassion. The classroom environment can be set up in such a way to make the students more attentive and conducive to learning. All teachers must be aware that AAE is not an impoverished version of more Standard English dialects, rather it is a separate but equivalent system, as complex and rule governed as Academic English (AE) but with some alternative rules and conventions for expressing the same syntactic relationships, semantic content, and verbal pronunciations (Labov, 1998). Speakers of AAE have to be made aware of the dialectical differences between AAE and AE used in classrooms and textbooks. Teachers can readily understand the difficulties experienced by many ESL students in learning to read, but they are typically unaware of the difficulties encountered by students who speak AAE. The boundaries of a foreign language and English are usually clear cut. However, due to the extensive overlap between the AAE dialect and AE, it is not easy to tell precisely where one leaves off and the other begins. This makes it difficult for the student to know what is acceptable and what is not acceptable in AE. Pittman, Joshi, and Carreker (2014) found that after nine weeks of systematic and explicit instruction that included teaching spelling through the use of morphemes, Greek and Latin roots, and word origins, poor-performing African-American students not only improved their spelling but also maintained it during the semester even after the instruction was discontinued.

Since there is a high percentage of Spanish-speaking children in US schools, knowing the regularity of Spanish orthography and the many cognate words of English and Spanish (e.g., *attention/atención*; *exceptional/excepcional*; *curious/curioso*) can help the teacher to modify instruction to meet the needs of Spanish-speaking ESL learners. There are also many students in US schools whose first language is other than English and Spanish. Knowing that Chinese is a morpho-syllabic language with the basic unit being a character at the morpheme level and not a letter of an alphabet can help teachers understand why children whose first language is Chinese make certain kinds of errors while learning to read and write English. Similarly, knowing that Arabic is written from right to left and many of the textbooks in Arabic, after about Grade 3, leave out the written vowels can also help teachers to understand the literacy problems of students whose first language is Arabic.

Motivation and teacher knowledge are two of the factors under the psychological domain. Motivation can be improved by Concept-Oriented Reading Instruction (CORI) (Wigfield & Guthrie, 1997; Wigfield et al., 2016) which focuses on enhancing children's reading motivation and comprehension in a content domain like science or social studies. By providing reading strategy instruction and implementing practices that focus motivation such as self-efficacy, value of reading, and collaboration, CORI has been a useful model in improving motivation as well as reading.

Teacher knowledge of the language constructs needed to teach literacy skills is very important, but unfortunately several studies have shown that teachers are not equipped with this knowledge (Binks-Cantrell, Joshi, & Washburn, 2012; Joshi et al., 2009). However, as McCutchen et al. (2002) demonstrated, even a short summer course providing the knowledge of language constructs and pedagogical knowledge cannot only improve the knowledge among teachers but also the literacy achievement of their students.

The cognitive aspects of CMR—decoding and comprehension—can be developed by many instructional activities that are based on empirical evidence, outlined by the National Reading Panel (NRP, 2000, see also Kilpatrick & O'Brien, Chap. 8 this volume). Phonemic awareness can benefit all children in various grade levels and reading levels and it is most effective when it is direct and systematic. Phoneme deletion and phoneme blending are useful activities and just about 10–15 minutes of instruction in a small group can have lasting effects. Similarly, decoding can be improved by explicit instruction through a synthetic phonics approach. Spelling instruction should include explicit instruction of letter-sound correspondences, history of English, and etymology. Emphasizing rote memory or expecting students to copy words ten times are not recommended. Joshi, Treiman, Carreker, and Moats (2008) provide a detailed outline of what concepts to teach at each grade level. Vocabulary can also be improved by analyzing morphemic patterns and etymology. Just knowing a few morphemes like *ology* (study of), *spect* (to see), *duct* (to lead), and *scribe* (to write) can literally make hundreds of words. Thus, it is extremely important to teach morphemic patterns in words in multiple contexts and multiple meanings to improve the depth and breadth of vocabulary. Comprehension can be improved through empirically based approaches such as reciprocal teaching (Brown & Palincsar, 1987). Most of the successful comprehension programs include some common themes, such as collaborative or cooperative learning, having activities before reading (such as what I know), during reading (what I want to know); and after reading (what I learned as a result of my reading); and comprehension monitoring (stopping and asking questions such as "Is it making sense?" "Am I understanding what I have read so far?"), and being an active reader by constantly predicting what is going to happen next. Detailed explanations of various methods and programs can be found in Aaron, Joshi, Boulware-Gooden et al. (2008).

One of the empirically based writing instructional approaches is Self-Regulated Strategy Development (SRSD) (Graham, Harris, & Mason, 2005) that can be used from Grade 2 through high school and has strong empirical support. SRSD for writing instruction is somewhat similar to reciprocal teaching in the sense that some of the steps in the program aim to develop background knowledge and model it, and then, students are guided to independent performance.

1.5 Summary and Conclusions

Reading problems are a huge concern in the USA and it affects individuals, society, and the nation, financially and academically. The NAEP (2017) data show that 64% of fourth-graders and 66% of eighth-graders perform at or below proficiency in reading—proficiency being defined as "solid academic performance." Further, 31% of fourth-graders and 24% of eighth-graders were at or below the basic level, referring to only partial mastery of the prerequisite knowledge and skills needed for successful academic performance. Performance at the end of Grade 1 in reading skills can predict the reading development in Grade 4 (Juel, 1995) and poor reading performance by Grade 3 is the strongest predictor of dropout from high school (Alexander, Entwisle, & Kabbini, 2001). Unfortunately, the statistics about poor performance in reading have remained the same for decades despite billions of dollars spent on improving reading skills. The traditional method of identifying reading problems using IQ scores as well as the recent implementation of RtI has not produced promising results (further see Kilpatrick & O'Brien, Chap. 8 this volume). Since literacy problems might be caused by various factors, a comprehensive model such as the CMR might help in the assessment and intervention in order to solve literacy problems and thus help the individual, society, and the nation.

References

Aaron, P. G. (1997). The impending demise of the discrepancy formula. *Review of Educational Research, 67,* 461–502.

Aaron, P. G., Joshi, R. M., Boulware-Gooden, R., & Bentum, K. (2008). Diagnosis and treatment of reading disabilities based on the Component Model of Reading: An alternative to the discrepancy model of learning disabilities. *Journal of Learning Disabilities, 41,* 67–84.

Aaron, P. G., Joshi, R. M., & Quatroche, D. (2008). *Becoming a professional reading teacher: What to teach, how to teach, and why it matters.* Baltimore, MD: Paul H. Brookes.

Aaron, P. G., Joshi, M., & Williams, K. A. (1999). Not all reading disabilities are alike. *Journal of Learning Disabilities, 32,* 120–137.

Adlof, S. M., Catts, H. W., & Little, T. D. (2006). Should the simple view of reading include a fluency component? *Reading and Writing: An Interdisciplinary Journal, 19,* 933–958.

Alexander, K. L., Entwisle, D. R., & Kabbini, N. S. (2001). The dropout process in life course perspective: Early risk factors at home and school. *Teachers College Record, 103,* 760–882.

Berkeley, S., Bender, W. N., Peaster, L. G., & Saunders, L. (2009). Implementation of response to intervention: A snapshot of progress. *Journal of Learning Disabilities, 42,* 85–95.

Binks-Cantrell, E., Joshi, R. M., & Washburn, E. (2012). Validation of an instrument for assessing teacher knowledge of basic language constructs of literacy. *Annals of Dyslexia, 62,* 153–171.

Binks-Cantrell, E., Washburn, E., Joshi, R. M., & Hougan, M. (2012). Peter effect in the preparation of reading teachers. *Scientific Studies of Reading, 16,* 526–536. https://doi.org/10.1080/10888438.2011.601434.

Braze, D., Tabor, W., Shankweiler, D. P., & Mencl, W. E. (2007). Speaking up for vocabulary: Reading skill differences in young adults. *Journal of Learning Disabilities, 40,* 226–243. https://doi.org/10.1177/00222194070400030401.

Brown, A. L., & Palincsar, A. S. (1987). Reciprocal teaching of comprehension strategies: A natural history of one program for enhancing learning. In J. D. Day & J. G. Borkowski (Eds.), *Intelligence and exceptionality: New directions for theory, assessment, and instructional practice* (pp. 81–132). Norwood, NJ: Ablex.

Carreker, S., & Joshi, R. M. (2010). Response to intervention: Are the emperor's clothes really new? *Psicothema, 22,* 943–948.

Carrow-Woolfolk, E. (2011). *Oral and written language scales—Second edition (OWLS-II).* Austin, TX: Pro-Ed.

Charity, A. H., Scarborough, H. S., & Griffin, D. M. (2004). Familiarity with school English in African American children and its relation to early reading achievement. *Child Development, 75,* 1340–1356. https://doi.org/10.1111/j.1467-8624.2004.00744.x.

Chiu, M. M., & McBride-Chang, C. (2006). Gender, context, and reading: A comparison of students in 43 countries. *Scientific Studies of Reading, 10,* 331–362. https://doi.org/10.1207/s1532799xssr1004_1.

Education for All Handicapped Children Act. Public Law 94–142, November 29, 1975.

Ehri, L. C. (1997). Learning to read and learning to spell are one and the same, almost. In C. Perfeti, L. Rieben, & M. Fayol (Eds.), *Learning to spell: Research, theory, and practice across languages* (pp. 237–268). Mahwah, NJ: Lawrence Erlbaum Associates.

Fletcher, J. M., Denton, C., & Francis, D. J. (2005). Validity of alternative approaches for the identification of learning disabilities: Operationalizing unexpected underachievement. *Journal of Learning Disabilities, 38,* 545–552.

Fuchs, D., & Fuchs, L. (2006). Introduction to response to intervention: What, why, and how valid is it. *Reading Research Quarterly, 41,* 93–99.

Goldenberg, C., Tolar, T. M., Reese, L., Francis, D. J., & Mejia-Arauz, R. (2014). How important is teaching phonemic awareness to children learning to read in Spanish? *American Educational Research Journal, 51,* 604–633. https://doi.org/10.3102/0002831214529082.

Gough, P. B., & Tunmer, W. E. (1986). Decoding, reading, and reading disability. *Remedial and Special Education, 7,* 6–10. https://doi.org/10.1177/074193258600700104.

Graham, S., Harris, K. R., & Mason, L. (2005). Improving the writing performance, knowledge, and self-efficacy of struggling young writers: The effects of self-regulated strategy development. *Contemporary Educational Psychology, 30,* 207–241.

Hammill, D. D., & Larsen, S. C. (2009). *Test of written language—Fourth edition (TOWL-IV).* Austin, TX: Pro-Ed.

Hinshelwood, J. (1895). Word-blindness and visual memory. *The Lancet, 1,* 1506–1508.

Hoover, W. A., & Gough, P. B. (1990). The simple view of reading. *Reading and Writing: An Interdisciplinary Journal, 2,* 127–160. https://doi.org/10.1007/bf00401799.

Individuals with Disabilities Education Improvement Act of 2004, H.R. 1350, 108 Cong., 2nd Sess (2004).

Joshi, R. M. (2018). Simple view of reading (SVR) in different orthographies: Seeing the forest with the trees. In T. Lachman & T. Weiss (Eds.), *Reading and dyslexia* (pp. 71–80). Dordrecht, The Netherlands: Springer Publications.

Joshi, R. M., & Aaron, P. G. (2000). The component model of reading: Simple view of reading made a little more complex. *Reading Psychology, 21,* 85–97.

Joshi, R. M., & Aaron, P. G. (Eds.). (2006). *Handbook of orthography and literacy.* Mahwah, NJ: Lawrence Erlbaum Associates.

Joshi, R. M., Binks, E., Hougen, M., Dahlgren, M., Dean, E., & Smith, D. (2009). Why elementary teachers might be inadequately prepared to teach reading. *Journal of Learning Disabilities, 42,* 392–402. https://doi.org/10.1177/0022219409338736.

Joshi, R. M., Ji, X., Breznitz, Z., Amiel, M., & Yulia, A. (2015). Validation of the simple view of reading in Hebrew—A semitic language. *Scientific Studies of Reading, 19,* 243–252. https://doi.org/10.1080/10888438.2015.1010117.

Joshi, R. M., Tao, S., Aaron, P. G., & Quiroz, B. (2012). Cognitive component of componential model of reading applied to different orthographies. *Journal of Learning Disabilities, 45*, 480–486. https://doi.org/10.1177/0022219411432690.

Joshi, R. M., Treiman, R., Carreker, S., & Moats, L. (2009). How words cast their spell: Spelling instruction focused on language, not memory, improves reading and writing. *American Educator, 32*(4), 6–16, 42–43.

Joshi, R. M., Williams, K., & Wood, J. (1998). Predicting reading comprehension with listening comprehension: Is this the answer to the IQ debate? In C. Hulme & R. M. Joshi (Eds.), *Reading and spelling: Development and disorders* (pp. 319–327). Mahwah, NJ: Lawrence Erlbaum.

Juel, C. (1995). *Learning to read and write in one elementary school.* New York, NY: Springer Verlag.

Keenan, J. M., Betjemann, R. S., & Olson, R. K. (2008). Reading comprehension tests vary in the skills they assess: Differential dependence on decoding and oral comprehension. *Scientific Studies of Reading, 12*, 281–300.

Keenan, J. M., & Meenan, C. E. (2014). Test differences in diagnosing reading comprehension deficits. *Journal of Learning Disabilities, 47*, 125–135.

Labov, W. (1995). Can reading failure be reversed? A linguistic approach to the question. In V. L. Gadsden & D. A. Wagner (Eds.), *Literacy among African-American youth* (pp. 39–68). Cresskill, NJ: Hampton Press.

Labov, W. (1998). Co-existent systems in African-American English. In S. Mufwene, J. Rickford, J. Baugh, & G. Bailey (Eds.), *The structure of African-American English* (pp. 110–153). London: Routledge.

Larsen, S. C., Hammill, D., & Moats, L. (2013). *Test of written spelling—Fifth edition (TWS-5).* Austin, TX: Pro-Ed.

Liberman, I. Y. (1987). Language and literacy: The obligation of the schools of education. In W. Ellis (Ed.), *Intimacy with language: A forgotten basic in teacher education* (pp. 1–9). Baltimore, MD: The Orton Dyslexia Society.

Lindamood, P. C., & Lindamood, P. (2004). *Lindamood auditory conceptualization test—Third edition (LAC–3).* Austin, TX: Pro-Ed.

Lyon, G. R. (2001). Measuring success: Using assessments and accountability to raise student achievement. In *Hearing Before House Committee on Education and the Workforce, Subcommittee on Education Reform, 107th Congress.* Available at http://www.nrrf.org/learning/statement-of-dr-g-reid-lyon-before-the-u-s-house-subcommittee-on-education-and-the-workforce-hearing/.

MacGinitie, W. H., MacGinitie, R. K., Katherine Maria, L., & Dreyer, L. G. (2000). *Gates-MacGinitie reading tests* (4th ed.). Itasca, IL: Riverside.

McCutchen, D, Abbott, R. D., Green, L. B., Beretvas, S. N., Cox, S., Potter, N. S., Quiroga, T, & Gray, A. L. (2002). Beginning literacy: Links among teacher knowledge, teacher practice, and student learning. *Journal of Learning Disabilities, 35*, 69–86. https://doi.org/10.1177/002221940203500106.

McIntosh, K., & Goodman, S. (2016). *Integrated multi-tiered system of support: Blending RtI and PBIS.* New York, NY: Guilford Press.

Moats, L. C. (1994). The missing foundation in teacher education: Knowledge of the structure of spoken and written language. *Annals of Dyslexia, 44*, 81–102.

Morgan, W. P. (1896). A case of congenital word-blindness. *British Medical Journal, 2*, 1368.

National Assessment of Educational Progress. (2017). *The nation's report card: Mathematics & Reading.* Washington DC: U.S. Government Printing Office. Available at https://www.nationsreportcard.gov/.

National Institute of Child Health and Human Development (NICHD). (2000). *Report of the National Reading Panel. Teaching children to read: An evidence-based assessment of the scientific research literature on reading and its implications for reading instruction: Reports of the subgroups* (NIH Publication No. 00-4754). Washington, DC: U.S. Government Printing Office.

Oakhill, J., Berenhaus, M. S., & Cain, K. (2015). Children's reading comprehension and comprehension difficulties. In A. Pollatsek & R. Treiman (Eds.), *The Oxford handbook of reading*. New
York, NY: Oxford University Press.
Pittman, R. T., Joshi, R. M., & Carreker, S. (2014). Improving the spelling ability among speakers
of African American English through explicit instruction. *Literacy Research and Instruction, 53,*
107–133. https://doi.org/10.1080/19388071.2013.870623.
Protopapas, A., Simos, P. G., Sideridis, G. D., & Mouzaki, A. (2012). The components of the simple
view of reading: A confirmatory factor analysis. *Reading Psychology, 33,* 217–240. https://doi.
org/10.1080/02702711.2010.507626.
Schrank, F. A., McGrew, K. S., Mather, N., & Woodcock, R. W. (2014). *Woodcock-Johnson tests
of achievement–IV*. Rolling Meadows, IL: Riverside.
Seidenberg, M. (2017). *Language at the speed of sight: How we read, why so many can't, and what
can be done about it*. New York, NY: Basic Books.
Shankweiler, D., Lundquist, E., Dreyer, L. G., & Dickinson, D. D. (1996). Reading and spelling
difficulties in high school students: Causes and consequences. *Reading and Writing: An Inter-
disciplinary Journal, 8,* 267–294. https://doi.org/10.1007/BF00420279.
Seymour, P. H. K., Aro, M., & Erskine, J. M. (2003). Foundation literacy acquisition in
European orthographies. *British Journal of Psychology, 94,* 143–174. https://doi.org/10.1348/
000712603321661859.
Seymour, H. N., Roeper, T., & de Villiers, J. G. (2009). *Diagnostic evaluation of language variation
screening test (DELV-ST)*. San Antonio, TX: The Psychological Corporation.
Stanovich, K. E. (1988). Explaining the differences between the dyslexic and the garden-variety
poor reader: The phonological-core variable-difference model. *Journal of Learning Disabilities,
21,* 590–604.
Stanovich, K. E. (1993). Does reading make you smarter? Literacy and the development of verbal
intelligence. *Advances in Child Development and Behavior, 24,* 133–180.
Stanovich, K. E., Cunningham, A. E., & Feeman, D. J. (1984). Relation between early reading
acquisition and word decoding with and without context: A longitudinal study of first-grade
children. *Journal of Educational Psychology, 76,* 668–677.
Sweet, R. W. (2004). The big picture: Where we are nationally on the reading front and how we got
there. In P. McCardle & V. Chhabra (Eds.), *The voice of evidence in reading research* (pp. 13–44).
Baltimore, MD: Paul H. Brookes.
Texas Education Agency. (2012). *Texas English language proficiency assessment system* (TELPAS).
Austin, TX: Texas Education Agency.
Torgesen, J. K., & Bryant, B. R. (2004). *Test of phonological awareness (TOPA 2)*. Austin, TX:
Pro-Ed.
Torgesen, J. K., Wagner, R. K., & Rashotte, C. A. (2012). *Test of word reading efficiency—Second
edition (TOWRE–2)*. Austin, TX: Pro-Ed.
Tran, L., Sanchez, B., Arellano, L., & Swanson, H. L. (2011). A meta-analysis of the literature for
children at-risk for reading disabilities. *Journal of Learning Disabilities, 44,* 283–205.
Treiman, R. (2004). Spelling and dialect: Comparisons between speakers of African American
vernacular English and white speakers. *Psychonomic Bulletin & Review, 11,* 338–342. https://
doi.org/10.3758/bf03196580.
Tunmer, W. E., & Chapman, J. W. (2012). The simple view of reading redux: Vocabulary knowledge
and the independent components hypothesis. *Journal of Learning Disabilities, 45,* 453–466.
Wagner, R. K. (2008). Rediscovering dyslexia: New approaches for identification and classification. In G. Reid, A. Fawcett, F. Manis, & L. Siegel (Eds.), *The SAGE handbook of dyslexia*
(pp. 174–191). London, UK: Sage Publications.
Wagner, R. K., Torgesen, J. K., Rashotte, C. A., & Pearson, N. A. (2013). *Comprehensive test of
phonological processing—Second edition (CTOPP-2)*. Austin, TX: Pro-Ed.
Washington, J. A., & Craig, H. K. (2002). Morphosyntactic forms of African American English
used by young children and their caregivers. *Applied Psycholinguistics, 23,* 209–231. http://doi.
org/10.1017.S0142716402002035.

Wiederholt, J. L., & Bryant, B. R. (2012). *Gray oral reading tests–Fifth edition (GORT-5)*. Austin, TX: Pro-Ed.

Wigfield, A., Gladstone, J., & Turci, L. (2016). Beyond cognition: Reading motivation and reading comprehension. *Child Development Perspectives, 10,* 190–195. https://doi.org/10.1111/cdep.12184.

Wigfield, A., & Guthrie, J. T. (1997). Relations of children's motivation for reading to the amount and breadth of their reading. *Journal of Educational Psychology, 89,* 420–432.

Wilkinson, G. S., & Robertson, G. J. (2017). *Wide range achievement test—Fifth edition (WRAT-5)*. San Antonio, TX: Psychological Corporation.

Woodcock, R. J. (2011). *Woodcock reading mastery test-III*. San Antonio, TX: Psychological Corporation.

Wolf, M., & Denckla, M. B. (2005). *Rapid automatized naming and rapid alternating stimulus tests (RAN/RAS)*. Austin, TX: Pro-Ed.

Woodcock, R. J., Schrank, F. A., Muñoz-Sandoval, A. F., McGrew, K. S., & Mather, N. (2005). *Woodcock-Muñoz Batería III*. Rolling Meadows, IL: Riverside.

Chapter 2
Reading-Related Phonological Processing in English and Other Written Languages

Richard K. Wagner, Rachel Joyner, Poh Wee Koh, Antje Malkowski, Sunaina Shenoy, Sarah G. Wood, Chong Zhang and Fotena Zirps

Abstract The three major phonological skills related to word-level reading are phonological awareness, phonological short-term/working memory, and phonological retrieval (i.e., rapid automatized naming). These skills and their relations to reading development in English and other alphabetic writing systems are presented. Then, the phonological processes in a non-alphabetic writing system, Chinese, are explored, as are the phonological skills of multi-lingual students. Research in these areas helps provide a better understanding of the nature of reading and reading development in English and other languages.

R. K. Wagner (✉) · R. Joyner · A. Malkowski · S. G. Wood · F. Zirps
Florida State University, Tallahasee, FL 32306, USA
e-mail: rkwagner@psy.fsu.edu

R. Joyner
e-mail: rjoyner@psy.fsu.edu

A. Malkowski
e-mail: amalkowski@fsu.edu

S. G. Wood
e-mail: sgw12@my.fsu.edu

F. Zirps
e-mail: fzirps@psy.fsu.edu

P. W. Koh
Texas A&M University, College Station, TX, USA
e-mail: pohwee.koh@gmail.com

S. Shenoy
University of New Mexico, Albuquerque, NM, USA
e-mail: shenoy@unm.edu

C. Zhang
China National Institute for Education Sciences, Beijing, China
e-mail: zhangchongchina@126.com

© Springer Nature Switzerland AG 2019
D. A. Kilpatrick et al. (eds.), *Reading Development and Difficulties*,
https://doi.org/10.1007/978-3-030-26550-2_2

All writing systems convey information about meaning and pronunciation. This is true regardless of what oral language or languages you know and which of the many written scripts you are reading. Reading-related phonological processing refers to the pronunciation aspect of the information that is represented by print. The Greek word *phōnē* (**fwnh/**) refers to sound or voice, and it is the root of the family of words that includes *phonological, phonemic, phone*, and *phoneme*. The general term phonological processing refers to use of speech-based sounds/codes for processing oral or written language (Wagner & Torgesen, 1987).

The present chapter is divided into four parts. In the first part, we provide a brief review of the three most widely known reading-related phonological processes and their relations to reading. Much of this research is based on studies using alphabetic orthographies. For many years, it was assumed that completely different requirements were associated with different kinds of scripts, such as alphabetic writing systems versus non-alphabetic writing systems. However, we now have a rapidly growing body of literature based on non-alphabetic orthographies such as Chinese, so we provide a brief review of this growing literature in the second part. Reflecting the growing interest in bi- and multi-lingual individuals, part three provides a brief review of phonological processing in individuals' non-native languages. In the fourth and final part, we address the assessment of phonological processing.

2.1 Three Kinds of Reading-Related Phonological Processing

Three kinds of phonological processing are most commonly associated with reading: phonological awareness, phonological memory, and phonological recoding in lexical access (Wagner & Torgesen, 1987).

2.1.1 Phonological Awareness

Phonological awareness refers to one's awareness and access to the sound structure of one's oral language (Mattingly, 1972). Sound structure refers to how the words in an oral language are pronounced, and this structure can be represented at several levels. At the lowest level, *phones* refer to all sounds that are made when pronouncing the words in one's language. For example, pronouncing the first sound in the English word "tuck" involves placing the tip of the tongue on the back of the upper front teeth, blocking off the airway and building up some pressure in it, then explosively releasing the pressure by opening the airway and dropping the tip of the tongue away from the back of the teeth. This sound is labeled a plosive stop consonant because of the way it is produced. The first sound in the word "puck" is produced in a similar manner except that the tongue is not placed against the back of the teeth, but rather the lips are closed and then opened. Relatedly, doing similar articulatory gestures but pushing air through the vocal cords to get them to vibrate changes the sound from the unvoiced first sound in "puck" to the voiced first sound in the word "buck."

At the next higher level of sound structure, related phones are categorized into abstract phonemes that signal differences in meaning. For example, "tuck" and "duck" mean two different things, and this is signaled by the fact that the words begin with different phonemes. In alphabetic writing systems, the sounds of letters of the alphabet correspond roughly to phonemes. The degree of correspondence varies depending on where the orthography falls on the continuum between transparent (e.g., Finnish, with a nearly perfect correspondence between letters and phonemes) to opaque (e.g., English, where there are many deviations from perfect correspondence). The sounds associated with the "t" in the words "top," "stop," and "pot" are identical phonemes but actually different phones in that there are subtle differences in the articulatory gestures used to pronounce them. To demonstrate this fact, hold your hand in front of your mouth while you say the words *top, stop,* and *pot.* You will notice differences in the degree to which you feel an explosive burst of air associated with the /t/ sound. The largest burst will be felt for the /t/ in *top.* Somewhat less of a burst will be felt for the /t/ in *pot,* and the least amount will be felt for the /t/ in *stop.* Different phones that are associated with the same phoneme, such as the three sounds of the /t/ are referred to as allophones of the phoneme /t/.

For Midwestern American English, which refers to the dialect spoken by most newscasters on national networks in the USA, all of the words in the language can be produced by stringing together a sequence taken from a basic list of just over 40 total phonemes. Combinations of phonemes give rise to additional levels of representation. A syllable, for example, is a unit of sounds that typically consists of an onset and a rime. The onset refers to the initial consonantal phoneme (e.g., the *h* in *hat*), and the rime refers to vowel and any trailing phonemes in that syllable (the *at* in *hat*). For example, the first syllable in the two-syllable word *subject* is made up of the onset /s/ and the rime /ub/. All whole words are made up of one or more syllables.

Different orthographies represent speech differently, depending on what the symbols signify. Japanese Kana is referred to as a syllabic orthography because the characters represent syllables for the most part. Regular or transparent alphabetic orthographies such as Finnish or Spanish are referred to as phonemic orthographies because the letters correspond to phonemes. Irregular or opaque alphabetic orthographies such as English or French are considered to be morphophonemic orthographies because the spellings represent sounds or phonemes but with exceptions that reflect morphemes or meaning (Seymour, Aro, & Erskine, 2003).

There is a well-established developmental order in which children are able to access levels of phonological representation. Larger units are easier to bring to awareness and manipulate than smaller units. The easiest and most accessible level for awareness and manipulation is compound words, which are composed of whole words (e.g., *cow-boy*). Next comes the ability to recognize and manipulate syllables within whole words (*en-ter*). Following that is an awareness of onsets (i.e., the initial consonant(s) of a syllable) and rimes (i.e., the vowel and remaining consonants within syllables) (e.g., *r-un*) and the ability to manipulate them. Then comes an awareness and ability to manipulate individual phonemes (e.g., /r/ /u/ /n/), followed by an awareness and ability to manipulate individual phonemes within phoneme clusters (e.g., /s/ /t/ /r/ /aw/) (Crowder & Wagner, 1992).

A practical application of this order of phonological development is in selecting test items for an assessment designed for individuals at different developmental levels. For example, blending is a common phonological awareness task in which separately presented speech segments are combined, often to form a whole word. The very easiest blending items, which can be performed by pre-readers, are blending two words together to form a compound word. The next easiest, which also can be performed by pre-readers, are items requiring blending syllables together to form a word. Then comes blending onsets and rimes into syllables, a task that can be difficult for pre-readers. Very difficult for most pre-readers are items that require blending of individual phonemes. By incorporating each of these kinds of items in the appropriate order, it is possible to come up with a blending task that can be used for all readers, from pre-readers to skilled readers.

2.1.2 Phonological Memory

Phonological memory refers to using phonological (i.e., speech-sound-based) codes for temporary storage of information. If you try to remember a series of numbers or letters, you typically will code them phonologically by saying and maybe repeating their names. This keeps them active in short-term memory. Information can be kept in short-term memory for short periods of time by using the phonological loop and an articulatory control process (Baddeley, 1986, 1992; Torgesen & Davis, 1996). The phonological loop can be thought of as a loop of recording tape that can store roughly the most recent 2 seconds worth of auditory input. The articulatory control process allows auditory information to enter the phonological loop and can also be used to refresh the information in the loop so that storage extends beyond 2 seconds.

Reading single words that are already known do not appear to rely heavily on phonological memory, but phonological memory appears to be more critical for other aspects of reading and language. First, phonological memory is used when a new word is encountered and one attempts to read it by sounding it out. What appears to be happening is that the sounds of individual letters are retrieved sequentially, and successfully sounding out the word requires storing the initial sounds while subsequent sounds are retrieved. Second, impaired phonological memory can make it more difficult to learn new words encountered in print and also appear to constrain adding new words to one's oral vocabulary (Gathercole & Baddeley, 1990; Gathercole, Willis, & Baddeley, 1991). The reason that impaired phonological processing appears to constrain adding new words to one's oral vocabulary may be the same reason that makes it difficult to read new words by sounding them out. New oral vocabulary words exist as a string of phonemes that must be stored in order to form a pronunciation that can be associated with meaning. Based upon David Share's *self-teaching hypothesis*, this sounding-out process plays an important role in remembering newly encountered words (see this volume Miles & Ehri, Chap. 4). Third, phonological memory appears to be required to support working memory when comprehending entire sentences. Although it is true that meaning is extracted when words are encountered in sentences, readers need a sense of the order of words in complex sentences to understand them. Phonological memory appears to facilitate this (see Oakhill, Cain, & Elbro, Chap. 5, this volume).

2.1.3 Phonological Recoding in Lexical Access

Phonological recoding in lexical access refers to coding information phonologically for the purpose of lexical entry, i.e., accessing the location in memory where a word's pronunciation, orthographic representation, and meaning are stored. Location may be the wrong metaphor because the three kinds of representations may be distributed rather than stored in a specific location in the brain. Yet the basic idea of using pronunciation to access a word's orthographic representation and meaning holds true regardless. Phonological recoding in lexical access is typically assessed by tasks that are commonly referred to as *rapid automatized naming* (RAN), or simply *rapid naming*. Such tasks require individuals to name strings of known items as quickly and accurately as possible. It has also been assessed in the laboratory using a computer presentation of single items and a voice-activated key measures, in milliseconds, when the pronunciation begins. Rapid naming of items such as the names of pictured objects, the names of the colors in colored squares, or the names of letters or digits requires efficient recall of the pronunciations that comprise the names from long-term or permanent memory. Although the name retrieval aspect of the task is clearly phonological in nature, rapid-naming tasks are different from phonological awareness and phonological memory tasks in that visual stimuli are required for such assessments. This makes the rapid-naming task a hybrid one in which a visual symbol must be processed or identified as an initial step in the name retrieval process. It has been assumed that the efficiency with which individuals are able to retrieve the phonological codes associated with individual phonemes, word segments, or pronunciations of complete words should influence the degree to which phonological information can be used to read words (Baddeley, 1986; Wolf, 1991).

The hybrid nature of rapid naming means that naming will depend on how well the items to be named are known, how well the associated phonological representation is known, and how strong the mapping is between the item and its pronunciation. Reading shares this hybrid nature, and this may be one reason why rapid naming is predictive of reading independently of measures of phonological awareness (Bowers & Swanson, 1991; Lervag & Hulme, 2009; Manis, Doi, & Badha, 2000; Parrila, Kirby, & McQuarrie, 2004).

Most of the research that was reviewed in the previous section was based on studies with participants who were learning alphabetic writing systems such as English. What is known about how phonological processing is related to reading non-alphabetic scripts such as Chinese?

2.2   Reading-Related Phonological Processing and Learning to Read Chinese

Decades ago, when research was primarily based on alphabetic writing systems, the most important link between phonological processing and reading was believed to be mapping phonemes onto letters. Alphabetic writing systems are designed to represent the spoken language at the level of individual letters, though as mentioned, some alphabet-based writing systems do so more transparently than others (Seymour et al., 2003). Impaired phonological processing was thought to interfere with developing tight connections between letters and sounds.

Non-alphabetic writing systems such as Chinese do not have alphabetic letters corresponding to individual phonemes/sounds. Consequently, learning to read Chinese does not involve learning to map phonemes onto letters. It was conjectured that it might be possible for individuals who struggled learning to read English to learn to read Chinese without difficulty. This conjecture was reinforced by the fact that reading disability has not been recognized as a problem for Chinese children by many parents and teachers. However, a growing body of research indicates that individuals who are impaired in phonological processing can be found regardless of the oral language they speak, and that phonological processing tasks predict learning to read regardless of the nature of the written script. This probably occurs because all written scripts convey information about both pronunciation and meaning, and phonological processing is related to the pronunciation aspect of what written scripts convey.

In this section of the chapter, we review empirical work examining (1) how different aspects of phonological processing relate to reading Chinese, drawing from investigations with typical and atypical readers, and (2) how these findings relate to the phonological structure of Chinese.

2.2.1   Phonological Awareness in Chinese

Among the three kinds of phonological processing, phonological awareness has been examined most extensively in Chinese. As mentioned, phonological processing is important for reading all written scripts because they convey information about pronunciation as well as meaning. Additionally, phonological awareness is important for reading Chinese because of several unique characteristics associated with the Chinese orthography (i.e., writing system). First, written Chinese maps primarily onto syllables (McBride-Chang, Bialystok, Chong, & Li, 2004). It is estimated that there are 400 and 600 syllables in Mandarin and Cantonese, respectively. The number of unique syllables in each of the two Chinese languages increases when tones are considered, which feature as the second unique characteristic of Chinese. Specifically, Mandarin has four tones and Cantonese has six. Third, syllables are commonly segmented into onsets and rimes in Chinese for instruction, at least in countries such as Mainland China and Taiwan, where phonological cueing systems such as *pinyin* and *zhuyin fuhao* are used to help children map sounds onto Roman characters (pinyin) or specialized non Roman characters (zhuyin fuhao) in the early stages of learning.

Similar to the developmental pattern observed in alphabetic languages in which young children are initially aware of larger phonological units and eventually become aware of smaller units, the development of phonological awareness in Chinese is characterized by larger sound units being acquired before more fine-grained ones (Ho & Bryant, 1997). Specifically, the development of phonological awareness in Chinese has been shown to progress from the awareness of syllables, to that of rimes and tones, and finally onsets (Ho & Bryant, 1997; Shu, Peng, & McBride-Chang, 2008).

Phonological awareness in Chinese takes the form of syllabic and tone awareness related to character reading across different Chinese learning contexts and ages (e.g., McBride-Chang & Kail, 2002; McBride-Chang et al., 2008; Shu et al., 2008; Tong et al., 2011; Tong, Tong, & McBride-Chang, 2015; Yeung & Ganotice, 2014). For example, Tong et al. (2015) found that the ability to detect tones was a significant predictor of character reading among kindergarteners in Hong Kong. In another study conducted by McBride-Chang et al. (2008) with kindergarteners in Hong Kong, both tone and syllable awareness were significant predictors of Chinese character reading.

Extending these findings, longitudinal studies suggest that syllable awareness is a predictor of subsequent reading in Chinese (Lei et al., 2011; Pan et al., 2016). For example, in the study conducted by Pan and colleagues (2016) children's syllable awareness assessed in kindergarten and Grade 1 remained a significant predictor of reading in Chinese in subsequent years. Intervention studies also suggest causal relationships between these two aspects of phonological awareness and character reading (e.g., Wang, Liu, Chung, & Yang, 2017). In the study conducted by Wang et al. (2017), Grade 2 children with dyslexia in Hong Kong showed an improvement in a character-naming task after receiving an intervention targeted at the development of tone awareness.

By contrast, studies that have examined the role of onset and rime awareness in character reading have yielded mixed findings (e.g., Ho & Bryant, 1997; So & Siegel, 1997; Wang, Lin, & Yang, 2014). On the one hand, Wang et al. (2014) found rime awareness to be a significant predictor of Chinese word reading among Grade 1 Chinese–English bilingual children in the USA. On the other hand, research conducted by McBride-Chang and colleagues (2008) showed that onset awareness did not predict Chinese word reading among kindergarteners in Hong Kong. In yet another study, Ho and Bryant (1997) found that rime awareness was a significant predictor of Chinese word reading among Grade 1 children but not Grade 2 children in Hong Kong. These inconsistent findings across studies are possibly attributed to differences in learning and instruction. Instead of using phonological cueing systems to aid character learning, Hong Kong children are taught using the whole word/look-say method (see Kilpatrick & O'Brien, Chap. 8, this volume) which encourages the rote memory of visual representations of characters (McBride-Chang et al., 2005), rather than the segmentation of character sounds into onsets and rimes. Therefore, the role of onset and rime awareness in predicting word reading is more unpredictable. By contrast, being in an English-majority environment might encourage children in the study conducted by Wang et al. (2014) to segment sounds into smaller units in a way similar to how they learn English.

2.2.2 Phonological Recoding in Lexical Access in Chinese

Phonological recoding in lexical access in Chinese is assessed using RAN tasks (Wagner & Torgesen, 1987) where participants verbally name objects, digits, colors, or characters/words presented to them in the shortest time possible. Why is phonological recoding in lexical access important for reading in Chinese? Chinese characters are phonologically opaque in that word identification, and naming is accomplished by accessing the character as a whole unit rather than segmenting the character into component sounds. The ability to rapidly access character names in the mental lexicon is thus important for success in reading in Chinese and RAN tasks tap into this rapid retrieval process (Liao, Georgiou, & Parrila, 2008). The role phonological recoding in lexical access plays in Chinese reading is also likely attributable to instructional practices (McBride-Chang & Ho, 2000). Chinese instruction in many Chinese-speaking contexts emphasizes the use of rote memory which likely promotes the automaticity of retrieval of words (McBride-Chang & Ho, 2000). In regard to the RAN-reading relation, three trends have been observed.

First, concurrent relations between different RAN tasks and Chinese character reading have been established across a number of studies (e.g., Chow, McBride-Chang, & Burgess, 2005; Hu & Catts, 1998; Liao et al., 2015; McBride-Chang, Liu, Wong, Wong, & Shu, 2012; McBride-Chang, Shu, Zhou, Wat, & Wagner, 2003; Xue, Shu, Li, Li, & Tian, 2013). For example, digit- and object-naming tasks were significant predictors of Chinese character reading in kindergarten and Grade 2 children in Hong Kong (McBride-Chang et al., 2003). Xue et al. (2013) also found that a digit-naming task was a significant predictor of character reading among children in Grades 2, 4, and 6 in China.

Second, findings of longitudinal relations between RAN tasks and Chinese character reading have been mixed (McBride-Chang & Zhong, 2003; Pan et al., 2011; Wei, Georgiou, & Deng, 2015). On the one hand, McBride-Chang and Zhong (2003) found that among kindergarteners in Hong Kong, RAN abilities measured in kindergarten significantly predicted later character reading. In another study with Taiwanese children (Chang et al., 2014), RAN was consistently a significant predictor of Chinese character reading across three years (Grades 1 to 3) for children who were identified as delayed in naming tasks in kindergarten. Pan and colleagues (2011) also found that among children in China, performance on a composite of the four RAN tasks measured at age 5 was a significant predictor of character reading at ages 7 through 10. These findings are in line with the view that the role of RAN in Chinese reading increases with age (Liao et al., 2008; Tan, Spinks, Eden, Perfetti, & Siok, 2005). By contrast, McBride-Chang and Ho (2005) found that kindergarteners' performance on an object-naming task did not predict character reading two years later. Similarly, Wei et al. (2015) also found no significant longitudinal relations between RAN and word reading in Chinese children who were assessed in Grades 3, 4, and 5.

Third, research has shown that RAN is more predictive of reading fluency as compared to reading accuracy in Chinese (Liao et al., 2015; Shum & Au, 2017; Wei et al., 2015). The explanation put forth is that reading fluency tasks in Chinese are made up of characters or words that are familiar to children and therefore, promote the automaticity of retrieval. In comparison, not all words are familiar in word recognition and character-reading tasks. Thus, automaticity of retrieval might not be as relevant a skill in such a task (Liao et al., 2015).

2.2.3 Phonological Memory

Compared to the other two aspects of phonological processing, there are very few empirical investigations on phonological memory in Chinese. It has been argued that phonological memory is important for Chinese reading for a somewhat unique reason relative to alphabetic orthographies. There are no spaces between characters in Chinese print, which makes word boundaries less obvious. Therefore, when encountering unfamiliar words or characters, readers often have to maintain sounds in memory while processing other characters until word boundaries are identified and word decoding and identification can proceed (Hu & Catts, 1998).

Several tasks have been used to assess phonological memory in Chinese reading. One such task is the short-term memory task developed by So and Siegel (1997). In this task, participants are initially presented with a set of four Chinese characters, after which they are asked to identify the character that was presented in the previous set among five options provided. Other commonly used tasks include digit, word, or nonword repetition tasks where participants are asked to repeat a series of numbers, real Chinese characters, or pseudo-characters, respectively (e.g., Ho & Lai, 1999; Hu & Catts, 1998).

In the limited literature available, findings point to the importance of phonological memory for Chinese reading (e.g., Chan & Siegel, 2001; Ho, Chan, Tsang, & Lee, 2002; Ho & Lai, 1999; Hu & Catts, 1998; So & Siegel, 1997; Xue et al., 2013). For example, Hu and Catts (1998) found that phonological memory, measured using a multi-syllable nonword repetition task, was a significant predictor of reading of Chinese characters among first-grade children in Taiwan. Studies with atypical readers have also yielded similar conclusions. Chan and Siegel (2001) found that poor readers between 7 and 12 years of age in Hong Kong performed significantly lower on a short-term memory task compared to typical readers matched on age. Similarly, Ho and colleagues (2002) found that dyslexic children in Hong Kong performed worse on a word repetition task compared to age-matched controls. It was interesting to note that no significant between-group differences were observed on the nonword repetition task in this study. Considering that different tasks were used across studies, future studies should examine how different tasks of phonological recoding in working memory relate to Chinese reading.

Several studies have compared the predictive performance of the three kinds of phonological processing tasks in the same study (Hu & Catts, 1998; McBride-Chang & Ho, 2000; Xue et al., 2013). For example, McBride-Chang and Ho (2000) showed that when all three components were considered in the same model predicting character recognition, phonological awareness was a stronger predictor of reading compared to phonological memory and rapid naming based on a study of preschoolers in Hong Kong. However, based on their findings with older dyslexic children, Ho et al. (2002) concluded that deficits in rapid naming were the most significant type of deficit among children with reading disabilities in Chinese. Although this difference in findings is in line with the notion that the strength of the relation between rapid naming and reading increases with age (Liao et al., 2008; Tan et al., 2005), further investigations that test children on the relevant constructs over time are needed to draw more definitive conclusions.

Regarding differences in findings described earlier, we speculate on a number of possible explanations. First, the differences in findings regarding the roles of onset and rime awareness in Chinese reading could be due to differences in instruction and learning across different Chinese learning contexts. Of particular importance is whether some phonological system such as pinyin is used in instruction. Turning to the mixed findings in regard to the longitudinal relations between RAN and reading, questions about the mechanisms underlying RAN and why this set of tasks that assess phonological recoding in lexical access predicts Chinese reading should be investigated further. Finally, a variety of tasks have been used across different studies to measure the same construct. Task differences could also have an impact on the associations observed. Thus, future studies should also examine how task differences contribute to the phonological processing–reading relations.

2.3 Reading-Related Phonological Processing Abilities in Multi-lingual Children

Many studies have shown that there is a proximal and likely if not causal relationship between phonological processing skills and reading in English and other alphabetic languages (e.g., Caravolas et al., 2012; Wagner & Torgesen, 1987; Ziegler et al., 2010). Recently, there has been an expansion of studies to measure the relationship between phonological processing skills and reading in other languages, including studies of individuals who know more than one language. This literature is guided by the psycholinguistic grain size theory (Ziegler & Goswami, 2005, 2006) which states that producing meaning from text is guided by the availability of sounds in the spoken language, the granularity of the writing system, and the overlap between the spoken and written systems. Thus, a writing system with a highly regular representation of phonemes (e.g., Spanish, Korean) would be easier in terms of phonological processing compared to a writing system with numerous irregularities (e.g., English, French) or one in which phonemes are not clearly represented (e.g., Chinese, Japanese). This is critical in examining cross-language relationships in phonological awareness tasks.

Melby-Lervag and Lervag (2011) conducted a meta-analysis on cross-linguistic transfer of oral language, decoding, phonological awareness, and reading comprehension. They found a small meta-correlation for the transfer of oral language between L1 and L2, but a moderate to large correlation for the transfer of phonological awareness and decoding between L1 and L2. According to Branum-Martin, Tao, Garnaat, Bunta, & Francis (2012), there is a high correlation between phonological tasks in English and other alphabetic languages. Similar findings were reported by Comeau, Cormier, Grandmaison, and Lacroix (1999) who found the relationship between phonological awareness and reading achievement were similar in both English and French, and confirmed a transfer of these skills between these two alphabetic languages. A study by LaFrance and Gottardo (2005) found that phonological awareness in both French and English were uniquely predictive of reading achievement in both languages, after accounting for the effects of cognitive ability, reading ability, working memory, and naming speed (see Geva, Xi, Massey-Garrison, & Mak, Chap. 6, this volume for a more extensive review of this research).

Phonological awareness skills in other languages are moderately to highly correlated with English phonological awareness tasks (Branum-Martin et al., 2012). According to Dickinson, McCabe, Clark-Chiarelli, and Wolf (2004), the development of phonological awareness in either Spanish or English among Spanish–English bilinguals is strongly predictive of the development of phonological awareness in the other language. Similar findings were reported for Persian–English bilinguals and Arabic–English bilinguals. Arab-Moghaddam and Senechal (2001) measured the concurrent development of reading and spelling in Persian and English bilinguals. They found the predictors of reading were similar across the two languages, with phonological and orthographic skills predicting variance in word reading in both English and Persian. Al Ghanem and Kerns (2015) conducted a synthesis of existing literature to measure whether orthographic, morphological, or phonological skills played a bigger role in learning to read in Arabic. They found that phonological skills had the strongest association with learning to read in Arabic, across vowelized and unvowelized texts.

By contrast, some researchers have found phonological processing skills to play a minimal role in reading acquisition in Korean and Chinese. According to Fraser (2010), phonological awareness was not predictive of Hangul word reading. Chen, Ku, Koyama, Anderson, and Li (2008) measured the development of phonological awareness in Chinese bilingual children and found that while onset-rime awareness had a more universal development pattern across Mandarin and Cantonese, tone awareness was a more language-specific construct which developed faster among Mandarin-speaking children compared to Cantonese-speaking children. Chow, McBride-Chang, and Burgess (2005) examined the relationship between Chinese phonological processing skills (phonological awareness, rapid automatized naming, and short-term verbal memory) in early Chinese and English readers who were kindergarten-aged in Hong Kong. They found that out of the phonological processing skills that were measured, only phonological awareness remained a significant predictor both concurrently and longitudinally for both Chinese- and English-reading skills.

Although more research remains to be done, the past decade has been characterized by a surge of studies with non-alphabetical writing systems. The main conclusion appears to be that the commonalities outweigh the differences in terms of how phonological processing is related to ostensibly very different writing systems.

2.4   Measuring Phonological Processing

A variety of tests are available that include measures of one or more of the three kinds of phonological processing abilities presented in this chapter—phonological awareness, phonological memory, and rapid naming. We will begin by describing a test that was developed specifically for measuring these three reading-related phonological processing abilities and then describe other measures that include subtests that measure various aspects of phonological processing.

The *Comprehensive Test of Phonological Processing—Second Edition* (CTOPP-2; Wagner, Torgesen, Rashotte, & Pearson, 2013) is an individually administered test battery that was specifically designed to measure phonological awareness, phonological memory, and rapid naming. It is appropriate for individuals from age 4 through 24. The CTOPP-2 differs from other tests in its comprehensive measurement of phonological processing (Dickens, Meisinger, & Tara, 2015), given that it includes multiple measures of each of the three types of phonological processing abilities. The multiple measures are combined into composite scores that are more reliable than are individual subtest scores. There are two versions of the test, one for children aged 4–6 and a second for individuals from age 7 to 24. The composite scores and the subtests that comprise them for both versions are presented in Tables 2.1 and 2.2. The composites are similar for both versions with a few differences. Rapid naming for the 4- to 6-year-old version has composites for both symbolic items (e.g., letters and digits) and non-symbolic items (e.g., colors and objects). There is an alternate phonological awareness composite for the 7- through 24-year-old version that is made up of two phonological awareness tasks with nonword items. Finally, the phonological awareness composite includes sound matching for the 4- to 6-year-old version, and this subtest is replaced by a phoneme isolation subtest in the 7- through 24-year-old version.

There are also phonological processing measures on achievement, language, and cognitive test batteries. The *Kaufman Test of Educational Achievement—Third Edition* (KTEA-III; Kaufman & Kaufman, 2014) includes individual subtests for measuring phonological awareness and rapid object naming. Multiple subtests are not provided, so composite scores are not available. The *Process Assessment of the Learner—Second Edition* (PAL II; Berninger, 2001) is a comprehensive system for screening, assessment, and ongoing monitoring of intervention. The PAL II includes

Table 2.1 CTOPP–2 composite scores and subtests for the 4 to 6-year-old version

Composites				
	Phonological awareness	Phonological memory	Rapid symbolic naming	Rapid non-symbolic naming
Core subtests				
Elision	X			
Blending words	X			
Sound matching	X			
Memory for digits		X		
Nonword repetition		X		
Rapid digit naming			X	
Rapid letter naming			X	
Rapid color naming				X
Rapid object naming				X
Supplemental subtests				
Blending nonwords				

measures of phonological awareness, phonological processing, and rapid automatized naming, but no composite scores and many subtests have a limited number of items. The *Woodcock Johnson Tests—Fourth Edition WJ IV* (LaForte, McGrew, & Schrank, 2014) include separate assessment batteries for *Oral Language (WJ IV OL)*, *Cognitive Abilities (WK IV COG)* and *Achievement (WJ IV ACH)*. The batteries include measures of phonological awareness, phonological processing, and rapid automatized naming. To get the three skills measured, however, requires use of multiple batteries (WJ IV OL and WJ IV COG). The *Woodcock Reading Mastery Test—Third Edition* (WRMT-III; Woodcock, 2011) was recently updated to include a phonological awareness subtest and rapid-naming subtests. The *Wechsler Individual Achievement Test—Third Edition* (WIAT-III; Wechsler, 2009) does not have any phonological processing subtests. However, the WIAT-IV, under development at this writing, is slated to have a phonological awareness subtest.

The *Emerging Literacy and Language Assessment* (ELLA; Wiig, & Secord, 2006) includes subtests that measure phonological awareness and rapid automatized naming. The *Gray Diagnostic Reading Test—Second Edition* (GDRT-2; Bryant, Wiederholt, & Bryant, 2004) includes supplemental subtests that assess rapid naming and phonological awareness. The *Dynamic Indicators of Basic Literacy Skills* (DIBELS;

Table 2.2 CTOPP 2 composite scores and subtests for the 7 to 24-year-old version

Composites

	Phonological awareness	Phonological memory	Rapid symbolic naming	Alternate phonological awareness
Core subtests				
Elision	X			
Blending words	X			
Phoneme isolation	X			
Memory for digits		X		
Nonword repetition		X		
Rapid digit naming			X	
Rapid letter naming			X	
Supplemental subtests				
Blending nonwords				X
Segmenting nonwords				X

Good & Kaminski, 2002) includes measures of phonological awareness in the form of initial sound fluency and phoneme segmentation fluency. The *Test of Preschool Early Literacy* (TOPEL; Lonigan, Wagner, Torgesen, & Rashotte, 2007) includes a measure of phonological awareness. The *Phonological Awareness Profile* (PAP; Robertson & Salter, 1995) is a criterion-referenced test that is administered individually and designed to track progress in phonological awareness skills. The *Phonological Awareness Test—Second Edition* (PAT-2) includes multiple phonological awareness subtests (Robertson & Salter, 2017). The *Rapid Automatized Naming and Rapid Alternating Stimulus Tests* (RAN/RAS; Wolf & Denkla, 2005) include subtests that measure rapid naming of letters, numbers, objects, and colors. The *Wechsler Intelligence Test for Children—Fifth Edition* (WISC-V; Wechsler, 2014) has subtests for phonological memory and rapid naming. The *Differential Abilities Scales—Second Edition* (DAS-2; Elliot, 2007) includes a rapid-naming subtest. Finally, the Phonological Awareness Screening Test (PAST; Kilpatrick, 2016) is a free, standardized but non-normed assessment of phonological awareness with a focus on the speed of responding to the individual test items.[1] It can function as a supplement to normed

---

[1] This is not to be confused with another free test with the same acronym of PAST which is the Phonological Awareness Skills Test, which approaches assessment of phonological awareness in a very different manner and has no focus on speed of response to test items.

assessments, such as the CTOPP-2 *Elision* and *Phoneme Isolation,* providing some information about the proficiency of phonological skills given the element of response time per item feature of the PAST

2.5 Summary

In this chapter, we addressed four topics regarding reading-related phonological processing. First, we reviewed the three most common reading-related phonological processes: Phonological awareness; phonological memory; and phonological recoding for lexical access (i.e., rapid naming or RAN). We discussed how they are related to reading. Second, we reviewed the literature on phonological processing and its relations with reading Chinese. It was shown that the similarities were greater than the differences in how phonological processing is related to alphabetic and non-alphabetic scripts. Third, given that an increasing number of children learning to read know more than one spoken language, we reviewed what is known about phonological processing in multi-lingual individuals. Finally, we did a brief review of measures of phonological processing available in English. This chapter functions as a primer on phonological processing, a theme that emerges over and over again in the other chapters throughout this volume, given the intimate relationship between phonological processes and reading.

References

Al Ghanem, R., & Kearns, D. M. (2015). Orthographic, phonological, and morphological skills and children's word reading in Arabic: A literature review. *Reading Research Quarterly, 50*(1), 83–109. https://doi.org/10.1002/rrq.84.

Arab-Moghaddam, N., & Sénéchal, M. (2001). Orthographic and phonological processing skills in reading and spelling in Persian/English bilinguals. *International Journal of Behavioral Development, 25*(2), 140–147. https://doi.org/10.1080/01650250042000320.

Baddeley, A. (1986). *Oxford Psychology Series, No. 11. Working Memory.* New York, NY: Oxford University Press.

Baddeley, A. (1992). Working memory and conscious awareness. In A. F. Collins, S. E. Gathercole, M. A. Conway, & P. E. Morris (Eds.), *Theories of memory* (pp. 11–20). Hove, UK: Lawrence Erlbaum Associates.

Berninger, V. (2001). *Process assessment of the learner (PAL) test battery for reading and writing.* San Antonio, TX: The Psychological Corporation.

Bowers, P. G., & Swanson, L. B. (1991). Naming speed deficits in reading disability: Multiple measures of a singular process. *Journal of Experimental Child Psychology, 51,* 195–219. https://doi.org/10.1016/0022-0965(91)90032-N.

Branum-Martin, L., Tao, S., Garnaat, S., Bunta, F., & Francis, D. J. (2012). Meta-analysis of bilingual phonological awareness: Language, age, and psycholinguistic grain size. *Journal of Educational Psychology, 104*(4), 932–944. https://doi.org/10.1037/a0027755.

Bryant, R. B., Wiederholt, J. L., & Bryant, D. P. (2004). *Gray diagnostic reading test—Second edition.* Austin, TX: PRO-ED.

Caravolas, M., Lervåg, A., Mousikou, P., Efrim, C., Litavský, M., Onochie-Quintanilla, E., ... & Seidlová-Málková, G. (2012). Common patterns of prediction of literacy development in different alphabetic orthographies. *Psychological Science, 23*(6), 678–686. https://doi.org/10.1177/0956797611434536.

Chan, C. K., & Siegel, L. S. (2001). Phonological processing in reading Chinese among normally achieving and poor readers. *Journal of Experimental Child Psychology, 80*(1), 23–43. https://doi.org/10.1006/jecp.2000.2622.

Chang, Y. J., Su, F. H., Tzeng, S. J., Ko, H. W., Wu, M. L., Yang, C. C., et al. (2014). The contribution of rapid automatized naming to Chinese character recognition. *Learning and Individual Differences, 34,* 43–50. https://doi.org/10.1016/j.lindif.2014.05.010.

Chen, X., Ku, Y. M., Koyama, E., Anderson, R. C., & Li, W. (2008). Development of phonological awareness in bilingual Chinese children. *Journal of Psycholinguistic Research, 37*(6), 405–418. https://doi.org/10.1007/s10936-008-9085-z.

Chow, B. W. Y., McBride-Chang, C., & Burgess, S. (2005). Phonological processing skills and early reading abilities in Hong Kong Chinese kindergarteners learning to read English as a second language. *Journal of Educational Psychology, 97*(1), 81–87. https://doi.org/10.1037/0022-0663.97.1.81.

Comeau, L., Cormier, P., Grandmaison, É., & Lacroix, D. (1999). A longitudinal study of phonological processing skills in children learning to read in a second language. *Journal of Educational Psychology, 91*(1), 29. https://doi.org/10.1037/0022-0663.91.1.29.

Crowder, R. G., & Wagner, R. K. (1992). *The psychology of reading.* New York: Oxford University Press.

Dickens, R. H., Meisinger, E. B., & Tarar, J. M. (2015). Test review CTOPP-2. *Canadian Journal of School Psychology, 30*(2), 155–162. https://doi.org/10.1177/0829573514563280.

Dickinson, D. K., McCabe, A., Clark-Chiarelli, N., & Wolf, A. (2004). Cross-language transfer of phonological awareness in low-income Spanish and English bilingual preschool children. *Applied Psycholinguistics, 25*(3), 323–347. https://doi.org/10.1017.S0142716404001158.

Elliott, C. (2007). *Differential ability scales—Second edition.* San Antonio, TX: Harcourt Assessment.

Fraser, C. M. (2010). *An exploration of levels of phonological awareness as predictors of word reading in Korean children learning English* (Unpublished doctoral dissertation).

Gathercole, S. E., & Baddeley, A. D. (1990). Phonological memory deficits in language disordered children: Is there a causal connection? *Journal of Memory and Language, 29,* 336–360. https://doi.org/10.1016/0749-596X(90)90004-J.

Gathercole, S. E., Willis, C., & Baddeley, A. D. (1991). Differentiating phonological memory and awareness of rhyme: Reading and vocabulary development in children. *British Journal of Psychology, 82*(3), 387–406. https://doi.org/10.1111/j.2044-8295.1991.tb02407.x.

Good, R. H., & Kaminski, R. A. (2002). *Dynamic indicators of basic early literacy skills—Sixth edition.* Eugene, OR: Institute for the Development of Educational Achievement.

Ho, C. S.-H., & Bryant, P. (1997). Phonological skills are important in learning to read Chinese. *Developmental Psychology, 33*(6), 946–951. https://doi.org/10.1037/0012-1649.33.6.946.

Ho, C. S. H., & Lai, D. N. C. (1999). Naming-speed deficits and phonological memory deficits in Chinese developmental dyslexia. *Learning and Individual Differences, 11*(2), 173–186. https://doi.org/10.1016/s1041-6080(00)80004-7.

Ho, C. S.-H., Chan, D. W.-O., Tsang, S.-M., & Lee, S.-H. (2002). The cognitive profile and multiple-deficit hypothesis in Chinese developmental dyslexia. *Developmental Psychology, 38*(4), 543–553. https://doi.org/10.1037/0012-1649.38.4.543.

Hu, C. F., & Catts, H. W. (1998). The role of phonological processing in early reading ability: What we can learn from Chinese. *Scientific Studies of Reading, 2*(1), 55–79. https://doi.org/10.1207/s1532799xssr0201_3.

Kaufman, A. S., & Kaufman, N. L. (2014). *Kaufman test of educational achievement—Third edition (KTEA-3).* Bloomington, MN: NCS Pearson.

Kilpatrick, D. A. (2016). *The phonological awareness screening test.* Syracuse, NY: Author (www.thepasttest.com).

LaForte, E. M., McGrew, K. S., & Schrank, F. A. (2014). *WJ IV technical abstract* (Woodcock-Johnson IV Assessment Service Bulletin No. 2). Rolling Meadows, IL: Riverside.

Lafrance, A., & Gottardo, A. (2005). A longitudinal study of phonological processing skills and reading in bilingual children. *Applied Psycholinguistics, 26*(4), 559–578. https://doi.org/10.1017/S0142716405050307.

Lei, L., Pan, J., Liu, H., McBride-Chang, C., Li, H., Zhang, Y., … & Shu, H. (2011). Developmental trajectories of reading development and impairment from ages 3 to 8 years in Chinese children. *Journal of Child Psychology and Psychiatry, 52*(2), 212–220. https://doi.org/10.1111/j.1469-7610.2010.02311.x.

Lervag, A., & Hulme, C. (2009). Rapid automatized naming (RAN) taps a mechanism that places constraints on the development of early reading fluency. *Psychological Science, 20*(8), 1040–1048. https://doi.org/10.1111/j.1467-9280.2009.02405.x.

Liao, C. H., Deng, C., Hamilton, J., Lee, C. S. C., Wei, W., & Georgiou, G. K. (2015). The role of rapid naming in reading development and dyslexia in Chinese. *Journal of Experimental Child Psychology, 30*, 106–122. https://doi.org/10.1016/j.jecp.2014.10.002.

Liao, C. H., Georgiou, G. K., & Parrila, R. (2008). Rapid naming speed and Chinese character recognition. *Reading and Writing: An Interdisciplinary Journal, 21*(3), 231–253. https://doi.org/10.1007/s11145-007-9071-0.

Lonigan, C. J., Wagner, R. K., Torgesen, J. K., & Rashotte, C. A. (2007). *Test of preschool early literacy.* Austin, TX: PRO-ED.

Manis, F. R., Doi, L. M., & Bhadha, B. (2000). Naming speed, phonological awareness, and orthographic knowledge in second graders. *Journal of Learning Disabilities, 33*(325–333), 374. https://doi.org/10.1177/002221940003300405.

Mattingly, I. G. (1972). Reading, the linguistic process and linguistic awareness. In J. Kavanagh & I. Mattingly (Eds.), *Language by ear and by eye* (pp. 133–147). Cambridge, MA: MIT Press.

McBride-Chang, C., Bialystok, E., Chong, K. K., & Li, Y. (2004). Levels of phonological awareness in three cultures. *Journal of Experimental Child Psychology, 89*(2), 93–111. https://doi.org/10.1016/j.jecp.2004.05.001.

McBride-Chang, C., Cho, J. R., Liu, H., Wagner, R. K., Shu, H., Zhou, A., … & Muse, A. (2005). Changing models across cultures: Associations of phonological awareness and morphological structure awareness with vocabulary and word recognition in second graders from Beijing, Hong Kong, Korea, and the United States. *Journal of Experimental Child Psychology, 92*(2), 140–160. https://doi.org/10.1016/j.jecp.2005.03.009.

McBride-Chang, C., & Ho, C. S.-H. (2000). Naming speed and phonological awareness in Chinese children: Relations to reading skills. *Journal of Psychology in Chinese Societies, 1*(1), 93–108.

McBride-Chang, C., & Ho, C.-S. (2005). Predictors of beginning reading in Chinese and English: A 2-year longitudinal study of Chinese kindergartners. *Scientific Studies of Reading, 9*(2), 117–144. https://doi.org/10.1207/s1532799xssr0902_2.

McBride-Chang, C., & Kail, R. V. (2002). Cross–cultural similarities in the predictors of reading acquisition. *Child Development, 73*(5), 1392–1407. https://doi.org/10.1111/1467-8624.00479.

McBride-Chang, C., Liu, P. D., Wong, T., Wong, A., & Shu, H. (2012). Specific reading difficulties in Chinese, English, or both: Longitudinal markers of phonological awareness, morphological awareness, and RAN in Hong Kong Chinese children. *Journal of Learning Disabilities, 45*(6), 503–514. https://doi.org/10.1177/0022219411400748.

McBride-Chang, C., Shu, H., Zhou, A., Wat, C. P., & Wagner, R. K. (2003). Morphological awareness uniquely predicts young children's Chinese character recognition. *Journal of Educational Psychology, 95*(4), 743–751. https://doi.org/10.1037/0022-0663.95.4.743.

McBride-Chang, C., Tardif, T., Cho, J. R., Shu, H. U. A., Fletcher, P., Stokes, S. F., et al. (2008). What's in a word? Morphological awareness and vocabulary knowledge in three languages. *Applied Psycholinguistics, 29*(3), 437–462. https://doi.org/10.1017/S014271640808020X.

McBride-Chang, C., & Zhong, Y. (2003). A longitudinal study of effects of phonological processing, visual skills, and speed of processing on Chinese character acquisition among Hong Kong Chinese kindergartners. In C. McBride-Chang & H. C. Chen (Eds.), *Reading development in Chinese children* (pp. 37–49). Westport, CT. Praeger Publishers.

Melby-Lervåg, M., & Lervåg, A. (2011). Cross-linguistic transfer of oral language, decoding, phonological awareness and reading comprehension: A meta-analysis of the correlational evidence. *Journal of Research in Reading, 34*(1), 114–135. https://doi.org/10.1111/j.1467-9817. 2010.01477.x.

Pan, J., McBride-Chang, C., Shu, H., Liu, H., Zhang, Y., & Li, H. (2011). What is in the naming? A 5-year longitudinal study of early rapid naming and phonological sensitivity in relation to subsequent reading skills in both native Chinese and English as a second language. *Journal of Educational Psychology, 103*(4), 897–908. https://doi.org/10.1037/a0024344.

Pan, J., Song, S., Su, M., McBride, C., Liu, H., Zhang, Y., et al. (2016). On the relationship between phonological awareness, morphological awareness and Chinese literacy skills: evidence from an 8-year longitudinal study. *Developmental Science, 19*(6), 982–991. https://doi.org/10.1111/desc. 12356.

Parrila, R., Kirby, J. R., & McQuarrie, L. (2004). Articulation rate, naming speed, verbal short-term memory, and phonological awareness: Longitudinal predictors of early reading development? *Scientific Studies of Reading, 8*(1), 3–26. https://doi.org/10.1207/s1532799xssr0801_2.

Robertson, C., & Salter, W. (1995). *The phonological awareness profile.* Austin, TX: PRO-ED.

Robertson, C., & Salter, W. (2017). *Phonological awareness test-second edition: Normative update.* Austin, TX: PRO-ED.

Seymour, P. K., Aro, M., & Erskine, J. M. (2003). Foundation literacy acquisition in European orthographies. *British Journal of Psychology, 94,* 143–174.

Shu, H., Peng, H., & McBride-Chang, C. (2008). Phonological awareness in young Chinese children. *Developmental Science, 11*(1), 171–181. https://doi.org/10.1111/j.1467-7687.2007.00654.x.

So, D., & Siegel, L. S. (1997). Learning to read Chinese: Semantic, syntactic, phonological and working memory skills in normally achieving and poor Chinese readers. *Reading and Writing: An Interdisciplinary Journal, 9*(1), 1–21. https://doi.org/10.1023/A:1007963513853.

Shum, K. K. M., & Au, T. K. F. (2017). Why does rapid naming predict Chinese word reading? *Language Learning and Development, 13*(1), 127–142. https://doi.org/10.1080/15475441.2016. 1232651.

Tan, L. H., Spinks, J. A., Eden, G. F., Perfetti, C. A., & Siok, W. T. (2005). Reading depends on writing, in Chinese. *Proceedings of the National Academy of Sciences of the United States of America, 102*(24), 8781–8785. https://doi.org/10.1073/pnas.0503523102.

Tong, X., McBride-Chang, C., Wong, A. M. Y., Shu, H., Reitsma, P., & Rispens, J. (2011). Longitudinal predictors of very early Chinese literacy acquisition. *Journal of Research in Reading, 34*(3), 315–332. https://doi.org/10.1111/j.1467-9817.2009.01426.x.

Tong, X., Tong, X., & McBride-Chang, C. (2015). Tune in to the tone: Lexical tone identification is associated with vocabulary and word recognition abilities in young Chinese children. *Language and Speech, 58*(4), 441–458. https://doi.org/10.1177/0023830914562988.

Torgesen, J. K., & Davis, C. (1996). Individual difference variables that predict response to training in phonological awareness. *Journal of Experimental Child Psychology, 63*(1), 1–21.

Wagner, R. K., & Torgesen, J. K. (1987). The nature of phonological processing and its causal role in the acquisition of reading skills. *Psychological Bulletin, 101*(2), 192–212. https://doi.org/10. 1037/0033-2909.101.2.192.

Wagner, R. K., Torgesen, J., Rashotte, C., & Pearson, N. (2013). *Comprehensive Test of Phonological Processing-Second Edition (CTOPP-2).* Austin, TX: Pro-Ed.

Wang, M., Lin, C. Y., & Yang, C. (2014). Contributions of phonology, orthography, and morphology in Chinese-English biliteracy acquisition: A one-year longitudinal study. In X. Chen, Q. Liu, & C. Y. Luo (Eds.), *Reading development and difficulties in monolingual and bilingual Chinese children* (pp. 191–211). Netherlands: Springer.

Wang, L. C., Liu, D., Chung, K. K. H., & Yang, H. M. (2017). Development of lexical tone awareness in Chinese children with and without dyslexia. *Contemporary Educational Psychology, 49,* 203–214. https://doi.org/10.1016/j.cedpsych.2017.02.002.

Wechsler, D. (2009). *Wechsler individual achievement test—Third edition.* Bloomington, MN: Pearson.

Wechsler, D. (2014). *Wechsler intelligence test for children—Fifth edition.* Bloomington, MN: Pearson.

Wei, W., Georgiou, G. K., & Deng, C. (2015). Examining the cross-lagged relationships between RAN and word reading in Chinese. *Scientific Studies of Reading, 19*(6), 446–455. https://doi.org/10.1080/10888438.2015.1077447.

Wiig, E., & Secord, W. (2016). *Emerging literacy and language assessment.* Greenville, SC.: Super Duper Publications.

Wolf, M. (1991). Naming speed and reading: The contribution of the cognitive neurosciences. *Reading Research Quarterly, 26,* 123–141. https://doi.org/10.2307/747978.

Wolf, M., & Denckla, M. B. (2005). *RAN/RAS: Rapid automatized naming and rapid alternating stimulus tests.* Austin, TX: Pro-Ed.

Woodcock, R. W. (2011). *Woodcock reading mastery test—Fourth edition.* San Antonio, TX: Pearson.

Xue, J., Shu, H., Li, H., Li, W., & Tian, X. (2013). The stability of literacy-related cognitive contributions to Chinese character naming and reading fluency. *Journal of Psycholinguistic Research, 42*(5), 433–450. https://doi.org/10.1007/s10936-012-9228-0.

Yeung, S. S., & Ganotice, F. A. (2014). The role of phonological awareness in biliteracy acquisition among Hong Kong Chinese kindergarteners who learn English-as-a-second language (ESL). *The Asia-Pacific Education Researcher, 23*(3), 333–343. https://doi.org/10.1007/s40299-013-0108-7.

Ziegler, J. C., & Goswami, U. (2005). Reading acquisition, developmental dyslexia, and skilled reading across languages: A psycholinguistic grain size theory. *Psychological Bulletin, 131*(1), 3–29.

Ziegler, J. C., & Goswami, U. (2006). Becoming literate in different languages: Similar problems, different solutions. *Developmental Science, 9*(5), 429–436. https://doi.org/10.1037/0033-2909.131.1.3.

Ziegler, J. C., Bertrand, D., Tóth, D., Csépe, V., Reis, A., Faísca, L., et al. (2010). Orthographic depth and its impact on universal predictors of reading: A cross-language investigation. *Psychological Science, 21*(4), 551–559.

Chapter 3
Phonics and Spelling: Learning the Structure of Language at the Word Level

Louisa Moats

Abstract This chapter discusses why phonics in beginning reading and spelling is a critical component of instruction, but more complex and challenging to implement than commonly portrayed. It will argue that phonics is better characterized as an aspect of structured language teaching requiring explicit and systematic skill building within several levels of language organization (phoneme-grapheme correspondences, orthographic patterns, morphology, and etymology). Well-conceived practices supported by theory and research are contrasted with others that do not align with scientific evidence, in spite of their ubiquity. The chapter concludes with a set of well-supported recommendations to improve phonics, word reading, and spelling instruction.

3.1 Most Reading Difficulties Originate from Problems with Decoding and Word Recognition

Our national data continue to show that nearly a third of school children fail to become skilled readers by fourth grade (National Assessment of Educational Progress, United States Department of Education, 2017). This grim statistic has not changed substantially over the last 20 years. Reading failure is associated with costly social, economic, and health impacts for the affected individuals and for our society (Sweet, 2004). Yet one must ask, if reading is one of the most studied of all psychological skills (Rayner, Foorman, Perfetti, Pesetsky, & Seidenberg, 2001; Seidenberg, 2017), why do so many students still not learn to read? This puzzle has many pieces, but a major one is the enduring chasm between scientific research and typical practices in our schools. At the center of the debates regarding reading instruction, there continues to be dissention over whether or not to teach phonics, as well as how to teach phonics.

Cognitive science has shown beyond doubt that fluent, accurate word recognition is a hallmark of skilled reading with comprehension (Adams, 1990; Rayner et al., 2001) and that poor readers are almost always limited by their inability to

L. Moats (✉)
Moats Associates Consulting, Sun Valley, ID, USA
e-mail: louisa.moats@gmail.com

© Springer Nature Switzerland AG 2019   39
D. A. Kilpatrick et al. (eds.), *Reading Development and Difficulties*,
https://doi.org/10.1007/978-3-030-26550-2_3

use letter-sound skills (e.g., phonics skills) to identify unfamiliar words (Ehri, 1998; Rack, Snowling, & Olson, 1992) and, consequently, to establish a sight recognition vocabulary sufficient for fluent reading (Ehri, 2014; Miles & Ehri, Chap. 4, this volume). Accurate and automatic mapping of print to speech, and speech to print (Treiman, 2017), depends first on knowing both sounds and symbols. Interestingly, this apparently easy task—learning letters, sounds, and their connections—ranges from somewhat difficult to very difficult for at least a third of the population (Denton, Fletcher, Taylor, Barth, & Vaughn, 2014). It is the most common impediment standing in the way of normal reading development.

The importance of teaching foundational reading skills in the regular classroom and in intervention programs has been established by meta-analyses and expert reviews over several decades, and these foundational skills include phonological awareness, phonics, and fluent word recognition (Adams, 1990; Anderson, Heibert, Scott, & Wilkinson, 1985; Chall, 1967; Gersten et al. 2008; Foorman et al., 2016; National Institute of Child Health and Human Development, 2000; Snow, Burns, & Griffin, 1998). Teaching phonics and phonological awareness explicitly, systematically, and sequentially, with phoneme-grapheme correspondence as the core focus of instruction, is essential if the goal is preventing reading failure and enabling most students to read. Nevertheless, instruction in how to read words and how to spell them during text reading and writing is often insufficient, haphazard, misinformed, or dissociated from reading and spelling (Moats, 2017). Consequently, reading problems that could be identified, resolved, and/or reduced in severity beginning in kindergarten are left untreated (Torgesen, 2004, 2005).

This chapter will discuss why the subject matter of phonics in beginning reading and spelling is more complex than commonly portrayed. It will argue that this component of instruction would be better characterized as an aspect of structured language teaching at several levels of language organization. Well-conceived practices supported by theory and research will be contrasted with others that do not align with scientific evidence. The chapter concludes with a set of well-supported recommendations to improve phonics, word reading, and spelling instruction.

3.2 Students' Instructional Needs Differ, But How?

Students vary greatly in their literacy knowledge when they arrive at school, for reasons ranging from genetic predispositions or natural aptitudes for processing written language (Olson, Keenan, Byrne, and Samuelsson, 2014; Byrne, Olson, and Samuelsson, Chap. 9, this volume) to their life experiences prior to entering school. Learning to read, however, makes similar cognitive and linguistic demands on everyone. To read English, we must learn the letters, learn to identify the speech sounds that letters represent, and learn to map symbols to sounds very efficiently. If we name a printed word accurately, and know the meaning, we can instantly make sense of it (Rayner et al., 2001).

To spell, we invert this process: We analyze the sounds in words, conjure their meanings (if known), and recall the complete orthographic image or letter sequence of the word if we know it (Treiman, 2017). There is no bypass around the alphabetic coding process in learning to read or spell English. We do not learn words as visual wholes (see Kilpatrick & O'Brien, Chap. 8, this volume). Recognizing words by sight and spelling them is the end result of a multi-phase developmental process described in detail by Ehri (1998, 2014) and colleagues (Ehri, Cardoso-Martins, & Carroll, 2014; Miles & Ehri, Chap. 4, this volume).

It is poor readers who turn to context, guesswork, and pictures to determine the identity of whole words as they read (Adams, 1990; Gough & Tunmer, 1986; Rayner et al., 2001). Those behaviors signify inadequate knowledge of phonic correspondences, print patterns, and decoding strategies. Such students are sometimes mistakenly called "visual learners," although there is no evidence that non-verbal, visual-spatial aptitudes are an asset for learning how to recode the alphabet into spoken language. Poor readers, in the beginning stages of learning to read, most commonly have a language-based learning problem that is interfering with progress in word recognition (Fletcher, Lyon, Fuchs, & Barnes, 2019; Lyon, Shaywitz, & Shaywitz, 2003).

Differentiation of instruction, therefore, should be predicated primarily on a student's levels of phonological awareness (Kilpatrick, 2015), knowledge of sound-symbol correspondences for reading and spelling, automaticity in word recognition, and language comprehension. The relative severity of students' problems in these areas should determine how instructional time is allocated, but phonics instruction will be one key component of effective intervention for the large majority of poor readers (Kilpatrick & O'Brien Chap. 8, this volume).

3.3 General Research Findings About Phonics Instruction

In 1998, the National Reading Panel (NRP) (National Institute of Child Health and Human Development (NICHD), 2000) was commissioned by Congress to resolve long-standing disputes about the best way(s) to teach reading. The report provided a comprehensive review and meta-analysis of scientific evidence on the teaching of reading accumulated to that date, much of it realized through research funded by the NICHD. At the time, 38 studies that met criteria for scientific rigor were included in the analysis of the effects of phonics instruction. The NRP found substantial support for systematic, sequential instruction in phonics, to include all the major letter–sound relationships of both consonants and vowels, and issued these summary recommendations:

- Systematic and explicit phonics instruction is more effective than non-systematic phonics instruction or reading instruction that includes no phonics component.
- Systematic and explicit phonics instruction significantly improves word recognition and spelling for kindergarten and first-grade students.

- Systematic and explicit phonics instruction significantly improves students' reading comprehension in the early grades.
- Systematic and explicit phonics instruction is effective for students from various socioeconomic levels. It helps students from various backgrounds make greater gains in reading than does non-systematic phonics instruction.
- Systematic and explicit phonics instruction is particularly beneficial for students who are having difficulty learning to read and who are at risk for developing future reading problems.
- Systematic and explicit phonics instruction is most effective when introduced early; instruction should start in kindergarten and first grade.
- Phonics instruction is not a complete reading program. Beginning readers should simultaneously be solidifying their knowledge of the alphabet, engaging in phonemic-awareness activities, and listening to stories and informational texts read aloud. They should also be reading texts as soon as possible and writing letters, words, messages, and stories.
- Phonics can be taught effectively to a whole class at once, in small groups, or to individual students.
- Approximately, two years of basic phonics instruction is sufficient for most students.

Motivated by unresolved questions of methodology and implementation, Brady (2011) subsequently reviewed relevant research on beginning reading instruction produced in the decade following the NRP. She found additional clear support for the practice of teaching phonics systematically and explicitly, with "advantages evident for complete analysis of the phoneme-grapheme composition of one-syllable words," (p. 80) and that the advantage accrued for all first graders—not just students with reading disabilities. In addition, she found that comprehensive programs that include all other essential components named by the NRP—phoneme awareness, fluency, vocabulary, and reading/language comprehension—yield the best results.

More recently, a panel of researchers convened by the Institute for Education Sciences (Foorman et al., 2016) analyzed the literature on foundational reading skills instruction for K-3. Support for teaching phoneme awareness and explicit phonics was again found to be strong. Further, the report pointedly warned against methods and programs that teach children to guess at words from pictures and context, citing them as harmful and contrary to scientific evidence of effectiveness.

In spite of consistent, overwhelming evidence for the importance and value of code-emphasis instruction for all, and systematic, explicit remediation in phonic decoding for most students with reading difficulties, our schools continue to embrace methods and programs that ignore these recommendations. For example, Denton et al. (2014) reported that two-thirds of the teachers in their study used Guided Reading (Fountas & Pinnell, 1996), an approach with no systematic phonics instruction. Reading Recovery (Clay, 1991), an intervention with no systematic phoneme awareness or phonics instruction, continues to have adherents in spite of its demonstrated ineffectiveness with students who have reading disabilities (Chapman & Tunmer, 2011; Chapman, Greaney, & Tunmer, 2015). Leveled Literacy Intervention (LLI, Fountas

& Pinnell, 2008) is used to complement Guided Reading, but phonics instruction is minimal, implicit, non-systematic, uninformative, and often unrelated to the texts students are reading (Murray, Munger, & Heibert, 2014). Two recent studies of LLI indicated little or no carry over to general reading improvement on assessments not affiliated with the underlying techniques taught in LLI (Ransford-Kaldon et al., 2010, 2012).

Popular practices, overall, are not aligned with research evidence. Children at risk for reading difficulties often do not receive the kind of instruction they need. Perhaps one way to redirect educators' attention toward phonics and foundational skills is to give the subject matter a new identity—as an aspect of language that is inherently interesting, enjoyable to study, and linked closely to vocabulary, spelling, and reading comprehension. Reconceptualizing the foundations of literacy may help move us beyond fruitless debates of the past.

3.4 More Than Phonics: Word Reading and Spelling Involve Awareness of Language at Several Levels of Language Organization

Learning to decode is not a low-level association skill that must be learned by rote drills. Good readers establish printed word representations in memory (unitized whole word letter sequences that can be recognized by sight) when they can map phonemes to letters or letter combinations, and vice versa (Ehri, 2014; Harris & Perfetti, 2017; Miles & Ehri, Chap. 4, this volume) and when these associations connect to meaning. In addition, fully specified or high quality mental representations of words include all of their linguistic features (Adlof & Perfetti, 2014), from their pronunciation to their semantic properties. Each aspect of language discussed below is represented in the English writing system and should be addressed during formal instruction.

Phonological awareness. An alphabetic orthography or writing system represents individual speech sounds or phonemes. Thus, for sound–symbol mapping to occur in the mind of the learner, he or she must establish mental representations for the speech sounds that the orthography represents. Those phoneme representations will be the template onto which the print symbols are mapped (Miles & Ehri, this volume). But herein is an under-appreciated fact: phonemes are more than sound frequencies. Their distinctive identities include the articulatory movements required to produce them. To establish a mental representation for a phoneme, the learner must differentiate phonemes by their acoustic and articulatory features (Fromkin, Rodman, & Hyams, 2014; Liberman, Shankweiler, & Liberman, 1989).

For example, the difference between /ch/ and /j/ is voicing; /ch/ is unvoiced, spoken with no activation of vocal cords while /j/ is voiced, with the vocal cords resonating. Except for the feature of voicing, the two consonants are articulated exactly the same way, with the mouth puckered, the teeth together, and single push of breath. English has nine pairs of consonant phonemes that differ only in voicing: /p/ /b/; /t/ /d/; /k/ /g/; /f/ /v/; /th/ /th̲/; /s/ /z/; /sh/ /zh/; /ch/ /j/; /wh/ /w/. Developing awareness of subtle differences among similar phonemes is challenging for students with phonological processing weaknesses, as their spelling errors attest (Bourassa & Treiman, 2014; Cassar, Treiman, Moats, Pollo, & Kessler, 2005; Moats, 2010).

In addition, English has sounds that are not represented by unique alphabet letters, and many letters are used in more than one way to represent various phonemes. Knowing letter names, while helpful for developing phoneme awareness, is not enough to learn the identity of the speech sounds. Children must become aware of phonemes for which there are no single visual symbols. For example, the consonant phonemes, including /ng/ as in *sing*, /zh/ as in *vision*, /th̲/ as in *them* or *bathe*, and a number of the 18 vowel phonemes, including /aw/ as in *saw*, /oo/ as in *book*, /oi/ as in *boy*, /ou/ as in *out*, /er/, /ar/, and /or/ are not consistently spelled with a single letter, or even the same letter(s).

Phoneme awareness eludes many students, moreover, because the identity of phonemes in connected speech is obscured by the properties of the speech stream (Fromkin et al., 2014; Liberman et al., 1989; Moats, 2010). Phonemes in words are not spoken individually, but rather are *co-articulated* in natural speech. Co-articulation means speaking together or saying a string of phonemes as one linguistic unit, usually organized around the central vowel in a syllable. Because phonemes are co-articulated, their phonetic properties (the way they are actually spoken) can vary, sometimes rather dramatically. Say the following words: *desk, dress, ladder, educate*. Each has the letter *d* but only in the first word, *desk*, does the mouth articulate a pure /d/. The phoneme /d/ in *dress* and *educate* is affricated or spoken more like /j/ because of the influence of the phoneme /r/ in *dress* and the hidden phoneme /y/ in the /yū/ in *educate*. The /d/ in *ladder* becomes a tap of the tongue against the back of the upper teeth. These variations are particularly problematic for students trying to spell words by the way they sound, who often produce attempts such as JRS (dress) and EJUKAT (educate) (Treiman, 2017; Moats, 2010).

These realities of spoken language suggest that the phonological awareness strand of literacy instruction should enable students to identify the 25 consonant phonemes and the 18 vowel phonemes of English (Table 3.1), plus schwa (the indistinct vowel, like the *a* in *about* or the last vowel in *wagon*). The ability to quickly map print to speech depends on it. Furthermore, this aspect of language instruction should be distinguished from learning about the alphabet and learning orthography because phonological awareness requires oral language analysis independent of print. Finally, as Boyer and Ehri (2011) demonstrated, instruction should reference mouth forms and articulatory features of phonemes, and acknowledge the phenomenon of co-articulation.

Phoneme-grapheme correspondences. One reason to teach phonics through encoding, or phoneme-grapheme correspondence, is that the logic of sound to symbol recapitulates history. Letters and graphemes do not "make sounds," as teachers often say, but rather, written symbols were invented over millennia to represent speech. Speech is the start point for understanding orthography. Second, English has a limited set of 44 speech sounds, including schwa, for which there are about 80–120

Table 3.1 Inventory of common consonant graphemes used to spell English phonemes

Phoneme	Word examples	Graphemes for spelling
/p/	pat, spa, stomp	p
/b/	but, brought, stubble	b
/m/	milk, bomb, autumn	m, mb, mn
/t/	tent, putt, missed	t, tt, ed
/d/	desk, summed	d, ed
/n/	neck, know, gnaw	n, kn, gn
/k/	cot, kettle, deck, chorus, unique, quit	k, c, ck, ch, que, q
/g/	get, ghost	g, gh
/ng/	rang, dank	ng, n
/f/	staff, asphalt, rough	f, ff, ph, gh
/v/	very, give	v, ve
/s/	suit, pass, scent, psycho	s, ss, sc, ps
/z/	zen, fuzz, rise, his, xerox	z, zz, se, s, x
/th/	thing, bath, ether	th
/t͟h/	that, seethe, weather	th
/sh/	shawl, pressure, sugar, chagrin, conscious, spatial, mission, special	sh, ss, s, ch, sc, ti, si, ci
/zh/	measure, seizure, vision, rouge	s, z, si, -ge
/ch/	cheese, sketch	ch, tch
/j/	jam, fudge, page	j, dge, ge
/l/	lice, pill, bubble	l, ll, le
/r/	rat, wrist	r, wr
/y/	your, euro, unique, onion	y, (u, eu), i
/w/	want, question	w, (q)u
/wh/[a]	whale	wh
/h/	harm, whose	h, wh

[a]The phoneme /wh/ is disappearing in American English; for many speakers, /w/ and /wh/ are identical sounds, so the sound represented by wh must be taught as a "phonics fiction."

teachable spellings (Moats, 2010). The smaller number of phonemes provides an easier organization for code-based instruction than the large number of letters and letter combinations that often serve multiple functions (e.g., *ea* in *meat*, *head*, and *great*). Third, there is evidence that a strong encoding (sound to symbol) component increases the effectiveness of beginning reading lessons (Weiser & Mathes, 2011).

The sound–symbol correspondence system in English uses both single letters and letter combinations to represent phonemes. The term *grapheme* means any letter or letter combination that represents a phoneme. Some graphemes are more than two letters, such as *igh* for /ī/ in *sight*, and *eigh* for /ā/ in *weigh*. Letter combinations are necessary because English has only 26 Roman alphabet symbols to represent

44 sounds. Further, the long historical evolution of English spelling, combined with changes of pronunciation, resulted in several ways to represent many phonemes (Venezky, 1999). The five single vowel letters *a, e, i, o,* and *u* can stand for short or long vowel sounds. Vowel phonemes, especially long vowels, are often represented with several graphemes. The unglided long u, /ū/, for example, can be spelled oo (*moon*), u (*truth*), ue (*blue*), u_e (*rude*), ou (*soup*), ough (*through*) and ew (*stew*). These complexities require several years to teach thoroughly, and certainly cannot be addressed by teaching students that "each letter makes a sound."

The most common graphemes that represent phonemes in English are listed in Table 3.1 (consonants) and Table 3.2 (vowels).

Table 3.2 Inventory of vowel graphemes most often used to spell English vowels	Vowel phoneme	Examples of words	Most common vowel graphemes
	ē (long e)	happy, me, see, meat	y, e, ee, ea
	ĭ (short i)	itch, gran*i*te, gym	i, i_e, y
	ā (long a)	*a*corn, date, pay, pail	a, a_e, ay, ai
	ĕ (short e)	echo, dead	e, ea
	ă (short a)	*a*pple	a
	ī (long i)	ride, idol, cry, night	i_e, i, y, ight
	ŏ (short o)	*o*ctopus	o, a
	ŭ (short u)	up, c*o*ver	u, o
	aw	lost, call, saw, *au*dio	o, al, aw, au
	ō (long o)	*o*pen, toe, boat, throw	o, oe, oa, ow
	oo	put, book, could	u, oo, ou
	ū (unglided long u)	duty, rude, noose, chew, blue	u, u_e, oo, ew, ue
	yū (glided long u)	*u*nicorn, cute, few	u, u_e, ew
	oi	boil, boy	oi, oy
	ou	ouch, cow	ou, ow
	er	her, fur, sir, cell*ar*, doct*or*	er, ur, ir, ar, or
	ar	star, are, heart	ar, a_e, ear
	or	sport, chore	or, ore
	schwa (/ə/)	circ*u*s, *a*bout, wag*o*n, *e*ffect, c*o*mmit	u, a, o, e, i (any vowel spelling)

Orthographic patterns. English orthography also encompasses many redundant patterns, conventions for letter sequences, and constraints on the placement of graphemes (beginning, middle, end; before or after other letters). For example, due to historical influences, no English word ends in the letters *v* or *j*. Words such as *have*, *give*, *dodge*, and *college* follow these constraints. The letter combinations *ng*, *ck*, *ll*, *ff*, *ss*, and *dge* occur right after vowels that are usually short, but never in the beginnings of syllables. Certain letters such as *h*, *i, x*, and *y* are never doubled. From their first exposure to print, children notice these patterns (or graphotactic characteristics) of orthography (Treiman, 2017). One characteristic of students who fail to automatize word recognition is their inattention to and poor memory for print patterns and the likelihood of their occurrence, referred to as statistical learning (Seidenberg, 2017).

At another level of representation, English orthography uses conventions known as written syllable types to represent vowel sounds in longer words. Familiarity with the six basic syllable-spelling conventions (Table 3.3) can help students decode longer words by breaking them into decodable chunks (Bhattacharya & Ehri, 2004) and can help them remember spellings. Notice that these written chunks do not correspond to the natural breaks in spoken word pronunciation—vocal pauses that tend to come after a vowel no matter what kind of vowel it is. Written syllable conventions are for representing pronunciation of a vowel sound.

Morphology and etymology. Morphemes are the smallest units of meaning. Words may contain one morpheme or many. A single morpheme may be one syllable (*bat*), or more than one (*tiger, banana*). Some morphemes are single phonemes, not pronounceable syllables, such as plural s, /s/ (*cats*) or /z/ (*dogs*), or two forms of the past tense -ed, /t/ (*wished*) or /d/ (*hummed*). Advanced decoding lessons should recognize the differences between syllables and morphemes. It is insufficient to call them all "word parts" as is common in superficial instruction.

Written forms of words often reveal their underlying morphological structures. We spell by sound–symbol correspondences and meaning. For example, *bookkeeper* has two k's because it is a compound; *attach* has two t's because it has a Latin prefix *at* (a variation of *ad*, "to" or "toward") and a Latin root *tach*. The word *mnemonic* begins with *mne* because that was the base of the Greek word for memory. To explain why words are spelled the way they are, a teacher must call students' attention to linguistic features beyond the basic alphabetic code.

Instruction in morphology is more meaningful if it is linked to word origin or etymology. Modern English is an amalgam of Anglo-Saxon, Latin, and Greek, and to a lesser extent, includes spellings from French, German, Italian, and Spanish. Each of these languages contributed spelling conventions that within the language of origin were predictable but that violate the patterns of another. For example, *ch* is used to spell /ch/ in Anglo-Saxon words such as *chair;* it is used to spell /k/ in Greek-derived words such as *chorus;* and it spells /sh/ in French-derived words such as *charade* and *machine.* Classes of morphemes in English are listed in Table 3.4 in relation to their language origin.

Learning to recognize morphemes helps students to decode morphologically complex words more quickly, to learn word meanings, and to spell (Carlisle & Goodwin, 2014).

3.5 More Than Phonics: A Multi-linguistic Approach Makes Sense

What are the implications of these linguistic realities for teaching students to read and spell words? First, the term *phonics* is insufficient for capturing the substance and nature of printed word learning. A better term, such as *structured language*, would signify the relevance and interconnectedness of all aspects of language represented in our orthography and the importance of explaining words from several angles.

Second, isolating phonics as a component of instruction has invited a piecemeal, incidental, and cursory approach to teach word identification that is often disconnected from other aspects of literacy. The separation of components diminishes the vital role that phonological awareness and linguistic awareness in general play in

Table 3.3 Six types of written syllables in English orthography

Syllable type	Examples	Definition
Closed	**dap**-ple **hos**-pital **bev**-erage	A syllable with a short vowel spelled with a single vowel letter ending in one or more consonants
Vowel-C-e ("Magic e")	com-**pete** in-**vite**	A syllable with a long vowel spelled with one vowel + one consonant + silent *e*
Open	**pro**-gram **ta**-ble **re**-cent	A syllable that ends with a long vowel sound, spelled with a single vowel letter
Vowel team	**aw**-ful **train**-er con-**geal** re-**coil** in-**sight**	Syllables with long or short vowel spellings that use two to four letters to spell the vowel. Diphthongs *ou/ow* and *oi/oy* are included in this category
Vowel-r (r-controlled)	in-**cur** con-**sort** **char-ter** **irk**-some	A syllable with **er, ir, or, ar,** or **ur**. Vowel pronunciation often changes before /r/
Consonant-le	drib-**ble** bea-**gle** bat-**tle** ma-**ple**	An unaccented final syllable containing a consonant before /l/followed by a silent *e*. Also, known as the stable final syllable
Non-conforming: Odd and Schwa syllables	dam-**age** act-**ive** na-**tion**	Usually, final, unaccented syllables with odd spellings. Many are spellings for derivational suffixes such as –ive, -age, -ine, and -tion

Table 3.4 Classes of morphemes in English, classified by language of origin

Language of origin	Type of morpheme	Example words
Anglo-Saxon	Base words	chair, father, love, night
	Compound words (base words combined)	highchair, turtledove, fishcake
	Inflectional suffixes -ed, -s, -es, -er, -est, -ing	climbs, climbed, climbing, higher, highest
	Prefixes such as fore-, be-	beforehand, foreman, begotten
	Derivational suffixes such as hood, -ward, -en, -less	neighborhood, backward, beholden, fatherless
Romance, Latin-based	Prefixes such as ad, re, ex, com, in (im)	admit, revise, exert, commend, innate
	Roots such as duct, tract, port, vert, vis(vid)	conduct, extract, import, revert, vision
	Suffixes such as –tion, -ize, -ity, -al	nation, nationalize, nationality, natural
Greek	Combining forms such as bio, logy, lex, graph, neuro, psych, archos	biology, lexicon, lexicographer, neuropsychology, architecture, monarch

processing the written word, for reading, spelling, and vocabulary development. It is common for programs to purport to teach phonics but to omit entirely any effective work on the phonological skills enumerated in Kilpatrick (2015) or any systematic application of phonics to reading, spelling, and understanding words in context.

Third, we should counter more vigorously the negative connotation held by the word *phonics* that is reinforced in schools of education and education textbooks (Binks-Cantrell, Washburn, Joshi, & Hougen, 2012; Joshi, Binks, Hougen, et al., 2009b; Joshi, Binks, Graham, et al. 2009a; Walsh, Glaser, & Dunne-Wilcox, 2006). Teachers may dislike and avoid teaching phonics because they have no background in the psychology of reading or the structure of language (Brady et al., 2009; Cunningham, Zibulsky, Stanovich, & Stanovich, 2009). Our experience has been that once teachers are introduced to information about spoken and written language necessary for explaining how the code works and why words are spelled the way they are, they are much more likely to embrace good teaching practices (Moats, 2004).

3.6 Structured Literacy in Practice

While this chapter cannot address or describe all the complexities of structured language and literacy teaching, some examples can illustrate the content and methods of the approach. Higher-quality programs of instruction that are linguistically informed are likely to have features such as these.

1. *Phonological awareness instruction* that progresses from early, to basic, to advanced (Kilpatrick, 2015). Lessons will teach students to identify 40–44 phonemes, taught cumulatively and systematically. Phoneme identification activities will include reference to articulation within the system of distinguishing phonetic features (voiced/unvoiced; continuous or stop; placement of the tongue, lips, and teeth).

2. *Pedagogical distinction between letter names and the sounds they represent.* The program will recognize that letter sounds and letter names such as /w/ and "Y", and /y/ and "U" may be confused, that some phonemes have no unique spellings, and that letters are used in various ways to represent speech sounds.

3. *Routines for introducing sound-letter correspondences.* Lessons will be structured so that students learn letter names, letter sounds, and letter formation in a coordinated sequence. Strong programs include sound–symbol association cards with picture mnemonics.

4. *Regular practice blending all the sounds in words, left to right.* Children may not develop the habit of sounding a word out from start to finish unless they are taught how and are given consistent practice applying this skill. Systematic programs begin with a limited set of sound–symbol correspondences—a few consonant letters (*b, f, h, j, k, m, p, t*) and one or two vowel letters (*a, i*) so that words can be built right away. Other consonants and vowels are added gradually to those already known. Once a correspondence is learned (e.g., /ĕ/, short e, is spelled with e), looking at graphemes and blending them to make whole words (*pet, red, hen*) should be routine.

5. *Phoneme-grapheme mapping.* This type of activity enhances students' attention to the internal structure of words, in both speech and spelling, and supports whole word identification. Students use grid paper ("sound boxes") or movable grapheme tiles to map graphemes to phonemes (Grace, 2007). For example, if a grid is used, each box stands for one phoneme in the word to be mapped. Words with digraphs and blends would be mapped in this way:

Word	1st sound	2nd sound	3rd sound	4th sound	5th sound
Champ	ch	a	m	p	
Brisk	b	r	i	s	k
Fresh	f	r	e	sh	
Sting	s	t	i	ng	
Croak	c	r	oa	k	

6. *Practice for automaticity.* What is taught must be practiced. Lesson routines will contain many kinds of practice, including word sorts, using words in fill-in-the-blank activities, and above all, reading phrases, sentences, and connected text that is decodable—that is, it contains a high percentage of words and patterns that have been explicitly taught.

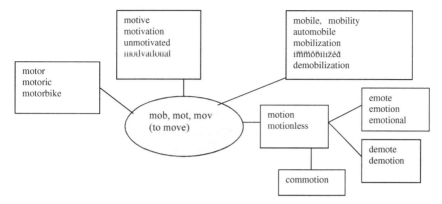

Fig. 3.1 Morphological Word Family Map

3.7   Beyond the Basic Code

To consolidate word recognition, students must become adept at deciphering longer words. Students need strategies for recognizing syllable chunks and common morphemes such as those discussed by Henry (2010). Beginning in late first or early second grade, students should practice combining syllable chunks and dividing words into pronounceable units. As their competence with decoding grows, students in grade three and beyond can enjoy discovering how many words there are in a morphological word family, and thereby expand their vocabularies (Fig. 3.1).

3.8   Explicit, Systematic, Code-Based, and Sequential Reading Instruction: What It Is and What It Is not

Identifying programs and approaches that embody the principles of instruction supported by extensive scientific research is not a simple matter for the consumer. After the National Reading Panel report, almost every publisher and author claimed to have a research-based program. More insidiously, authors and publishers would use the terms systematic, sequential, and explicit to describe visual and context-driven word recognition strategies (e.g., Fountas & Pinnell, 1996, 2008; Hall & Cunningham, 2003). Instead of teaching students to map a whole printed word to its sounds, teachers are coached to correct student errors by drawing attention to meaning, syntax, and visual cues. Sounding out a word is a strategy of last resort, after looking at pictures, thinking about the whole sentence, or looking at the first letter and guessing at something that would make sense. In Guided Reading, the optional component of "word work" merits one or two minutes per day (Fountas & Pinnell, 1996). In contrast, beginning reading programs that get the best results devote 30–45 minutes per day to teaching the code and its application to word reading out of context and in context (Al Otaiba & Torgesen, 2007; Denton et al., 2014; Foorman et al., 2006; Torgesen, 2004; Torgesen et al., 2001).

Explicit versus non-explicit teaching. To be explicit, the instructor explains how a pattern or correspondence works and leaves little to chance (Archer & Hughes, 2011; Christensen & Bowey, 2005; Connor et al., 2011; Rosenshine, 2012). He or she assumes that decoding is challenging and minimizes exercises where students must intuit the code on their own. Guesswork is discouraged. Table 3.5 illustrates the differences between the instructional dialogue of explicit teaching and the instructional dialogue typical of non-explicit phonics instruction in a lesson on the long-*i*, Vowel-Consonant-*e* (VCe) spelling pattern.

The underlying assumptions of non-explicit approaches such as Reading Recovery, Balanced Literacy, Leveled Literacy Intervention, and Guided Reading are that students do not need to know sound–symbol correspondences to decode unknown words, and that words will be learned globally as visual wholes during meaning-emphasis instruction. These underlying but inaccurate assumptions were promoted under the "whole language" umbrella by Goodman (1986) and Smith (1979) in the 1980s. In spite of overwhelming evidence to the contrary, such assumptions are alive and well in our classrooms.

Table 3.5 Examples of explicit and non-explicit explanation of a phonics pattern

Example of explicit instruction	Example of non-explicit instruction
Teacher: "Today we will study another Vowel-Consonant-e or VCe pattern, this one for /ī/ or 'long i.' We've already learned the VCe pattern for /ā/ as in *cake, safe*, and *tape.*"	While reading a leveled book, students read *hid* for *hide* in the sentence, *We played hide and seek*
"First, let's listen for the sound. If you hear /ī/ in the word I say, put thumbs up (*ride, hike, made, fit, bite*, etc.). Look in the mirror as you say the vowel /ī/. What is your mouth doing?"	The teacher asks, "Does that sound like a game you know? Read that again and think of a game you know."
"A letter pattern that represents long vowels is VCe: one vowel letter, a single consonant, and a silent *e* at the end."	Students say, "It's hide and seek."
"Let's say the sounds in the word *side*. /s/ /ī/ /d/." Teacher writes three lines or moves blocks into three sound boxes as students say the three sounds, raising a finger for each sound.	Teacher later writes these words on the board or chart paper: *hide, ride, side, tide*, and leads students in choral reading of the word list.
Teacher writes the word *side* on the lines or in the boxes. "Look at the word *side*. How many letters are there?" (Four.) "How many sounds?" (Three)	Teacher says, "These words are all part of the *ide* family. If you can read *ride* you can read *hide*."
"Which letter represents no sound by itself? (*e*). The letter *e* does not get its own box [or its own line] because it does not represent a vowel sound by itself. Its job is to reach back over the consonant, tap the vowel, and make it say its own name." (Teacher draws arrow from the silent *e* back to the sounded vowel letter)	

During text reading, if the instruction is implicit, students typically are asked to decode words in context on the basis of the meaning of the sentence, passage, or accompanying illustrations. This strategy is known as a "cueing systems" approach. For example, in a context-based, non-explicit approach based on a cueing systems strategy, teachers encourage students to follow these steps when they come across an unknown word:

(1) Think about what would make sense here.
(2) Skip the word and read the whole sentence.
(3) Look at the pictures for help.
(4) Look at the first letter; what sound?
(5) Sound out the whole word.

In contrast, an explicit, code-based word recognition routine, for use while reading text, follows these steps:

(1) Look carefully at the whole word. [Name the letters, if necessary.]
(2) Sound it out, left to right.
(3) Check it; does the word make sense here?

The first approach, the "cueing systems" strategy, conveys to the student that he or she need not know exactly how the correspondences work and that guessing from the meaning or syntax is a productive way of approaching unknown words. The second approach depends on whether the student has—or should have—learned the major correspondences that can be relied upon to recover a reasonable pronunciation from the print.

One of the reasons why contextual guessing is the strategy of choice in programs like Leveled Literacy Intervention (LLI) is that the texts that accompany a "word study" lesson often contain few or no words with the phonics pattern that presumably has been taught. Murray et al. (2014) documented that the texts used in Leveled Literacy sometimes had no words with the phonics pattern. Further, the lesson texts contained many multi-syllabic words that the students could not yet read. Contextual guessing is the only strategy available in LLI because students cannot rely on what they have learned when they attempt to read the words.

Systematic versus non-systematic decoding instruction. The term *systematic* has two connotations: instruction that is carried out through step-by-step procedures or routines; instruction that explicates the system of correspondence between speech and print (Ehri, Nunes, Stahl, & Willows, 2001).

Step-by-step routines and procedures are customary in systematic code-based approaches. These typically employ learned hand gestures, signals, or response formats that enable students to respond quickly and frequently during teacher-led instruction. The lesson structure proceeds from teacher explanation and modeling, to guided practice, to independent practice monitored by the teacher.

A system for explicit teaching usually follows a format for introducing a new phonics concept, such as the following:

- Identify the target phoneme in spoken words
- Pronounce and describe articulatory features of the phoneme, with mirrors
- Write letter(s) that are used to represent the phoneme
- Learn a mnemonic or keyword for the sound–symbol correspondence
- Decode and spell words with the correspondence
- Read decodable text with words and patterns that have been taught during the phonics instruction.

A systematic approach to the content means that any explicitly taught concept about language or orthography is situated within a system that has a defined and overarching conceptual structure. The teacher can place each element of the system in relation to language organization as a whole. In reading and spelling, systematic instruction places each linguistic element (sound, syllable, morpheme, word, phrase, or sentence) within a larger category or in relation to a general principle of oral or written language organization.

For example, a lesson about the suffix -ful would do more than state its pronunciation. It would explain that -ful, like all suffixes, does not stand alone as a word. It is a morpheme, or meaningful part, related to but not the same as the Anglo-Saxon word full. The suffix -ful begins with a consonant, and therefore does not change the spelling of a base word when it is added. Doubling a final consonant or dropping a final e when we add -ful to a base word is unnecessary, as in *harmful, spiteful, useful,* or *cupful.* Within the whole system of printed English, -ful is one of many suffixes that mark words as adjectives (as in *graceful* and *beautiful*) or nouns (as in *hatful* or *handful*).

Non-systematic programs lack detailed, organized, teacher-led lessons on the specifics of the orthographic code. In the absence of a systematic approach, students are left to infer how orthography works from random exposure to words in print. Information about phonics, syllabification, orthographic conventions, and morphology is scarce and often inaccurate. Some non-systematic programs include a phonics workbook or phonics activities but instruction in decoding remains incomplete, incidental, and disconnected from the reading and writing components of the program.

For example, students might have a lesson on "short o" (as in *hot*), but then be asked to read a leveled book that uses the words *from, of, one, rope,* and *off*—none of which have the sound of /ŏ/. Or, instruction might begin with rote memorization of 50–100 words as wholes, on flash cards. The emphasis is not on print-to-speech or speech-to-print correspondences.

To summarize, non-systematic programs:

- teach concepts "as they come up"—during reading and writing;
- do not teach the entire system of sound–symbol correspondences or other aspects of word structure in relation to a complete framework;
- do not follow established teaching routines in each lesson;
- do not categorize concepts or place them within language systems. For example, *igh* may be taught in a family of *ight* rhyming words, but students are not taught that it is a low frequency, Old English, three-letter grapheme that is one of at least six spellings for the long vowel /ī/; and

- do not provide practice materials, such as decodable books, that offer children the opportunity to apply what they are learning about letter–sound relationships. The reading materials these programs do provide for children are selected according to other criteria, such as their topic.

Sequential reading instruction. Print-to-speech concepts and correspondences range from simple to complex, from transparent to elusive, and from highly reliable (e.g., -*ck* occurs immediately after a short vowel) to highly variable (e.g., sounds represented by *ough*). While there is no single, superior pathway through this content, well-designed programs follow a progression from easier to more difficult language constructs. For example, simple syllables without consonant blends are easier for learners to process than words with blends (Bourassa & Treiman, 2014). Learners who cannot easily learn print-to-speech correspondences must learn them cumulatively, with one building on the next.

Table 3.6 provides a general outline for a sequence of instruction that is typical of an organized, code-emphasis program (Birsh, 2010; Moats & Hall, 2010).

Table 3.6 A general sequence for beginning phonics instruction

Phonics concept	Example graphemes or patterns	Example words
Single, highly reliable consonants and a short vowel	b, s, t, d, m	sad, mat, mad, bat
More single consonants	r, l, f, z, v, g, p, n	red, fit, got, zip, pup
Short vowels/ă/,/ŏ/,/ĭ/,/ŭ/,/ĕ/, introduced gradually	a, o, i, u, e	wag, top, zip, rub, jet
Consonant digraphs	th, ch, sh, ng, wh, also -ck	thing, chunk, shop, when
Consonant blends	st, lk, mp, br, cl	stop, milk, camp, bran, must
Inflections	-s, -ed, -ing	wishes, wished, wishing
VCe for long vowels	a_e, i_e, o_e, u_e	lake, ride, rope, cute
Odd consonants	x, qu	box, quit
"Floss" pattern	-ff, -ll, -ss, -zz	stuff, well, grass, jazz
Vowel teams	ee, ea, oa, ai, ay	meet, heap, boat, mail, play
Vowel-r patterns	er, or, ur, ar	her, for, fur, star
Complex consonants	ge/dge, ch/tch, hard and soft c and g	wage, dodge; church, catch; cell, city, gem, gym
Multi-syllable words, gradual introduction	(six syllable types)	napkin, playground, compete

3.9   What About Irregular Words?

Students must learn to recognize and remember some high-frequency words that do not follow regular correspondence patterns in English. Many of these are grammatical function words necessary to form sentences that are among the oldest in the language (*do, does, were, are, was, of, said, any, who, what*). Irregularly spelled words, however, comprise no more than a quarter of the most frequent 300–500 words. The rest have regular sound–symbol correspondences (*when, is, he, them, day, us, for, not, with*) or conform to orthographic patterns that can be taught (*have, by, will, all, most, year, good*). Even the so-called irregular words usually have some correspondences that are predictable. Therefore, students can be taught most high-frequency words either by including them in a lesson on predictable correspondences and patterns (*he, she, we, be, the*), by using a spelling pronunciation to aid memory (said = say + ed), or by contrasting the letters with the word's pronunciation ("was = /w/ /ă/ /s/... but we don't say /w/ /ă/ /s/, we say /w/ /ŭ/ /z/").

Irregular words should be introduced gradually, perhaps three to five per week in first grade. The recent advisory on foundational reading skills published by the Institute for Education Sciences (Foorman et al., 2016) encourages the teaching of irregular words using whole word methods, including tracing and saying the letters until the word can be memorized or reciting words from flash cards. Current theories of word learning processes (Miles & Ehri, this volume; Kilpatrick & O'Brien, this volume), however, do not support the idea that so-called visual learning of orthography is independent of phonology or sound–symbol mapping. While repeated exposure to these words may be necessary, initial presentation and practice routines can place those words in relation to regularities in the orthography.

3.10   Barriers to Better Implementation

Let us return to the question posed at the beginning of this chapter: Why do so many students continue to struggle with reading and spelling when so much research has been done on the prevention and amelioration of these difficulties? Clearly, the promise of research—to enable early identification of reading difficulties and to promote informed, effective instruction—remains unrealized in many schools.

One well-documented reason for this gap between scientific findings and common practices is simply that teachers and school psychologists (Nelson & Machek, 2007) are not prepared to understand or deliver explicit, systematic instruction in foundational reading skills. Teachers' preparatory courses often do not address the essential components of instruction (Greenberg, McKee, & Walsh, 2013; National Council on Teacher Quality, 2016). Neither do they require any coursework in language structure or language development. Likewise, their professors may not themselves know the structures of language, the scientific literature on reading development or reading difficulties, or the evidence regarding best practices (Binks-Cantrell et al., 2012).

Reading education textbooks contain errors such as confusion of phonics and phoneme awareness, and fail to provide information that would enable effective teaching of foundational reading skills (Joshi, Binks, Graham, et al., 2009b). This state of affairs means that teachers can only learn what they need to know after they have entered the profession, through courses, workshops, and the instructional materials they are given. Such professional development is uncommon.

A second and related issue is that acquiring the knowledge necessary for informed, structured, language-based literacy instruction is a protracted process that cannot be accomplished in one or two workshops. Phoneme awareness, for example, is often written and talked about as if it should be simple to understand and simpler to teach. In contrast, teachers typically score very low on surveys of their knowledge of phoneme awareness and phonics (Cunningham, Perry, Stanovich, & Stanovich, 2004; Moats, 1994, 2009; Spencer, Schuele, Guillot, & Lee, 2008) and in our experience, need at least six to ten hours of instruction and practice to learn the English phonemes, to accurately segment English words, and to understand more advanced ideas such as co-articulation and allophonic variation. We need at least another ten hours of coursework to educate teachers about English orthography and how to teach it. Learning the structure of language is not much easier for teachers than it is for younger students; the content and concepts are challenging and should be treated as such. Nor is having a scripted program sufficient for educators to acquire the requisite knowledge base or overcome a lack of knowledge pertaining to language and reading (Piasta, Connor, Fishman, & Morrison, 2009).

Third, some widely used instructional materials and programs are not designed in accordance with current recommendations from the research community (e.g., Foorman et al., 2016). These include Balanced Literacy, Four Blocks, Reading Recovery, Leveled Language Intervention and others. Objective analyses and critiques of these approaches abound (Chapman & Tunmer, 2011; Chapman, Greaney, & Tunmer, 2015; Denton et al. 2014; Kilpatrick, 2015; Moats, 2017; Seidenberg, 2017) but critiques from scientists seem to have little impact on the choices that district administrators make with regard to programs of instruction. As long as this trend continues, rates of reading and overall literacy failure will be higher than they need to be.

Fourth, guidelines for implementation of the Common Core State Standards minimized the importance of foundational reading and writing skills toward meaning-emphasis instruction beginning in kindergarten (Common Core, Inc., 2012). The organization of the standards document spoke volumes: foundational reading skills were relegated to the back of the English Language Arts section in favor of comprehension-focused literature standards, from kindergarten onward. The lofty goals for comprehension and composition have overshadowed the necessity of teaching students to recognize and form letters, identify speech sounds, decode words using phonics, establish a sight vocabulary, and formulate grammatical sentences.

And finally, while the shortcomings of teacher training have been well documented, the training of principals, school psychologists, and curriculum specialists has neglected to address the science of reading. Knowledgeable leadership is essential if we are to do better for students who struggle with literacy.

3.11 Recommendations

1. School psychologists, curriculum directors, and other leaders are encouraged to consult reliable, scientifically informed sources before investing in instructional programs and other services. Better sources include the consensus reports referenced here; the practice guides published by the Institute for Education Sciences; and public interest white papers by reading researchers from the Society for the Scientific Study of Reading, the American Psychological Association, the American Speech Hearing and Language Association, the International Dyslexia Association, among others.

2. Structured literacy or explicit teaching of phonics, augmented by attention to other aspects of language, should be bedrock practice in every school, in regular classrooms *and* in intervention programs. Characteristics of the most effective approaches for building foundational skills for reading and writing are:

   - explicit, sequential, systematic instruction in phoneme awareness, phonic decoding with sound blending, recognition of print patterns in words, and spelling;
   - explication of language structure at the level of speech sounds, graphemes, syllables, morphemes, and whole words;
   - error correction that calls attention to sound–symbol correspondence first, not the context or pictures, and that discourages guessing;
   - inclusion of spelling instruction and coordination of spelling with reading;
   - application of skills to read fully decodable text;
   - supervised text reading practice to build fluency.

3. Instruction must be sufficiently intensive to help students in the lower third of the population accelerate their growth. Effective instruction of foundational reading and spelling skills should take at least 30–40 minutes per day in first grade, and somewhat less time as proficiency increases. Studies of successful interventions typically call for 80–120 hours of instruction if students are to gain in relative standing. Older students from third grade onward need even more intensive instruction to close the reading gap (Calhoon & Petscher, 2013; Torgesen et al., 2001).

4. Phonics and basic language instruction must be augmented by vocabulary and language comprehension instruction, through read-alouds and oral language activities if necessary.

5. Teachers and others require and deserve substantial training and support to implement programs with these characteristics.

References

Adams, M. (1990). *Beginning to read. Thinking and learning about print.* Cambridge, MA. MIT.

Adlof, S. M., & Perfetti, C. A. (2014). Individual differences in word learning and reading ability. In C. A. Stone, B. J. Ehren, E. R. Silliman, & G. P. Wallach (Eds.), *Handbook of language and literacy development and disorders* (2nd ed., pp. 246–264). New York, NY: Guilford Press.

Al Otaiba, S., & Torgesen, J. (2007). Effects from intensive standardized kindergarten and first-grade interventions for the prevention of reading difficulties. In S. R. Jimerson, M. K. Burns, & A. M. VanDer Heyden (Eds.), *Handbook of response to intervention* (pp. 212–222). New York, NY: Springer.

Anderson, R. C., Heibert, E. H., Scott, J. A., & Wilkinson, I. A. G. (1985). *Becoming a nation of readers: The report of the commission on reading.* Washington, DC: National Academy of Education.

Archer, A. L., & Hughes, C. A. (2011). *Explicit instruction: Effective and efficient teaching.* New York: Guilford.

Bhattacharya, A., & Ehri, L. (2004). Graphosyllabic analysis helps adolescent struggling readers read and spell words. *Journal of Learning Disabilities, 37,* 331–348.

Binks-Cantrell, E., Washburn, E. K., Joshi, R. M., & Hougen, M. (2012). Peter effect in the preparation of reading teachers. *Scientific Studies of Reading, 16,* 526–536.

Birsh, J. (Ed.). (2010). *Multisensory teaching of basic language skills* (2nd ed.). Baltimore, MD: Paul Brookes Publishing.

Bourassa, D., & Treiman, R. (2014). Spelling development and disability in English. In C. A. Stone, E. R. Silliman, B. J. Ehren, & G. P. Wallach (Eds.), *Handbook of language and literacy: Development and disorders* (2nd ed., pp. 569–583). New York, NY: Guilford Press.

Boyer, N., & Ehri, L. C. (2011). Contribution of phonemic segmentation instruction with letters and articulation pictures to word reading and spelling in beginners. *Scientific Studies of Reading, 15*(5), 440–470.

Brady, S. (2011). Efficacy of phonics teaching for reading outcomes: Implications from Post-NRP research. In S. Brady, D. Braze, & C. Fowler (Eds.), *Explaining individual differences in reading* (pp. 69–96). London: Psychology Press.

Brady, S., Gillis, M., Smith, T., Liss-Bronstein, L., Lowe, E., Russo, E., et al. (2009). First grade teachers' knowledge of phonological awareness and code concepts: Examining gains from an intensive form of professional development. *Reading and Writing: An Interdisciplinary Journal, 22,* 425–455.

Calhoon, M. B., & Petscher, Y. (2013). Individual and group sensitivity to remedial reading program design: examining reading gains across three middle school reading projects. *Reading and Writing, 26,* 565–592.

Carlisle, J. F., & Goodwin, A. P. (2014). Morphemes matter: How morphological knowledge contributes to reading and writing. In C. A. Stone, E. R. Silliman, B. J. Ehren, & G. P. Wallach (Eds.), *Handbook of language and Literacy: Development and disorders* (2nd ed., pp. 265–282). New York, NY: Guilford Press.

Cassar, M., Treiman, R., Moats, L., Pollo, T. C., & Kessler, B. (2005). How do the spellings of children with dyslexia compare with those of nondyslexic children? *Reading and Writing, 18,* 27–49.

Chall, J. S. (1967). *Learning to read: The great debate.* New York: McGraw-Hill.

Chapman, J., & Tunmer, W. (2011). Reading recovery: Does it work? *Perspectives on Language and Literacy, 37*(4), 21–24.

Chapman, J. W., Greaney, K. T., & Tunmer, W. E. (2015). Is reading recovery an effective early literacy intervention programme for children who most need literacy supports? In W. E. Tunmer & J. W. Chapman (Eds.), *Excellence and equity in literacy education: The case of New Zealand* (pp. 41–70). London, England: Palgrave Macmillan.

Christensen, C. A., & Bowey, J. A. (2005). The efficacy of orthographic rime, grapheme-phoneme correspondence, and implicit phonics approaches to teaching decoding skills. *Scientific Studies of Reading, 9*(4), 327–349.

Clay, M. (1991). *Becoming literate: the construction of inner control.* Taylor & Francis.

Common Core, Inc. (2012). *Common core curriculum maps: English language arts, Grades K-5.* San Francisco, CA: Jossey-Bass.

Connor, C. M., Morrison, F. J., Schatschneider, C., Toste, J., Lundblom, E. G., Crowe, E., et al. (2011). Effective classroom instruction: Implications of child characteristic by instruction interactions on first graders' word reading achievement. *Journal for Research on Educational Effectiveness, 4*(3), 173–207.

Cunningham, A., Perry, K., Stanovich, K., & Stanovich, P. (2004). Disciplinary knowledge of K-3 teachers and their knowledge calibration in the domain of early literacy. *Annals of Dyslexia, 54,* 139–168.

Cunningham, A., Zibulsky, J., Stanovich, K., & Stanovich, P. (2009). How teachers would spend their time teaching language arts: The mismatch between self-reported and best practices. *Journal of Learning Disabilities, 42,* 418–430.

Denton, C. A., Fletcher, J. M., Taylor, W. P., Barth, A. E., & Vaughn, S. (2014). An experimental evaluation of Guided Reading and explicit interventions for primary-grade students at-risk for reading difficulties. *Journal of Research on Educational Effectiveness, 7*(3), 268–293.

Ehri, L., Nunes, R. S., Stahl, S., & Willows, D. (2001). Systematic phonics instruction helps students learn to read: Evidence from the National Reading Panel's meta-analysis. *Review of Educational Research, 71,* 393–447.

Ehri, L. C. (1998). Grapheme-phoneme knowledge is essential for learning to read words in English. In J. L. Matsala & L. C. Ehri (Eds.), *Word recognition in beginning literacy* (pp. 3–40). Mahwah, NJ: Lawrence Erlbaum.

Ehri, L. C. (2014). Orthographic mapping in the acquisition of sight word reading, spelling memory, and vocabulary learning. *Scientific Studies of Reading, 18*(1), 5–21.

Ehri, L. C., Cardoso-Martins, C., & Carroll, J. M. (2014). Developmental variation in reading words. In C. A. Stone, E. R. Silliman, B. J. Ehren, & G. P. Wallach (Eds.), *Handbook of language and Literacy: Development and disorders* (2nd ed., pp. 285–407). New York, NY: Guilford Press.

Fletcher, J., Lyon, G. R., Fuchs, L., & Barnes, M. A. (2019). *Learning disabilities: From identification to intervention* (2nd ed.). New York: Guilford Press.

Foorman, B., Schatschneider, C., Eakin, M., Fletcher, J., Moats, L., & Francis, D. (2006). The impact of instructional practices in Grades 1 and 2 on reading and spelling achievement in high poverty schools. *Contemporary Educational Psychology, 31*(1), 1–29.

Foorman, B., Beyler, N., Borradaile, K., Coyne, M., Denton, C. A., Dimino, J., Furgeson, J., Hayes, L., Henke, J., Justice, L., Keating, B., Lewis, W., Sattar, S., Streke, A., Wagner, R., & Wissel, S. (2016). *Foundational skills to support reading for understanding in kindergarten through 3rd grade* (NCEE 2016–4008). Washington, DC: National Center for Education Evaluation and Regional Assistance (NCEE), Institute of Education Sciences, U.S. Department of Education. Retrieved from the NCEE website http://whatworks.ed.gov.

Fountas, I. C., & Pinnell, G. S. (1996). *Guided reading: Good first teaching for all children.* Portsmouth, NH: Heinemann.

Fountas, I. C., & Pinnell, G. S. (2008). *Leveled literacy intervention.* Portsmouth, NH: Heinemann.

Fromkin, V., Rodman, R., & Hyams, N. (2014). *An introduction to language* (10th ed.). Boston, MA: Wadsworth, Cengage Learning.

Gersten, R. Compton, D., Connor, C. M., Dimino, J., Santoro, L., Linan-Thompson, S., & Tilly, W. D. (2008). *Assisting students struggling with reading: Response to intervention and multitier intervention for reading in the primary grades. A practice guide* (NCEE 2009–4045) Washington, DC: U.S. Department of Education, National Center for Education Evaluation and Regional Assistance, Institute of Education Sciences.

Goodman, K. (1986). *What's whole in whole language.* Richmond Hill, Ontario: Scholastic.

Gough, P., & Tunmer, W. (1986). Decoding, reading, and reading disability. *Remedial and Special Education, 7,* 6–10.

Grace, K. (2007). *Phonics and spelling through phoneme-grapheme mapping.* Longmont, CO: Sopris West.

Greenberg, J., McKee, A., & Walsh, K. (2013). *Teacher prep review: A review of the nation's teacher preparation programs.* Washington, DC: National Council on Teacher Quality.

Hall, D. P., & Cunningham, P. M. (2003). *Month-by-month phonics for second grade: Systematic, multi-level instruction.* Greensboro, NC: Carson-Dellosa Publishing.

Harris, L. N., & Perfetti, C. A. (2017). Individual differences in phonological feedback effects: Evidence for the orthographic recoding hypothesis of orthographic learning. *Scientific Studies of Reading, 21,* 31–45.

Henry, M. (2010). *Unlocking literacy: Effective decoding and spelling instruction.* Baltimore: MD: Brookes.

Joshi, R. M., Binks, E., Graham, L., Ocker-Dean, E., Smith, D., & Boulware-Gooden, R. (2009a). Do textbooks used in university reading education courses conform to the instructional recommendations of the National Reading Panel? *Journal of Learning Disabilities, 42,* 458–463.

Joshi, R. M., Binks, E., Hougen, M., Dahlgren, M., Ocker-Dean, E., & Smith, D. (2009b). Why elementary teachers might be inadequately prepared to teach reading. *Journal of Learning Disabilities, 42,* 392–402.

Kilpatrick, D. A. (2015). *Essentials of assessing, preventing, and overcoming reading difficulties.* Hoboken, NJ: Wiley.

Liberman, I. Y., Shankweiler, D., & Liberman, A. M. (1989). The alphabetic principle and learning to read. In D. Shankweiler & I. Y. Liberman (Eds.), *Phonology and reading disability: Solving the reading puzzle.* Ann Arbor: University of Michigan Press.

Lyon, R., Shaywitz, S., & Shaywitz, D. (2003). A definition of dyslexia. *Annals of Dyslexia, 53,* 1–14.

Moats, L. C. (1994). The missing foundation in teacher education: Knowledge of the structure of spoken and written language. *Annals of Dyslexia, 44,* 81–102.

Moats, L. C. (2004). Language, science, and imagination in the professional development of teachers of reading. In P. McCardle & V. Chhabra (Eds.), *The voice of evidence in reading research* (pp. 269–287). Baltimore, MD: Brookes Publishing.

Moats, L. (2009). Still wanted: Teachers with knowledge of language. *Journal of Learning Disabilities, 42,* 387–391.

Moats, L. C. (2010). *Speech to print: Language essentials for teachers* (2nd ed.). Baltimore, MD: Brookes.

Moats, L. C. (2017) Can prevailing approaches to reading instruction accomplish the goals of RTI? *Perspectives on Language and Literacy, publication of the International Dyslexia Association.*

Moats, L. C., & Hall, S. (2010). *LETRS module 7: Teaching phonics, word study, and the alphabetic principle* (2nd ed.). Boston, MA: Cambium/Sopris West.

Murray, M. S., Munger, K. A., & Hiebert, A. H. (2014). An analysis of two reading intervention programs: How do the words, texts, and programs compare? *The Elementary School Journal, 114,* 479–500.

National Assessment of Educational Progress (NAEP). (2017). National assessment of educational progress reading assessment. Washington DC: National Center for Education Statistics, US Department of Education. https://nces.ed.gov/nationsreportcard/.

National Council on Teacher Quality. (2016). *Landscapes in teacher prep: Undergraduate elementary ed.* Washington, DC: NCTQ. Available at http://www.nctq.org/dmsView/UE_2016_Landscape_653385_656245.

National Institute of Child Health and Human Development (NICHD). (2000). *Report of the national reading panel: Teaching children to read: An evidence-based assessment of the scientific research literature on reading and its implications for reading instruction.* Washington, DC: U.S. Government Printing Office.

Nelson, J. M., & Machek, G. R. (2007). A survey of training, practice, and competence in reading assessment and intervention. *School Psychology Review, 36,* 311–327.

Olson, R. K., Keenan, J. M., Byrne, B., & Samuelsson, S. (2014). Why do children differ in their development of reading and related skills? *Scientific Studies of Reading, 18,* 38–54.

Piasta, S., Connor, C., Fishman, B., & Morrison, F. (2009). Teachers' knowledge of literacy concepts, classroom practices, and student reading growth. *Scientific Studies of Reading, 13*(3), 224–248.

Rack, J. P., Snowling, J. J., & Olson, R. K. (1992). The nonword reading deficit in developmental dyslexia: A review. *Reading Research Quarterly, 27,* 28–53.

Ransford-Kaldon, C. R., Flynt, E. S., Ross, C. L., Franceschini, L., Zoblotsky, T., Huang, Y., et al. (2010). *An empirical study to evaluate the efficacy of Fountas & Pinnell's leveled literacy intervention system (LLI) (2009–2010).* Memphis, TN: Center for Research in Educational Policy, University of Memphis.

Ransford-Kaldon, C. R., Ross, C. L., Lee, C. C., Flynt, E. S., Franceschini, L., & Zoblotsky, T. (2012). *An empirical evaluation of LLI in Denver Public Schools.* Memphis, TN: Center for Research in Educational Policy, University of Memphis.

Rayner, K., Foorman, B., Perfetti, C., Pesetsky, D., & Seidenberg, M. (2001). How psychological science informs the teaching of reading. *Psychological Science in the Public Interest, 2,* 31–74.

Rosenshine, B. (2012). Principles of instruction: Research-based strategies that all teachers should know. *American Educator, 36*(Spring), 12–19, 39.

Seidenberg, M. (2017). *Language at the speed of sight: How we read, why so many can't, and what can be done about it.* New York: Basic Books.

Smith, F. (1979). *Reading without nonsense.* New York: Teachers College.

Snow, C. E., Burns, E. S., & Griffin, P. (Eds.). (1998). *Preventing reading difficulties in young children.* Washington, DC: National Academy Press.

Spencer, E. J., Schuele, C. M., Guillot, K. M., & Lee, M. W. (2008). Phonemic awareness skill of speech-language pathologists and other educators. *Language, Speech, and Hearing Services in Schools, 39*(4), 512–520.

Sweet, R. W. (2004). The big picture: Where we are nationally on the reading front and how we got there. In P. McCardle & V. Chhabra (Eds.), *The voice of evidence in reading research* (pp. 13–34). Baltimore, MD: Brookes.

Torgesen, J. K. (2004). Lessons learned from the last 20 years of research on interventions for students who experience difficulty learning to read. In P. McCardle & V. Chhabra (Eds.), *The voice of evidence in reading research* (pp. 355–382). Baltimore, MD: Brookes.

Torgesen, J. K. (2005). Recent discoveries on remedial interventions for children with dyslexia. In M. J. Snowling & C. Hulme (Eds.), *The science of reading: A handbook* (pp. 521–537). UK, Oxford: Blackwell.

Torgesen, J. K., Alexander, A. W., Wagner, R. K., Rashotte, C. A., Voeller, K., Conway, T., et al. (2001). Intensive remedial instruction for children with severe reading disabilities: Immediate and long-term outcomes from two instructional approaches. *Journal of Learning Disabilities, 34,* 33–58.

Treiman, R. (2017). Learning to spell words: Findings, theories, and issues. *Scientific Studies of Reading.* http://dx.doi.org/10.1080/10888438.2017.1296449.

Venezky, R. (1999). *The American way of spelling.* New York: Guilford.

Walsh, K., Glaser, D., & Dunne-Wilcox, D. (2006). *What elementary teachers don't know about reading and what teacher preparation programs aren't teaching.* Washington, DC: National Council for Teacher Quality.

Weiser, B., & Mathes, P. (2011). Using encoding instruction to improve the reading and spelling performances of elementary students at risk for literacy difficulties: A best-evidence synthesis. *Review of Educational Research, 81*(2), 170–200. https://doi.org/10.3102/0034654310396719.

Chapter 4
Orthographic Mapping Facilitates Sight Word Memory and Vocabulary Learning

Katharine Pace Miles and Linnea C. Ehri

Abstract Efficient word reading involves retrieving familiar written words from memory automatically by sight, and sounding out letters or guessing from context only when unfamiliar words are encountered. The process of storing written words for later immediate recall occurs through a process called orthographic mapping. This process involves connecting pronunciations to the written letters that represent those pronunciations in memory. It is not based upon visual memorization of picture-like forms of words. Letter sound knowledge and phonemic awareness are central to the orthographic mapping process. Four phases of development portray sight word learning that results from orthographic mapping. Studies show that orthographic mapping facilitates vocabulary learning.

To read text efficiently, one must be able to retrieve words from memory automatically by sight without analyzing letter by letter to decode them. This reliance on sight word reading frees up mental space for comprehending the meaning of the text. Efficient adult readers have a vast sight word memory bank from which to instantaneously retrieve the pronunciations and meanings of words. Emergent readers face the task of building their sight word memories through repeated exposure to written words. To understand how reading skill develops, one must explain how emergent readers achieve competence in reading words accurately and automatically. This chapter explains how the ability to store words in memory as sight words is governed by the reader's orthographic mapping skill.

Orthographic mapping refers to the process of connecting letters in the spellings of words to sounds in their pronunciations. This becomes possible once readers learn the alphabetic writing system, that is, how letters systematically symbolize sounds and how to distinguish those sounds in pronunciations of the words. Orthographic mapping is applied when words are read and also when words are spelt. This secures

K. P. Miles (✉)
Brooklyn College, Brooklyn, NY, USA
e-mail: kpmiles@brooklyn.cuny.edu

L. C. Ehri
City University of New York Graduate Center, New York, NY, USA
e-mail: LEhri@gc.cuny.edu

© Springer Nature Switzerland AG 2019
D. A. Kilpatrick et al. (eds.), *Reading Development and Difficulties*,
https://doi.org/10.1007/978-3-030-26550-2_4

spellings of the words in memory and enables students to read words by sight and to spell words. Note that this is very different from the commonly held view that sight words are read by ignoring letter-sound relations in words and reading them in another way, by implanting strictly visual, picture-like forms of words in memory through repeated practice and memorization. Research has shown that this is not the case. More will be said about this subsequently.

It is important to clarify our view of sight word learning. The term may be interpreted in one of the three ways. To some, it refers to a method of instruction to teach sight words by giving students a set of flashcards to practice reading. To some, it is limited to the learning of irregularly spelled, high-frequency words. To others including us, it designates a process that involves readers' storing the spellings, pronunciations, and meanings of words in the brain for later activation when a text is read. It is important to recognize these distinctions. In the current chapter, the *process* of sight word acquisition is discussed separately from any method of instruction and is not limited to any specific word type. We use the term sight word to refer to what the mind does to store all types of written words in memory so that the spellings, pronunciations, and meanings of these words can be retrieved as soon as the readers' eyes alight upon the words, hence the term *sight* word (Ehri, 1992, 1998, 2005b; Kilpatrick, 2015). In this chapter, studies that support the explanation of sight word acquisition are discussed along with studies clarifying the effects of different instructional methods on sight word learning.

For proficient readers, practically all words are read from memory by sight (Ehri, 2014). Accumulation of sight words has occurred over time and through repeated exposure to spellings of words in and out of text (Ehri, 1992, 1998, 2005b). These readers are proficient because pronunciations and meanings are activated automatically when the written words are seen, allowing readers to expend their mental energy comprehending the text (Ehri, 2005b). Not only do proficient readers have the ability to automatically recognize words in print, but also they are able to read the words as single written units, without any pauses between parts of the word (Ehri, 2014).

Evidence that readers recognize words as single whole units (called *unitization*) was demonstrated in an experiment by Ehri and Wilce (1983) in which they assessed younger (second grade) and older (fourth grade) readers' ability to read familiar object words (i.e., *book*), consonant-vowel-consonant (CVC) nonwords (i.e., *baf*), and to name single digits (i.e., *4, 3,* or *6*). Response latencies were measured. Results showed that the words children had already learned to read were read more quickly than unfamiliar nonwords and in fact were read as quickly as naming single digits. These findings indicate that familiar words are read as single whole units rather than as letters processed sequentially. Dehaene (2009) also found evidence that sight words are read by parallel processing, that is, with all the letters in a word processed at once, instead of sequentially.

All written words when practiced become sight words, not just high frequency or irregularly spelled words (Ehri, 1992, 2005b, 2014). However, even proficient readers come across words in print that are unfamiliar. In these instances, they must fall back on word-reading strategies in order to determine the pronunciation and meaning of the words. These are the same strategies that beginning readers use in order to determine the correct pronunciation of unfamiliar words. These word-reading strategies may be applied by readers more than once until the word is stored as a sight word.

One possible strategy for reading an unfamiliar word is analogizing (Goswami, 1986; Ehri, 1998, 2005b, 2014). This entails finding a similarly spelled known word in memory and using it to read the new word. An example is using the word *mountain* to read *fountain*. Another strategy is prediction (Ehri, 1998, 2005b, 2014; Goodman, 1970; Tumner & Chapman 1998). This involves relying on picture, sentence, and letter clues to guess the unknown word. A third strategy is to apply knowledge of graphemes and phonemes in order to decode the unknown word. Phonemes are the smallest sounds in words (e.g., the word *she* has two phonemes), and graphemes are the letters that regularly symbolize phonemes in the writing system (e.g., *she* has two graphemes, SH and E). In order to apply a decoding strategy effectively, readers must match the graphemes to their corresponding phonemes blend the sequence to pronounce the unit, and then find the word in their mental lexical to recognize its meaning (Ehri, 2014).

As readers advance in their grapheme–phoneme knowledge of the writing system and their memory for sight words, they acquire and apply their knowledge of larger grapho-syllabic units (e.g., *-tion, -ing, -ump*) in order to make the decoding process more efficient (Bhattacharya & Ehri, 2004; Ehri, 2014; Moats, 2010). Due to the variability and irregularity of the English writing system, grapheme–phoneme decoding may not produce a recognizable word match in memory. In these cases, readers must be flexible and try out alternative pronunciations of the words in order to uncover the appropriate pronunciation matching a real word (Elbro, de Jong, Houter, & Neilsen, 2012; Tumner & Chapman, 2012).

Ehri (1992, 1998, 2005b, 2014) explains that through repeated practice forming connections between graphemes and phonemes or grapho-syllabic relations, the spellings of words become bonded to their pronunciations via orthographic mapping. This connection-forming process stores words in memory by gluing spellings to their pronunciations and meanings to enable automatic sight word reading (Ehri, 1980, 1992, 1998, 2005b, 2014; Perfetti, 1992; Rack, Hulme, Snowling, & Wightman, 1994). Similarly, Share's (2004, 2008) self-teaching hypothesis suggests that decoding supports orthographic learning of words. According to the self-teaching hypothesis, translating the printed version of a word into its spoken form is the primary way in which the orthographic representations of words are learned. The decoding process directs readers' attention to the individual grapheme–phoneme relations in specific words and thus supports storage of the order and identity of the letter strings.

Examples of connections (both grapho-phonemic and grapho-syllabic) that readers may form to learn sight words are illustrated in Fig. 4.1. Capital letters represent the spellings of the words. Spaces are used to distinguish the letter units that map onto phonemes, syllables, or morphemes (i.e., smallest meaningful units in words). Arrows represent connections between the written and spoken units.

This connection-forming process also bonds letters to sounds in irregularly spelled words. As depicted in Fig. 4.1, most graphemes in irregularly spelled words map onto predictable phonemes. The letters that do not conform or are unpredictable include

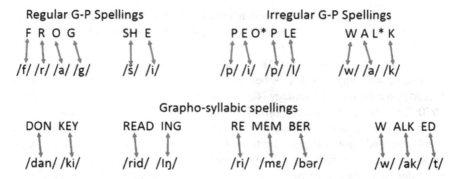

Fig. 4.1 Examples of connections to retain sight words in memory. *Note GP* grapho-phonemic. Capital letters = spellings. Spaces separate graphemes or spellings of syllables or morphemes. Lower case letters and symbols between slashes are IPA phonetic symbols far phonemes. Arrows = connections. * = silent letter

silent letters (indicated by an asterisk) and letters representing schwa vowels that lack a distinctive sound in unstressed syllables (e.g., schwa pronounced "uh" in the second syllable of *chicken*). Silent letters or letters spelling schwa vowels might be remembered as extra visual letter units. Alternatively, they might be more easily remembered if students create special mnemonic spelling pronunciations (e.g., *listen* pronounced "lis-ten"; *chocolate* pronounced "choc-o-late;" *chicken* pronounced "chick-en"), or if they recognize the letter as a member of a familiar multi-letter spelling pattern (e.g., *-alk* with a silent L in *talk, walk, chalk*) (Drake & Ehri, 1984; Landerl & Reitsma, 2005; Ocal, 2015). Thus, most if not all of the letters in irregularly spelled words can be stored in memory using the same connection-forming process as is used to remember regularly spelled words.

4.1 Requisite Skills for Successful Orthographic Mapping

Readers' phonemic awareness and knowledge of letter-sound regularities enable them to form connections between the spellings and pronunciations of words in order to store the bonded word units in memory (Ehri & Roberts, 2006; Ehri, 2005b, 2014). Studies show that children who have the ability to segment words into sounds and to identify letter names and sounds progress faster in their ability to learn to read than children who do not have these skills (National Reading Panel, 2000; Share, Jorm, MacLean, & Matthews, 1984). Phonemic awareness enables readers to segment and blends the sounds in pronunciations of words. Letter-sound knowledge enables readers to match graphemes in spellings to their corresponding phonemes in pronunciations of words. These grapheme–phoneme connections provide the glue for sight word storage. Studies have demonstrated how training in phonemic awareness and letter knowledge improves readers' ability to read words from memory (Boyer & Ehri, 2011; Ehri & Wilce, 1987; Shmidman & Ehri, 2010). Also phonemic proficiency, that is, the ability to process the phonemes in mapping relations quickly, contributes to word-learning skill (Kilpatrick, 2018; Kilpatrick & O'Brien, Chap. 8 this volume).

4.1.1   Phonemic Awareness

Castiglioni-Spalten and Ehri (2003) investigated the impact of phonemic segmentation instruction on beginning readers' ability to read new words. Kindergartners were assigned to three conditions: mouth treatment, ear treatment, and no-treatment control. In the mouth condition, students were trained to identify pictures of articulatory gestures that corresponded to the sequence of sounds in pronunciations of target words. The ear treatment was taught to represent the sequence of sounds in the target words with blocks. At the end of the training, both treatment groups outperformed the control group in phoneme segmentation skill. In addition, both treatment groups were able to spell the sounds in target words even though spelling words with letters was not taught. Interestingly, the mouth group trained with articulatory gestures was the only group to show the benefit of segmentation training in a sight word learning task. In this task, children practiced learning to read words over several trials.

In a follow-up study, Boyer and Ehri (2011) trained preschoolers to segment CV (consonant-vowel), VC, and CVC words into phonemes using either mouth pictures and letters, or only letters. Students were randomly assigned to one of two training conditions or to a control condition: (1) letters plus pictures of articulatory gestures (LPA), (2) letters only (LO), and (3) no treatment. Students in the LPA group were taught relationships between 15 graphemes and phonemes as well as relationships between pictures of articulatory gestures and spoken phonemes. Then they learned how to segment the training words into phonemes by representing them with these mouth pictures as well as with the letters. For example, segmentation of the nonword "po" was depicted with two pictures, the first showing lips closed and the second showing lips open and rounded; "po" was spelled with the letters P and O. Students in the LO group learned 15 grapheme-phoneme associations and how to use these associations to segment and spell the same words and nonwords. On a sight word-learning task following training, students in the LPA group learned to read the words more easily than the other two groups, and this advantage persisted on a one-week delayed posttest. The findings from both Castiglioni-Spalten & Ehri (2003) and Boyer and Ehri (2011) demonstrate the facilitative effect of phonemic segmentation training with articulatory pictures on sight word reading for beginning readers.

4.1.2   Letter Knowledge

As previously mentioned, grapheme–phoneme knowledge is essential for sight word learning. Studies have shown that children who have knowledge of letter shapes and sounds are better able to read words they have previously read than children who do not know letter names or sounds. Ehri and Wilce (1985) demonstrated that as children progress into learning to read words, they shift from processing their visual features to processing connections between letters and sounds. Roberts (2003) trained preschool children who were non-readers for 16 weeks on either letter names or comprehension-focused instruction (the control group) and then examined whether letter name training improved children's ability to learn to read two types of words. One set was spelled phonetically with letters mapping sounds in the words (e.g., LFT to spell "elephant"). The other set was spelled non-phonetically with letters that did not represent any sounds in the words but were more salient visually (e.g., XKO to spell "elephant"). Students who received letter name training learned to read words spelled phonetically better than the non-phonetic words, whereas the control group showed the opposite pattern, with the non-phonetic set learned more easily. These results show that when prereaders learn letter names, they can apply them in remembering how to read words. This is their entre into the alphabetic writing system and into building a sight word vocabulary by forming letter-sound connections.

The contribution of grapheme–phoneme knowledge to building a sight vocabulary has also been studied in a classroom-based longitudinal study. Ehri, Satlow, and Gaskins (2009) worked with first, second, and third graders enrolled in a school for struggling readers. They compared two-word reading instructional programs. The Key method trained students to read new words by analogy to keywords. The Key-Plus method also taught analogizing to keywords. In addition, Key-Plus students learned to retain spellings of the keywords in memory by analyzing mapping relations between graphemes and phonemes within the words. To learn a keyword, students first counted phonemes in its pronunciation, then they matched graphemes in its spelling to its phonemes and explained the regularities, then they spelled the word from memory. Students who received the Key-Plus program showed superior word reading and spelling abilities during the first two years compared to students in the Key program. However, differences were diminished during the third year as the latter group caught up. This study provides further evidence for the contribution of grapheme–phoneme knowledge and orthographic mapping to word reading during the primary grades.

Learning letter names and their corresponding sounds is essential knowledge for beginning readers because it is the basis for grapheme–phoneme mapping which is essential for sight word learning. Learning associations between all the letters and their sounds can be a tedious task for young children. Studies have shown that it can be made easier with the use of *embedded picture mnemonics*. This involves imposing letter shapes on drawings of objects whose shapes resemble the letters and whose names begin with the sound of the letter (e.g., the letter *h* drawn as a house or *s* drawn as a snake). Ehri, Deffner, and Wilce (1984) demonstrated the benefit of this approach with preschoolers, kindergartners, and first graders. Students were taught each of several letters, either with embedded picture mnemonics, or with disasso-ciated pictures whose names began with sounds represented by letters but whose shapes did not resemble the letters (e.g., *s* associated with a snake coiled up), or letters without any pictures. Results showed that students taught with embedded picture mnemonics performed significantly better learning letter-sounds than students in the other two groups. Interestingly, the other two groups did not differ, showing that pictures unrelated to the shapes of letters did not facilitate letter sound learning, even though their names began with the relevant letter sounds. The reason is that they failed to provide a memorable link between letter shapes and sounds.

Schmidman and Ehri (2010) replicated and extended these findings with English-speaking 5-year-old children learning Hebrew letters. Because the children did not speak Hebrew, letter-sound associations were taught with English labels for pictures. Children were taught Hebrew letter-sound relations either with embedded pictures mnemonics (i.e., Hebrew letter ש symbolizing the sound /sh/ was embedded in a drawing of a ship with the hull as the base and sails resembling the vertical lines) or with disassociated mnemonics (i.e., letter ש associated with a ship drawn as an ocean liner with no resemblance to the letter's shape). Letter-sound relations were practiced until children learned them all. Results supported previous findings (Ehri, Deffner, & Wilce, 1984). Letter-sounds taught with embedded pictures were learned more easily and were remembered significantly better in a one-week follow-up test. In addition, the embedded letters enhanced children's ability to learn to read English words written with Hebrew letters and to spell English words using Hebrew letters. These results underscore the foundational role of letter-sound knowledge in learning to read and spell words and the value of embedded picture mnemonics for teaching letter-sound relations.

4.2 Phases in the Development of Sight Word Reading

Beginning readers follow a developmental trajectory as they acquire reading and spelling skills. Ehri (2005a, 2014) has proposed four developmentally distinct phases that depict the progression in sight word reading and spelling abilities of beginning and emergent readers. Rather than being discrete non-overlapping stages, the phases are conceptualized as fluid and overlapping in the processes and knowledge sources used to read words. The phases are labeled to reflect the predominant type of spelling-sound connection that students use to remember how to read and spell words. The connections advance from non-alphabetic, visually salient connections to partial grapho-phonemic connections, to full grapho-phonemic connections, to grapho-syllabic connections. Characteristics and abilities of learners at the various phases are summarized in Table 4.1.

The *pre-alphabetic phase* is characterized by a lack of knowledge of the alphabetic system. Children in this phase do not possess knowledge of letter name or sound connections and therefore are unable to apply these skills to read and spell words (Ehri, 2005a). If children read words, it is because they remember some visual feature of the word. They may read *camel* by remembering the two humps or *look* by the two eyeballs in the middle (Gough, Juel, & Griffith, 1992). Children at this phase also rely on visual contextual clues from the environment. Examples include reading

Table 4.1 Summary of the emergence of knowledge, skills, and strategies characterizing Ehri's pre-alphabetic, partial alphabetic, full alphabetic, and consolidated alphabetic phases of development in learning to read and spell words

Pre-alphabetic	Partial alphabetic	Full alphabetic	Consolidated alphabetic
Limited or no letter knowledge	Most letter names and some GPCs	Major GPCs and some larger spelling units	Many grapho-syllabic and morphemic spelling units
Lack of phoneme segmentation	Partial phoneme segmentation	Full phoneme segmentation	
No GPC mapping	Partial GPC mapping; correct directional orientation to print	Complete GPC mapping	Grapho-syllabic and morphemic mapping as well as GPC mapping
Growing knowledge of spoken language: pronunciations, syntax, meanings of words	Growing knowledge of spoken language continues	Growing knowledge of spoken language continues	Growing knowledge of spoken language including morphemic units continues
Sight word memory			
Reading words by remembering salient visual or context cues; semantic substitution errors; no letter-sound connections; memory unreliable except for personal name	Reading words by remembering partial GPC connections; confusing similarly spelled words	Reading words by remembering full GPC connections; accuracy, automaticity, and unitization of word recognition are emerging	Reading words by remembering larger spelling units as well as GPC connections; accuracy, automaticity, unitization established for known words
Strategies to read unfamiliar words			
No word decoding ability	Little or no word decoding ability	Growing ability to decode unfamiliar words using GPCs	Proficient decoding of unfamiliar words using GPCs and larger units
Cannot analogize	Cannot analogize	Limited use of analogizing due to small sight vocabulary	Greater use of analogizing as sight word vocabulary grows
Words predicted from visual cues, context, pictures	Words predicted using initial letters and context	Prediction to support and confirm words decoded or read by analogy	Prediction to support and confirm words decoded or read by analogy
Spelling			
Non-phonetic spellings of unfamiliar words using scribbling, pseudo-letters, or letters	Partial phonetic spellings of unfamiliar words using letter names or GPCs	Complete phonetic spellings of unfamiliar words using GPCs	Grapho-syllabic and morphemic units as well as GPCs to spell unfamiliar words
No memory for correct spellings except for personal name	Limited memory for correct spellings	Good memory for correct spellings of many known words	Proficient memory for correct spellings of known words

Note: *GPC* grapheme–phoneme correspondences/connections

a *McDonald's* sign by recognizing the golden arches and reading a *STOP* sign by recognizing the red octagonal shape.

Masonheimer, Drum, and Ehri (1984) demonstrated pre-alphabetic children's reliance on visual and contextual clues in an experiment. The researchers took familiar signs and logos, such as the *PEPSI* logo, and changed one letter in the spelling (e.g., XEPSI). Children in the pre-alphabetic phase did not notice the difference and continued to read the label as if it was spelled properly. This occurred even when the experimenter warned children that there may be a mistake in the spelling. This showed that children were reading the environment rather than the print.

Reading words based on the visual clues is unreliable and insufficient to accommodate all the words necessary to become a proficient reader. As children begin to learn the names and sounds of letters, they transition to the *partial alphabetic phase*. Knowledge of letter names and sounds is used to read and spell words, although the connections made are incomplete. Children at this phase rely on the most salient sounds in a word (e.g., the /m/ and /d/ in *mud*), often the beginning and ending sounds, to form connections to letters. This creates confusion and causes reading errors when the beginning and ending sounds in two words are similar, for example, *step* and *stop*.

Children in the partial phase lack the ability to segment pronunciations into their full array of phonemes. They have difficulty blending a sequence of sounds to form words. They lack complete knowledge of grapheme–phoneme relations, especially vowel spellings. These limitations make it difficult for children in the partial alphabetic phase to remember how to read and spell words reliably, and to decode and generate spellings of unknown words. Children may use partial cues to guess words when they read, for example, reading *spin* as *spoon,* and they may spell *spoon* with only an *s* and *n*.

Ehri and Wilce (1985) examined the difference between pre-alphabetic and partial alphabetic phase readers. Kindergartens were distinguished by their phase of development. They were given practice learning to read two types of words, like those used by Roberts (2003) mentioned previously. One set of words contained visually distinct spellings that bore no relationship to the phonetic spelling of the word (e.g., *mask* spelled uHo). In the other set of words, letters represented sounds phonetically (e.g., *giraffe* spelled JRF). The results demonstrated that pre-alphabetic phase children learned to read the visually distinct spelling more readily than the phonetic spellings, whereas the partial-phase readers were better able to learn the phonetically spelled words than the visual words. These results support the claim that pre-alphabetic readers rely on visual cues to recall how to read words, but as children transition into reading, they focus on relations between letters and sounds, or phonetic cues in letters, to read words. Several researchers have replicated and extended these findings (deAbreu & Cardoso-Martins, 1998; Rack et al., 1994; Roberts, 2003; Scott & Ehri, 1989; Treiman & Broderick, 1998; Treiman & Rodriguez, 1999).

When children are able to form complete connections between letters in spellings and phonemes in pronunciations, children transition into the *full alphabetic phase*. This transition becomes possible when they learn the major grapheme–phoneme relations of the alphabetic system. To read an unfamiliar word, children in the full alphabetic phase are able to decode, that is, to transform graphemes into a sequence of phonemes and to blend the phonemes to pronounce a recognizable word. To spell a word, children in this phase are able to segment a pronunciation into phonemes and match each phoneme with a letter that typically represents that sound. Readers learn sight words at this phase by forming complete connections between graphemes and phonemes and storing the spelling in memory bonded to its pronunciation and meaning. These processes work for the majority of words learned by readers at the full alphabetic phase. However, if spellings are irregular or contain letter-sound relations that children have not yet learned, they may have difficulty decoding the words or remembering complete spellings, and the connections stored in memory in these cases may remain partial.

Miles (2015) studied differences between children in the partial and full alphabetic phases in various literacy tasks. Kindergartners were grouped by phase based on their ability to decode CVC nonwords. Students were given practiced learning to read a set of sight words on flashcards over trials. Full-phase readers learned the words more readily than partial phase readers. On posttests, full-phase readers remembered the spellings of the words better than partial readers. Also they performed better on tasks to assess orthographic mapping, spelling, and sentence generation. Miles concluded that full-phase readers were better able to form full grapheme–phoneme connections of the words, as evidenced on the spelling task, and this enabled them to store more stable representations of pronunciations, spellings, and meanings of the word amalgams in memory.

As more words are retained in memory, readers transition into the *consolidated alphabetic phase*. At this phase, the increase in storage of written words is supported mainly by readers' ability to form grapho-syllabic connections. Use of larger letter chunks involving spelling patterns that recur in different words, including rimes, syllables, morphemes, and whole unitized words makes decoding and encoding sight words, especially multi-syllabic words, more efficient, and accurate than in the full phase. Whereas full-phase readers would need to process seven grapheme–phoneme connections to remember how to read and spell *computer*, readers in the consolidated phase would need only three grapho-syllabic connections, *com-put-er*, thus reducing the memory load.

The benefit of grapho-syllabic mapping was investigated by Bhattacharya and Ehri (2004). Adolescents who were reading substantially below grade level (i.e., third, fourth, and fifth grade-equivalent levels) were randomly assigned to two treatment groups or a no-treatment control group. The two treatment groups practiced reading 100 multi-syllabic words broken into four lists taught on different days. The syllable group analyzed grapho-syllabic units in the words by counting spoken syllables and then matching each to its spelling within the word. They read the lists in this way four times. The whole word group practiced reading the same words as whole units and practiced reading the lists six times. Results indicated that students who received grapho-syllabic mapping instruction performed better on tasks of reading and spelling practiced words and on a transfer task decoding novel words than the other two groups. These results support the claim that multi-syllabic words are more effectively stored in memory when grapho-syllabic connections are processed.

4.3 Word-Reading Experiences: Impact on Orthographic Mapping

As children progress through the primary grades, their word-reading skills are strengthened by various experiences reading words. They may receive intentional and explicit instruction in decoding new words, or they may simply be exposed to new words as they read books independently, or as they read labels posted around the classroom, or as they read single words on flashcards. It is important to consider the impact of these word-reading experiences. The ultimate goal is to have all words stored in memory as sight words. As previously explained, the most effective way to secure new words in memory is through orthographic mapping, that is, analyzing the grapheme–phoneme or grapho-syllabic units in words. Several researchers have investigated the effect of word-learning experiences on students' ability to store words in memory.

Ehri and Roberts (1979) examined how different word-reading experiences facilitate learning the identities of written words, including their pronunciations, meanings, and spellings. The authors hypothesized that different experiences may strengthen one identity more than another. First graders were randomly assigned to two groups. One group read target words embedded in meaningful sentences. The other group read single target words on flashcards and then heard each word spoken in a meaningful sentence. Homonym pairs such as *rows/rose* and *chews/choose* were used as the target words to study the process of attaching meanings to spellings while controlling for the pronunciations of words. Performance on posttests following learning supported the idea that word-reading experiences influence which identities of words are strengthened. Students who read words in context learned more about the semantic identities of words than students in the isolation group, as indicated by their ability to embed the words in semantically accurate sentences. However, students in the isolation group could read the words faster and remembered their spellings better than students who read the words in sentences.

Ehri and Wilce (1980) replicated and extended these findings by targeting only function words which are high-frequency words that include determiners (e.g., *the*, *that*), conjunctions (*and*, *but*), prepositions (*in*, *of*), pronouns (*she*, *they*), auxiliary verbs (*be*, *have*), modals (*may*, *could*), and quantifiers (*some*, *both*). The grammatical functions and meanings of these words are activated mainly when they accompany other words in sentences. Importantly, many function words appear on pre-primer and primer word lists and are among the first words taught to beginning readers because they are needed to construct a meaningful text.

Ehri and Wilce (1980) examined the role of word-reading experiences on first-graders' acquisition of the syntactic/semantic and orthographic identities of a set of function words. One group of first graders read function words embedded in meaningful sentences, while the other group read each word in isolation and then heard it used in a meaningful sentence. Results supported the previous findings of Ehri and Roberts (1979). The sentence reading group learned more about the syntactic/semantic identities of the words whereas the isolation group learned more about their orthographic identities. One explanation for poorer orthographic learning in the sentence context group is that context readers spent less time looking at and decoding words in sentences because the context helped them identify the words and because their eyes quickly moved on to subsequent words in the sentence. Greater attention to and reliance on context reduced the opportunity for orthographic mapping to occur so that letters in spellings could become bonded to phonemes in their pronunciations. An explanation for weaker syntactic/semantic learning in the isolation condition is that when this group read the function words outside of a written sentence context, the grammatical relations of the words were not activated when they were read. It was only afterward when children heard the sentences that the relations were exposed. However, because the function words were buried in the spoken sentences, this very likely obscured readers' awareness of their grammatical role.

Word-reading experiences were also assessed by Johnston (2000) in first graders using predictable text in three different ways. The repeated reading group read the same predictable text ten times over the course of four days. The sentence context group read the predictable text chorally and then read the text on a chart without the illustrations and built the story using sentence strips. The word bank group underlined words they could read in the predictable text while they read unillustrated copies silently. The underlined words were then written on flashcards and practiced. Performance on immediate and delayed word recall tests revealed that the students in the word bank group learned to read the most words. While these results support the use of reading words in isolation, it is important to note that the words were taken from a meaningful text that the students practiced reading. This is unlike having students repeatedly read lists of isolated words such as Dolch words that remain disconnected from any context activating their meanings.

Because many common high-frequency words are irregularly spelled, it is believed that children learn to read and spell these words differently from regularly spelled words. Wang, Castles, Nickles, and Nation (2011) investigated whether embedding words in context or isolation impacts the orthographic learning of regularly and irregularly spelled words differently. These researchers first introduced the second graders to target nonwords orally by pronouncing the words and pairing them with picture cards showing their made-up meanings. After children learned the spoken words, they practiced reading their written forms four times either in a story context or in isolation on a list. Results showed that both regularly and irregularly spelled words were read more accurately in context than in isolation, presumably because context activated meanings to prime word memory. However, spellings of the words were not better remembered when the words were read in isolation than in context, contrary to findings cited earlier in other studies with younger children. On average over half of the regular spellings were recalled whereas only 15% of the irregular spellings were recalled correctly. Both reading and spelling errors on irregular words involved regularizations of the letter-sound correspondences. These findings show that the same processes affect the learning of regular and irregular words. Because spellings of the latter deviate from expected grapheme–phoneme relations, they are simply harder to learn.

Miles (2015) investigated the impact of word-learning experiences on native and nonnative English-speaking kindergarten students. They were taught to read words either embedded in meaningful sentences or displayed in isolation on flashcards. Results supported previous findings by showing that learning to read words was superior when words were read in isolation, whereas learning the words' syntactic and semantic identities was better when the words were read in contexts. The latter finding was evident in students' ability to produce more grammatically correct and contextually rich sentences. The same pattern held for both native and nonnative speakers.

Taken together, these studies show that word-learning experiences matter. The type or extent of information that is remembered about newly encountered words is influenced by whether the word is read in isolation or context and whether the word is regularly or irregularly spelled. To have a word securely stored in memory as a sight word, it is important for all of its identities to be represented, including its pronunciation, spelling, syntactic function, and meaning. Any instructional program designed for beginning readers should make provisions for all of these identities to become bonded together in memory to support growth in children's sight vocabularies.

4.4 Impact of Orthographic Mapping on Vocabulary Learning

The aforementioned theory and research reveal the essential role that orthographic mapping plays in sight word learning. In addition, orthographic mapping, the process that establishes the spellings of words in memory has been shown to be instrumental in vocabulary learning. This role is not commonly recognized. Vocabulary learning has been regarded mainly as a process of learning associations between pronunciations and meanings of new words without much regard for the involvement of word spellings. Rosenthal and Ehri (2008) point out that it is common for instructional programs to suggest many strategies that help students' learn new vocabulary words but to ignore the value of attending to the spellings of words. Recently several studies have shown that exposing learners to the spellings of words whose pronunciations and meanings are being learned boosts their memory for the words (Ehri, 2005b; Miles, Ehri, & Lauterbach, 2016; Lucas & Norbury, 2014; Mengoni, Nash, & Hulme, 2013; Ricketts, Bishop, & Nation, 2009; Rosenthal & Ehri, 2008).

A study by Rosenthal and Ehri (2008) reported also in Ehri (2005b) was one of the first to investigate this role. In two experiments, students were taught the pronunciations and meanings of several very low-frequency words. Second graders were taught six words, for example, *tot* (a young child) and *gam* (a family of whales), and fifth graders were taught ten words, for example, *vibrissa* (the whiskers on a cat), and *scrivello* (the tusks on an elephant). In both experiments, the words were pronounced, defined, presented in sentences, and accompanied by drawings of their meanings on flashcards. Students were given several practice trials through the words to learn them. The words were divided into two sets for each age group. One set displayed the spelling of the word below the picture on study and feedback trials, but not when word pronunciations and meanings were being recalled. The experimenter did not draw attention to the spelling of the words but just exposed them beneath the drawings on the cards. The other set of words was not accompanied by any spellings during the study or feedback periods. However, students pronounced these words extra times.

Results showed that spellings facilitated vocabulary learning for both grade levels. Second graders performed better recalling pronunciations of words when they had seen spellings than when they had not seen spellings. Fifth graders were divided into high and low groups based on their reading and spelling ability. Both high- and low-ability groups remembered pronunciations better when words were accompanied by spellings than when they were not. This effect was especially strong for high readers. Seeing spellings also significantly boosted the fifth graders' memory for the meanings of words. Results demonstrated that spellings contribute to vocabulary learning in both younger and older readers. The explanation rests on facilitation from orthographic mapping. Seeing spellings of the words activates connections between graphemes and phonemes and bonds spellings to their pronunciations in memory. This serves to better secure these previously unfamiliar pronunciations and meanings in memory.

Phonological working memory has been regarded as playing a critical role in readers' memory for vocabulary words (Gathercole, 2006). However, results of Rosenthal and Ehri's (2008) study suggest that vocabulary learning is more reliant on orthographic memory than on phonological memory. Findings of their study showed very little difference between high- and low-ability readers in their memory for pronunciations of vocabulary words when spellings were not provided during learning, indicating an inconsequential difference in the phonological memory of stronger and weaker readers. However, there was a substantial difference between high and low readers in their memory for pronunciations of vocabulary words when they did see the spellings of words, suggesting that orthographic mapping skill, not phonological memory skill, is a better explanation of why good word-level readers have superior vocabulary learning skill compared to students with weaker word-reading skill.

Supporting Rosenthal and Ehri's (2008) findings, Rickets, Bishop, and Nation (2009) also detected orthographic facilitation in a vocabulary learning study with 8–9 year-olds who were taught pseudowords paired with novel meanings. In addition, the authors investigated the influence of orthographic consistency. Words were spelled either with reliable or variable grapheme–phoneme mappings (i.e., cases where consonants or vowels could be spelled in more than one way, for example, long *e* could be spelled *jeet* or *jeat*). Children learned pronunciations of the vocabulary words better when spellings were shown during study periods than when spellings were not seen. There was some evidence that variable vowel spellings produced more limited orthographic facilitation during learning, but by the final session, consistency exerted no differential effects. This indicates that in order to produce orthographic facilitation, it is more important for spelling-sound relations to be systematic than to have only one unique orthographic form.

To further investigate the role of orthography in vocabulary learning, Rosenthal and Ehri (2011) examined the effect of reading novel words aloud versus silently. Fifth graders were randomly assigned either to an oral or a silent word-reading condition. Eight low-frequency words were selected from their previous study (Rosenthal & Ehri, 2008). A passage was created to teach the meaning of each word which was repeated three times and underlined in the passage. Students read the passages silently. However, students in the oral condition were instructed to say the underlined target words out loud when they came to them. Students in the silent condition were instructed to put a check next to the underlined words if they had seen them before. Results demonstrated that the oral decoding strategy better supported vocabulary learning. Students who read the words aloud performed significantly better on pronunciation-meaning association and spelling tasks. The authors note that while these effects were evident for both stronger and weaker readers, they were especially large for weaker readers. Results provide evidence for orthographic mapping effects. Pronouncing embedded words aloud while looking at the spelling of the words supports the formation of connections between spellings, pronunciations, and meanings, and this better secures the new vocabulary words in memory. Because weaker readers are more likely to skip over unfamiliar words without decoding them, being required to decode the words exerts a bigger impact on their vocabulary learning.

Miles et al. (2016) also examined the effect of orthography on vocabulary learning for native and nonnative English speakers. College students who had learned English as a second language and native English speakers were both taught the meanings and pronunciations of very low-frequency words. Words were pronounced, defined orally, and depicted. Learners were exposed to spellings during learning but not during testing in one condition but they were not shown spellings in the other condition. Results indicated that exposure to spellings improved memory for the words' pronunciations but not for their meanings. The authors note that ceiling effects may have precluded the detection of a difference on the meaning task. Interestingly, native English speakers outperformed nonnative speakers on memory for pronunciations even though the two groups were enrolled at the same university and did not differ in GPA, word decoding ability, or English vocabulary knowledge. Why orthographic facilitation was not as strong among nonnative speakers awaits further study.

4.5   Types of Words Read by Beginning Readers

Words differ in the extent that the activation of their meanings is dependent on the presence of other words. Whereas nouns can be meaningful by themselves, verbs and function words require contexts. Both Ehri (1975) and Morris (1992) found that context -dependent words were more difficult for children to distinguish and use than context-independent words. Children who had not yet learned to read were unable to distinguish context-dependent words as separate units in sentence segmentation tasks. Often they combined these words with adjacent content words and based segmentation on stress points rather than word units. For example, three words were detected in the following sentence, with stress points in bold: The**dog** /is**sleeping**/onthe**rug**/. Beginning readers also demonstrated difficulty distinguishing context-dependent words as separate units in a finger-point reading task requiring them to point to each word as they recited a sentence (Morris, 1992). Both studies revealed that young children lack awareness of context-dependent words as separate units of speech. It is not until they see these words in print and learn to read them that they become aware of their separate identities (Ehri, 1975).

To confirm that activation of meanings is diminished for context-dependent words compared to nouns and adjectives when the words are presented out of context, Ehri (1976) investigated the impact of word class in a paired associate word-learning task. Five high-frequency unambiguous words from each of the following word classes were taught: a noun, adjective, past tense verb, preposition, and function word. Each word was paired with a distinctive visual squiggle. Results showed that kindergartners and first graders were better able to remember content-rich words than context-dependent words. Memory for associations between words and their squiggles were much easier to learn when the words were nouns and adjectives than when the words were verbs, prepositions, and function words.

As these studies show, context-dependent words are more difficult to learn than context-independent words. Morris (2001) extended these findings to fifth and sixth graders. Native English speakers and English language learners' (ELLs) writing samples were examined. The analysis showed that ELLs left out more function words than content words in their writing, and they spelled content words more accurately than function words. ELLs demonstrated the ability to spell complex spelling patterns in content words, but often misspelled high-frequency function words. Unstressed function words were most often spelled incorrectly. This pattern of spelling errors was not observed with native English speakers. These findings suggest that ELLs require additional instruction in order to learn the distinct identities of function words, and that their phonological, syntactic, and semantic identities are more influential than their high word frequency in learning their spellings (for more discussion of teaching ELLs to read, see Geva, Xi, Massey-Garrison, & Mak, Chap. 6, this volume).

Miles (2015) also investigated whether there was a difference in native and non-native English speakers' ability to learn to read content and function words. Kindergarteners were taught two sets of words each containing three content and three function words. Students were taught the words and then tested on their ability to read the words over three trials. After the word-reading activity, students were asked to spell each word and use the word in a sentence. Results confirmed those of previous studies. Content words were easier to read, spell, and embed in grammatically correct, contextually rich sentences than function words. This occurred even though the content words were of lower frequency than the function words and thus presumably more difficult to learn. Additionally, results of hierarchical linear models showed that language proficiency as measured by a vocabulary test accounted for variance in function word reading but not content word reading, suggesting that familiarity with colloquial English impacts beginners' ability to learn to read context-dependent words (Miles, 2015).

4.6 Conclusions

Sight word reading is the most efficient way to read words. Research has demonstrated that sight words are acquired through a grapho-phonemic-based process called orthographic mapping. Orthographic mapping involves forming connections between graphemes in spellings of words and phonemes in their pronunciations. As a result, the spellings of words enter memory bonded to their pronunciations and meanings. Subsequently when eyes alight on these words, they are recognized immediately. Also students' ability to spell the words is supported. Knowledge of grapheme–phoneme relations combined with the ability to distinguish separate phonemes in spoken pronunciations provides the glue that secures the spellings in memory.

In order to retain sight words in memory, beginners need to possess some requisite skills including knowledge of grapheme–phoneme relations and phonemic awareness, especially segmentation and blending. Segmentation facilitates the activation of connections between graphemes and phonemes when words are read. Blending facilitates the application of a decoding strategy to read unfamiliar words. This initiates the process of retaining written words in memory, so they can be read by sight. Learning letter names and letter sounds enables children to acquire the letter knowledge that is needed for mapping.

Beginners progress through four phases of development in learning to read words by sight. Growth is characterized by their knowledge of the alphabetic writing system as it is used for orthographic mapping, from pre-alphabetic involving the use of non-phonetic visually salient cues, to partial alphabetic connections, to full alphabetic grapheme–phoneme connections, to consolidated alphabetic connections involving multi-letter units and spelling patterns.

The conditions for reading words influence what aspects of words are learned. Syntactic and semantic identities of words are better learned when the words are read in context, whereas orthographic identities are better learned when words are read outside of contexts in isolation. It is especially important for beginners to learn to read context-dependent words such as function words in context to establish connections between spellings and meanings of these words.

Research into sight word learning helps us understand why teaching letter knowledge and phonemic awareness at the outset should be a priority in early literacy instruction. That way, beginners possess the foundation needed to acquire decoding skill, spelling skill, and memory for sight words. Indeed, this is precisely what research into preventing and intervening with reading difficulties has shown (Kilpatrick, 2015; National Reading Panel, 2000; O'Connor & Vadasy, 2011; Shaywitz, 2003; Snow, Burns, & Griffith, 1998).

References

Bhattacharya, A., & Ehri, L. C. (2004). Graphosyllabic analysis helps adolescent struggling readers read and spell words. *Journal of Learning Disabilities, 37*(4), 331–348.

Boyer, N., & Ehri, L. C. (2011). Contribution of phonemic segmentation instruction with letters and articulation pictures to word reading and spelling in beginners. *Scientific Studies of Reading, 15*(5), 440–470.

Castiglioni-Spalten, M. L., & Ehri, L. C. (2003). Phonemic awareness instruction: Contribution of articulatory segmentation to novice beginners' reading and spelling. *Scientific Studies of Reading, 7*(1), 25–52.

DeAbreu, M. D., & Cardoso-Martins, C. (1998). Alphabetic access route in beginning reading acquisition in Portuguese: The role of letter-name knowledge. *Reading and Writing, 10*(2), 85–104.

Dehaene, S. (2009). *Reading in the brain: The new science of how we read.* Penguin.

Drake, D. A., & Ehri, L. C. (1984). Spelling acquisition; Effects of pronouncing words on memory for their spellings. *Cognition and Instruction, 1*(3), 297–320.

Ehri, L. C. (1975). Word consciousness in readers and prereaders. *Journal of Educational Psychology, 67*(2), 204.

Ehri, L. C. (1976). Word learning in beginning readers and prereaders: Effects of form class and defining contexts. *Journal of Educational Psychology, 68*(6), 832.

Ehri, L. C. (1980). The development of orthographic images. In U. Frith (Ed.), *Cognitive processes in spelling* (pp. 311–338). San Diego, CA: Academic.

Ehri, L. C. (1992). Reconceptualizing the development of sight word reading and its relationship to recoding. In P. B. Gough, L. C. Ehri, R. Treiman, P. B. Gough, L. C. Ehri, & R. Treiman (Eds.), *Reading acquisition* (pp. 107–143). Hillsdale, NJ, England: Lawrence Erlbaum Associates Inc.

Ehri, L. C. (1998). Grapheme-phoneme knowledge is essential to learning to read words in English. In J. L. Metsala, L. C. Ehri, J. L. Metsala, & L. C. Ehri (Eds.), *Word recognition in beginning literacy* (pp. 3–40). Mahwah, NJ, US: Lawrence Erlbaum Associates Publishers.

Ehri, L. C. (2005a). Development of sight word reading: Phases and findings. In M. Snowling & C. Hulme (Eds.), *The science of reading: A handbook* (pp. 135–154). Malden, MA: Blackwell.

Ehri, L. C. (2005b). Learning to read words: Theory, findings, and issues. *Scientific Studies of Reading, 9*(2), 167–188.

Ehri, L. C. (2014). Orthographic mapping in the acquisition of sight word reading, spelling memory, and vocabulary learning. *Scientific Studies of Reading, 18*(1), 5–21.

Ehri, L. C., Deffner, N. D., & Wilce, L. S. (1984). Pictorial mnemonics for phonics. *Journal of Educational Psychology, 76*(5), 880–893.

Ehri, L. C., & Roberts, K. T. (1979). Do beginners learn printed words better in contexts or in isolation? *Child Development,* 675–685.

Ehri, L. C., & Roberts, T. (2006). The roots of learning to read and write: Acquisition of letters and phonemic awareness. *Handbook of Early Literacy Research, 2,* 113–131.

Ehri, L. C., Satlow, E., & Gaskins, I. (2009). Grapho-phonemic enrichment strengthens keyword analogy instruction for struggling young readers. *Reading & Writing Quarterly, 25*(2–3), 162–191.

Ehri, L., & Wilce, L. (1980). Do beginners learn to read function words better in sentences or in lists? *Reading Research Quarterly, 15*(4), 451–477.

Ehri, L. C., & Wilce, L. S. (1983). Development of word identification speed in skilled and less skilled beginning readers. *Journal of Educational Psychology, 75*(1), 3.

Ehri, L. C., & Wilce, L. S. (1985). Movement into reading: Is the first stage of printed word learning visual or phonetic? *Reading Research Quarterly, 20*(2), 163–179.

Ehri, L. C., & Wilce, L. S. (1987). Cipher versus cue reading: An experiment in decoding acquisition. *Journal of Educational Psychology, 79*(1), 3.

Elbro, C., de Jong, P., Houter, D., & Neilsen, A. (2012). From spelling pronunciation to lexical access: A second step in word decoding? *Scientific Studies of Reading, 16,* 341–359.

Gathercole, S. E. (2006). Nonword repetition and word learning: The nature of the relationship. *Applied Psycholinguistics, 27*(04), 513–543.

Goodman, K. S. (1970). Behind the eye: What happens in reading. In K. Goodman & O. Niles (Eds.), *Reading: Process and program* (pp. 3–38). Urbana, IL: National Council of Teachers of English.

Goswami, U. (1986). Children's use of analogy in learning to read: A developmental study. *Journal of Experimental Child Psychology, 42*(1), 73–83.

Gough, P. B., Juel, C., & Griffith, P. L. (1992). Reading, spelling, and the orthographic cipher. In P. B. Gough, L. C. Ehri, R. Treiman, P. B. Gough, L. C. Ehri, & R. Treiman (Eds.), *Reading acquisition* (pp. 35–48). Hillsdale, NJ, England: Lawrence Erlbaum Associates Inc.

Johnston, F. R. (2000). Word learning in predictable text. *Journal of Educational Psychology, 92*(2), 248.

Kilpatrick, D. (2015). *Essentials of assessing, preventing, and overcoming reading difficulties.* Hoboken, NJ: Wiley.

Kilpatrick, D. A. (2018). Incorporating recent advances in understanding word-reading skills into SLD diagnoses: The case of orthographic mapping. In D. P. Flanagan, & E. M. McDonough (Eds.). *Contemporary intellectual assessment–fourth edition: Theories, tests, and issues.* New York, NY: Guilford.

Landerl, K., & Reitsma, P. (2005). Phonological and morphological consistency in the acquisition of vowel duration spelling in Dutch and German. *Journal of Experimental Child Psychology, 92*(4), 322–344.

Lucas, R., & Norbury, C. F. (2014). Orthography facilitates vocabulary learning for children with autism spectrum disorders (ASD). *The Quarterly Journal of Experimental Psychology, 67*(7), 1317–1334.

Masonheimer, P. E., Drum, P. A., & Ehri, L. C. (1984). Does environmental print identification lead children into word reading? *Journal of Reading Behavior, 16*(4), 257–271.

Mengoni, S. E., Nash, H., & Hulme, C. (2013). The benefit of orthographic support for oral vocabulary learning in children with Down syndrome. *Journal of Child Language, 40,* 221–243.

Miles, K. P. (2015). *The effect of orthographic mapping, context, and word class on sight word learning for native and nonnative English-speakers* (Doctoral dissertation). Retrieved from PsycInfo. (2016-99011-013).

Miles, K. P., Ehri, L. C., & Lauterbach, M. D. (2016). Mnemonic value of orthography for vocabulary learning in monolinguals and language minority English-speaking college students. *Journal of College Reading and Learning, 46*(2), 99–112.

Moats, L. C. (2010). *Speech to print: Language essentials for teachers* (2nd ed.). Baltimore, MD: Brookes.

Morris, D. (1992). Concept of word: A pivotal understanding in the learning-to-read process. In S. Templeton & D. Bear (Eds.), *Development of orthographic knowledge and the foundations of literacy: A memorial festschrift for Edmund H. Henderson* (pp. 53–77). Hillsdale, NJ: Erlbaum.

Morris, L. (2001). Going through a bad spell: What the spelling errors of young ESL learners reveal about their grammatical knowledge. *Canadian Modern Language Review/La Revue Canadienne des Langues Vivantes, 58*(2), 273–286.

National Reading Panel. (2000). *Report of the National Reading Panel: Teaching children to read.* National Institute of Child Health and Human Development: Washington D.C.

Ocal, T. (2015). *A spelling pronunciation strategy helps college students remember how to spell difficult words* (Unpublished doctoral dissertation). Graduate Center of The City University of New York, New York, NY.

O'Connor, R., & Vadasy, P. (Eds.). (2011). *Handbook of reading interventions.* New York: Guilford.

Perfetti, C. A. (1992). The representation problem in reading acquisition. In P. Gough, L. Ehri, & R. Treiman (Eds.), *Reading acquisition* (pp. 145–174). Hillside, NJ: Lawrence Erlbaum Associates Inc.

Rack, J., Hulme, C., Snowling, M., & Wightman, J. (1994). The role of phonology in young children learning to read words: The direct-mapping hypothesis. *Journal of Experimental Child Psychology, 57*(1), 42–71.

Ricketts, J., Bishop, D. M., & Nation, K. (2009). Orthographic facilitation in oral vocabulary acquisition. *The Quarterly Journal of Experimental Psychology, 62*(10), 1948–1966.

Roberts, T. A. (2003). Effects of alphabet-letter instruction on young children's word recognition. *Journal of Educational Psychology, 95*(1), 41–51.

Rosenthal, J., & Ehri, L. C. (2008). The mnemonic value of orthography for vocabulary learning. *Journal of Educational Psychology, 100*(1), 175–191.

Rosenthal, J., & Ehri, L. C. (2011). Pronouncing new words aloud during the silent reading of text enhances fifth graders' memory for vocabulary words and their spellings. *Reading and Writing: An Interdisciplinary Journal, 24*(8), 921–950.

Scott, J., & Ehri, L. (1989). Sight word reading in prereaders: Use of logographic versus alphabetic access routes. *Journal of Reading Behavior, 22*(2), 149–166.

Share, D. L. (2004). Orthographic learning at a glance: On the time course and developmental onset of self-teaching. *Journal of Experimental Child Psychology, 87*(4), 267–298.

Share, D. L. (2008). Orthographic learning, phonological recoding, and self-teaching. *Advances in Child Development and Behavior, 36,* 31.

Share, D. L., Jorm, A. F., Maclean, R., & Matthews, R. (1984). Sources of individual differences in reading acquisition. *Journal of Educational Psychology, 76*(6), 1309–1324.

Shaywitz, S. (2003). *Overcoming dyslexia: A new and complete science-based program for reading problems at any level.* New York: Knopf.

Shmidman, A., & Ehri, L. (2010). Embedded picture mnemonics to learn letters. *Scientific Studies of Reading, 14*(2), 159–182.

Snow, C., Burns, M., & Griffin, P. (Eds.). (1998). *Preventing reading difficulties in young children.* Washington, DC: National Academy Press.

Treiman, R., & Broderick, V. (1998). What's in a name: Children's knowledge about the letters in their own names. *Journal of Experimental Child Psychology, 70*(2), 97–116.

Treiman, R., & Rodriguez, K. (1999). Young children use letter names in learning to read words. *Psychological Science, 10*(4), 334–338.

Tunmer, W., & Chapman, J. W. (1998). Language prediction skill, phonological recoding ability, and beginning reading. *Reading and Spelling: Development and Disorders,* 33.

Tunmer, W. E., & Chapman, J. W. (2012). Does set for variability mediate the influence of vocabulary knowledge on the development of word recognition skills? *Scientific Studies of Reading, 16*(2), 122–140.

Wang, H. C., Castles, A., Nickels, L., & Nation, K. (2011). Context effects on orthographic learning of regular and irregular words. *Journal of Experimental Child Psychology, 109*(1), 39–57.

Chapter 5
Reading Comprehension and Reading Comprehension Difficulties

Jane Oakhill, Kate Cain and Carsten Elbro

Abstract The Simple View of Reading indicates that reading comprehension is based upon two broad skills, language comprehension and word reading. This chapter explores the many factors that directly impact language comprehension and reading comprehension apart from word reading skills. Vocabulary, inferencing, background knowledge, comprehension monitoring, and knowledge of text structure are all explored in detail. How these factors interact with reading comprehension and with one other is described, and how to best improve these skills in struggling comprehenders is also presented.

5.1 Introduction

Reading comprehension is crucial not just for understanding text, but for learning more generally and thus education more broadly. It is also requisite for social activities because of email, texting, and the numerous Web applications that people use on an everyday basis. In this chapter, we will explore how successful reading comprehension requires the orchestration of a number of different abilities and processes for its success.

J. Oakhill (✉)
University of Sussex, Brighton, UK
e-mail: j.oakhill@sussex.ac.uk

K. Cain
Lancaster University, Lancashire, UK
e-mail: k.cain@lancaster.ac.uk

C. Elbro
University of Copenhagen, Copenhagen, Denmark
e-mail: ce@hum.ku.dk

© Springer Nature Switzerland AG 2019   83
D. A. Kilpatrick et al. (eds.), *Reading Development and Difficulties*,
https://doi.org/10.1007/978-3-030-26550-2_5

5.1.1 The Simple View of Reading

In this chapter, we focus on the language skills that underpin successful reading comprehension. It goes without saying that readers will not be able to understand a text if they cannot decode a reasonable number of the words in it. But effective reading comprehension also requires good language understanding more generally. Critically, reading comprehension cannot take place in the absence of either one of these components: If a child cannot read any words and/or if a child has no language comprehension ability, their reading comprehension will be zero. This is the essence of the Simple View of Reading (originally proposed by Gough & Tunmer, 1986; see also Joshi, Chap. 1, this volume). The Simple View of Reading does not imply that reading, or learning to read, is "simple" but, rather, that variation in reading ability can be captured (simply) by variation in these two skills. It is a useful framework for understanding not only reading development, but also reading difficulties.

The development of reading. For the beginning reader, word reading is new, and children will differ substantially in how quickly they acquire the ability to decode the words on the page. Language comprehension, on the other hand, is quite well developed when children start school. So, in beginning readers the variation in reading comprehension is almost identical to the variation in word reading. As children become competent at decoding the words, good language comprehension will be more crucial to their overall reading comprehension than word recognition.

This change in the influence of word reading and language skills in the first few years of reading development does not mean that early reading instruction should focus solely on teaching children how to decode words. Even though children typically have a high level of communicative competence by the time they begin to learn to read, written texts are, in important ways, different from spoken interactions and typically require memory abilities and other cognitive skills that are not so crucial in understanding everyday face-to-face spoken interactions, that typically happen in the "here and now." We review the critical skills for reading comprehension under different categories below.

Reading difficulties. The Simple View of Reading is often presented schematically, as in Fig. 5.1, to illustrate the sources of variability among students in their reading skills. This schematic representation shows how problems with one component of reading can occur independently of problems with the other. For example, children with specific comprehension problems can be differentiated from children who have specific word reading problems (i.e., dyslexics) or generally poor readers (sometimes termed "garden variety" poor readers; Gough & Tunmer, 1986).

Children with specific comprehension problems (often simply termed "poor comprehenders") have difficulties with reading comprehension, despite having age-appropriate word reading skills. The problems of such children often do not become apparent before the 3rd or 4th year of schooling, because such children are perceived as "good readers" (i.e., good at word decoding) and the material they are being asked to read and understand in the early years of school is typically not very demanding in terms of language comprehension (which encompasses a number of skills we will

	Language comprehension	
Word reading	Poor	Good
Poor	Generally poor reader	Dyslexic
Good	Poor comprehender	Good reader

Fig. 5.1 Simple View of Reading

outline below). Thus, as the texts they are expected to read and understand become increasingly complex, some children who initially seemed quite competent at reading might turn out to have reading comprehension problems (e.g., Catts, Compton, Tomblin, & Bridges, 2012). These children with *specific reading comprehension problems*, i.e., the poor comprehenders, will be the focus of this chapter.

5.1.2 What Does It Mean to Comprehend a Text?

Whatever the modality in which a text is presented (i.e., whether written down or read aloud), successful comprehension involves the construction of an integrated representation of the overall meaning of the text. This example (taken from a study of reading comprehension) will give you an idea of the importance of building this representation.

> The man was worried. His car came to a halt and he was all alone. It was extremely dark and cold. The man took off his overcoat, rolled down the window, and got out of the car as quickly as possible. Then he used all his strength to move as fast as he could. He was relieved when he finally saw the lights of the city, even though they were far away. (from Bransford & Nitsch, 1978)

If you are like most readers, you may say that there is nothing exactly wrong with the text. However, you may find it hard to understand and hard to recall. The problem is that it is difficult to set up a suitable mental model from the start of the text. What is the setting? Why is the man worried? On closer inspection, some things do not fit with the text: Why does the man take off his coat and roll down the window when it is extremely cold?

A suitable mental model could be "man escapes from car driven into water." With that model in mind, each piece of information from the text makes sense, i.e., can be integrated. The text will also be much easier to remember at a later point. That is because you remember your mental model of the text, not the text itself. This integrated representation of the meaning of a text has been termed a *mental model* (Johnson-Laird, 1983) or a *situation model* (Kintsch, 1998).

In the remainder of this chapter, we consider the skills and processes that are needed in order to understand a text. The comprehension processes we outline are central not only to reading comprehension but also to listening comprehension, with an important caveat: Listening comprehension is intended as the understanding of a text read out loud, and not listening in the sense of everyday conversations and interactions.

5.2   Vocabulary and Word Meanings

It is possible for a competent decoder to read out loud all the words in a text, but to understand very little of the actual text, as in this example

> The first model that was able to explain the full spectrum of thermal radiation was put forward by *Max Planck* in 1900. He proposed a mathematical model in which the thermal radiation was in equilibrium with a set of *harmonic oscillators*. To reproduce the experimental results, he had to assume that each oscillator emitted an integer number of units of energy at its single characteristic frequency, rather than being able to emit any arbitrary amount of energy. In other words, the energy emitted by an oscillator was *quantized*. The *quantum* of energy for each oscillator, according to Planck, was proportional to the frequency of the oscillator; the constant of proportionality is now known as the *Planck constant*. (from "Introduction to Quantum mechanics", Wikipedia)

Good reading comprehension depends on knowledge of the meanings of the words in the text. The strong relations between vocabulary knowledge and reading comprehension have been acknowledged for many years (e.g., Carroll, 1993; Davis, 1944, 1968; Thorndike, 1973). Some estimate that about 90% of the words need to be known for a reader to have a good chance of understanding a text (Nagy & Scott, 2000).

However, good reading comprehension is also an invaluable source of word knowledge. For a start, it is not necessary to know all the words in a text or to stop to look up all unknown words because, to some extent, the meanings of unknown words can be worked out from the context. New items are added to our vocabularies throughout our lifetimes, and, similarly, existing vocabulary is refined through reading. Once children become fluent readers, written text will be a major source of new vocabulary items (Cunningham, 2005; Nagy & Scott, 2000).

The relation is reciprocal: vocabulary development and reading comprehension can have a beneficial effect on each other (e.g., Seigneuric & Ehrlich, 2005). This relation of mutual reciprocity between vocabulary and comprehension means that readers can enter either virtuous or vicious circles. With limited vocabulary knowledge, comprehension is likely to suffer, and without a basic level of comprehension, the ensuing vocabulary learning is likely to be minimal. Conversely, a skilled reader with relevant prior knowledge and good vocabulary can learn a lot from the same text. These positive or negative circles are frequently referred to as the Matthew effect in reading (Stanovich, 1986).

5.2.1 Different Aspects of Vocabulary and Their Relation with Reading Comprehension

It is not easy to say what it means to know a word. It is difficult because "knowing" a word spans all the way from superficial recognition—"I think I have heard the word *pelagic* before, but I am not sure I know what it means"—to being able to explain the word's meaning in depth and providing appropriate examples of usage.

In other words, vocabulary knowledge is not all or none; there are different degrees of knowledge of the meaning(s) of a word. Measures of vocabulary knowledge at *shallow levels* are also known as measures of vocabulary *breadth*. Such measures typically require simple recognition or production of single words as in the *British Picture Vocabulary Scale*, (BPVS: Dunn, Dunn, Whetton, & Pintillie, 1992).

The amount and detail of knowledge of words is often referred to as *depth* of vocabulary knowledge, and this can include not only definitional knowledge of a word, but also the relations and associations between individual words and concepts. For example, knowledge about *pulmonary barotrauma* might include the information that it is something SCUBA divers might be prone to. More "in-depth" knowledge might include the fact that it typically occurs if a diver holds his/her breath while ascending and that it is a serious and potentially fatal condition. Even deeper knowledge would include the information that a pulmonary barotrauma occurs when the pressure inside the lungs becomes too great so that the lung is ruptured. Incidentally, in this instance morphological decomposition can also help with working out (and remembering) the meaning of the expression. You would need to know that *pulmonary* relates to lungs (as in *pulmonary disease, pulmonary embolism*, etc.), and consideration of the composition of *barotrauma* makes it obvious that it has two morphemes: *baro*, meaning pressure (as in *bar, barometer*), and *trauma*, meaning some sort of damage. So a morphological analysis of *pulmonary barotrauma* may lead to the meaning "pressure damage to the lung," or more colloquially "burst lung."

There is now increasing evidence that comprehension is particularly dependent on vocabulary knowledge at relatively *deep* levels (Ouellette, 2006; Tannenbaum, Torgesen, & Wagner, 2006). There are many reasons why readers need a relatively deep understanding of words: First, when concepts that have names occur in a text, such as *barotrauma* or *table*, it will be easier for the reader to understand the text the more s/he knows about those words. If the reader can activate an appropriate, more detailed and contextually relevant, instance at the first encounter of the key word (e.g., Anderson, Stevens, Shifrin, & Osborn, 1978) that is likely to facilitate subsequent comprehension. For instance, if a reader sees the text "The fish attacked the surfer," the instantiated representation of the fish in question is some sort of large and aggressive fish, most likely a shark, not just any old generic fish. A related issue is that a reader might have quite a detailed meaning representation of a word, but might fail to activate and use that knowledge to make appropriate inferences during comprehension (Cain & Oakhill, 1999; Cain, Oakhill, Barnes, & Bryant, 2001).

Reading comprehension occurs in real time, so it is crucial that the reader is able to access word meanings (and, indeed, other sorts of knowledge), rapidly and accurately. If the activation of meanings is too slow, it will be difficult to process the links with other words in the text before the next word is encountered. Thus, *speed of activation* should be added to the requirements for having a rich vocabulary. It is not enough to know lots of word meanings if it takes a long time to activate them. In our own recent research, for example (see Oakhill, Cain, & McCarthy, 2015; Oakhill, Cain, McCarthy, & Field, 2012), we explored different aspects of children's vocabulary knowledge and the relation between those different aspects of knowledge and comprehension skill. We assessed not only children's knowledge of words at deeper levels, but also assessed their facility of access to the word meanings. The children in the study were asked to produce synonyms or hypernyms, e.g., "an apple is a sort of what?" (answer: fruit), and were also asked to do speeded synonym and hypernym judgments on word pairs. So, for example, they had to judge as quickly as possible whether the first item was a "type of" the second, e.g., *bread-food, fox-vegetable*. The results showed that children's vocabulary knowledge at deep levels, and in particular the speed with which that knowledge could be accessed, was predictive of their comprehension skill even when word reading ability and general speed of responding were taken into account.

5.2.2 Vocabulary Development

Even in very young children, vocabulary learning is already dependent on inference making (see the next section), because very young children cannot be taught word definitions. Instead, they typically have things labeled for them and have to extract and refine meanings themselves by working out what the crucial features are. Indeed, they might focus on salient, but not necessarily definitional features. For example, a child might learn the word *dog* and apply it appropriately to refer to dogs, or pictures of dogs, but might also overextend the meaning to cats, pigs, cows, horses, and, indeed, all four-legged animals.

The reciprocity between vocabulary development and reading comprehension is apparent in young children (prereaders). Lepola, Lynch, Laakkonen, Silven, and Niemi, (2012) assessed children's ability to make inferences about stories in picture books, and they found that this skill when the children were age 4 predicted their vocabulary knowledge one year later, which subsequently predicted their listening comprehension at 6. This finding indicates that it is important to foster and develop children's inference skills even before they can read. Not only are inference skills important for text comprehension (as we outline later in the chapter), but they are also important in developing vocabulary knowledge.

Once children start reading, most new vocabulary is learned through reading, not from being directly taught word meanings (Cunningham, 2005). Hence, the quality and the amount of reading is important for the further development of vocabulary—and thereby for reading comprehension. The mediating variable seems to be amount of reading experience. Children who have good comprehension (or good vocabulary, or both) are likely to read more (and enjoy reading more) and thus improve their vocabulary (and comprehension) through practice in reading.

There are very substantial differences in the amount of reading that children do voluntarily. It has been estimated that during the middle grades an average reader might read 100,000 words a year, while a more highly motivated child might read 1,000,000 words. Really voracious readers might read 10 million or even up to 50,000,000 words in a year (Nagy & Anderson, 1984). These very substantial individual differences between readers will lead to similarly substantial differences in vocabulary and comprehension in later years.

The relation between vocabulary knowledge and reading comprehension changes developmentally. Vocabulary becomes more important as a predictor of comprehension skill between about 7 and 10 years (Protopapas, Siderisis, Mouzaki, & Simos, 2007). This change probably occurs because, as children become more skilled and fluent word decoders, vocabulary knowledge becomes more crucial and also because as children get older, the books that they need to read become more challenging in terms of vocabulary (reading books for beginners are typically written with a restricted word set).

5.2.3 Vocabulary and Reading Comprehension

There are different ways in which vocabulary knowledge and reading comprehension may be related:

First, poor comprehension restricts vocabulary growth: Children with specific reading comprehension difficulties have slower rates of vocabulary growth than same-age peers with good reading comprehension (Cain & Oakhill, 2011).

Second, there is not a clear causal link between vocabulary breadth (see above) and comprehension. Children identified as poor comprehenders typically perform within the normal range on measures of receptive vocabulary, but such children may have problems with other aspects of vocabulary (Cain, Oakhill, & Lemmon, 2004).

Third, some poor comprehenders also perform relatively poorly on measures of *activation of word meanings and related words*, for example, on tests of vocabulary fluency. They generate fewer category instances than good comprehenders (e.g., name as many kinds of *farm animals* as you can), but do not have similar problems when asked to generate words that rhyme with a given word (name as many words that rhyme with *farm* as you can). Thus, the problem is specific to tasks requiring access to word *meanings* (Nation & Snowling, 1998).

In addition, there is evidence that poor comprehenders are less likely than good comprehenders to activate meaning-related words automatically. For instance, we used a false memory task to assess good and poor comprehenders' gist memory for word lists (Weekes, Hamilton, Oakhill, & Holliday, 2008). This task employs the DRM paradigm (Deese, 1959; Roediger & McDermott, 1995) in which people are required to remember (recall or recognize) a list of words, such as: *bed, rest, tired, dream, wake, snooze, blanket, doze, slumber, snore, nap, peace, blanket, yawn, drowsy.* In such tasks, both adults and children very often recall or recognize words that were not in the list, but which capture the gist, or theme, of the list (i.e., *sleep,* in the above list). It was the good comprehenders who were *more* likely to misremember the theme words, although there were no differences in memory for the words that actually appeared in the lists.

5.2.4 Teaching Vocabulary

There is evidence that reading comprehension can be improved by substituting easier vocabulary words for harder words, and instruction in the meaning of more difficult words can improve comprehension (Kameenui, Carnine, & Freschi, 1982). However, the adaptation of texts for children with poor vocabularies is clearly not a viable strategy in the longer term. First, logistically, this is not practicable, and second, it is important that children learn to infer meanings from context so that they increase their vocabulary and not just have texts simplified to the level of their existing vocabulary.

There have been a number of studies of different methods of teaching vocabulary to children, but none of these methods will dramatically expand and deepen their vocabulary. The immediate results of vocabulary training are moderate, and the transfer effects to reading comprehension are even less substantial and have only been demonstrated in a small number of studies (NRP, 2000). However, there are promising ways in which the interplay between vocabulary knowledge and reading comprehension may be improved.

Two different approaches to teaching vocabulary can be distinguished. The most obvious is simply to help children learn the meanings of *specific* words. The other is to help children become better at *figuring out meanings of new* words through independent reading. Both methods can support reading comprehension. These methods are described in turn in the next section.

Teaching specific words. The authors of school texts often take word knowledge for granted even though many words may be unfamiliar to children. In such cases, it can be helpful to explain the key words and to link them to topic knowledge *before* the children read the text. When such words are known, it is much easier to use them to build mental models of the content of the text. For instance, for fifth-grade students, teaching relevant vocabulary has an effect on learning of, and memory for, a social studies text (Carney, Anderson, Blackburn, & Blessings, 1984), and Medo and Ryder (1993) found that vocabulary instruction helped eighth-grade students to make causal connections in an informational text, a method that was beneficial across a wide range of ability levels.

In addition to key words, other words may also be targeted for direct teaching. These are words that children are likely to encounter frequently in texts in a variety of content areas as they enter higher-grade level words such as *coincidence, absurd, hasty, perseverance* ("tier two words"[1] in the USA, Beck, McKeown, & Kucan, 2005). They are neither the most frequent and early-acquired words ("tier one" words,

---

[1] It should be noted that the usage of the term "tier" by Beck et al. (to denote three levels of vocabulary) is unrelated to the use of that term in the context of Response to Intervention (RTI).

such as *clock, baby, happy*) nor infrequent, topic-specific words ("tier three" words, such as *osmosis, nucleus, archeologist*). Since words are learned in approximately the same order no matter whether they are learned at the age of 7 or 10, tier two words are the ones that are either just included or about to be included in the child's vocabulary (Biemiller, 2005). As such, they are among the most useful words to teach.

There are numerous ways to teach vocabulary but, based on the research thus far, some methods and strategies are likely to be more helpful than others. First, as would be expected given the links between vocabulary and reading comprehension, the successful teaching of vocabulary needs to be aimed at deeper levels of vocabulary knowledge. This means that children should not just learn word definitions, but also how unfamiliar words relate to other words. So, for example, it is not enough to learn that a "shitzou" is a name of a particular animal. It is much more efficient to know that a shitzou is a type of dog, in which ways it is a typical dog, and how it differs from most other dogs. In this way, shitzou will be linked to many other words and concepts in a "semantic network" (or meaning network). In practice, this means that vocabulary teaching should take place in a rich context (Beck, Perfetti, & McKeown, 1982; NRP, 2000), and the formation of connections (networks) between words should be actively encouraged. Second, vocabulary learning is also enhanced when children are given opportunities to detect and to use new words, e.g., during dialogues with the teacher (Coyne, McCoach & Kapp, 2007). The teacher can support learning by asking increasingly demanding questions about new words (e.g., Blewitt, Rump, Shealy, & Cook, 2009). Third, repetitions of new vocabulary items are also supportive of learning, as pointed out in the survey of training studies by Stahl and Fairbanks (1986). So, for example, prereading activities with key words should be followed up by activities on what has been learned about these words during reading, and follow-up activities on later occasions. For younger children, simple re-reading of storybooks will provide them with important opportunities to rehearse the meaning of new words (Biemiller & Boote, 2006).

Teaching children to acquire new vocabulary. Even though it may be possible for children to learn 10 new words a week through a well-structured vocabulary training program (Biemiller, 2005), such a program would help children to acquire only about 400 new words a year. This would still only be a small fraction of the words that children typically acquire in a year. A further complication is that it would be difficult for the teacher to predict which key content words the children would need to know in the longer run. Thus, some more recent programs (see below) teach children word knowledge and inference making abilities that can help them acquire new word knowledge during independent reading.

There are two main ways in which children can be helped to improve their incidental learning of new vocabulary. These are not mutually exclusive; rather, they may supplement each other. One way is to instruct children in ways to derive meanings from context. Children can be taught to search the context for clues about the category of the unknown word ("what sort of thing is it?"), for defining characteristics ("how can you describe it?") and for likes and opposites ("do you know of something similar or the opposite?"). For instance, Tomesen and Aarnoutse (1998) found that such direct instruction was helpful in improving the text comprehension of both poor and average readers. However, the skills did not transfer to the children's reading comprehension more generally.

Another way is to teach word knowledge through morphology, that is, through knowledge of the smallest significant units of words: prefixes, roots, suffixes, inflections, e.g., *mis/read/ing/s* (see Bowers & Kirby, 2010). The same root morphemes occur in several different words; for example, the root *read* is part of *reads, reader, unread, reading,* etc., and derivations and inflections apply to whole classes of words. So, learning a morpheme in one word is potentially beneficial for recognizing and understanding many new words in which the morpheme occurs. For example, if you know that the morpheme *eval* relates to "age," then you will see that medieval means "middle age," primeval means "first age" and you can probably work out the meaning of "coeval" if you do not already know it. Numerous studies have found that teaching morphology to children has significant effects on the development of both vocabulary and reading comprehension. Such effects are enhanced if teaching does not just focus on the analysis of single words but is combined with comprehension instruction (see Bowers, Kirby, & Deacon, 2010).

Successful training programs typically explicitly emphasize the interrelations between the orthographic, phonological, morphological, semantic, and syntactic aspects of reading (so-called lexical quality of the word; Perfetti, 2007). The idea behind such training is that the more one knows about a word (i.e., its phonemes, orthographic patterns, semantic meanings, syntactic uses, and morphological roots and affixes), the more efficiently the word can be decoded, retrieved, and comprehended. Such a program, called RAVE-O (Barzillai, Morris, Lovett, & Wolf, 2010), which focuses on training meaning in the context of the other linguistic properties of the word to be learned, has been shown to improve second- and third-grade poor readers' vocabulary knowledge. This training was effective not only for the multiple meanings of the words taught within the program, but also improved the children's knowledge of the meanings of words not taught within the program. Importantly, these gains were maintained one year later.

5.3   Inferences

Most texts are far from explicit, and, indeed, they would be very long and tedious if they were. Inferences are licensed by the text, but they go beyond the information that is stated explicitly. Good stories, and novels in particular, create opportunities for the reader to make inferences to work out what is going on. Consider the following three sentences:

Mary heard the ice-cream van coming.

She remembered her pocket money.

She rushed into the house to get it.

You almost certainly spontaneously made links between those sentences so that they were no longer independent. *She* in the second and third sentences refers back to

Mary in the first sentence and thus provides a link between those sentences. Similarly, *it* in the final sentence refers back to *Mary's pocket money*. The inferences that you made to link these sentences are *local cohesion inferences* (often called bridging inferences). The need to generate a local cohesion inference is often signaled by pronouns, and other explicit cues in the text. Another critical type of inference is a *global coherence inference*. The reasons for Mary's thoughts and actions are not stated in the text but, like most readers, you most probably made a global coherence inference to understand that Mary has the *intention* to buy an ice cream, using her pocket money. In doing so, you drew on your background knowledge about such events. Global coherence inferences such as these contribute to the meaning and coherence of the text overall.

This example shows that even a very short, apparently simple, text requires numerous inferences. What is important to note is that the examples above are of inferences that are *necessary* to understand the essence of the text. For example, a reader might infer that Mary cannot find her pocket money in time and does not succeed in her goal of buying an ice cream, or that Mary's favorite ice cream is strawberry, but those inferences are not necessary to construct a coherent representation of the three sentences. Such inferences can be considered as *elaborative* in that they embellish the mental model. Although they might be helpful in some circumstances, they could actually be detrimental to understanding because they are not licensed by the text, and might turn out to be not just irrelevant, but wrong (as well as being time-consuming and distracting). It is connecting inferences, which help to establish local and global coherence in text that needs to be encouraged and facilitated in young readers.

5.3.1 The Development of Inference Making

Inference making is important for understanding the world, not just for text comprehension. Thus, it is not surprising that children have the ability to make the types of inferences necessary to understand text from an early age, before formal reading instruction begins. Preschool children are able to generate inferences from picture books, stories read aloud to them, and animated cartoon sequences (Kendeou, Lynch, van den Broek, Espin, White, & Kremer, 2005; Language and Reading Research Consortium, 2015; Silva & Cain, 2015). However, inference making ability continues to improve between the ages 6 and 15 years, with not even the oldest children achieving 100% accuracy (Barnes, Dennis, & Haefele-Kalvaitis, 1996). So what are the key factors that support developmental improvements?

First, it is clear that younger children's memory limitations might restrict their ability to make inferences. Memory capacity develops across a wide age range (Gathercole, Pickering, Ambridge, & Wearing, 2004). Children need to remember accurately key parts of the text to construct a mental model. One aspect of memory that is particularly important for inference making is *working memory*. Working memory refers to the ability to process information while storing previously read or heard information used when the reader (or listener) needs to link information between different sentences in a text and/or incorporate background knowledge to make sense of implicit details. Memory capacity is associated with children's ability to generate inferences between 6 and 12 years (Cain, Oakhill, & Bryant, 2004; Chrysochoou, Bablekou, & Tsigilis, 2011; Currie & Cain, 2015). If a child has difficulty with inferential questions, it may be helpful to check that they remember the crucial pieces of information on which the inferences depend and also to check their working memory capacity.

A second factor that likely influences developmental differences in inference making is knowledge: both vocabulary knowledge and background knowledge related to the topic of the text. In order make the inferences outlined above, for example, the reader has to know the meanings of key words and also know that we need money to purchase ice cream, etc. Depth of vocabulary knowledge (what we know about a word's meaning) is more strongly related to inference skill than breadth of vocabulary knowledge (how many words are known; Cain & Oakhill, 2014). Thus, building up rich, interconnected, semantic networks as vocabulary knowledge expands may, in part, explain developmental improvements.

The contribution that background knowledge makes to inference skills developmentally has been explored in beginner readers through to mid-adolescence (Barnes et al., 1996). Of course, lack of relevant knowledge can limit inference making, but even when they have the relevant knowledge, some children do not access it and apply it to their understanding of text. It appears that not only depth of knowledge, but also facility of access to that knowledge, may be a critical determinant of children's inference making (see also Oakhill, et al., 2012).

A third factor to consider is a reader's (or listener's) *standard for coherence* and their active attempts to make the text cohere (van den Broek, 1997). This standard for coherence can vary both inter-individually (i.e., between readers) and intra-individually (i.e., within readers, e.g., depending on the purpose of reading). For instance, when adults are required to read to study for a test they generate more inferences than when required to read for entertainment (van den Broek, Lorch, Linderholm, & Gustafson, 2001). Thus, it seems that readers set goals, and when it is important to make all of the critical links between information in a text and to derive conclusions from that text, they are able to do so. In contrast, when reading for pleasure, they might make a less deliberate effort because they regard the purpose as being entertained rather than to learn from the text. However, some children might not set appropriate standards for coherence and/or might not be able to make task-relevant adjustments to those standards.

5.3.2 Difficulties with Inference Making

Children with reading comprehension problems do not generate as many necessary local cohesion and global coherence inferences as their peers (Cain & Oakhill, 1999; Cain et al., 2001; Oakhill, 1984). As was the case with developmental differences, three main factors seem to be particularly important: memory, knowledge, and a reader's standard for coherence.

Children with poor comprehension skills tend to have lower working memory capacity than children with good comprehension (Cain, 2006; Nation, Adams, Bowyer-Crane, & Snowling, 1999; Oakhill, Yuill, & Parkin, 1986), and independent measures of working memory predict inference making skill in typically developing readers (Cain et al., 2004). For children with poor comprehension skills, memory is particularly predictive of their performance when the inference required the integration of information in sentences separated by several additional sentences (Barnes, Faulkner, Wilkinson, & Dennis, 2004; Cain et al., 2004).

Vocabulary and background knowledge are important for inference making, as shown in our earlier example about Mary and the ice-cream van. Even very simple inferences cannot be made if the reader does not have the requisite background knowledge. However, when knowledge is carefully controlled for, poor comprehenders still make fewer inferences than good comprehenders (Cain et al., 2001). So, as was the case with younger readers, inferencing failures do not occur simply because poor comprehenders lack relevant knowledge. It may be that it is the activation of knowledge, and the speed with which that knowledge can be activated, rather than having knowledge per se, that are critical limiting factors.

Children's *standard for coherence* may also explain inference making difficulties between good and poor comprehenders. Children who are good comprehenders are sensitive to different task goals. For instance, when told that they will be tested on their memory for the content of a text, they take longer to read it and also remember more of its content compared to a "reading for pleasure" goal. However, poor comprehenders do not adjust their reading in response to different goals (Cain, 1999).

5.3.3 How Can Inference Making Ability Be Improved?

It seems that there are, at least, three reasons why inference making might be hard for younger readers and poor comprehenders: poor memory, access to knowledge, and how able a reader is to set appropriate standards for coherence. Interventions to improve working memory have met with limited success, and transfer to reading comprehension has not been demonstrated (Melby-Lervåg & Hulme, 2013). Here, we briefly summarize the essence of two approaches to intervention that seek to raise awareness of when inferences are needed and also to show readers how to generate inferences from vocabulary and background knowledge. Thus, although not directly, these techniques both speak to access to knowledge and setting appropriate standards of coherence.

To raise awareness of the need to make an inference, children can be taught to quite literally question the text. In a recent classroom intervention, three questioning techniques were compared: Wh-questions, which in this study were: *who, what, when,* and *where*; causal inference questions; and also a general questioning technique in which students were asked, "How does the sentence you just read connect with something that happened before in the story?" Each method resulted in gains in understanding, suggesting that a range of questioning protocols can be used to get students thinking about text and generating inferences (McMaster et al., 2012). One successful technique for teaching children how to make inferences from information in the text is to show them how to analyze the text for clues. Consider the sentence: "Sleepy Jack was late for school again." *Sleepy* suggests that the character may have overslept, thus providing a reason for being late for school, *Jack* combined with school suggests that this is a schoolchild and not a teacher who would most probably be introduced as Mr. X, and *again* indicates that Jack is habitually late. Such interventions, combined with question generation, have resulted in gains in standardized assessments of reading comprehension (Yuill & Oakhill, 1988).

A different approach uses graphic organizers to make students aware of their own contributions to inferences, by drawing on their background knowledge. Here is an example:

> During the 20th century, fishing boats became hugely more efficient so that it was possible to catch large quantities of fish in a short time. Towards the end of the century it became necessary to regulate fishing, for example by setting limits (quotas) on the catches of each fisherman or boat. (from Elbro & Buch-Iversen, 2013)

An obvious question is *why* it has become necessary to regulate fishing. The answer requires a (causal) inference that draws on information *both* from the text *and* the reader's background knowledge, as illustrated in Fig. 5.2.

In one study, 10- to 11-year-old students worked primarily with non-fiction texts and this technique had a strong and significant positive impact on the students' inference making during reading in general–and even a long-term positive effect on their general reading comprehension (Elbro & Buch-Iversen, 2013).

Thus, ways to improve inference making involve training children in different techniques that make them aware of the need to generate an inference, and also how

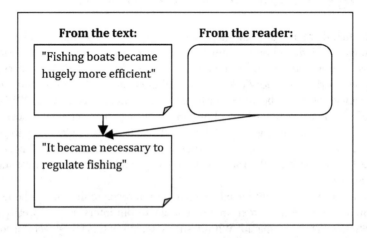

Fig. 5.2 A graphic organizer can elucidate the contributions from both the texts—and the reader, e.g., "there is a limited amount of fish to be caught."

to make those inferences by analyzing the text and drawing on their background knowledge.

What about knowledge and vocabulary in inference making? Knowing the meanings of words is obviously crucial for reading comprehension and, as we have discussed above, for inference making in particular. So should inference training also focus on expanding vocabulary knowledge? As we noted above, speed of access to critical vocabulary and background knowledge appears to be more critical to inference making than knowledge per se, so training might usefully seek to focus on how to enable fast and accurate access to relevant information. One way to support fast access to vocabulary might be to foster rich and well-connected semantic networks. Our own work has shown that depth of vocabulary knowledge (what one knows about a word's meaning) is a stronger predictor of inference making than just breadth of vocabulary (how many words you know) (Cain & Oakhill, 2014). There is also evidence that good comprehenders are more likely than poor comprehenders to activate meaning-related words automatically (Weekes, et al., 2008). Thus, vocabulary instruction that emphasizes the links between related words might help in this respect.

5.4 Monitoring for Meaning

Comprehension monitoring is the process by which a reader (or listener) reflects on his or her own understanding. To be effective comprehenders, readers must not only be able to assess their understanding of what they have read, but also be able to apply appropriate strategies if they detect a comprehension failure. Such failures might arise for a number of different reasons. For example, a reader might simply have a lapse of attention and continue to "read" the text, without really taking it in. Or, they may lack relevant knowledge: They might not know the meanings of critical words or they may lack the relevant background knowledge that enables them to make sense of the text more generally. If readers are able to monitor their understanding, then they will have the opportunity to fix lapses in understanding, providing they have the strategic abilities to do so. Thus, being aware of one's one understanding is important to ensuring adequate comprehension. However, younger children, and those with language and reading difficulties, may find it difficult to engage in comprehension monitoring because it depends on cognitive resources such as memory and attention.

5.4.1 The Development of Comprehension Monitoring

Children have the ability to monitor information for sense even before they begin to receive instruction in reading. Comprehension monitoring is often assessed by asking children to detect errors and inconsistencies in texts. For example, if a character is altered, or there is a change in the order of events in a familiar storybook, 3- to 4-year-old children will show surprise, an indication that they are monitoring their understanding (Skarakis-Doyle, 2002). However, children do not engage spontaneously in comprehension monitoring a lot of the time. Some classic examples of children's difficulties with comprehension monitoring come from studies by Ellen Markman. For example, Markman (1979) used texts with inconsistencies, such as those shown below.

Explicit Condition

> One of the things children like to eat everywhere in the world is ice cream. Some ice cream stores sell many different flavors of ice cream, but the most popular flavors are chocolate and vanilla. Lots of different kinds of desserts can be made with ice cream. Some fancy restaurants serve a special dessert made out of ice cream called Baked Alaska. To make it they put the ice cream in a very hot oven. The ice cream in Baked Alaska melts when it gets that hot. Then they take the ice cream out of the oven and serve it right away. When they make Baked Alaska, the ice cream stays firm and it does not melt. (The inconsistent information is underlined).

Implicit Condition

> *as above until* … To make it they bake the ice cream. As soon as it is finished baking they cut it into pieces with a knife and serve it right away.

Markman found that, in a sample of 8- to 11-year-olds, the majority of children failed to spot even quite blatant (explicit) inconsistencies, and even when asked explicit questions, such as "Did I forget to tell you anything?" and "Did everything make sense?" they still did not pick out problems with the text about 50% of the time.

Markman's studies highlighted the difficulties that children have with comprehension monitoring tasks. There are a number of reasons why children might fail to spot even quite obvious problems, such as those in the example text above. First, they might be reluctant to criticize printed texts that are given to them by adults. Indeed, when children are explicitly informed that some texts contain errors, which gives them a license to be critical, their rates of detection improve. Second, children may be using different standards for monitoring to the one targeted by the experimenter. For instance, in Markman's (1979) study, the children's comments often indicated that they were engaging in monitoring behavior, but not in the way intended by the experimenter. For example, several of the children stated that they were checking that they knew the meaning of the words.

A subsequent study by Baker (1984) included texts with three different types of error: nonwords (as a proxy for unfamiliar vocabulary items), information that was inconsistent with general knowledge (external to the text) and information that was inconsistent with information presented elsewhere in the text (internal inconsistencies, similar to those used by Markman). In Baker's study, the children (aged 5–11) were told in advance that some of the texts contained errors, but those up to 7 years of age found the internal inconsistencies particularly difficult to detect.

Thus, there is evidence that children can monitor their understanding and, thus, spot errors and inconsistencies in texts, but they also indicate that it is important to develop sensitive methods to assess monitoring so that young children's abilities in this domain are not underestimated. Some further reasons as to why children might fail to adequately monitor their own comprehension are discussed in the next section.

5.4.2   Difficulties with Comprehension Monitoring

Not only young children, but also those with reading difficulties, and specifically those with specific reading comprehension problems, often fail to monitor their comprehension adequately. For example, a study by Oakhill, Hartt and Samols (2005) showed that children identified as poor comprehenders have difficulties in spotting internal inconsistencies in texts (of the sort described above), but have particularly marked problems when the inconsistencies are not in adjacent sentences in the text (i.e., the information that had to be integrated in order for the inconsistency to become apparent was separated by several sentences in the texts). Thus, memory limitations might, at least in part, explain why younger children and poorer comprehenders have difficulties with comprehension monitoring. A related possibility is that the poor comprehenders do not set up an adequate text representation (or mental model) as they read so that information later in the text is not necessarily recognized as being in conflict with information presented earlier because the representation of the earlier text was inadequate or incomplete.

In sum, the research into children's comprehension monitoring shows that children are able to evaluate their comprehension from an early age, but the particular task they are set, as well as memory and attentional demands, is likely to influence how well they perform on monitoring tasks. Children with specific comprehension difficulties in particular show problems with comprehension monitoring, and there is evidence that comprehension monitoring skills are causally implicated in the development of good reading comprehension (Oakhill & Cain, 2012).

5.4.3   Teaching Comprehension Monitoring

Good comprehenders can be characterized as active readers, who engage with a text during reading, and evaluate their own comprehension both during and after reading. Thus, it would seem that activities that encourage children to engage with the construction of meaning during reading are likely to improve their comprehension monitoring. One way of training children to better monitor their comprehension is to present them with a specific task, such as pretending to be a detective. De Sousa and Oakhill (1996) found that children with comprehension problems were much better at detecting several types of text inconsistency (nonsense words, internal inconsistencies, and conflicts with prior knowledge) when they were told to pretend to be a detective and to read statements from witnesses to a crime, compared to when they were simply reading passages with the aim of spotting errors. Interestingly, the children in the comparison group of good comprehenders were not influenced by the instructions, presumably because they were already good at comprehension monitoring and had little scope to improve their skills.

As mentioned above, merely alerting children to the fact that a text contains errors is often enough to improve their monitoring performance. This technique could be useful in modeling comprehension monitoring behavior, to demonstrate to children the types of comprehension problems they might encounter in naturalistic texts, such as unfamiliar words, inconsistencies within the text, and conflicts with prior knowledge.

Another, more general, strategy that could be used to enhance comprehension monitoring could be to encourage children to stop and produce a summary at set points during reading or listening activities. It is not possible to produce a good summary unless you have understood the main points and ideas in a text, and the act of trying to produce a summary can be used as a tool to identify whether or not comprehension is progressing adequately, and there is evidence that comprehension monitoring is related to summarization skills. Indeed, self-directed summarization was one of the techniques included by Palincsar and Brown (1984) in a package of skills designed to help children to foster and monitor their own comprehension. The poor readers who were taught in that way produced better summaries than a control group and also performed better on a transfer test of comprehension monitoring.

A rather different technique–encouraging children to visualize a story as a sequence of mental images–has also been shown to improve comprehension monitoring. This technique is relatively easy to teach to children older than about 9 (Pressley, 1976), and supports memory for stories not only in poor comprehenders but also in typically developing readers. It has been shown that poor readers who were taught to use mental imagery improved their detection of inconsistencies in a comprehension monitoring task (Gambrell & Bales, 1986), perhaps because the requirement to construct images helped the children to remember, and to compare, details from the stories. Although, at first gloss, the use of imagery may seem very different from summarization techniques, to be successful both require the comparison and integration of information from different parts of a text.

5.5   Awareness and Use of Text Structure

Although all the letters have been replaced with x's, you can probably tell what sort of text it is and even answer some questions about the contents:

Xxxxxx xx xxxxxxxxxx

xxxxxxx xxx xx xxx

Xxxxxxx: Xxx xx xx xxxxxx xxx xxx xxx x xxxxxx xx xxx xxxxxxxxxx xxxxxxxxxxxxx, xxx xxxxxx xxxxxxxx.

Xxxx xxxx xxxxxxxxx xxx xxxxxx xx xxx xxxxxx, xxx xxxxxx xxx xxxxx xx xxxxx. Xx xxxxxxxx xx xxxx xxx xxxx xxxxx, xx xxxxxx xxxxxx. Xxxx xxxxxxx xx xxxx xx xxx xxxxx, xxx xx xx xxxx, xxxxx xx xxxxxxx xxxxxxxx, xxxxxxx xxxxxxxxxxx Xxxxx Xxxxxxxx.

Xxx xxxxxxx xx xxxx xx xxx xxxxx xxx xx, xxx xx xx xxxx, xxxxx xx xxxxxxx xxxxxxxx, xxxxxxx xxxxxxx. xxx xxxx xxxxx, xx xxxxxx xxxxxx. Xxxx xxxxxxx xx xxxx xx xxx xxxxx, xxx xx xx xxxx xx.

Xx xxxxxxxx xx xxxx xxx xxxx xxxxx, xx xxxxxx xxxxxx. Xxxx xxxxxxx xx xxxx xx xxx xxxxx, xxx xx xx xxxx, xxxxx xx xxxxxxx xxxx xxxx xxxxxxx.

Xx Xxxxxxxxx Xxxxxx.

What sort of text do you think it is? Where do you think you could find a brief summary of the contents? And where would you look for the author's name? Imagine that a British news article–that is a likely genre–is about a managing director who stole $250 million from her company. The article tells how the theft was discovered and what she was sentenced to. What could be the contents of the last paragraph?

Text genres are just conventional text structures used for specific purposes of communication. There are genres for personal updates (blog posts, postcards, etc.) for fairy tales and other narratives, for information about nutritional facts (labels), for brief scientific reports (journal papers), meal choices (menus), and so on. Text genres are useful once they have been learned because the reader will quickly know what to expect from the text and where to read for certain types of information.

Another way of looking at text structure is to look at the underlying logical structure–across genres (e.g., Meyer & Freedle, 1984). One way to group the structures is the following:

Description: A topic is described by listing various characteristics, features, and also examples.
Sequence: Items are presented in an order, typically chronological.
Compare and contrast: Two or more items are presented, and how they are similar and also different is discussed.
Cause and effect: One or more causes and effects are detailed.
Problem and solution: A problem is stated, and various solutions are then presented.

These underlying logical structures have typically been observed and taught in informational (expository) texts even though they also apply to narratives. The reader can benefit from identifying such underlying structures: The general idea of the text (or passage) becomes much simpler and thereby clearer, and the types of inferences needed are usually much easier to identify. Imagine, for example, that a text *contrasts* organic foods with traditionally produced foods. The text mentions some quality of organic foods, but says nothing about this quality or lack of it in traditional produce. Within the context of the compare-contrast structure, the reader would probably be right in inferring that the traditional produce does not have the same quality (to the same extent).

5.5.1   How Does Awareness of Text Structure Develop?

Before school entry, most children are familiar with at least one (major) text genre, that of stories (narratives). They have experiences with stories from cartoons and movies, picture books, spoken stories, and books that they have listened to. However, there is also evidence that young children do not represent stories in quite the same hierarchically structured manner as older children and adults do. For example, young children are less likely than older children and adults to pay attention to characters' superordinate goals and to include them in their recalls of stories. The younger children may not pay as much attention to the character's main aim, for example, to retrieve a lost pet frog, as adults do. Instead of goals and internal states, the younger children recall concrete events (Mandler & Johnson, 1977; van den Broek, Lorch, & Thurlow, 1996).

Some children are better than others at recalling the key events in stories. It is well documented that a child's ability to recall stories is predictive of how well the child will do in reading comprehension with stories later in school (Kendeou, van den Broek, White, & Lynch, 2009; Oakhill & Cain, 2012). Interestingly, this correlation over time is independent on the type of media in which the story was presented in early childhood. Hence, comprehension of the story in televised cartoons in 6-year-olds is as predictive of later reading comprehension as early story comprehension is in other media, such as listening comprehension, at the age of 6 (Kendeou et al., 2009). This independence of the medium suggests that what matters is the child's ability to represent the story in a structured way. Obviously, relevant background knowledge is important for such representation.

5.5.2 Difficulties with Text Structures

Consider these stories about recent vacations told by three 6-year-olds from the same class:

Esther: We saw a whole lot of animals. I must not open the car window. I have a game with wild animals on my computer. My ice cream dripped on the seat. The end.

Luke: I helped my grandpa feed the geese. Then we had lunch. Afterwards it rained and we played cards. Then we went down to the sea. And then we had to go home.

Karen: We were in France to visit my aunt. We saw a big lion on the television. It had escaped from a circus. It was dangerous. So we made lassos to catch the lion. We caught it right after it had gone dark. But it was the neighbour's cat.

The three stories are structured in very different ways. Esther's story is not a conventional story at all but more a description of a situation with an association to a computer game. Luke, on the other hand, tells a story with a series of events. His story could be an entry into a diary. The structure is the simplest possible, a string of events connected by *and then, and then*. Karen's story has a different structure; it has a setting, internal causality, and even a point. Clearly, the three "stories" are structured at very different levels.

The quality of their story structures is linked with children's reading comprehension and reading difficulties (Cain, 2003; Shapiro & Hudson, 1997). Cain (2003) found that 7- to 8-year-old children with reading comprehension difficulties were poorer at telling well-structured stories than their peers. They were even poorer than 6- to 7-year-old children who matched the older children on reading comprehension. The poor comprehenders were more likely to tell a non-story like Esther's, especially when they were only given a title as a starting point.

The link between story structure awareness and reading comprehension is further supported by other findings. For example, poor comprehenders have been found to be less likely than their peers to produce continuations of stories that fit in with the structure of the stories (Englert & Thomas, 1987). Even with informational text, poor structure awareness is linked to poorly structured understanding and recall even with well-structured texts (Taylor & Samuels, 1983).

5.5.3 How Can Awareness and Use of Text Structure Be Improved?

There are at least three major paths to help readers gain awareness of text structures.

First, it is well documented that direct instruction in narrative structures, such as story grammar, is beneficial (e.g., Paris & Paris, 2007; Stetter & Hughes, 2010, provide an overview). During such instruction, the readers will learn about the typical structure of stories. First, there is a setting (e.g., "once upon a time there was a …"). But something is missing or the harmony is broken ("the terrible dragon abducted the little prince"). Several attempts are made to solve the problem ("Braveheart Victoria stepped in …"), before a resolution is reached ("and they lived happily ever after"). When children know this structure, it becomes easier for them to orient themselves in similar stories, to predict the events, and to produce well-organized summaries.

Second, it is possible to teach even children in the early grades logical structures of informational texts. For example, children can learn to spot key words that signal a compare-contrast structure: *but, however, both, on the other hand*. They can learn to apply generalizable questions, like "Which are the two things that were being compared in this paragraph?" "How are they alike?" "How are they different?" Importantly, it has been found that children can work at this more general level and even learn as many details from the texts as when they are taught to focus on the informational details (Williams et al., 2007, 2009).

Third, readers can be taught graphic organizers and how to use them to represent the logical structure of texts. Such organizers comprise simple compare-contrast tables, Venn diagrams, flowcharts, tree diagrams (for general concept and their more specific parts or examples). Such graphic organizers use the spatial orientation to represent logical relations (contrasts, causes and consequences, etc.), and thus, they make the logical structure directly visible to the reader.

5.6 Teaching the Components of Comprehension

When a reader comprehends a text, the components of reading comprehension are weaved tightly together. This means that weaknesses in just one component can weaken comprehension significantly. It also means that the reader must know when to make use of each component. Consider the following short text:

> The door suddenly opened and a young woman entered the office. The school psychologist looked up and said, "do come in!" A little boy was trying to hide behind the woman. "Why didn't you do a vergence test?" asked the woman and continued, "we took Peter to the optometrist who discovered insufficient vergence".

The *monitoring* reader detects an inconsistency right at the beginning of this meeting: The school psychologist says, "do come in" when the woman is already in the office. There is no immediate reason to issue this invitation.

One possible *inference* is that the psychologist offers the invitation as a polite way of reproaching the woman for not knocking on the door first. Perhaps the psychologist is annoyed with being disturbed and vents this in a mild way. Many other inferences are necessary to establish a coherent mental model of the situation: The woman is probably the boy's, Peter's, mother and has probably been to see the school psychologist before about some problem of Peter's. Now, she is annoyed with the psychologist because he or she has not diagnosed Peter properly earlier. She is probably also worried about Peter which may explain (but not excuse) her inconsiderate manners. Do her worries transfer to Peter? What does he think of his mother's behavior?

The word *vergence* is likely to present a *vocabulary* challenge to the reader. Potentially, the context provides a bit of a clue depending on the reader's knowledge of what optometrists do. The reader may *infer* that *vergence* is likely to have something to do with eyes and vision. The reader may also draw morphological analogies to *convergence* and *divergence*, again depending on his or her vocabulary knowledge.

The use of the definite form of nouns, "the door," "the office," and "the school psychologist," indicates that the text should be read as fiction. The definite forms invite the reader to think of the office and the psychologist as well-known entities, though they have not been introduced and described. Assuming that the text is a piece of fiction, the reader can set up a number of expectations about the *structure of the text*. There will be a protagonist; perhaps, it is the psychologist because he or she is part of the scene that is presented as already given. The reader may expect that the conflict escalates, and if it does, the boy is likely to be a victim–very much depending on the knowledge and skills of the psychologist.

A teacher of reading comprehension must know such components of comprehension to assess them and to teach them (see Oakhill, Cain, & Elbro, 2014, for a detailed account). However, there is no strong evidence that teaching single components of reading comprehension separately will lead to large and sustained gains in comprehension. There may be several reasons for this lack of transfer. One is that there are so many components that each of them only has modest influence on reading comprehension in general. Another is that children do not know *when* to use a particular component. For example, children may be good at understanding compare-contrast type texts when this structure is pointed out to them, but very poor at identifying texts with that structure (Williams et al., 2009).

A more productive way ahead is to teach the components of comprehension in an integrated fashion driven by reading for specific purposes. One simple reason is that fulfilling the purpose of reading is the only lasting motivation for reading. It is also the reading purpose that sets the criteria for the necessary quality (specification) of the reader's mental model of the text. The model is set up and specified by means of an integrated set of component processes.

In order to teach component processes in the complex context of text comprehension, the teacher needs to be able to identify the components that are needed. Important inferences make a lot of sense to students who need them to make sense of a text. Monitoring may turn an uninteresting text into a fascinating riddle. A search for context clues—and inference making—may give the hint that is needed to add new vocabulary knowledge and link a new bit of information to the reader's knowledge. The well-informed teacher will be able to seize such opportunities to help students become better comprehenders.

References

Anderson, R. C., Stevens, K. C., Shifrin, Z., & Osborn, J. H. (1978). Instantiation of word meanings in children. *Journal of Literacy Research, 10*(2), 149–157.

Arnold, J. E., Brown-Schmidt, S., & Trueswell, J. (2007). Children's use of gender and order-of-mention during pronoun comprehension. *Language and Cognitive Processes, 22*(4), 527–565.

Baddeley, A. D. (1986). *Working memory*. Oxford: Oxford University Press.

Baddeley, A. D. (1996). *Your memory: A user's guide* (3rd ed.). London: Prion Books.

Baddeley, A. D., & Hitch, G. J. (1974). Working memory. In G. A. Bower (Ed.), *Recent advances in learning and motivation* (Vol. 8, pp. 47–90). New York: Academic Press.

Baker, L. (1984). Spontaneous versus instructed use of multiple standards for evaluating comprehension: Effects of age, reading proficiency, and type of standard. *Journal of Experimental Child Psychology, 38*(2), 289–311.

Barnes, M. A., & Dennis, M. (1998). Discourse after early-onset hydrocephalus: Core deficits in children of average intelligence. *Brain and Language, 61*(3), 309–334.

Barnes, M. A., Dennis, M., & Haefele-Kalvaitis, J. (1996). The effects of knowledge availability and knowledge accessibility on coherence and elaborative inferencing in children from six to fifteen years of age. *Journal of Experimental Child Psychology, 61*(3), 216–241.

Barnes, M. A., Faulkner, H., Wilkinson, M., & Dennis, M. (2004). Meaning construction and integration in children with hydrocephalus. *Brain and Language, 89*, 47–56.

Barzillai, M., Morris, R., Lovett, M. & Wolf, M. (2010). Poster Presented at the Annual Meeting of the Society for Scientific Studies in Reading.

Bast, J., & Reitsma, P. (1998). Analyzing the development of individual differences in terms of Matthew effects in reading: Results from a Dutch longitudinal study. *Developmental Psychology, 34*(6), 1373–1399.

Beck, I. L., & McKeown, M. G. (2001). Inviting students into the pursuit of meaning. *Educational Psychology Review, 13*(3), 225–241.

Beck, I. L., McKeown, M. G., & Kucan, L. (2005). Choosing words to teach. In A. Hiebert & M. Kamil (Eds.), *Teaching and learning vocabulary: Bringing research to practice* (pp. 209–222). Mahwah, NJ: Erlbaum.

Beck, I., Perfetti, C., & McKeown, M. (1982). Effects of long-term vocabulary instruction on lexical access and reading comprehension. *Journal of Educational Psychology, 74*, 506–521.

Best, R. M., Floyd, R. G., & McNamara, D. S. (2008). Differential competencies contributing to children's comprehension of narrative and expository texts. *Reading Psychology, 29*(2), 137–164.

Biemiller, A. (2005). Size and sequence in vocabulary development: Implications for choosing words for primary grade vocabulary instruction. In A. Hiebert & M. Kamil (Eds.), *Teaching and learning vocabulary: Bringing research to practice* (pp. 223–242). Mahwah, NJ: Erlbaum.

Biemiller, A., & Boote, C. (2006). An effective method for building meaning vocabulary in primary grades. *Journal of Educational Psychology, 98*(1), 44–62.

Bishop, D. V. M. (1997). *Uncommon understanding: Development and disorders of language comprehension in children.* Hove: Psychology Press.

Bishop, D. V. M. (2001). *Uncommon understanding.* East Sussex, England: Psychology Press.

Blewitt, P., Rump, K. M., Shealy, S. E., & Cook, S. A. (2009). Shared book reading: When and how questions affect young children's word learning. *Journal of Educational Psychology, 101*(2), 294–304.

Bloom, L., Lahey, M., Hood, L., Lifter, K., & Fiess, K. (1980). Complex sentences: Acquisition of syntactic connectives and the semantic relations they encode. *Journal of Child Language, 7*(2), 235–261.

Bormuth, J. R. (1967). Cloze readability procedure. CSEIP Occasional Report 1. Los Angeles, CA: University of California.

Bowers, P. N., & Kirby, J. R. (2010). Effects of morphological instruction on vocabulary acquisition. *Reading and Writing, 23*(5), 515–537.

Bowers, P. N., Kirby, J. R., & Deacon, S. H. (2010). The effects of morphological instruction on literacy skills A systematic review of the literature. *Review of Educational Research, 80*(2), 144–179.

Brady, S. A. (2011). Efficacy of phonics teaching for reading outcomes: Indications from post NRP research. In S. A. Brady & D. Braze & C. A. Fowler (Eds.), *Explaining individual differences in reading. Theory and evidence* (pp. 69–96). New York: Psychology Press.

Bransford, J. D., & Johnson, M. K. (1972). Contextual prerequisites for understanding: Some investigations of comprehension and recall. *Journal of Verbal Learning and Verbal Behavior, 11*(6), 717–726.

Bransford, J. D., & Nitsch, K. E. (1978). Coming to understand things we could not previously understand. In J. F. Kavanaugh & W. Strange (Eds.), *Speech and language in the laboratory, school, and clinic* (pp. 267–307). Cambridge, MA: MIT Press.

Cain, K. (1996). Story knowledge and comprehension skill. In C. Cornoldi & J. Oakhill (Eds.), *Reading comprehension difficulties: processes and remediation* (pp. 167–192). Mahwah, NJ: LEA.

Cain, K. (1999). Ways of reading: How knowledge and use of strategies are related to reading comprehension. *British Journal of Developmental Psychology, 17*(2), 293–309.

Cain, K. (2003). Text comprehension and its relation to coherence and cohesion in children's fictional narratives. *British Journal of Developmental Psychology, 21*(3), 335–351.

Cain, K. (2006). Individual differences in children's memory and reading comprehension: An investigation of semantic and inhibitory deficits. *Memory, 14*, 553–569.

Cain, K. (2007). Syntactic awareness and reading ability: Is there any evidence for a special relationship? *Applied Psycholinguistics, 28*(4), 679–694.

Cain, K., & Nash, H. M. (2011). The influence of connectives on young readers' processing and comprehension of text. *Journal of Educational Psychology, 103*(2), 429–441.

Cain, K., & Oakhill, J. V. (1999). Inference making and its relation to comprehension failure. Reading and Writing. *An Interdisciplinary Journal, 11*(5–6), 489–503.

Cain, K., & Oakhill, J. V. (2006). Profiles of children with specific reading comprehension difficulties. *British Journal of Educational Psychology, 76*(4), 683–696.

Cain, K., & Oakhill, J. V. (2011). Matthew effects in young readers reading comprehension and reading experience aid vocabulary development. *Journal of Learning Disabilities, 44*(5), 431–443.

Cain, K., & Oakhill, J. (2014). Reading comprehension and vocabulary: Is vocabulary more important for some aspects of comprehension? *L'Année psychologique, 114*, 647–662.

Cain, K., & Oakhill, J. V. (in press). Reading comprehension and vocabulary: Is vocabulary more important for some aspects of comprehension? *L'Année Psychologique/Topics in Cognitive Psychology.*

Cain, K., Oakhill, J. V., Barnes, M. A., & Bryant, P. E. (2001). Comprehension skill, inference making ability and their relation to knowledge. *Memory and Cognition, 29*(6), 850–859.

Cain, K., Oakhill, J. V., & Bryant, P. E. (2004a). Children's reading comprehension ability: Concurrent prediction by working memory, verbal ability, and component skills. *Journal of Educational Psychology, 96*(1), 671–681.

Cain, K., Oakhill, J. V., & Lemmon, K. (2004b). Individual differences in the inference of word meanings from context: the influence of reading comprehension, vocabulary knowledge, and memory capacity. *Journal of Educational Psychology, 96*(4), 671–681.

Cain, K., Oakhill, J. V., & Lemmon, K. (2005a). The relation between children's reading comprehension level and their comprehension of idioms. *Journal of Experimental Child Psychology, 90*(1), 65–87.

Cain, K., Patson, N., & Andrews, L. (2005b). Age-and ability-related differences in young readers' use of conjunctions. *Journal of Child Language, 32*(4), 877–892.

Cain, K., & Towse, A. S. (2008). To get hold of the wrong end of the stick: Reasons for poor idiom understanding in children with reading comprehension difficulties. *Journal of Speech, Language, and Hearing Research, 51*(6), 1538–1549.

Cain, K., Towse, A. S., & Knight, R. S. (2009). The development of idiom comprehension: An investigation of semantic and contextual processing skills. *Journal of Experimental Child Psychology, 102*(3), 280–298.

Carney, J. J., Anderson, D., Blackburn, C., & Blessing, D. (1984). Preteaching vocabulary and the comprehension of social studies materials by elementary school children. *Social Education, 48*(3), 195–196.

Carroll, J. B. (1993). *Human cognitive abilities: A survey of factor-analytic studies.* New York: Cambridge University Press.

Catts, H. W., Compton, D., Tomblin, J. B., & Bridges, M. S. (2012). Prevalence and nature of late-emerging poor readers. *Journal of Educational Research, 104*(1), 166–181.

Catts, H. W., Hogan, T. P., & Adlof, S. M. (2005). Developmental changes in reading and reading disabilities. In H. W. Catts & A. G. Kamhi (Eds.), *The connections between language and reading disabilities* (pp. 25–40). Mahwah, NJ: Lawrence Erlbaum.

Chall, J. S., Jacobs, V. A., & Baldwin, L. E. (1990). *The reading crisis: Why poor children fall behind.* Cambridge, Mass: Harvard University Press.

Chapman, L. J. (1983). *Reading development and cohesion.* Exeter: Heinemann.

Charniak, E. (1972). *Toward a model of children's story comprehension* (Technical Report 266). Cambridge, MA: Artificial Intelligence Laboratory, MIT.

Chien, Y. C., & Wexler, K. (1990). Children's knowledge of locality conditions in binding as evidence for the modularity of syntax and pragmatics. *Language Acquisition, 1*(3), 225–295.

Chomsky, C. (1969). *The acquisition of syntax in children from 5 to 10.* Cambridge, Mass.: M.I.T. Press.

Chrysochoou, E., Bablekou, Z., & Tsigilis, N. (2011). Working memory contributions to reading comprehension components in middle childhood children. *American Journal of Psychology, 124,* 275–289.

Connolly, J. (1999). *Every dead thing.* New York: Simon & Schuster.

Coyne, M. D., McCoach, D. B., & Kapp, S. (2007). Vocabulary intervention for kindergarten students: Comparing extended instruction to embedded instruction and incidental exposure. *Learning Disability Quarterly, 30*(2), 74–88.

Crosson, A. C., Lesaux, N. K., & Martiniello, M. (2008). Factors that influence comprehension of connectives among language minority children from Spanish-speaking backgrounds. *Applied Psycholinguistics, 29*(4), 603–625.

Cunningham, A. E. (2005). Vocabulary growth through independent reading and reading aloud to children. In E. H. Hiebert & M. L. Kamhi (Eds.), *Teaching and learning vocabulary: Bringing research to practice* (pp. 45–68). Mahwah, NJ: LEA

Currie, N. K., & Cain, K. (2015). Children's inference generation: The role of vocabulary and working memory. *Journal of Experimental Child Psychology, 137*, 57–75.

Cutting, L. E., & Scarborough, H. S. (2006). Prediction of reading comprehension: Relative contributions of word recognition, language proficiency, and other cognitive skills can depend on how comprehension is measured. *Scientific Studies of Reading, 10*(3), 277–299.

Daneman, M., & Carpenter, P. A. (1980). Individual differences in working memory and reading. *Journal of Verbal Learning and Verbal Behavior, 19*(4), 450–466.

Davis, F. B. (1944). Fundamental factors of comprehension in reading. *Psychometrika, 9*(3), 185–197.

Davis, F. B. (1968). Research in comprehension in reading. *Reading Research Quarterly, 3*(4), 499–545.

de Sousa, I., & Oakhill, J. V. (1996). Do levels of interest have an effect on children's comprehension monitoring performance? *British Journal of Educational Psychology, 66*(4), 471–482.

de Jong, P. F., & van der Leij, A. (2002). Effects of phonological abilities and linguistic comprehension on the development of reading. *Scientific Studies of Reading, 6*(1), 51–77.

Deese, J. (1959). On the prediction of occurrence of particular verbal intrusions in immediate recall. *Journal of Experimental Psychology, 58*(1), 17–22. https://doi.org/10.1037/H0046671.

Duke, N. K. (2000). 3.6 minutes per day: The scarcity of informational texts in first grade. *Reading Research Quarterly, 35*(2), 202–224.

Dunn, L. M., Dunn, L. M., Whetton, C., & Pintilie, D. (1992). *British picture vocabulary scale.* London: NFER-Nelson.

Ehrlich, M. F., Rémond, M., & Tardieu, H. (1999). Processing of anaphoric devices in young skilled and less skilled comprehenders: Differences in metacognitive monitoring. *Reading and Writing, 11*(1), 29–63.

Elbro, C., & Arnbak, E. (2002). Components of reading comprehension as predictors of educational achievement. In E. Hjelmquist & C. von Euler (Eds.), *Dyslexia and literacy* (pp. 69–83). London: Whurr.

Elbro, C., & Buch-Iversen, I. (2013). Activation of background knowledge for inference making: Effects on reading comprehension. *Scientific Studies of Reading, 17*(6), 435–452.

Elbro, C., & Knudsen, L. (2010). *The importance of genre knowledge for text comprehension. Insights from a training study.* Paper presented at the Annual meeting of the Society for Text and Discourse, August 16–18. Chicago, USA.

Englert, C. S., & Hiebert, E. F. (1984). Children's developing awareness of text structures in expository materials. *Journal of Educational Psychology, 76*(1), 65–74.

Englert, C. S., & Thomas, C. C. (1987). Sensitivity to text structure in reading and writing: A comparison between learning-disabled and non-learning disabled students. *Learning Disability Quarterly, 10*(2), 93–105.

Florit, E., Roch, M., & Levorato, M. C. (2011). Listening text comprehension of explicit and implicit information in preschoolers: The role of verbal and inferential skills. *Discourse Processes, 48*(2), 119–138.

Gallini, J., Spires, H., Terry, S., & Gleaton, J. (1993). The influence of macro and micro-level cognitive strategies training on text learning. *Journal of Research and Development in Education, 26*(3), 164–178.

Gambrell, L. B., & Bales, R. J. (1986). Mental imagery and the comprehension-monitoring performance of fourth- and fifth-grade poor readers. *Reading Research Quarterly, 21*(4), 454–464.

Gathercole, S. E., Pickering, S. J., Ambridge, B., & Wearing, H. (2004). The structure of working memory from 4 to 15 years of age. *Developmental Psychology, 40*, 177–190.

Gellert, A. S., & Elbro, C. (2013). Cloze tests may be quick, but are they dirty? Development and preliminary validation of a Cloze test of reading comprehension. *Journal of Psychoeducational Assessment, 31*(1), 16–28.

Gernsbacher, M. A., & Hargreaves, D. J. (1988). Accessing sentence participants: The advantage of first mention. *Journal of Memory and Language, 27*(6), 699–717.

Gernsbacher, M. M., Varner, K. R., & Faust, M. E. (1990). Investigating individual differences in general comprehension skill. *Journal of Experimental Psychology. Learning, Memory, and Cognition, 16*(3), 430–445.

Geva, E., & Ryan, E. B. (1985). Use of conjunctions in expository texts by skilled and less skilled readers. *Journal of Reading Behavior, 17*(4), 331–346.

Gough, P. B., & Hillinger, M. L. (1980). Learning to read: An unnatural act. *Bulletin of the Orton Society, 30*(1), 179–196.

Gough, P. B., Hoover, W. A., & Peterson, C. L. (1996). Some observations on a simple view of reading. In C. Cornoldi & J. Oakhill (Eds.), *Reading comprehension difficulties. Processes and intervention* (pp. 1–13). Mahwah, NJ: Erlbaum.

Gough, P. B., & Tunmer, W. E. (1986). Decoding, reading, and reading disability. *Remedial and Special Education, 7*(1), 6–10.

Hall, K. M., Markham, J. C., & Culatta, B. (2005). The development of the Early Expository Comprehension Assessment (EECA): A look at reliability. *Communication Disorders Quarterly, 26*(4), 195–206.

Halliday, M. A. K., & Hasan, R. (1976). *Cohesion in English*. London: Longman.

Irwin, J. W., & Pulver, C. J. (1984). Effects of explicitness, clause order, and reversibility on children's comprehension of causal relationships. *Journal of Educational Psychology, 76*, 399–407.

Johnson-Laird, P. N. (1983). *Mental models: Towards a cognitive science of language, inference, and consciousness*. Cambridge, MA: Harvard University Press.

Kail, M. l. (1976). Strategies of comprehension of personal pronouns among young children. *Enfance, 4–5*, 447–466.

Kail, M., & Weissenborn, J. (1991). Connectives: Developmental issues. In G. Piéraut-le-Bonniec & M. Dolitsky (Eds.), *Language bases … discourse bases: Some aspects of contemporary French-language psycholinguistics research* (pp. 125–142). Amsterdam: Benjamins.

Kameenui, E. J., Carnine, D. W., & Freschi, R. (1982). Effects of text construction and instructional procedures for teaching word meanings on comprehension and recall. *Reading Research Quarterly*, 367–388.

Keenan, J. M., & Betjemann, R. S. (2006). Comprehending the gray oral reading test without reading it: Why comprehension tests should not include passage-independent items. *Scientific Studies of Reading, 10*(4), 368–380.

Keenan, J. M., Betjemann, R. S., & Olson, R. K. (2008). Reading comprehension tests vary in the skills they assess: Differential dependence on decoding and oral comprehension. *Scientific Studies of Reading, 12*(3), 281–300.

Kendeou, P., Bohn-Gettler, C., White, M. J., & van Den Broek, P. (2008). Children's inference generation across different media. *Journal of Research in Reading, 31*(3), 259–272.

Kendeou, P., Lynch, J. S., van den Broek, P., Espin, C., White, M., & Kremer, K. E. (2005). Developing successful readers: Building early narrative comprehension skills through television viewing and listening. *Early Childhood Education Journal, 33*, 91–98.

Kendeou, P., van den Broek, P., White, M., & Lynch, J. S. (2009). Predicting reading comprehension in early elementary school: The independent contributions of oral language and decoding skills. *Journal of Educational Psychology, 101*(4), 765–778.

Kintsch, W. (1998). *Comprehension: A paradigm for cognition*. New York: Cambridge University Press.

Language and Reading Research Consortium. (2015). The dimensionality of language ability in young children. *Child Development, 86*, 1948–1965. https://doi.org/10.1111/cdev.12450.

Leach, J. M., Scarborough, H. S., & Rescorla, L. (2003). Late-emerging reading disabilities. *Journal of Educational Psychology, 95*(2), 211–224.

Lepola, J., Lynch, J., Laakkonen, E., Silvén, M., & Niemi, P. (2012). The role of inference making and other language skills in the development of narrative listening comprehension in 4–6-year-old children. *Reading Research Quarterly, 47*(3), 259–282.

Levorato, M. C., Nesi, B., & Cacciari, C. (2004). Reading comprehension and understanding idiomatic expressions: A developmental study. *Brain and Language, 91*(3), 303–314.

Levorato, M. C., Roch, M., & Nesi, B. (2007). A longitudinal study of idiom and text comprehension. *Journal of Child Language, 34*(3), 473–494.

Lynch, J. S., & van den Broek, P. (2007). Understanding the glue of narrative structure: Children's on- and off-line inferences about characters' goals. *Cognitive Development, 22*(3), 323–340.

Lynch, J. S., van den Broek, P., Kremer, K., Kendeou, P., White, M. J., & Lorch, E. P. (2008). The development of narrative comprehension and its relation to other early reading skills. *Reading Psychology, 29*(4), 327–365.

Mandler, J. M., & Johnson, N. S. (1977). Remembrance of things parsed: Story structure and recall. *Cognitive Psychology, 9*(1), 111–151.

Markman, E. M. (1979). Realizing that you don't understand: Elementary school children's awareness of inconsistencies. *Child Development, 50,* 643–655.

Mayer, M. (1969). *Frog, where are you?.* New York: Penguin Putnam Inc.

McMaster, K. L., van den Broek, P., Espin, C. A., White, M. J., Rapp, D. N., Kendeou, P., et al. (2012). Making the right connections: Differential effects of reading intervention for subgroups of comprehenders. *Learning and Individual Differences, 22*(1), 100–111.

McNamara, D. S., & Kintsch, W. (1996). Learning from texts: Effects of prior knowledge and text coherence. *Discourse Processes, 22,* 247–288.

Medo, M. A., & Ryder, R. J. (1993). The effects of vocabulary instruction on readers' ability to make causal connections. *Literacy Research and Instruction, 33*(2), 119–134.

Megherbi, H., & Ehrlich, M. F. (2005). Language impairment in less skilled comprehenders: The on-line processing of anaphoric pronouns in a listening situation. *Reading and Writing, 18*(7–9), 715–753.

Mehegan, C., & Dreifuss, F. E. (1972). *Hyperlexia. Neurology, 22*(11), 1105–1111.

Melby-Lervåg, M., & Hulme, C. (2013). Is working memory training effective? A met analytic review. *Developmental Psychology, 49,* 270–291. https://doi.org/10.1037/a0028228.

Meyer, B. J., & Freedle, R. O. (1984). Effects of discourse type on recall. *American Educational Research Journal, 21*(1), 121–143.

Muter, V., Hulme, C., Snowling, M. J., & Stevenson, J. (2004). Phonemes, rimes, vocabulary, and grammatical skills as foundations of early reading development: Evidence from a longitudinal study. *Developmental Psychology, 40*(5), 665–681.

Nagy, W. E., & Anderson, R. C. (1984). How many words are there in printed school English? *Reading Research Quarterly, 19*(3), 304–330.

Nagy, W. E., & Herman, P. A. (1987). Breadth and depth of vocabulary knowledge: Implications for acquisition and instruction. In M. G. McKeown & M. E. Curtis (Eds.), *The nature of vocabulary acquisition* (pp. 19–36). Hillsdale, NJ: Erlbaum.

Nagy, W. E., & Scott, J. (2000). Vocabulary processes. In M. Kamil, P. Mosenthal, P. D. Pearson, & R. Barr (Eds.), *Handbook of reading research* (Vol. III, pp. 269–284). Mahwah, NJ: Erlbaum.

Nation, K. (1999). Reading skills in hyperlexia: A developmental perspective. *Psychological Bulletin, 125*(3), 338–355.

Nation, K., Cocksey, J., Taylor, J. S., & Bishop, D. V. (2010). A longitudinal investigation of early reading and language skills in children with poor reading comprehension. *Journal of Child Psychology and Psychiatry, 51*(9), 1031–1039.

Nation, K., & Norbury, C. F. (2005). Why reading comprehension fails: Insights from developmental disorders. *Topics in Language Disorders, 25*(1), 21–32.

Nation, K., & Snowling, M. J. (1998). Semantic processing and the development of word-recognition skills: Evidence from children with reading comprehension difficulties. *Journal of Memory and Language, 39*(1), 85–101.

National Reading Panel. (2000). *Teaching children to read: An evidence-based assessment of the scientific research literature on reading and its implications for reading instruction.* Washington, DC: The National Institute of Child Health and Human Development (http://www.nichd.nih.gov/publications/nrp/smallbook.htm).

Neale, M. D. (1997). *The Neale analysis of reading ability—Revised (NARA–II)*. Windsor, England: NFER-Nelson.

Oakhill, J. V. (1984). Constructive processes in skilled and less-skilled comprehenders' memory for sentences. *British Journal of Psychology, 75(1), 13–20.*

Oakhill, J. (1984). Inferential and memory skills in children's comprehension of stories. *British Journal of Educational Psychology, 54*, 31–39. https://doi.org/10.1111/j.2044-8279.1984.tb00842.x.

Oakhill, J. V., & Cain, K. (2012). The precursors of reading ability in young readers: Evidence from a four-year longitudinal study. *Scientific Studies of Reading, 16*(2), 91–121.

Oakhill, J. V., & Cain, K. (2017). Children with specific text comprehension problems. In K. Cain, D. Compton, & R. Parrila (Eds.), *Theories of reading development*. John Benjamins: Amsterdam, The Netherlands.

Oakhill, J. V., Cain, K., & Bryant, P. E. (2003). The dissociation of word reading and text comprehension: Evidence from component skills. *Language and Cognitive Processes, 18*(4), 443–468.

Oakhill, J., Cain, K., & Elbro, C. (2014). *Understanding and teaching reading comprehension. A handbook*. London: Routledge.

Oakhill, J. V., Cain, K., & McCarthy, D. (2015). Inference processing in children: the contributions of depth and breadth of vocabulary knowledge. In E. O'Brien, A. Cook & R. Lorch (Eds.), *Inferences during reading*, Cambridge University Press.

Oakhill, J. V., Cain, K., McCarthy, D., & Field, Z. (2012). Making the link between vocabulary knowledge and comprehension skill. In A. Britt, S. Goldman, & J.-F. Rouet (Eds.), *From words to reading for understanding* (p. 101). Hoboken, NJ: Routledge.

Oakhill, J. V., & Yuill, N. (1986). Pronoun resolution in skilled and less-skilled comprehenders: Effects of memory load and inferential complexity. *Language and Speech, 29*(1), 25–37.

Oakhill, J. V., Yuill, N., & Donaldson, M. L. (1990). Understanding of causal expressions in skilled and less skilled text comprehenders. *British Journal of Developmental Psychology, 8*(4), 401–410.

Oakhill, J. V., Yuill, N. M., & Parkin, A. (1986). On the nature of the difference between skilled and less-skilled comprehenders. *Journal of Research in Reading, 9*, 80–91.

Oakhill, J. V., Hartt, J., & Samols, D. (2005). Levels of comprehension monitoring and working memory in good and poor comprehenders. *Reading and Writing, 18,* 657–686.

Ouellette, G. P. (2006). What's meaning got to do with it: The role of vocabulary in word reading and reading comprehension. *Journal of Educational Psychology, 98*(3), 554–566.

Palinscar, A. S., & Brown, A. L. (1984). Reciprocal teaching of comprehension-fostering and comprehension-monitoring activities. *Cognition and Instruction, 1*(2), 117–175.

Pappas, C. C. (1993). Is narrative 'primary'? Some insights from kindergarteners' pretend readings of stories and information books. *Journal of Reading Behavior, 25*(1), 97–129.

Paris, S. G. (2005). Reinterpreting the development of reading skills. *Reading Research Quarterly, 40*(2), 184–202.

Paris, A. H., & Paris, S. G. (2003). Assessing narrative comprehension in young children. *Reading Research Quarterly, 38*(1), 36–76.

Paris, A. H., & Paris, S. G. (2007). Teaching narrative comprehension strategies to first graders. *Cognition and Instruction, 25*(1), 1–44.

Paris, S. G., & Jacobs, J. E. (1984). The benefits of informed instruction for children's reading awareness and comprehension skills. *Child Development, 55*(6), 2083–2093.

Perfetti, C. A. (1985). *Reading ability*. New York, NY: Oxford University Press.

Perfetti, C. (2007). Reading ability: Lexical quality to comprehension. *Scientific Studies of Reading, 11*(4), 357–383. https://doi.org/10.1080/10888430701530730.

Peterson, C. (1986). Semantic and pragmatic uses of 'but'. *Journal of Child Language, 13*(3), 583–590.

Peterson, C., & McCabe, A. (1987). The connective 'and': Do older children use it less as they learn other connectives. *Journal of Child Language, 14*(2), 375–381.

Pichert, J. W., & Anderson, R. C. (1977). Taking different perspectives on a story. *Journal of Educational Psychology, 69,* 309–315.

Pike, M. M., Barnes, M. A., & Barron, R. W. (2010). The role of illustrations in children's inferential comprehension. *Journal of Experimental Child Psychology, 105*(3), 243–255.

Pinker, S. (1994). *The language instinct, The new science of language and mind.* London: Allen Lane.

Pressley, G. M. (1976). Mental imagery helps eight-year-olds remember what they read. *Journal of Educational Psychology, 68*(3), 355–359.

Pressley, M., & Afflerbach, P. P. (1995). *Verbal protocols of reading: The nature of constructively responsive reading.* Hillsdale, NJ: Erlbaum.

Protopapas, A., Sideridis, G. D., Mouzaki, A., & Simos, P. G. (2007). Development of lexical mediation in the relation between reading comprehension and word reading skills in Greek. *Scientific Studies of Reading, 11*(3), 165–197.

Pyykkonen, P., & Jarvikivi, J. (2012). Children and situation models of multiple events. *Developmental Psychology, 48,* 521–529.

Reid, J. (1972). *Children's comprehension of syntactic features found in some extension readers.* Occasional paper: Centre for Research in Educational Sciences, University of Edinburgh.

Roediger, H. L., & McDermott, K. B. (1995). Creating false memories: Remembering words not presented in lists. *Journal of Experimental Psychology: Learning Memory and Cognition, 21*(4), 803–814. https://doi.org/10.1037/0278-7393.21.4.803.

Rosenshine, B., Meister, C., & Chapman, S. (1996). Teaching students to generate questions: A review of the intervention studies. *Review of Educational Research, 66*(2), 181–221.

Sachs, J. S. (1967). Recognition memory for syntactic and semantic aspects of connected discourse. *Perception and Psychophysics, 2*(9), 437–442.

Scarborough, H. (2001). Connecting early language and literacy to later reading (dis)abilities: Evidence, theory, and practice. In S. B. Neuman & D. K. Dickinson (Eds.), *Handbook of early literacy* (pp. 97–110). New York: Guilford Press.

Seigneuric, A., & Ehrlich, M. F. (2005). Contribution of working memory capacity to children's reading comprehension: A longitudinal investigation. *Reading and Writing, 18*(7–9), 617–656.

Seymour, P. H. K., & Elder, L. (1986). Beginning reading without phonology. *Cognitive Neuropsychology, 3*(1), 1–36.

Shanahan, T., Kamil, M. L., & Tobin, A. W. (1982). Cloze as a measure of intersentential comprehension. *Reading Research Quarterly, 17*(2), 229–255.

Shapiro, B. K., & Hudson, J. A. (1997). Coherence and cohesion in children's stories. In J. Costermans & M. Fayol (Eds.), *Processing interclausal relationships: Studies in the production and comprehension of text* (pp. 23–48). Mahwah, NJ: Lawrence Erlbaum Associates.

Share, D. L. (1995). Phonological recoding and self-teaching: Sine qua non of reading acquisition. *Cognition, 55*(2), 151–218.

Skarakis-Doyle, E. (2002). Young children's detection of violations in familiar stories and emerging comprehension monitoring. *Discourse Processes, 33*(2), 175–197.

Silva, M. T., & Cain, K. (2015). The relations between lower- and higher-level oral language skills and their role in prediction of early reading comprehension. *Journal of Educational Psychology, 107,* 321–331. https://doi.org/10.1037/a0037769.

Smith, E. E., & Swinney, D. A. (1992). The role of schemas in reading text: A real-time examination. *Discourse Processes, 15*(3), 303–316.

Snowling, M., & Frith, U. (1986). Comprehension in "hyperlexic" readers. *Journal of Experimental Child Psychology, 42*(3), 392–415.

Snowling, M. J., & Hulme, C. (2005). Learning to read with a language impairment. In M. J. Snowling & C. Hulme (Eds.), *The science of reading: A handbook* (pp. 397–412). Oxford: Blackwell.

Song, H. J., & Fisher, C. (2005). Who's "she"? Discourse prominence influences preschoolers' comprehension of pronouns. *Journal of Memory and Language, 52*(1), 29–57.

Sparks, E., & Deacon, S. H. (2013). Morphological awareness and vocabulary acquisition: A longitudinal examination of their relationship in English-speaking children. *Applied Psycholinguistics,* 1–23.

Spooren, W., & Sanders, T. (2008). The acquisition order of coherence relations: On cognitive complexity in discourse. *Journal of Pragmatics, 40*(12), 2003–2026.

Spörer, N., Brunstein, J. C., & Kieschke, U. (2009). Improving students' reading comprehension skills. Effects of strategy instruction and reciprocal teaching. *Learning and Instruction, 19*(3), 272–286.

Stahl, S. A., & Fairbanks, M. M. (1986). The effects of vocabulary instruction: A model-based meta-analysis. *Review of Educational Research, 56*(1), 72–110.

Stanovich, K. E. (1986). Matthew effects in reading: Some consequences of individual differences in the acquisition of literacy. *Reading Research Quarterly, 21*(4), 360–407.

Stein, N. L., & Glenn, C. G. (1982). Children's concept of time: The development of story schema. In W. Friedman, J. (Ed.), *The developmental psychology of time* (pp. 255–282). New York: Academic Press.

Stetter, M. E., & Hughes, M. T. (2010). Using story grammar to assist students with learning disabilities and reading difficulties improve their comprehension. *Education & Treatment of Children, 33*(1), 115–151. https://doi.org/10.1353/etc.0.0087.

Taylor, B. M., & Samuels, S. J. (1983). Children's use of text structure in the recall of expository material. *American Educational Research Journal, 20*(4), 517–528.

Tannenbaum, K. R., Torgesen, J. K., & Wagner, R. K. (2006). Relationships between word knowledge and reading comprehension in third-grade children. *Scientific Studies of Reading, 10*(4), 381–398.

Thorndike, R. L. (1973). Reading as reasoning. *Reading Research Quarterly, 9*(2), 135–147.

Tomesen, M., & Aarnoutse, C. (1998). Effects of an instructional programme for deriving word meanings 1. *Educational Studies, 24*(1), 107–128.

Tompkins, V., Guo, Y., & Justice, L. M. (2013). Inference generation, story comprehension, and language skills in the preschool years. *Reading & Writing, 26*(3), 403–429.

Tong, X., Deacon, S. H., Kirby, J. R., Cain, K., & Parrila, R. (2011). Morphological awareness: A key to understanding poor reading comprehension in English. *Journal of Educational Psychology, 103*(3), 523–534.

Tunmer, W. E., Nesdale, A. R., & Pratt, C. (1983). The development of young children's awareness of logical inconsistencies. *Journal of Experimental Child Psychology, 36*(1), 97–108.

Tyler, L. K. (1983). The development of discourse mapping processes: The on-line interpretation of anaphoric expressions. *Cognition, 13*(3), 309–341.

van den Broek, P. W. (1997). Discovering the cement of the universe: The development of event comprehension from childhood to adulthood. In P. W. van den Broek, P. J. Bauer, & T. Bourg (Eds.), *Developmental spans in event comprehension and representation* (pp. 321–342). Mahwah, NJ: Lawrence Erlbaum Associates.

van den Broek, P. W., Lorch, R. F., Linderholm, T., & Gustafson, M. (2001). The effects of readers' goals on inference generation and memory for text. *Memory and Cognition, 29*(8), 1081–1087.

van den Broek, J., Lorch, E. P., & Thurlow, R. (1996). Children's and adults memory for television stories: The role of causal factors, story-grammar categories, and hierarchical structure. *Child Development, 67*(6), 3010–3028.

Venezky, R. (2000). The origins of the present-day chasms between adult literacy needs and school literacy instruction. *Scientific Studies of Reading, 4*(1), 19–39.

Walberg, H. J., Strykowski, B. F., Rovai, E., & Hung, S. S. (1984). Exceptional performance. *Review of Educational Research, 54*(1), 87–112.

Weekes, B. S., Hamilton, S., Oakhill, J. V., & Holliday, R. E. (2008). False recollection in children with reading comprehension difficulties. *Cognition, 106*(1), 222–233.

Whaley, J. F. (1981). Readers' expectations for story structure. *Reading Research Quarterly, 17*(1), 90–114.

Williams, J. P., Nubla-Kung, A. M., Pollini, S., Stafford, K. B., Garcia, A., & Snyder, A. E. (2007). Teaching cause–effect text structure through social studies content to at-risk second graders. *Journal of Learning Disabilities, 40*(2), 111–120.

Williams, J. P., Stafford, K. B., Lauer, K. D., Hall, K. M., & Pollini, S. (2009). Embedding reading comprehension training in content-area instruction. *Journal of Educational Psychology, 101*(1), 1–20.

Yuill, N. M., & Oakhill, J. V. (1988). Effects of inference awareness training on poor reading comprehension. *Applied Cognitive Psychology, 2*(1), 33–45.

Yuill, N. M., & Oakhill, J. V. (1991). *Children's problems in text comprehension: An experimental investigation.* Cambridge: Cambridge University Press.

Yuill, N. M., Oakhill, J. V., & Parkin, A. (1989). Working memory, comprehension ability and the resolution of text anomaly. *British Journal of Psychology, 80*(3), 351–361.

Zwaan, R. A. (1994). Effect of genre expectations on text comprehension. *Journal of Experimental Psychology. Learning, Memory, and Cognition, 20*(4), 920–933.

Chapter 6
Assessing Reading in Second Language Learners: Development, Validity, and Educational Considerations

Esther Geva, Yueming Xi, Angela Massey-Garrison and Joyce Y. Mak

Abstract The overall objective of this chapter is to provide educational professionals with an overview of theory and research findings about the field of second language (L2) reading development in typically developing learners and those with reading difficulties. We also intend to inform readers of the implications of this research for the development of culturally and linguistically sensitive, reliable, and valid strategies for the assessment of L2 learners who may have a reading difficulty. For both monolinguals and L2 learners, phonological awareness, rapid automatized naming, and working memory are significant early predictors of reading comprehension and reading fluency later on. L2 learners in early grades can develop word reading skills at a level that approximates their monolingual peers even when their oral language proficiency is still developing. Oral language proficiency becomes the most prominent predictor of reading comprehension and reading fluency around fourth grade when the text becomes more cognitively demanding. Therefore, early cognitive skills measured in the first language can be used reliably to merit a diagnosis of reading disability in the L2. When word reading and text reading of L2 learners is persistently dysfluent in comparison with other students with similar linguistic and educational backgrounds, the reading difficulties cannot be attributed to their L2 status and may reflect underlying cognitive deficits.

E. Geva (✉) · Y. Xi · A. Massey-Garrison · J. Y. Mak
Surrery Place, Toronto, Canada
e-mail: esther.geva@utoronto.ca

Y. Xi
e-mail: y.xi@mail.utoronto.ca

A. Massey-Garrison
e-mail: angela.massey.garrison@mail.utoronto.ca

J. Y. Mak
e-mail: Joyce.Mak@surreyplace.ca

© Springer Nature Switzerland AG 2019
D. A. Kilpatrick et al. (eds.), *Reading Development and Difficulties*,
https://doi.org/10.1007/978-3-030-26550-2_6

6.1 Aya's Story

Aya is a nine year old girl who arrived in Canada at age five with her mother as Syrian refugees. Her father was killed in the war when she was three years old, and she has no siblings. Both of her parents had graduated from high school and received some college education. After her father died, Aya and her mother relocated to a refugee camp for two years where Aya attended school on an inconsistent basis. She speaks Arabic fluently, but her Arabic literacy skills are minimal.

After moving to Canada, Aya was placed in an English as a second language (ESL) classroom for four years. Her ESL teacher reports that despite Aya's well-developed English skills, she is behind her peers in reading and writing, even when compared to those who also came from Syria around the same time. Aya is slow in decoding new words, developing fluent word reading skills, and remembering academic vocabulary. As the demands on reading to learn increase significantly in Grade 4, Aya is at risk of falling further behind her peers in academic achievement.

As you read this chapter, think about whether Aya's profile is typical of a student with interrupted schooling or whether perhaps she also has a reading disability. If so, what diagnostic approaches and measurement tools should be used to assess Aya's reading ability considering her English Language Learner (ELL) status? What reading intervention strategies should be implemented to help Aya learn to read and optimize her academic achievement? What are the contextual factors that impact Aya's current life and schooling that should be taken into consideration?

6.2 Introduction

Aya is one of an increasingly large population of immigrant and refugee children and adolescents who need to develop their language and reading skills in the language of their new country of residence (OECD, 2010; UNESCO, 2005). Some of these students are able to accommodate and achieve academically, while others struggle academically and could benefit from policies and programs that support their educational, emotional, and social needs. As L2 learners, these students often struggle not only because of the challenges involved in learning to speak and read in a new language and adapting culturally, but also because they have significant learning, behavioral, social, and emotional difficulties. As a result, they require the services of psychologists and other mental health professionals. Traditional psychological assessment methods may not be valid for these children.

Much of the research described in this chapter focuses on ELLs whose families arrived as refugees or immigrants to countries such as the USA, Canada, the UK, or Australia, where the societal language is English. However, the principles that we discuss are relevant to countries where a language other than English is the official language, to indigenous peoples, to marginalized cultural groups, and to emerging bilingual learners. It is also important to recognize that due to migration and demographic factors, English may in fact be the students' L3 or even L4. Some children may be speaking a dialect or a language that is different from the language they were accustomed to in their country of origin. For example, the home language of refugees from Syria may not be Arabic but rather Aramaic, Armenian, Kurdish, or Azeri. For these children, the language of schooling in the country of origin (e.g., Arabic) is different from the language(s) spoken at home, and therefore, English may be their third or fourth language. In other words, even the term ELL is complex and will require some unpacking and fact finding by the school psychologist.

The assessment of children and adolescents who come from linguistically and culturally diverse backgrounds and experience persistent academic and language difficulties at school is complex. School psychologists are faced with the challenge of understanding what factors contribute to the academic difficulties that some ELLs experience. A partial list of factors to consider includes:

(a)   an understanding of the typical course of learning to speak and read in an L2;
(b)   the age of onset of learning to read in the L2;
(c)   the similarities between the L1 and L2 in terms of features of the spoken and written language;
(d)   the extent to which various aspects of L2 reading and writing are related to language proficiency in the L2 (and the L1);
(e)   the extent of exposure to the L2;
(f)   quality of instruction in the L2;
(g)   quality and extent of exposure to schooling prior to immigration;
(h)   parental education;
(i)   access to resources (assessment instruments, cultural interpreters); and
(j)   a range of socio-emotional issues such as parental pressures to succeed, maltreatment, trauma, and changes in family dynamics.

Teasing apart the contribution of these factors from a bona fide learning disability is not a simple task, neither are these factors mutually exclusive. In addition, it is important to consider other L2 educational contexts that may be included in the school psychologists' portfolio and that are not as easy to classify. For example, L2 learners include international students who are sent by their families overseas to study in English-speaking schools, students who attend bilingual programs, students from aboriginal backgrounds who are expected to learn to read and speak in the societal language with varying degrees of support for their indigenous language, and students who undertake foreign language study as school subjects. The distinction between immigrant and refugee status is also relevant when considering the academic and socio-emotional well-being of the client; immigrants may have time to prepare the family for the transition whereas refugees do not. Clearly, one size does *not* fit all.

Furthermore, the parents of children and adolescents may not speak the societal language of their receiving country, they may be struggling financially, and their attributions about their children's academic and socio-emotional functioning may differ from those held by teachers and mental health professionals in the receiving society. Systemic bias toward immigrant groups and policies that discriminate culturally and linguistically diverse children and youth are important to acknowledge as well. It is not possible to cover all of these intra-individual, family, school, and policy-related factors and how they might inform culturally sensitive practices by school psychologists in one chapter (for a more comprehensive discussion, see Geva & Wiener, 2015). Instead, the intent of this chapter is to inform educational professionals about reading in the L2 and issues that they need to consider when assessing children and adolescents who are developing bilingually, struggling with the development of language and reading skills in the societal language, and who may also present with learning and/or socio-emotional difficulties.

The chapter is divided into four sections. In the first section, we discuss cross-linguistic transfer and its relevance to understanding the research on the relationship between L1 and L2 reading skills and the implications of this research for assessment and intervention. We do not expand here on other frameworks that are highly relevant such as the simple view of reading because these are treated carefully in Chap. 1 of this volume. In the second section, we briefly review research on the developmental trajectories of three aspects of reading: decoding, reading comprehension, and reading fluency among typically and atypically developing children who speak more than one language. In the third section, we discuss complementary strategies for assessing L2 learners with reading difficulties, and the factors that might influence the identification, classification, and diagnosis of reading difficulties among L2 learners. We close this chapter with a list of misconceptions concerning L2 reading development and common diagnostic procedures in the assessment of reading disabilities for L2 learners and how research findings discussed in this chapter can be best used as valid guidelines for educational professionals.

6.3   Why Is It Important to Consider Cross-Linguistic Transfer?

One prevalent theme when assessing L2 learners concerns cross-linguistic transfer. This has to do with the various ways in which learners' L1 might impact the development of specific features in their L2, and how specific language and reading features of the L1 can hinder (i.e., negative transfer) or support (i.e., positive transfer) the development of reading in another language. Transfer is a complex construct involving interactions of different units and levels of language and print that are affected by multiple factors (for a literature review on cross-language transfer, see Chung, Chen, and Geva, 2019). There are two primary complementary and relevant frameworks for thinking about transfer. One is referred to as the contrastive or typological hypothesis (Lado, 1957), and the other is often referred to as the linguistic interdependence hypothesis (Cummins, 1981, 2012). In more recent years, variants of the linguistic and interdependence hypothesis such as the common underlying cognitive processes theory (Geva & Ryan, 1993) and the transfer facilitation model (Koda, 2008) have been gaining momentum as well. In this section, we review briefly each of these frameworks.

6.3.1   Contrastive/Typological Hypothesis

The contrastive/typological perspective framework involves comparing and contrasting two or more languages to determine similarities and differences of *specific* components of the spoken language, such as phonics, vocabulary, and morpho-syntax (Fisiak, 1981), and features of the writing system or orthography (Seymour, Aro, & Erskine, 2003; Ziegler & Goswami, 2005). *Positive transfer* occurs when two languages share certain characteristics, while *negative transfer* occurs when specific features of the L2 bear little or no similarity to the L1. For example, not only do English and Spanish use the same alphabet, but words such as *organización* in Spanish and *organization* in English are "cognates" that originate from the same Latin root; their pronunciation and spelling are rather similar, as is their meaning. Provided that individuals are familiar with the word *organización* in Spanish, Spanish-speaking ELLs may have an advantage in learning the meaning and pronunciation of English words such as *organization.* English and Spanish share a large number of cognates, which can invariably help ELLs to learn Spanish words that are cognates, provided they are familiar with the meaning of these words in Spanish (Nagy, García, Durgunoğlu, & Hancin-Bhatt, 1993; Proctor & Mo, 2009).

Consider another, less intuitive, example. While English does not share many cognates with Chinese, a study by Ramirez, Chen, Geva, and Luo (2011) has shown that Chinese-speaking ELLs can acquire novel English compound vocabulary (words such as *baseball, cupcake,* and *blueberry* that consist of two morphemes) more easily than their Spanish-speaking ELL peers. Researchers explained that this is because compound words are extremely frequent in Chinese and the rules of forming compound words are shared between English and Chinese. In contrast, compounds are not as prevalent in Spanish.

Another example that illustrates how the contrastive/typological framework helps to think about the possible source of errors that L2 learners make as they develop their language and literacy skills comes from a study that focused on what it takes for ELLs to learn to distinguish between familiar and unfamiliar phonemes. The study (Wang & Geva, 2003) followed ELLs whose home language was Cantonese for 2 years. In Grade 1, these ELLs had difficulty distinguishing the phoneme /th/ from the phoneme /s/ in pseudowords such as "thop" and "sop" because the phoneme /th/ does not exist in Cantonese. When they listened to such word pairs, students were more likely to say that these two "made up words" were the same. However, over the course of grades 1 and 2, with systematic exposure and literacy instruction in English at school, they gradually learned to distinguish these two phonemes. Their acquisition of new phonemes and subsequent increased sensitivity to new phonemes also contributed to improvements in spelling (e.g., they were more likely to correctly hear and spell the sound /th/ in words such as *thick* and the sound /s/ in words such as *stick*).

Another perspective that should not be ignored concerns how writing systems vary from each other and how these differences may highlight differences in how children learn to develop their reading skills. Some languages can be characterized as having *transparent* or *shallow orthographies* where the correspondence between letters or letter clusters and phonemes is consistent. Spanish is an example of such a writing system. On the other hand, English is considered as having a *deep* or *opaque orthography* because there is less systematic correspondence between letters and phonemes. This is often illustrated by the inconsistencies in the letter cluster *ough*. This cluster in English words can represent six different vowel pronunciations (i.e., *thought, though, through, tough, cough,* and *bough*). While *ough* is arguably the most inconsistent pattern in English, it illustrates how such inconsistencies make learning to read words and decode unknown words in English especially challenging (Frost & Katz, 1992; Seymour et al., 2003; Ziegler & Goswami, 2005). Educational professionals should be aware of orthographic depth and how it can affect the ease of learning to decode in different languages. In regular or shallow writing systems, typically developing children can build their decoding accuracy very quickly, often in the first year of school. However, when young children learn to decode in deep orthographies such as English, it takes longer to acquire fluent decoding skills, even for typically developing children. A good illustration of this comes from a study involving English L1 children who attended an English–Hebrew bilingual school from age 5 (Geva & Siegel, 2000). The study showed that these children who had minimal command of Hebrew were able to read words with more accuracy in Hebrew than in English, despite English being their home language. These differences were attributed to the fact that when Hebrew is fully vowelized it is a highly consistent and shallow orthography, whereas English is not.

The contrastive framework is useful because it provides a mechanism for understanding the source of some errors that ELLs may make but also because it can highlight subtle differences in the development of reading skills in different languages. The study by Wang and Geva (2003) illustrates the benefits of considering jointly the cross-linguistic and developmental perspectives. This study shows that typically developing ELLs gradually acquire the new phonemes that are not shared with their L1. The contrastive/typological framework is useful for understanding which *specific* elements in the spoken or written language are easier or harder to acquire in the L2, and to consider these errors in a developmental framework. It also means that in a multilingual classroom where children come from different L1 backgrounds, different elements of English may pose a challenge to ELLs. At the same time, when students (1) continue to experience persistent difficulties in acquiring new distinctions, (2) have persistent difficulties despite ample learning opportunities, and (3) struggle above and beyond their peers coming from similar backgrounds, this may be a warning sign that perhaps the errors are not merely reflecting "negative" transfer, but that they may be pertinent to an underlying learning difficulty.

6.3.2   Linguistic Interdependence Hypothesis

Another transfer framework highly relevant for understanding how L2 learners develop their language and reading skills comes from the linguistic interdependence hypothesis (Cummins, 1981) that emphasizes the transfer of higher-level metacognitive strategies. According to this framework, skills developed in children's home language can transfer and enhance learning in the societal language (i.e., L2), and students learn best when they can draw on skills and knowledge that they have already developed through the L1 (Cummins, 2008). Cummins has emphasized that the transfer of knowledge and strategies from the L1 to the L2 is not automatic and that it depends on the extent to which students have had quality instruction in the L1 and sufficient language proficiency in the L2 (Cummins, 2012).

Metacognitive skills such as monitoring comprehension, inferencing, accessing and using prior knowledge, using knowledge of text genre conventions, and noticing the author's point of view involve the ability to decide what strategies one should use to regulate the reading process (Baker & Beall, 2009; Oakhill, Cain, & Elbro, Chap. 5, this volume; Schoonen, Hulstijn, & Bossers, 1998). Such strategies can transfer across languages, provided that the L2 learners have sufficient language and reading skills in the L1 and L2 to make use of such higher-order cognitive skills.

Ample research on reading comprehension across languages supports the interdependence hypothesis and the notion that L2 learners can transfer higher-level conceptual and strategic skills (Genesee, Geva, Dressler, & Kamil, 2006; Royer & Carlo, 1991). For example, even though English and Chinese have very different writing systems (and do not share any cognates), Li, McBride-Chang, Wong, and Shu (2012) reported strong correlations between English and Chinese reading comprehension in 10-year-old Chinese-speaking ELLs. Such results suggest that higher-level reading comprehension strategies acquired in one language can be transferred and used in the other, despite typological differences. As another example of transfer, Abu-Rabia, Shakkour, and Siegel (2013) reported significantly better performance in both Arabic and English reading comprehension after Grade 6 Arabic-speaking ELLs received English-only (L2) reading intervention.

6.3.3   Underlying Common Cognitive Processes Hypothesis

The underlying common cognitive processes' perspective (Geva & Ryan, 1993) adds nuance to the linguistic interdependence hypothesis by focusing on basic cognitive processes rather than higher-level metacognitive strategies. It proposes that cross-language correlations may be attributed not only to metacognitive skills but also to underlying cognitive processes such as working memory, phonological awareness, rapid automatized naming, and executive functioning. With the exception of phonological awareness, these processes are not easily modified through training and reflection, and are tied instead to basic processes that are activated when reading or writing in any language. These largely innate universal cognitive abilities predict word reading, reading comprehension, and reading fluency cross-linguistically even when the oral language proficiency of the L2 learners is still developing (Durgunoğlu, 2002). For example, it argues that individual differences in rapid automatized naming will correlate with reading fluency in any language, regardless of whether it is one's L1 or L2.

6.3.4 Transfer Facilitation Hypothesis

The transfer facilitation model (Koda, 2008) suggests that metalinguistic awareness–the ability to identify, analyze, and manipulate language forms–establishes the basis of interdependence because this ability provides the learner with linguistic knowledge to break down words into phonological and morphological components. Such transfer occurs at the phonological, morphological, and orthographic processing levels.

Phonological awareness is a person's awareness of smaller units in words and the awareness that these units can be manipulated in various ways (e.g., deleting phonemes from words, or assembling phonemes). Studies have shown that phonological awareness skills transfer across languages despite linguistic or typological differences (Durgunoğlu, 2002). To illustrate, phonological awareness in Spanish can predict word reading in English (Durgunoğlu, 2002; Durgunoğlu, Nagy, & Hancin-Bhatt, 1993). Likewise, phonological awareness in Spanish and English correlates highly in English–Spanish bilinguals (Dickinson, McCabe, Clark-Chiarelli, & Wolf, 2004). In fact, this is true even among highly dissimilar language pairs such as Arabic–English (Saiegh-Haddad & Geva, 2008). Clinically, this means that phonological awareness assessed in one language could be used to predict word reading in another language. It also suggests that if an ELL student shows difficulties in developing phonological and decoding skills in their stronger language, they will likely demonstrate similar difficulties in the other language as well.

Morphological awareness involves the ability to recognize and manipulate morphemes (which are the smallest units of meaning; word roots, prefixes, suffixes, etc.) and to use word formation rules in oral language communication, reading, and writing (Kuo & Anderson, 2006). Morphological skills involve three categories: inflectional (e.g., *boy-boys; eat-ate*), derivational (e.g., *farm-farmer; eat-edible*), and compound (e.g., fire + works = *fireworks*). Morphological skills play an important role in word reading, vocabulary knowledge, spelling, reading comprehension, and listening comprehension of L2 learners (e.g., Carlisle, 2000; Pacton & Deacon, 2008; Ramirez, Chen, Geva, & Luo, 2011). Transfer of morphological awareness skills tends to occur from the morphologically more complex language to the less complex language (e.g., Ramírez, Chen, Geva, & Kiefer, 2010; Saiegh-Haddad & Geva, 2008; Schiff & Calif, 2007), and from the more proficient language (typically the L1) to the less proficient language (or the L2) (e.g., Bérubé & Marinova-Todd, 2014; Deacon, Wade-Woolley,

& Kirby, 2007; Pasquarella, Chen, Lam, Luo, & Ramírez, 2011; Schiff & Calif, 2007; Zhang, Koda & Sun, 2014).

Orthographic processing, which is the "ability to form, store, and access the orthographic representation" of words (Stanovich & West, 1989, p. 404), connects the way a word sounds with the way that word is spelled (Ehri, 1995). It also includes orthographic processing involved in recognizing morphological units in word spellings (e.g., the /s/ or /z/ representing plurality, or the /un/, /believe/ and /able/ in *unbelievable*). These subskills, in turn, impact word reading skills (Cunningham, 2006; Deacon, Wade-Woolley, & Kirby, 2009; Roman, Kirby, Parrila, Wade-Woolley, & Deacon, 2009). Transfer of the ability to efficiently create orthographic memories of words (see Miles & Ehri, Chap. 4 and Kilpatrick & O'Brien, Chap. 8, this volume) tends to be specific to the writing system. For example, the skills used to establish Chinese orthographic memories do not help ELLs to remember orthographic spelling patterns of words in English (their L2) (Keung & Ho, 2009; Wang, Perfetti, & Liu, 2005). Nor can ELLs whose first language is Korean (Wang, Park, & Lee, 2006), Russian (Abu-Rabia, 2001), or Persian (Arab-Moghaddam & Sénéchal, 2001) transfer their L1 morphological skills to help them write and spell in English. However, when languages are represented by the same alphabetic script and share cognates and morphological rules, as is the case for English and French or English and Spanish, there is evidence of positive transfer of orthographic learning (Commissaire, Pasquarella, Chen, & Deacon, 2014; Deacon, Chen, Luo, & Ramírez, 2013; Sun-Alperin & Wang, 2011). Therefore, school psychologists and teachers can expect that individuals who have difficulties in remembering how to spell words in their L1 will have more difficulty in spelling words in their L2 if the languages are related to each other (e.g., Spanish–English) than when the languages do not share common features (e.g., Chinese–English).

The transfer frameworks we highlighted in this section have significant implications for the assessment of the language, cognitive, and academic skills of ELLs. L1–L2 transfer is associated with the transfer of both lower-level basic skills such as phonological awareness, orthographic skills, rapid automatized naming, working memory, and higher-level skills such as inferencing and metacognitive strategies. When feasible, gathering relevant formal and informal assessment data based on the L1 can help validate a possible diagnosis. For example, evidence from sources such as L1 assessments and report cards pointing to difficulties in developing decoding skills in the L1 can help validate similar trends in the child's L2. Likewise, evidence of difficulties with higher-order aspects of reading comprehension and writing in the L1 can help validate similar observations in the L2. Error analysis in the L2 may point to negative transfer from the L1. At the same time, persistent difficulties may point to a learning disability. As we argue in the next section, some skills are more related to proficiency in the L2 than others.

6.4   What Does Typical L2 Reading Development Look Like?

6.4.1   Word-Level Reading

Research has consistently demonstrated that, in general, accurate and fluent word-level reading skills of L2 learners (1) develop relatively quickly, (2) depend less on language proficiency in the L2, and (3) can be on par with their L1 peers after a couple of years, provided that they begin schooling in the L2 at an early age (Droop & Verhoeven, 2003; Geva, Yaghoub-Zadeh, & Schuster, 2000; Lesaux & Siegel, 2003; Swanson, Rosston, Gerber, & Solari, 2008). For example, Abu-Rabia and Siegel (2002) explored the word recognition and pseudoword decoding skills of bilingual Arabic–English learners and monolingual English learners. They found that word recognition and decoding skills of the Arabic–English learners did not differ from that of their monolingual peers. These results have been supported with other language combinations, including English–Portuguese (Da Fontoura & Siegel, 1995), English–Spanish (Durgunoğlu et al., 1993), and Chinese–English (Keung & Ho, 2009). The fact that ELLs can learn to decode and recognize words even when their L2 language proficiency is still developing is illustrated in Fig. 6.1. The figure summarizes the outcomes of a longitudinal study where the language and literacy skills of ELLs, coming from a variety of home language backgrounds, and their monolingual peers were tracked from grades 1–6. As can be seen in this figure, the general trajectories of word recognition skills are similar for the ELL and monolingual samples, even though the language skills of the ELLs continued to be less developed (as illustrated in Fig. 6.3) (Geva & Wiener, 2015).

There is less research on the word reading skill development of older L2 learners, especially those that began learning English as adolescents. One such study involving Grade 9 and Grade 10 ELLs who arrived in Canada in Grade 7 and Grade 8 showed that they performed significantly below their L1 peers on word reading skills. Further,

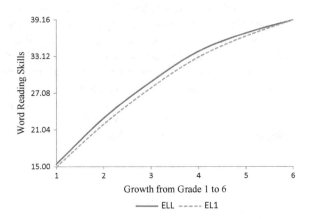

Fig. 6.1 Developmental trajectory of word reading skills in monolingual and ELL students from Grade 1 to Grade 6

accurate word reading skills for this group continued to predict reading comprehension, despite this not being the case with typically developing high school L1 readers (Pasquarella, Grant, & Gottardo, 2012). These findings serve as a reminder that one reason that ELLs who begin to learn the language as adolescents are at risk is because they have had fewer opportunities to develop accurate and fluent word reading skills in English, though are still expected to comprehend academic texts.

Several underlying cognitive processes are needed for efficient word reading regardless of language status, including phonological awareness, working memory, and rapid automatized naming (see Chaps. 1, 2, and 4, this volume). Research suggests that ELLs can perform these tasks well even in their developing L2. Figure 6.2 is based on the same Canadian study that was mentioned earlier in relation to Fig. 6.1. Figure 6.2a shows that the developmental trajectories of phonological awareness are highly similar for these monolingual and ELL students. Figure 6.2b demonstrates the same point with regard to rapid automatized naming. Both Fig. 6.2a and b demonstrate that, in general, ELLs and their monolingual peers who receive instruction in English from the onset of schooling develop these skills at the same rate. From the perspective of school psychologists and other educational evaluators, it is important to bear in mind that individual differences in these cognitive processes predict L1 and L2 reading development, and these findings hold true with ELLs who come from a variety of language backgrounds (Geva, Yaghoub-Zadeh, & Schuster, 2000). Overall, among both L1 and L2 learners, individual differences on these basic cognitive processes are associated with word reading and spelling skills.

Fig. 6.2 Developmental trajectory of phonological awareness (**a**) and rapid automatized naming (**b**) in monolingual and ELL students from Grade 1 to Grade 6

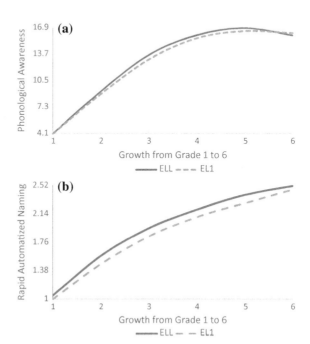

Phonological awareness is one of the most widely studied areas and one of the best predictors of word reading skills for both L1 and L2 learners (Gottardo, Collins, Baciu, & Gebotys, 2008; Jared, Cormier, Levy, & Wade-Woolley, 2010; Lindsey, Manis, & Bailey, 2003; Wagner, Torgesen, & Rashotte, 1994). Many studies have demonstrated that phonological awareness assessed in the L2 predicts basic word reading skills in L2 learners both concurrently and longitudinally (Chiappe & Siegel, 1999; Commeau, Cormier, Grandmaison, & Lacroix, 1999; Durgunoğlu et al., 1993; Geva & Farnia, 2012; Geva & Ryan, 1993; Gholamain & Geva, 1999; Gottardo, Yan, Siegel, & Wade-Woolley, 2001). Additionally, phonological awareness assessed in the L1 can predict word reading skills in the L2. This observation has been established with similar language pairs such as English–French (Erdos, Genesee, Savage, & Haigh, 2014; Jared et al., 2010) and English–Spanish (Durgunoğlu et al., 1993). More than that, this relationship has also been shown when the L1 and L2 involve different writing systems such as English–Hebrew (Wade-Woolley & Geva, 2000), English–Arabic (Saiegh-Haddad & Geva, 2010), Persian–English (Gholamain & Geva, 1999), and English–Chinese (Marinova-Todd, Zhao, & Bernhardt, 2010). Clinically, this means that one can assess phonological awareness in one language and use the information to reliably predict word recognition in both the L1 and the L2 (Bialystok, McBride-Chang, & Luk, 2005; Branum-Martin et al., 2006; Nakamura, Koda, & Joshi, 2014).

These findings are important for educational professionals because a consistent misconception is that one must wait until a child's oral language proficiency is well-developed before an assessment of their reading or language difficulties can be reliably carried out in English. The research shows (1) that phonological processing skills such as phonological awareness and rapid automatized naming are not strongly associated with language proficiency, (2) that they can be reliably assessed in the L2, and (3) that they can be used to predict word reading skills to help understand the source of difficulties in learning to develop word-level reading and spelling skills in the L2. This highlights the fact that L2 assessment measures can be used reliably to assess L2 word reading skills.

Processing speed, often measured with rapid automatized naming tasks, is implicated in the development of word-level reading skills in L1 and L2 learners. Research has demonstrated that L2 learners perform equally and sometimes better than L1 learners on rapid automatized naming tasks in the early stages of reading acquisition even though their skills in language and reading comprehension are weaker (Chiappe & Siegel, 1999; Chiappe, Siegel, & Gottardo, 2002; Chiappe, Siegel, & Wade-Woolley, 2002; Lesaux & Siegel, 2003). A longitudinal study by Nakamoto, Lindsey, and Manis (2007) involving Spanish-speaking ELLs investigated decoding and reading comprehension from first to sixth grade. Their findings indicated that along with phonological awareness, rapid automatized naming was a significant predictor of basic English word decoding (e.g., word reading and pseudoword decoding). As a result, performance on rapid automatized naming tasks in the L2 (such as rapid automatized letter and digit naming subtests of the *Comprehensive*

Test of Phonological Processing [CTOPP] test battery) can be used to predict L2 word reading skills for a variety of ELL groups (Chung & Ho, 2010; Geva & Farnia, 2012).

Another important cognitive process is working memory. Research with L1 students has shown that working memory plays a vital role in word-level reading processes (Lesaux & Siegel, 2003). Beginning readers face a heavy demand on working memory when learning to decode. Some research suggests that depending on the measures used, assessment of working memory in the L2 may be less reliable when language proficiency is less developed. Lipka, Siegel, and Vukovic (2005) assessed working memory with a sentence-based task. They found that the working memory of L2 students was weaker than that of their L1 peers in kindergarten and Grade 1. However, by Grade 2 the working memory differences between the L1 and L2 students disappeared, likely due to increased L2 English language proficiency. In other words, L2 students may require a certain amount of exposure and command of English syntax before performance on verbal working memory tasks is at a level approximate to that of their L1 counterparts. To overcome this challenge, in another study (Farnia & Geva, 2013), working memory was assessed using the digit backward task, a task that is linguistically less demanding than working memory tasks that rely on syntactic skills. Nevertheless, the study also showed that in the lower grades, ELLs performed more poorly than their L1 peers, and again, the gap in working memory closed within 2–3 years. Other studies with L2 learners in later elementary grades (between 9 and 14 years of age) have shown no differences between L1 and L2 learners on verbal working memory tasks (Abu-Rabia & Siegel, 2002; D'Angiulli, Siegel, & Serra, 2001). Taken together, these studies underline the importance of taking a developmental perspective and considering carefully the language proficiency of the reference group. They suggest that in the early elementary years or when the L2 proficiency is not yet well established, the assessment of verbal working memory in ELLs may be less reliable than that of their L1 peers, but that as proficiency increases the assessment becomes more reliable and valid.

This discussion is highly relevant for school psychologists and other educational evaluators because of the language demands that characterize many of the assessment tools currently in use. It appears that L2 learners who enter school with little English might perform below their L1 peers on tests of verbal memory, not because of a specific processing deficit but instead because of the language demands (e.g., vocabulary, syntax) of verbal memory tasks. This discussion suggests that evaluators should be careful when interpreting the performance of ELL children on working memory tasks. Further, if feasible, it may be beneficial to assess working memory in the L1 to get a refined picture of their working memory profile. At the same time, it is important to remember that a weaker performance on verbal working memory tasks after ELLs have had adequate exposure to English language instruction and opportunities to learn may be indicative of an actual processing deficit rather than merely reflecting a language proficiency issue.

6.4.2   Reading Fluency and Reading Comprehension

Reading fluency is important for reading comprehension in L2 learners just the way it is for L1 readers. Reading fluency involves "a level of reading competence at which textual material can be effortlessly, smoothly, and automatically understood" (Wolf & Katzir-Cohen, 2001, p. 177). According to automaticity theory (LaBerge & Samuels, 1974) and the verbal efficiency theory (Perfetti, 1985), the connection between reading fluency and reading comprehension can be attributed to faster, consistent, and reliable word recognition processes. This enables fluent readers to allocate their attention to meaning and comprehension of the text rather than to decoding (Perfetti, 1985) of individual words. Fluent and automatic word reading reduces processing demands and frees up mental capacity needed for text comprehension. The simple view of reading, described in Chap. 1, illustrates the necessity of both fluent decoding and language comprehension in enabling effective reading comprehension skills. From a developmental perspective, it is helpful to think of a transition that usually occurs around Grade 4 from learning to read (with a heavier focus on word reading skills) to reading to learn (with heavier language demands and more complex content) (Chall, 1996). At the same time, it is important to remember that when ELLs begin to learn to speak and read in English at an older age, the transition from "learning to read English" to "reading to learn in English" will occur later.

Reading fluency contributes to reading comprehension, and reading researchers have demonstrated that for both monolinguals and L2 learners, reading fluency is a key component of reading comprehension, in addition to fluent decoding and language comprehension (Geva & Farnia, 2012; Verhoeven & van Leeuwe, 2012; Yaghoub-Zadeh, Farnia, & Geva, 2012). It is useful to distinguish, both clinically and developmentally, between word reading fluency and text reading fluency. Research has shown, for example, that the ability to read isolated words fluently is not as strongly related to having well-developed oral language proficiency in the L2. Despite L2 learners having a lower command of the L2 than their L1 peers, word reading accuracy and fluency scores are rather similar across ELLs and their L1 peers who have been learning to read and speak English from Grade 1 (Geva, Wade-Woolley, & Shany, 1997; Geva & Yaghoub-Zadeh, 2006; Lesaux & Siegel, 2003). On the other hand, text reading fluency is more closely aligned with oral language skills. That is, better developed L2 language proficiency is associated with more fluent L2 text reading in typically developing L2 learners (Al Otaiba et al., 2009; Crosson & Lesaux, 2010; Geva & Farnia, 2012; Nakamoto et al., 2007). At the same time, L1 children demonstrate better text reading fluency than their ELL peers due to their better developed oral language skills (Geva & Yaghoub-Zadeh, 2006). This highlights the importance of cautiously interpreting timed reading comprehension tasks among L2 learners as they can be expected to be slower when they read texts in the L2, because their language proficiency is still developing.

Research on reading fluency in L2 learners has shown that the same underlying cognitive processing factors can explain individual differences in reading fluency and reading comprehension, including phonological awareness, working memory, and rapid automatized naming (Geva & Ryan, 1993; Geva & Yaghoub-Zadeh, 2006; Lipka & Siegel, 2012; Wolf & Katzir-Cohen, 2001). In general, research demonstrates that these cognitive factors influence reading fluency and reading comprehension similarly among L1 and L2 learners. For example, Solari et al. (2014) studied the longitudinal predictors of English oral reading fluency among 150 Spanish-speaking ELLs and their monolingual peers from kindergarten to Grade 2. They found that the same early literacy measures in kindergarten such as phonological awareness, letter knowledge, and word reading predicted English oral reading fluency later on.

Although these research findings can be used as guideposts for educators and school psychologists, it is important to remember that there are specific circumstances under which these research findings cannot be generalized to all L2 learners. For example, it is reasonable to expect that typically developing L2 learners who have first been exposed to the L2 in the upper elementary years will usually perform more poorly on language comprehension tasks, word reading, and reading fluency. Similarly, L2 learners that have had interrupted schooling or no schooling in their L1 may develop their reading fluency more slowly than typically developing L2 learners who have had consistent schooling and more extensive exposure to English from an earlier age. The challenge for the educational professionals is to be mindful of the potential sources of dysfluent reading–this means consideration of evidence about how these individuals read in their L1 and how they perform in comparison to other newcomers from similar backgrounds and with similar educational experiences.

6.4.3 Considering Development Over Time

A few studies examined development over time on various language and reading skills. Such studies are important because they help to delineate what skills are indicative of typical development of language and literacy skills in L2 learners and what patterns of development are indicative of a reading disability or language impairment. An important research finding for both L1 and L2 learners is that predictors of reading comprehension change over time. Generally, in the primary grades accurate and fluent word-level reading skills are a main predictor of reading comprehension. But in later years, as word-level reading becomes more fluent and proficient, oral language proficiency becomes a stronger predictor of reading fluency and reading comprehension than word reading skills (Francis et al., 2005; Geva & Farnia, 2012; Storch & Whitehurst, 2002; Verhoeven & van Leeuwe, 2012). At the same time, newcomer adolescents may read with less fluency not only because their L2 language proficiency is still developing but also because their word reading skills are also developing.

Listening comprehension, syntactic knowledge, morphological skills, and vocabulary knowledge are all components of L2 proficiency that are associated with reading comprehension in L2 children (August & Shanahan, 2006; Babayiğit, 2014; Droop & Verhoeven, 2003; Farnia & Geva, 2011; Geva, 2006; Hutchinson, Whitely, Smith, & Connors, 2003; Lam, Chen, Geva, Luo, & Li, 2012; Lesaux, Rupp, & Siegel,

Fig. 6.3 Developmental
trajectory of English
vocabulary in monolingual
and ELL students from
Grade 1 to Grade 6

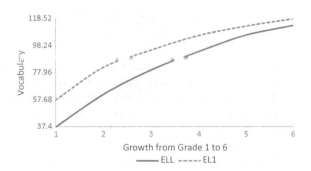

2007; Proctor, Carlo, August, & Snow, 2005; Verhoeven, 2000). Research shows
a consistent gap between vocabulary skills of L1 and L2 learners (Farnia & Geva,
2011, 2013; Nakamoto et al., 2007). For example, Farnia and Geva (2011) studied the
development of English vocabulary of ELLs and their monolingual peers from Grade
1 to Grade 6. They found that while, in general, the gap between English vocabulary
knowledge narrowed over time, the English vocabulary skills of L2-English learners
continued to lag behind their L1 counterparts, even after 6 years of English language
instruction from grades 1–6 (Fig. 6.3). This is an important finding because this gap
in vocabulary knowledge helps to explain to a large extent why ELLs perform below
their L1 counterparts on reading comprehension tasks.

It is also important to be mindful of the subtle distinction between everyday
vocabulary used for informal basic communication and academic vocabulary. Typically, L2 learners will acquire the everyday informal language rather quickly but
will take much longer to develop academic language, which includes both content
words and function words, such as connectives. Limited academic vocabulary knowledge explains poor reading comprehension and poor academic performance among
all readers (August & Shanahan, 2006; Geva, 2006; Snow, Burns, & Griffin, 1998;
Stahl & Nagy, 2006). ELLs' reading comprehension is challenged as the academic
language demands of texts in content areas increase (e.g., Geva & Ramírez, 2015;
Proctor, Carlo, August, & Snow, 2005; Roessingh & Kover, 2003).

By definition, ELLs can be expected to have English language skills that are lower
than the English language skills of their monolingual peers. This can be noted with
regard to various aspects of language including vocabulary, grammar, and familiarity
with idioms. This means that even when ELLs have had high-quality education in
their L1, they may not be familiar with academic vocabulary or have the same depth
of vocabulary knowledge in their L2 as do their monolingual counterparts. Of course
the situation may be even more difficult when ELLs have had poor, inconsistent, or
interrupted education.

Of particular importance for school psychologists and literacy specialists are the
research findings suggesting that vocabulary and reading comprehension skills of
ELLs are expected to be typically lower than those of their monolingual peers. As a
result, standardized test results need to be interpreted cautiously and complementary
assessment methods should be employed. At the same time, some ELLs may also

have difficulties in developing language skills in spite of consistent and high-quality instruction. These students perform more poorly than their typically developing ELL peers, and they may require some adaptive programming. We return to this issue later in the chapter. School psychologists and literacy specialists should not ignore these difficulties—the challenge is to figure out what is the source of difficulties and what interventions can enhance learning (see Oakhill et al., Chap. 5, this volume).

6.5 What Do Atypically Developing ELL Students Look like?

In this section, we discuss research based on the development of reading for L2 learners pertaining to three diagnostic subtypes: (a) decoding difficulties (i.e., dyslexia), (b) oral language deficiencies (for higher-level aspects of comprehension), and (c) dysfluency. These three subtypes can be mapped onto various conditions in the *neurodevelopmental disorders* category in the Diagnostic and Statistical Manual of Mental Disorders (DSM-5; American Psychiatric Association, 2013) and other diagnostic manuals, as well as the three subtypes of specific learning disability in the Individuals with Disabilities Education Improvement Act (IDEA, 2004) in the USA (basic reading, reading fluency, and reading comprehension). It is important to note from the outset that children may qualify for the diagnosis of disabilities in more than one domain. In this section, we examine the common underlying cognitive deficits associated with decoding, comprehension, and fluency in L1 and L2 learners. At the end of this section, we briefly address validity considerations of various assessment tools and other options available to educational evaluators. We also provide a brief discussion of alternative strategies for assessment.

6.5.1 Decoding Difficulties (Dyslexia)

As discussed earlier, phonological processing such as phonological awareness and rapid automatized naming are essential for learning to read in alphabetic languages. Individual differences on these processing skills predict individual differences on word reading and spelling skills in L1 and cross-linguistically. It is important to remember that deficits in phonological awareness and rapid automatized naming are associated with decoding and spelling difficulties in both monolinguals (Shaywitz & Shaywitz, 2005; Wagner & Torgesen, 1987; Wolf & Bowers, 1999; Yopp, 1992) and L2 learners (Geva et al., 2000; Jared et al., 2010; Lipka & Siegel, 2012; McBride-Chang, Liu, Wong, Wong, & Shu, 2012; Wagner et al., Chap. 2, this volume; For a review see Lesaux & Geva, 2006). Children who have deficits in both phonological awareness and rapid automatized naming constitute a group of individuals often referred to as having a "double deficit." Their reading difficulties tend to be more severe than those with deficits in only one domain.

The challenge of diagnosing dyslexia in L2 learners concerns the extent to which difficulties in developing word-level reading and spelling skills are related to language proficiency. After all, one would not want to diagnose dyslexia in L2 learners just because they are L2 learners (over-diagnosis), nor would one want to make the opposite error of attributing persistent difficulties in developing decoding and spelling skills to a lack of L2 language proficiency (under-diagnosis). In general, we should expect the same percentage of monolinguals and ELLs to be diagnosed with word-based reading difficulties such as dyslexia. There is a common misperception that reading difficulties are more common in English due to its orthographic depth. However, studies show a roughly equivalent percentage of weak readers across various orthographies, though the presenting symptoms may differ. In shallow orthographies, poor fluency rather than decoding accuracy characterize weak readers, while in deep orthographies such as English, both accuracy and fluency tend to be problematic.

The conclusions we draw from the literature we reviewed earlier is that it is possible to diagnose dyslexia in ELLs even though their language proficiency is still behind that of their monolingual peers. For example, Geva et al. (2000) have shown that the cognitive and reading profiles of ELLs with decoding difficulties are similar to those of their L1 counterparts with decoding difficulties. In another study, Geva and Massey-Garrison (2013) used a cut-off score of the 30th percentile on a standardized word reading task to define children "at risk for dyslexia." They found that the proportion of individuals with decoding difficulties was equally represented in the L1 and L2 groups. Students with decoding difficulties also displayed similar cognitive profiles on working memory, vocabulary, listening comprehension, and syntactic skills, which were distinct from those displayed by poor comprehenders or typical readers, even though those who were L2 learners performed worse on language measures than their L1 peers.

In this chapter, we have touched upon research demonstrating L1 to L2 transfer concerning basic processes that underlie word-based reading and spelling skills in different languages and in various groups of L2 learners. We have also cited research showing that in the case of L2 learners, performance on these processing skills is less closely associated with language proficiency than are higher-order skills such as reading comprehension. These general points can provide school psychologists and literacy specialists with the evidence needed to appreciate inter-lingual transfer, to trust the reliability of assessments of phonological processing components in the L1 and L2, and to consider the implications of deficits on these skills for acquiring decoding and spelling skills in the L1 and L2.

The implication is that L2 students' reading disability can be reliably predicted from their early performance on cognitive processing skills associated with word reading and spelling skills such as phonological awareness, rapid automatized naming and working memory, as well as from their performance on decoding and word recognition skills. A diagnosis should be made at the earliest time possible in order to provide support for L2 learners with reading disability. That is, there is no need to wait until students' oral language proficiency is fully developed to assess or diagnose L2 students who are struggling in reading.

6.5.2 Language and Reading Comprehension Difficulties

In this section, we focus on children whose reading comprehension skills reflect persistent poor language skills over and above what may be associated with their L2 status and their word reading skills. Research with English monolinguals suggests that different types of poor comprehenders emerge at different times in reading development. Typically, the difficulties poor decoders experience emerge in the primary grades when the impact of poor decoding on reading comprehension is first appreciated (Catts, Adlof, & Ellis-Weismer, 2006). Poor comprehenders, sometimes referred to as "unexpected poor comprehenders" or as "late-emerging" poor comprehenders (Farnia & Geva, 2019; Li & Kirby, 2014), are students who do not have difficulties with decoding but have difficulties with oral language skills such as vocabulary, syntactic skills, morphological awareness, listening comprehension, storytelling, and ability to comprehend figurative language (Lesaux & Kieffer, 2010; Lesaux, Lipka, & Siegel, 2006). Importantly, they have persistent difficulties with higher-order language and cognitive skills such as inference making, comprehension monitoring, and the ability to utilize conjunctions and other connectives to help them with text comprehension (Cain, Oakhill, & Bryant, 2004; Catts et al., 2006; Geva & Fraser, 2018; Li & Kirby, 2014).

Late-emerging poor comprehenders may have intact word reading skills compared with their L1 peers and even other L2 learners who come from similar backgrounds (Geva & Herbert, 2012; Geva & Massey-Garrison, 2013; Li & Kirby, 2014). The difficulties of late-emerging poor comprehenders are more likely to be noticed when the nature of reading tasks change, and the impact of persistent poor language skills becomes more noticeable, often around Grade 4. These reading comprehension difficulties may not be as noticeable when the reading material is less demanding in terms of content and cognitive demands. When the focus of reading instruction is mostly on developing fluent word reading and decoding skills, their difficulties may be attributed to lacking L2 proficiency. However, the story changes once the material becomes more demanding, when the nature of reading undergoes additional qualitative changes and students need to be able to learn from the text they read. Some children may be able to read single word or text involving high-frequency words with fluency but experience difficulty with reading texts fluently, because as the texts become more linguistically demanding, the content is novel and more dense (Oakhill & Cain, 2012), requires inferencing, and readers need to pay attention to macro level aspects of the texts they read (Afflerbach, Pearson, & Paris, 2008; Oakhill et al., Chap. 5, this volume; Prior, Goldina, Shany, Geva, & Katzir, 2014).

Assessing ELLs with underlying problems in language processing is difficult because it is not easy to tease apart the extent to which poor reading comprehension is related to their general L2 proficiency or to additional underlying difficulties. Even though there is little research in this area, we know from our experience of working with ELLs in our university clinic that it is possible to identify "unexpected" poor comprehenders among ELLs just as we can with L1 students. Like their L1 peers, these individuals may have relatively intact decoding skills. However, their poor language and comprehension skills are often attributed to their ELL status.

Highlighting the word *relative* in referring to the methodology used to identify this group among ELLs is not a trivial matter. In the absence of reliable and valid means of distinguishing ELLs who have underlying comprehension problems from their typically developing ELL peers, it is prudent to compare them to their typically developing peers. We argue that is it useful to compare ELLs with severe and persistent reading comprehension problems to their peers who are also ELLs, come from similar educational backgrounds, but have better reading comprehension skills. Stated differently, if the bulk of ELLs in a group with similar educational background is doing well on reading comprehension tasks, it indicates that the difficulties experienced by this subgroup of ELLs do not merely reflect their ELL status. This approach can help distinguish between ELLs whose reading comprehension difficulties can be attributed primarily to their L2 status, from ELLs whose reading comprehension difficulties reflect underlying difficulties with learning new vocabulary, processing language, inferencing, using metacognitive strategies, poor working memory, and so on. This approach should help minimize both over- and under-diagnosis of ELLs who have a learning disability.

6.5.3   Reading Fluency Difficulties

In the previous section, we focused on issues related to the assessment of learners whose difficulties are primarily in decoding and developing word recognition skills or with reading comprehension. Yet, as we suggested earlier, it is possible to identify a group of L1 and L2 learners who struggle with reading fluency (e.g., Geva et al., 1997; Quiroga, Lemos-Britton, Mostafapour, Abbott, & Berninger, 2002). L1 and L2 children who have reading fluency difficulties showed similar linguistic and cognitive profiles regardless of their language status (i.e., L1 or L2 learners). Subtypes of students with reading fluency difficulties are identifiable in L1 and L2 readers (e.g., Geva et al., 1997; Quiroga, Lemos-Britton, Mostafapour, Abbott, & Berninger, 2002). For example, Geva and Yaghoub-Zadeh (2006) distinguished three subgroups of L1 and L2 learners: accurate and fluent decoders, accurate but slow decoders, and inaccurate and slow decoders. They found that accurate and fluent decoders performed significantly better than accurate but slow decoders on all literacy and cognitive measures (e.g., phonological awareness, rapid automatized naming, and working memory). Subsequently, accurate but slow decoders performed better than inaccurate and slow decoders. L1 and L2 learners were highly similar in their literacy and cognitive abilities, but the L2 learners had a lower command of English vocabulary than their L1 peers, as might be expected.

As discussed earlier, L2 learners often have word reading accuracy and fluency scores that are similar to their L1 peers. However, while the fluent reading of single words may not be closely aligned with L2 oral language proficiency, it appears that the fluent reading of texts is closely aligned with L2 oral language proficiency (e.g., Al Otaiba et al., 2009; Crosson & Lesaux, 2010; Geva & Farnia, 2012; Nakamoto, Lindsey, & Manis,   2008). In other words, typically developing L2 readers with relatively better developed English language skills can read texts more fluently than their peers whose L2 language skills are less developed. When the text reading of L2 children and adolescents is consistently dysfluent relative to other L2 learners with similar educational histories, the basis of their dysfluent reading needs to be carefully analyzed. It is possible that dysfluent reading may not simply reflect poorer L2 proficiency, but could be attributed to poor decoding skills, language impairment, or a slow but accurate reading profile. In turn, each of these profiles requires different instructional and intervention approaches.

6.6   How Do We Assess ELL Students' English Reading Disability?

A well-informed assessment of a learning disability (LD) in reading is a critical step in facilitating timely and appropriate interventions and accommodations (Geva & Wiener, 2015). Assessment of academic achievement alone is not sufficient to merit a diagnosis of an LD (Hale et al., 2010; Stuebing, Barth, Cirino, Francis, & Fletcher, 2008; Tannock, 2013), especially in relation to L2 students, as their academic performance may not be a true reflection of their actual abilities due to their restricted language proficiency, and at times, educational history. Differentiating reading difficulties associated with an LD from typical development for an ELL is challenging. As noted earlier, school psychologists and evaluation teams should be aware of both the tendencies to over-identify L2 learners as having reading difficulties (Artiles, Harry, Reschly, & Chinn, 2010; Geva & Herbert, 2012; Klingner, Artiles, & Barletta, 2006; Zehler, Fleischman, Hopstock, Pendzick, & Stepheson, 2003) or under-identify L2 learners with reading difficulties when they actually do (Limbos & Geva, 2001).

As discussed earlier in this chapter, a growing body of research has shown that deficits in underlying cognitive skills in the early years reliably predict reading difficulties later in life, and that such cognitive skills assessed in students' L1 are valid predictors of reading difficulties in their L2s as well. Instead of waiting for L2 learners to develop proficiency in the target language to make a diagnosis, schools should work toward timely and unbiased assessments and interventions for L2 learners who have reading difficulties.

In this regard, it is especially important to be mindful of the pitfalls of the IQ-achievement discrepancy framework when assessing for learning disabilities. This precaution is based on two points. First, over the past four decades, a growing literature has provided evidence that IQ is irrelevant for diagnosing a word-level reading disability (dyslexia or the word reading skills of garden-variety poor readers, see Chap. 1, this volume) (e.g., Catts, 1989; Das, Mishra, & Kirby, 1994; Fletcher, 1992; Lyon, 1995; Rack, Snowling, & Olson, 1992; Reed, 1970; Siegel, 1992; Vellutino, Fletcher, Snowling, & Scanlon, 2004). Notably, the revised DSM-5 abandoned the discrepancy approach when making a diagnosis of a learning disability. Second, IQ tests often disadvantage L2 learners, both culturally and linguistically, and it may therefore be more difficult to establish reliable and valid IQ scores, and therefore to establish a discrepancy between IQ and achievement. In other words, the IQ-achievement discrepancy framework may be especially biased against L2 learners (Geva & Wiener, 2015).

Caution also needs to be exercised when L2 learners are compared with their L1 peers on standardized tests that are normed on more homogenous populations. A more relevant reference group should be used to make an unbiased assessment (Geva & Herbert, 2012). An example would be asking the teacher how an L2 client is doing in comparison with other similar children the teacher has taught before. Over-reliance on normed tests makes it difficult to distinguish L2 reading difficulties that merely reflect L2 language and reading development from difficulties that truly reflect an LD in reading. To this end, in addition to traditional assessments, alternative assessment techniques focusing on early identification and the use of evidence-based instruction with ongoing assessment and monitoring (Fuchs & Fuchs, 2006) can be highly informative in guiding clinicians toward a fairer and more realistic interpretation of performance on reading and achievement tests (for a more detailed description of these complementary assessment techniques, see Geva & Wiener, 2015).

Some of the complementary techniques school psychologists may use for assessing reading difficulties in L2 include classroom observation, examining report cards, teacher and parent interviewing, error analysis, dynamic assessment (Swanson & Lussier, 2001), curriculum-based measurement (Deno, 1985; Deno & Fuchs, 1987), and response to intervention (Fuchs & Vaughn, 2012). These assessment techniques can be beneficial as the psychologists and teachers can observe how the L2 student responds to specific interventions targeting their reading or language difficulties. In addition, one should consider comparison with peers and siblings, interviews with parents, examination of prior assessments and report cards, and formal and informal assessment in the L1, when it is justified and feasible. The psychologist needs to remember that when an ELL learner has not been exposed to systematic instruction in the L1 for some time, assessment in the L1 may not provide reliable information. A diagnosis of a reading disability can be reliably made by assembling information from these complementary data sources. When the L2 learner shows difficulties on relevant standardized tests and does not improve through these alternative approaches, and where there is other evidence of difficulties, a diagnosis may be justified. As noted earlier, another piece of this puzzle is consideration of the development of literacy and language skills within similar groups of L2 learners. Alternative assessment approaches help the clinician make an accurate diagnosis of a reading disability by comparing performance with that of typically developing L2 children from a similar background. In addition, in recent years there has been an increased momentum in promising studies that deemphasize assessment and emphasize instead dynamic assessment and response to intervention (RTI). There is research evidence that ELLs at risk for reading disabilities benefit when an RTI approach is implemented (Linan-Thompson, Vaughn, Prater, & Cirino, 2006; Lovett et al., 2008). In addition to considering test and interview factors, psychologists and educators need to also be aware of external contextual risk factors that influence the assessment of L2 learners. These include cultural background, interrupted schooling, SES, educational experience, parental education, and parental attributions about the source of difficulties, all of which should be taken into consideration in the assessment process as well. Of course, poor performance attributed to these factors should not be used as a basis for a diagnosis of a reading disability. In the next section, we address briefly these contextual factors.

6.7 What Are the Factors Influencing the Assessment of ELL Students' English Reading Ability?

6.7.1 Oral Language Proficiency

Often, L2 students need to learn to read and develop their oral language proficiency in synchrony. This contrasts with L1 learners who usually learn to read with oral language skills that are commensurate with their age. Cummins (1979) highlights the distinction between basic interpersonal communication skills (BICS) and cognitive academic language proficiency (CALP). BICS refers to language that people need for day-to-day social communication. CALP refers to the academic language students need to understand academic materials and texts used in the classroom. Most L2 students can acquire basic interpersonal communication skills (BICS) within one to two years after their arrival; however, cognitive academic language proficiency (CALP) may lag behind other L1 students for up to 5–7 years (Cummins, 1981; Thomas & Collier, 1997). Awareness of the distinction between BICS and CALP is important for both educators and school psychologists. Even though L2 learners may sound fluent in the societal language, or when they read simple texts, they are likely to struggle with the subtle and more advanced academic components of language (e.g., vocabulary, syntactic knowledge, morphological skills, and figurative language). These difficulties may negatively influence the performance of L2 students on academic tasks and standardized tests that rely heavily on verbal skills (e.g., Verbal Comprehension Index of the WISC-V), and lead to an underestimation of verbal abilities. It is important for school psychologists to understand the characteristics of typical and atypical L2 language and reading development. This will enable them to effectively synthesize aspects of the assessment that are associated with L2 language proficiency versus those indicating an underlying language reading difficulty.

6.7.2 School Experience

Typically, children who have had learning difficulties in the L1 will experience diffi
culties in the L2 as well. Prior placements in remedial programs and teachers' comments about academic delays may support the validity of an assessment. Interrupted
schooling may also be associated with significant educational gaps in language and
literacy acquisition in the L1, prior knowledge, behavioral expectations, and cultural
understandings (Brown, Miller, & Mitchell, 2006). One should also be aware that
children coming from school systems that emphasize skill-based rote memory may
need to adapt to approaches that emphasize constructivist, inquiry-based curriculum,
self-regulation, and problem-based learning (Bransford, Vye, Kinzer, & Risko, 1990;
Hmelo-Silver, Duncan, & Chinn, 2007).

6.7.3 Family Literacy

Students begin language and literacy learning before starting formal schooling. Studies (Heath, 1983; Snow et al., 1998) have shown that early literacy experiences significantly predict reading performance later on. When compared with illiterate parents,
educated parents are more likely to have higher expectations for their children's academic attainment and are able to mobilize educational and organizational resources
to promote children's literacy experiences. Engagement in family literacy activities,
regardless of the language used in such activities, helps to improve monolingual and
L2 students' reading performance (Evans, Kelley, Sikora & Treiman, 2010; Karlson,
Geva, & Halaas-Lyster, 2015; Snow & Dickinson, 1990).

6.7.4 Family History

Learning difficulties such as dyslexia are highly heritable (Haworth & Plomin, 2010;
Kovas et al., 2007; Mascheretti et al., 2015; also see Chaps. 9, 10, this volume).
Genetic factors that may have affected language and reading development for parents
may be transmitted to their children. Therefore, inquiring about whether biological
siblings, parents, and biological aunts, uncles, and grandparents had difficulties in
school or were diagnosed with LD may provide valuable insight.

Ample research shows that early language and literacy skills correlate with various socio-economic indices such as parental education and number of books at
home (Hart & Risley, 1999; Karlsen et al., 2015; Solari et al., 2014). There is a
tendency to think that immigrant parents may not be educated, especially when they
are not professionally employed. However, one should beware of overgeneralizations. Immigrant parents may be highly educated and in countries such as Canada,
a higher percentage of immigrant parents have university education than the general

population. Therefore, psychologists should not arbitrarily assume that students' low reading performance can be attributed to low SES status and a lack of print exposure at home (see Geva & Wiener, 2015 for a review). Immigrant parents may be educated, and their children may be exposed to relevant and helpful literacy activities at home in the L1, L2, or both (Karlsen et al., 2015; Schwartz & Shaul, 2013). Moreover, one should be aware of within-group variation and avoid ethnically based overgeneralizations. A carefully conducted investigation of family history should consider parental education and occupation, family literacy experience, familial LD history, and the value systems specific to the ethnic group and to the individual.

6.7.5 Social and Emotional Considerations

Learning a second language is a challenging task that is greatly aided by personal factors such as motivation, self-efficacy, personal values, and self-regulation (Phakiti, Hirsh, & Woodrow, 2013). Students also learn best in settings that support social and emotional learning, which involves developing emotional awareness, empathy for others, positive relationships, and learning to make responsible decisions and handle challenging situations effectively (CASEL, 2013). Asking children and parents about their social and emotional well-being may provide insight into how well the children are learning in school (for a more comprehensive discussion of this topic, see Geva & Wiener, 2015).

6.8 How Can School Psychologists Best Address the Needs of L2 Learners with Reading Difficulties?

In general, research findings indicate that L2 learners with reading difficulties benefit from the same type of instruction as struggling L1 readers (Cirino et al., 2009; Geva & Herbert, 2012; Lovett et al., 2008; Wise & Chen, 2010). Support for this general conclusion comes from various studies. For example, Lovett et al. (2008) found that L1 and L2 students with reading difficulties improved their word reading skills after being trained by a phonology-based reading program (PHAST). Such improvement was also reported by Carlo et al. (2004) and Goodwin and Ahn (2010), concluding that intervention programs designed to promote oral language skills (e.g., morphological awareness and vocabulary) can also improve reading comprehension for ELL students with and without reading difficulties. Additional information about research-based strategies and interventions for decoding and reading comprehension difficulties is provided in greater depth in Chap. 5, this volume. There is evidence that L2 students with reading difficulties can benefit from systematic phonological awareness instruction (Lovett et al., 2008), morphological-based instruction (Goodwin & Ahn, 2010), and explicit and intensive vocabulary instruction (Carlo et al., 2004;

Shanahan & Beck, 2006; U.S. Department of Education, 2006). Focused instruction on higher-order skills is especially beneficial for students with comprehension difficulties and language impairments (LaRusso et al., 2016).

6.9 Conclusion

This chapter has highlighted recent research into typical and atypical reading development in L2 learners. Despite the accumulated research on best practices for the assessment and treatment of reading difficulties in L2 students, common misconceptions remain among practitioners, leading to over- and under-identification of L2 students with reading disabilities. We wish to leave our readers with the most salient points from our review of the L2 reading research of typically and atypically developing ELLs, and underscore the implications of this growing body of research for sensitive and well-informed practices. The chart below summarizes common misconceptions and the implications of research for informed practice.

Common misconceptions	What the research says and implies for practice
Once L2 speakers can communicate with their peers, they should also be able to learn like their peers	• Typically developing L2 learners become proficient in the societal language (BICS) in 1–2 years. However, more complex academic aspects of language (e.g., vocabulary, syntactic knowledge, morphological skills) are challenging for L2 learners; it can take at least 5–7 years for typically developing L2 learners to develop academic language (CALP) at a level similar to their L1 peers
L2 learners should only read in their L2 since they are trying to improve their L2 reading skills	• Activities that promote knowledge about print and literacy skills are important for subsequent literacy achievement regardless of whether the L1 or L2 is used at home • L2 students should read in either the L1 or L2 to improve reading skills; if L1 is stronger it can actually help with L2 reading (transfer of metalinguistic and metacognitive skills; background knowledge)

(continued)

(continued)

Common misconceptions	What the research says and implies for practice
Children experience difficulties in reading in their L2 because their oral language proficiency is not adequate—yet	• Word-based reading processes in children are less closely related to oral language proficiency • ELLs have no problem decoding words even as their oral language proficiency is developing. In fact, some children can even decode more accurately in the L2 depending on the relative shallowness or depth of the writing system • Reading comprehension *is* tied to oral language proficiency (e.g., vocabulary) and is weaker in ELLs but should still develop and progress in typical L2 readers
The relationship between word reading processes and reading comprehension is different in L1 and L2	• Key factors that contribute to reading comprehension, such as efficient word reading and oral language proficiency (e.g., vocabulary), are essentially the same for L1 and L2 learners • Individual differences on these prerequisite skills for reading can indicate either seamless or problematic reading acquisition later (good predictors of later reading)
Poor phonological processing skills may contribute to poor word recognition in L1 children, but are less informative when oral language proficiency is still developing	• Individual differences in phonological processing skills are related to individual differences in word recognition skills • Evidence of cross-linguistic transfer of PA—phonological processing in either the L1 or L2—can explain significant amounts of variance on the word recognition skills in another language • Oral language proficiency is not necessary to assess phonological processing skills (independent of each other)

(continued)

(continued)

Common misconceptions	What the research says and implies for practice
Weaknesses in language comprehension and reading comprehension are attributed to ELL status and "still developing" L2 oral language proficiency	• Some late-emerging poor reading comprehenders demonstrate difficulties with underlying language comprehension and processing, but their word-level reading skills may be intact • Deficits in the same cognitive skills (e.g., working memory, rapid automatized naming) and higher-order language and cognitive skills (e.g., inference making, syntactic awareness, comprehension monitoring) are implicated in both L1 and L2 learners with language and reading comprehension weaknesses • L2 weaknesses in vocabulary, especially academic vocabulary, are normal and expected in comparison to L1 peers. However, persistent difficulties in L2 vocabulary, delays in language processing and comprehension skills, and lack of progress despite structured support may indicate difficulties beyond L2 status
Dysfluent reading in L2 learners is attributed to lack of adequate oral language proficiency	• Word reading fluency is not strongly related to having well-developed oral language proficiency. In fact, accurate and fluent word reading fluency can be similar across L1 and L2 learners with the same amount of reading experience in the L2. The same underlying cognitive–linguistic factors that are needed for word recognition are also needed for efficient word reading fluency • In addition to having good word reading skills, text reading fluency is closely aligned with oral language skills • L2 learners whose text reading is dysfluent in comparison to L2 peers from a similar language background may have fluency and language difficulties that cannot be attributed simply to their L2 status

(continued)

(continued)

Common misconceptions	What the research says and implies for practice
L2 students with reading disabilities need different reading interventions than those used for L1 students with reading disabilities	• The same deficits in cognitive processes (e.g., deficits in RAN, WM, PA) are implicated in children with decoding problems regardless of language and the interventions that are used for L1 children are effective with L2 children with reading disabilities • There is less research on interventions focusing on dysfluent readers or "unexpected" poor comprehension among L2 learners. Using intervention approaches that work for L1 students is likely a safe strategy
Once the student is fluent in the L2, it is possible to interpret test performance using published norms	• Language takes a long time to develop. While performance on standardized tests can be highly informative, interpreting behavior on the basis of L1-based test norms should be done with caution • Use a combination of standardized tests, tasks designed to measure specific processes, RTI, observations of academic improvement, and authentic oral language samples
Applying a one-size-fits-all, "consistent", assessment strategy minimizes bias in assessment	• In interpreting assessment data gathered from a variety of sources, consider age of arrival, exposure and opportunities to acquire the L2, prior schooling, typological differences between the L1 and L2, and various sources of positive and negative transfer • Select and interpret tests, including intelligence tests, on the basis of degree of linguistic and cultural loading

References

Abu-Rabia, S. (2001). Testing the interdependence hypothesis among native adult bilingual Russian-English students. *Journal of Psycholinguistic Research, 30,* 437–455. https://doi.org/10.1023/A:1010425825251.

Abu-Rabia, S., & Siegel, L. (2002). Reading, syntactic, orthographic, and working memory skills of bilingual Arabic-English speaking Canadian children. *Journal of Psycholinguistic Research, 31,* 661–678. https://doi.org/10.1023/A:1021221206119.

Abu-Rabia, S., Shakkour, W., & Siegel, L. (2013). Cognitive retroactive transfer (CRT) of language skills among bilingual Arabic-English readers. *Bilingual Research Journal, 36,* 61–81. https://doi.org/10.1080/15235882.2013.775975.

Afflerbach, P., Pearson, P. D., & Paris, S. G. (2008). Clarifying differences between reading skills and reading strategies. *The Reading Teacher, 61,* 364–373. https://doi.org/10.1598/RT.61.5.

Al Otaiba, S., Petscher, Y., Pappamihiel, N. E., Williams, R. S., Drylund, A. K., & Connor, C. M. (2009). Modeling oral reading fluency development in Latino students: A longitudinal study across second and third grade. *Journal of Educational Psychology, 101,* 315–329. https://doi.org/10.1037/a0014698.

American Psychiatric Association. (2013). *Diagnostic and statistical manual of mental disorders* (DSM, 5th ed.).

Arab-Moghaddam, N., & Sénéchal, M. (2001). Orthographic and phonological processing skills in reading and spelling in Persian/English bilinguals. *International Journal of Behavioral Development, 25*(2), 140–147. https://doi.org/10.1080/01650250042000320.

Artiles, A. J., Harry, B., Reschly, D. J., & Chinn, P. C. (2010). Over-identification of students of color in special education: A critical overview. *Multicultural Perspectives, 4,* 3–10. https://doi.org/10.1207/S15327892MCP0401_2.

August, D., & Shanahan, T. (Eds.). (2006). *Developing literacy in second language learners: Report of the national literacy panel on language minority youth and children.* Mahwah, NJ: Erlbaum.

Babayiğit, S. (2014). The role of oral language skills in reading and listening comprehension of text: A comparison of monolingual (L1) and bilingual (L2) speakers of English language. *Journal of Research in Reading, 37*(S1), S22–S47. https://doi.org/10.1111/j.1467-9817.2012.01538.

Baker, L., & Beall, L. C. (2009). Metacognitive processes and reading comprehension. In S. E. Israel & G. G. Duffy (Eds.), *Handbook of research on reading comprehension* (pp. 373–388). New York, NY: Routledge.

Bérubé, D., & Marinova-Todd, S. H. (2014). The effect of sociolinguistic factors and English language proficiency on the development of French as a third language. *International Journal of Bilingual Education and Bilingualism, 17*(4), 465–483. https://doi.org/10.1080/13670050.2013.820686.

Bialystok, E., McBride-Chang, C., & Luk, G. (2005). Bilingualism, language proficiency, and learning to read in two writing systems. *Journal of Educational Psychology, 97,* 580–590. https://doi.org/10.1037/0022-0663.97.4.580.

Bransford, J. D., Vye, N., Kinzer, C., & Risko, V. (1990). Teaching thinking and content knowledge: Toward an integrated approach. In B. F. Jones & L. Idol (Eds.), *Dimensions of thinking and cognitive instruction* (pp. 381–413). Hillsdale, NJ: Lawrence Earlbaum Associates.

Branum-Martin, L., Mehta, P. D., Fletcher, J. M., Carlson, C. D., Ortiz, A., & Carlo, M. (2006). Bilingual phonological awareness: Multilevel construct validation among Spanish-speaking kindergarteners in transitional bilingual education classrooms. *Journal of Educational Psychology, 98,* 170–181. https://doi.org/10.1037/0022-0663.98.1.170.

Brown, J., Miller, J., & Mitchell, J. (2006). Interrupted schooling and the acquisition of literacy: Experiences of Sudanese refugees in Victorian secondary schools. *Australian Journal of Language and Literacy, 29,* 150–162.

Cain, K., Oakhill, J. V., & Bryant, P. (2004). Children's reading comprehension ability: Concurrent prediction by working memory, verbal ability, and component skills. *Journal of Educational Psychology, 96,* 31–42. https://doi.org/10.1037/0022-0663.96.1.31.

Carlisle, J. F. (2000). Awareness of the structure and meaning of morphologically complex words: Impact on reading. *Reading and Writing: An Interdisciplinary Journal, 12,* 169–190. https://doi.org/10.1023/A:1008131926604.

Carlo, M. S., August, D., McLaughlin, B., Snow, C. E., Dressler, C., Lippman, D. N.,…White, C. E. (2004). Closing the gap: Addressing the vocabulary needs of English-language learners in bilingual and mainstream classrooms. *Reading Research Quarterly, 39,* 188–215. https://doi.org/10.1598/rrq.39.2.3.

Catts, H. W. (1989). Defining dyslexia as a developmental language disorder. *Annals of Dyslexia, 39*(1), 50–64. https://doi.org/10.1007/BF02656900.

Catts, H. W., Adlof, S. M., & Weismer, S. W. (2006). Language deficits in poor comprehenders: A case for the simple view of reading. *Journal of Speech, Language, and Hearing Research: JSLHR, 49*(2), 278–293. https://doi.org/10.1044/1092-4388(2006/023)

Chall, J. S. (1996). *Stages of reading development* (2nd ed.). Fort Worth, TX: Harcourt Brace College Publishers.

Chiappe, P., & Siegel, L. S. (1999). Phonological awareness and reading acquisition in English- and Punjabi-speaking Canadian children. *Journal of Educational Psychology, 91*, 20–28. https://doi.org/10.1037/0022-0663.91.1.20.

Chiappe, P., Siegel, L., & Gottardo, A. (2002). Reading-related skills of kindergartners from diverse linguistic backgrounds. *Applied Psycholinguistics, 23*, 95–116. https://doi.org/10.1017/S014271640200005X.

Chiappe, P., Siegel, L., & Wade-Woolley, L. (2002). Linguistic diversity and the development of reading skills: A longitudinal study. *Scientific Studies of Reading, 6*, 369–400. https://doi.org/10.1207/S1532799XSSR0604_04.

Chung, K., & Ho, C. (2010). Second language learning difficulties in Chinese children with dyslexia: What are the reading-related cognitive skills that contribute to English and Chinese word reading? *Journal of Learning Disabilities, 43*, 195–211. https://doi.org/10.1177/0022219409345018.

Chung, S. C., Chen, X., & Geva, E. (2019). Deconstructing and reconstructing cross-language transfer in bilingual reading development: An interactive framework. *Journal of Neurolinguistics Special Issue: Cross-linguistic Perspectives on Second Language Reading, 50*, 149–161. Verhoeven, L., A. Perfetti, C. A., & Pugh, K. Editors.

Cirino, P. T., Vaughn, S., Linan-Thompson, S., Cardenas-Hagan, E., Fletcher, J. M., & Francis, D. J. (2009). One-year follow-up outcomes of Spanish and English interventions for English language learners at risk for reading problems. *American Educational Research Journal, 46*(3), 744–781. https://doi.org/10.3102/0002831208330214.

Collaborative for Academic, Social, and Emotional Learning (CASEL). (2013). *The CASEL guide: Effective social and emotional learning programs.* Retrieved from http://www.casel.org/guide.

Commeau, L., Cormier, P., Grandmaison, E., & Lacroix, D. (1999). A longitudinal study of phono- logical processing skills in children learning to read in a second language. *Journal of Educational Psychology, 91*(1), 29–43. https://doi.org/10.1037/0022-0663.91.1.29.

Commissaire, E., Pasquarella, A., Chen, X., & Deacon, S. H. (2014). The development of ortho- graphic processing skills in children in early French immersion programs. *Written Language & Literacy, 17*(1), 16–39. https://doi.org/10.1075/wll.17.1.02com.

Crosson, A. C., & Lesaux, N. K. (2010). Revisiting assumptions about the relationship of flu- ent reading to comprehension: Spanish-speakers' text-reading fluency in English. *Reading and Writing: An Interdisciplinary Journal, 23*, 475–494. https://doi.org/10.1007/s11145-009-9168-8.

Cummins, J. (1979). Linguistic interdependence and the educational development of bilin- gual children. *Review of Educational Research, 49*, 222–251. https://doi.org/10.3102/00346543049002222.

Cummins, J. (1981). The role of primary language development in promoting educational success for language minority students. In California State Department of Education (Ed.), *Schooling and language minority students: A theoretical framework* (pp. 3–49). Los Angeles, CA: National Dissemination and Assessment Center. https://doi.org/10.13140/2.1.1334.9449.

Cummins, J. (2008). Teaching for transfer: Challenging the two solitudes assumption in bilingual education. In N. H. Hornberger (Ed.), *Encyclopedia of language and education* (pp. 1528–1538). https://doi.org/10.1007/978-0-387-30424-3_116.

Cummins, J. (2012). The intersection of cognitive and sociocultural factors in the development of reading comprehension among immigrant students. *Reading and Writing: An Interdisciplinary Journal, 25*, 1973–1990. https://doi.org/10.1007/s11145-010-9290-7.

Cunningham, A. E. (2006). Accounting for children's orthographic learning while reading text: Do children self-teach? *Journal of Experimental Child Psychology, 95*, 56–77. https://doi.org/10.1016/j.jecp.2006.03.008, https://doi.org/10.1016/j.jecp.2006.03.008.

D'Angiulli, A., Siegel, L. S., & Serra, E. (2001). The development of reading in English and Italian in bilingual children. *Applied Psycholinguistics, 22,* 479–507. https://doi.org/10.1017/S0142716401004015.

Da Fontoura, H., & Siegel, L. S. (1995). Reading, syntactic, and working memory skills of bilingual Portuguese-English Canadian children. *Reading and Writing: An Interdisciplinary Journal, 7,* 139–153. https://doi.org/10.1007/BF01026951.

Das, J. P., Mishra, R. K., & Kirby, J. R. (1994). Cognitive patterns of children with dyslexia: A comparison between groups with high and average nonverbal intelligence. *Journal of Learning Disabilities, 27,* 235–242. https://doi.org/10.1177/002221949402700405.

Deacon, S. H., Chen, X., Luo, Y. C., & Ramírez, G. (2013). Beyond language borders: Orthographic processing and word reading in Spanish-English bilinguals. *Journal of Research in Reading, 36*(1), 58–74. https://doi.org/10.1111/j.1467-9817.2011.01490.x.

Deacon, S. H., Wade-Woolley, L., & Kirby, J. R. (2007). Cross-over: The role of morphological awareness in French immersion children's reading. *Developmental Psychology, 43,* 732–746. https://doi.org/10.1037/0012-1649.43.3.732.

Deacon, S. H., Wade-Woolley, L., & Kirby, J. R. (2009). Flexibility in young second-language learners: Examining the language specificity of orthographic processing. *Journal of Research in Reading, 32*(2), 215–229. https://doi.org/10.1111/j.1467-9817.2009.01392.x.

Deno, S. L. (1985). Curriculum-based measurement: The emerging alternative. *Exceptional Children, 52,* 219–232. https://doi.org/10.1177/001440298505200303.

Deno, S. L., & Fuchs, L. S. (1987). Developing curriculum-based measurement systems for databased special education problem solving. *Focus on Exceptional Children, 19*(8), 1–16.

Dickinson, D. K., McCabe, A., Clark-Chiarelli, N., & Wolf, A. (2004). Cross-language transfer of phonological awareness in low-income Spanish and English bilingual preschool children. *Applied Psycholinguistics, 25,* 323–347. https://doi.org/10.1017/s0142716404001158.

Droop, M., & Verhoeven, L. (2003). Language proficiency and reading ability in first- and second-language learners. *Reading Research Quarterly, 38*(1), 78–103. https://doi.org/10.1598/RRQ.38.1.4.

Durgunoğlu, A., Nagy, W., & Hancin-Bhatt, B. (1993). Cross-language transfer of phonological awareness. *Journal of Educational Psychology, 85*(3), 453–465.

Durgunoğlu, A. Y. (2002). Cross-linguistic transfer in literacy development and implications for language learners. *Annals of Dyslexia, 52,* 189–204. https://doi.org/10.1007/s11881-002-0012-y.

Ehri, L. C. (1995). Phases of development in learning to read words by sight. *Journal of Research in Reading, 18,* 116–125. https://doi.org/10.1111/j.1467-9817.1995.tb00077.x.

Evans, M. D. R., Kelley, J., Sikora, J., & Treiman, D. J. (2010). Family scholarly culture and educational success: Books and schooling in 27 nations. *Research in Social Stratification and Mobility, 28,* 171–197. https://doi.org/10.1016/j.rssm.2010.01.002.

Erdos, C., Genesee, F., Savage, R., & Haigh, C. (2014). Predicting risk for oral and written language learning difficulties in students educated in a second language. *Applied Psycholinguistics, 35,* 371–398. https://doi.org/10.1017/S0142716412000422.

Farnia, F., & Geva, E. (2013). Growth and predictors of change in English language learners' reading comprehension. *Journal of Research in Reading, 36*(4), 389–421. https://doi.org/10.1111/jrir.12003.

Farnia, F., & Geva, E. (2011). Cognitive correlates of vocabulary growth in English language learners. *Applied Psycholinguistics, 32,* 711–738. https://doi.org/10.1017/S0142716411000038.

Farnia, F., & Geva, E. (2019). Late-emerging developmental language disorder in english-speaking monolinguals and english language learners: A longitudinal perspective. *Journal of Learning Disabilities.* https://doi.org/10.1177/0022219419866645

Fisiak, J. (1981). *Contrastive linguistics and the language teacher.* Oxford: Pergamon Press.

Fletcher, J. M. (1992). The validity of distinguishing children with language and learning disabilities according to discrepancies with IQ: Introduction to the special series. *Journal of Learning Disabilities, 25*(9), 546–548.

Francis, D. J., Fletcher, J. M., Stuebing, K. K., Lyon, G. R., Shaywitz, B. A., & Shaywitz, S. (2005). Psychometric approaches to the identification of LD IQ and achievement scores are not sufficient. *Journal of Learning Disabilities, 38,* 98–102. https://doi.org/10.1177/00222194050380020101.

Frost, R., & Katz, L. (Eds.). (1992). *Orthography, phonology, morphology, and meaning.* New York, NY: North-Holland.

Fuchs, D., & Fuchs, L. S. (2006). Introduction to response to intervention: What, why, and how valid is it? *Reading Research Quarterly, 41*(1), 93–99. https://doi.org/10.1598/RRQ.41.1.4.

Fuchs, L. S., & Vaughn, S. (2012). Responsiveness-to-Intervention: A decade later. *Journal of Learning Disabilities, 45*(3), 195–203. https://doi.org/10.1177/0022219412442150.

Genesee, F., Geva, E., Dressler, C., & Kamil, M. (2006). Synthesis: Cross-linguistic relationships in working memory, phonological processes, and oral language. In D. August & T. Shanahan (Eds.), *Developing literacy in second-language learners: A report of the National Literacy Panel on language-minority children and youth* (pp. 153–174). Mahwah, NJ: Erlbaum.

Geva, E. (2006). Second-language oral proficiency and second-language literacy. In D. August & T. Shanahan (Eds.), *Developing literacy in second-language learners: A report of the National Literacy Panel on language-minority children and youth* (pp. 123–139). Mahwah, NJ: Erlbaum.

Geva, E., & Farnia, F. (2012). Developmental changes in the nature of language proficiency and reading fluency paint a more complex view of reading comprehension in ELL and EL1. *Reading and Writing, 25*(8), 1819–1845. https://doi.org/10.1007/s11145-011-9333-8.

Geva, E., & Farnia, F. (2015). Cognitive and neural basis of learning: Abilities and disabilities. Invited presentation at the International conference in Memory of Professor Zvia Breznitz, Haifa, Israel. May 19–21. Retrieved from https://sites.google.com/a/edu.haifa.ac.il/cnal/videos/cognitive-predictors-of-late-emerging-language-impairment-in-el1-and-ell-school-children.

Geva, E., & Fraser, C. (2018). Multilingual learners: Vocabulary and beyond. In E. Segers & P. van den Broek (Eds.), *Developmental Perspectives in Written Language and Literacy.* pp. 199–-217. John Benjamin's

Geva, E., & Herbert, K. (2012). Assessment and interventions in English language learners with LD. In B. Wong & D. Butler (Eds.), *Learning about learning disabilities* (4th ed., pp. 271–298). San Diego, CA: Elsevier.

Geva, E., & Massey-Garrison, A. (2013). A comparison of the language skills of ELLs and monolinguals who are poor decoders, poor comprehenders, or normal readers. *Journal of Learning Disabilities, 46*(5), 387–401. https://doi.org/10.1177/0022219412466651.

Geva, E., & Ramírez, G. (2015). *Focus on reading.* Oxford: Oxford University Press.

Geva, E., & Ryan, E. B. (1993). Linguistic and cognitive correlates of academic skills in first and second language. *Language Learning, 43,* 5–42. https://doi.org/10.1111/j.1467-1770.1993.tb00171.x.

Geva, E., & Siegel, L. (2000). Orthographic and cognitive factors in the concurrent development of basic reading skills in two languages. *Reading and Writing, 12,* 1–30. https://doi.org/10.1023/A:1008017710115.

Geva, E., Wade-Woolley, L., & Shany, M. (1997). The development of reading efficiency in first and second language. *Scientific Studies of Reading, 1*(2), 119–144. https://doi.org/10.1207/s1532799xssr0102_2.

Geva, E., & Wiener, J. (2015). *Psychological assessment of culturally and linguistically diverse children—A practitioner's guide.* New York: Springer.

Geva, E., & Yaghoub-Zadeh, Z. (2006). Reading efficiency in native English-speaking and English-as-a-second-language children: The role of oral proficiency and underlying cognitive-linguistic processes. *Scientific Studies of Reading, 10,* 31–58. https://doi.org/10.1207/s1532799xssr1001_3.

Geva, E., Yaghoub-Zadeh, Z., & Schuster, B. (2000). Understanding individual differences in word recognition skills of ESL children. *Annals of Dyslexia, 50,* 121–154. https://doi.org/10.1007/s11881-000-0020-8.

Gholamain, M., & Geva, E. (1999). Orthographic and cognitive factors in the concurrent development of basic reading skills in English and Persian. *Language Learning, 49,* 183–217. https://doi.org/10.1111/0023-8333.00087.

Goodwin, A. P., & Ahn, S. (2010). A meta-analysis of morphological interventions: Effects on literacy achievement of children with literacy difficulties. *Annals of Dyslexia, 60,* 183–208. https://doi.org/10.1007/s11881-010-0041-x.

Gottardo, A., Collins, P., Baciu, I., & Gebotys, R. (2008). Predictors of grade 2 word reading and vocabulary learning from grade 1 variables in Spanish-speaking children: Similarities and differences. *Learning Disabilities Research & Practice, 23,* 11–24. https://doi.org/10.1111/j.1540-5826.2007.00259.x.

Gottardo, A., Yan, B., Siegel, L., & Wade-Woolley, L. (2001). Factors related to English reading performance in children with Chinese as a first language: More evidence of cross-language transfer of phonological processing. *Journal of Educational Psychology, 93*(3), 530–542. https://doi.org/10.1037/0022-0663.93.3.530.

Hale, J., Alfonso, V., Berninger, V., Bracken, B., Christo, C., Clark, E., et al. (2010). Critical issues in response-to-intervention, comprehensive evaluation, and specific learning disabilities identification and intervention: An expert white paper consensus. *Learning Disability Quarterly, 33,* 223–236. https://doi.org/10.1177/073194871003300310.

Hart, B., & Risley, T. R. (1999). *The social world of children: Learning to talk.* Baltimore, MD: Brookes Publishing.

Haworth, C. M. A., & Plomin, R. (2010). Quantitative genetics in the era of molecular genetics: Learning abilities and disabilities as an example. *Journal of the American Academy of Child and Adolescent Psychiatry, 49,* 783–793. https://doi.org/10.1016/j.jaac.2010.01.026.

Heath, S. B. (1983). *Ways with words: Language, life, and work in communities and classrooms.* New York, NY: Cambridge University Press.

Hmelo-Silver, C. E., Duncan, R. G., & Chinn, C. A. (2007). Scaffolding and achievement in problem-based and inquiry learning: A response to Kirschner, Sweller, and Clark (2006). *Educational Psychologist, 42,* 99–107. https://doi.org/10.1080/00461520701263368.

Hutchinson, J. M., Whiteley, H. E., Smith, C. D., & Connors, L. (2003). The developmental progression of comprehension-related skills in children learning EAL. *Journal of Research in Reading, 26,* 19–32. https://doi.org/10.1111/1467-9817.261003.

Individuals with Disabilities Education Act (IDEA). (2004). US Department of Education.

Jared, D., Cormier, P., Levy, B. A., & Wade-Woolley, L. (2010). Early predictors of biliteracy development in children in French immersion: A 4-year longitudinal study. *Journal of Educational Psychology, 103,* 119–139. https://doi.org/10.1037/a0021284.

Karlsen, J., Geva, E., & Halaas Lyster, S. A. (2015). Cognitive, linguistic and contextual factors in Norweigian second language learners narrative production. *Applied Psycholinguistics, 37,* 1117–1145. https://doi.org/10.1017/S014271641500051X.

Keung, Y. C., & Ho, C. S. H. (2009). Transfer of reading-related cognitive skills in learning to read Chinese (L1) and English (L2) among Chinese elementary school children. *Contemporary Educational Psychology, 34*(2), 103–112. https://doi.org/10.1016/j.cedpsych.2008.11.001.

Klingner, J. K., Artiles, A. J., & Barletta, L. M. (2006). English language learners who struggle with reading: Language acquisition or learning disabilities? *Journal of Learning Disabilities, 39*(2), 108–128.

Koda, K. (2008). Impacts of prior literacy experience on second-language learning to read. In K. Koda & A. M. Zehler (Eds.), *Learning to read across languages: Cross-linguistic relationships in first- and second-language literacy development* (pp. 68–96). Mahwah, NJ: Routledge.

Kovas, Y., Haworth, C. M. A., Dale, P. S., Plomin, R., Weinberg, R. A., Thomson, J. M., et al. (2007). The genetic and environmental origins of the learning abilities and disabilities in the early school years. *Monographs of the Society for Research in Child Development, 72,* 1–156.

Kuo, L. J., & Anderson, R. C. (2006). Morphological awareness and learning to read: a cross-language perspective. *Educational Psychologist, 41*(3), 161–180. https://doi.org/10.1207/s15326985ep4103_3.

LaBerge, D., & Samuels, S. J. (1974). Toward a theory of automatic information processing in reading. *Cognitive Psychology, 6,* 293–323. https://doi.org/10.1016/0010-0285(74)90015-2.

Lado, R. (1957). *Linguistics across cultures: Applied linguistics for language teachers.* Ann Arbor: University of Michigan Press.

Lam, K., Chen, X., Geva, E., Luo, Y. C., & Li, H. (2012). The role of morphological awareness in reading achievement among young Chinese-speaking English language learners: A longitudinal study. *Reading and Writing, 25*(8), 1847–1872. https://doi.org/10.1007/s11145-011-9329-4.

LaRusso, M., Kim, H, Y., Selman, R., Uccelli, P., Dawson, T., Jones, S., Donovan, D., & Snow, C. (2016). Contributions of academic language, perspective taking, and complex reasoning to deep reading comprehension. *Journal of Research on Educational Effectives, 9*(2), 201–222. https://doi.org/10.1080/19345747.2015.1116035.

Lesaux, N. K., & Kieffer, M. J. (2010). Exploring sources of reading comprehension difficulties among language minority learners and their classmates in early adolescence. *American Educational Research Journal, 47*(3), 596–632. https://doi.org/10.3102/0002831209355469.

Lesaux, N. K., Lipka, O., & Siegel, L. S. (2006). Investigating cognitive and linguistic abilities that influence the reading comprehension skills of children from diverse linguistic backgrounds. *Reading and Writing, 19*(1), 99–131. https://doi.org/10.1007/s11145-005-4713-6.

Lesaux, N. K., Rupp, A. A., & Siegel, L. S. (2007). Growth in reading skills of children from diverse linguistic backgrounds: Findings from a 5-year longitudinal study. *Journal of Educational Psychology, 99,* 821–834. https://doi.org/10.1037/0022-0663.99.4.821.

Lesaux, N., & Geva, E. (2006). Synthesis: Development of literacy in language-minority students. In D. August & T. Shanahan (Eds.), *Developing literacy in second-language learners: Report of the National Literacy Panel on language-minority children and youth* (pp. 53–74). Mahwah, NJ: Erlbaum.

Lesaux, N., & Siegel, L. S. (2003). The development of reading in children who speak English as a second language (ESL). *Developmental Psychology, 39,* 1005–1019. https://doi.org/10.1037/0012-1649.39.6.1005.

Li, M., & Kirby, J. R. (2014). Unexpected poor comprehenders among adolescent ESL students. *Scientific Studies of Reading, 18*(2), 75–93. https://doi.org/10.1080/10888438.2013.775130.

Li, T., McBride-Chang, C., Wong, A. M.-Y., & Shu, H. (2012). Longitudinal predictors of spelling and reading comprehension in Chinese as an L1 and English as an L2 in Hong Kong Chinese children. *Journal of Educational Psychology, 104*(2), 286–301. https://doi.org/10.1037/a0026445.

Limbos, M. J., & Geva, E. (2001). Accuracy of teacher assessments of second-language students at risk for reading disability. *Journal of Learning Disabilities, 34,* 136–151. https://doi.org/10.1177/002221940103400204.

Lindsey, K. A., Manis, F. R., & Bailey, C. E. (2003). Prediction of first-grade reading in Spanish-speaking English-language learners. *Journal of Educational Psychology, 95,* 482–494. https://doi.org/10.1037/0022-0663.95.3.482.

Linan-Thompson, S., Vaughn, S., Prater, K., & Cirino, P. (2006). The response to intervention of English language learners at risk for reading problems. *Journal of Learning Disabilities, 39*(5), 390–398. https://doi.org/10.1177/00222194060390050201.

Lipka, O., & Siegel, L. S. (2012). The development of reading comprehension skills in children learning English as a second language. *Reading and Writing, 25*(8), 1873–1898. https://doi.org/10.1007/s11145-011-9309-8.

Lipka, O., Siegel, L. S., & Vukovic, R. (2005). The literacy skills of english language learners in Canada. *Learning Disabilities Research & Practice, 20,* 39–49. https://doi.org/10.1111/j.1540-5826.2005.00119.x.

Lovett, W. M., De Palma, M., Frijters, J., Steinbach, K., Temple, M., Benson, N., et al. (2008). Interventions for reading difficulties a comparison of response to intervention by ELL and EFL struggling readers. *Journal of Learning Disabilities, 41,* 333–352. https://doi.org/10.1177/0022219408317850

Lyon, G. R. (1995). Toward a definition of dyslexia. *Annals of Dyslexia, 45,* 3–27. https://doi.org/10.1007/BF02648210.

Marinova-Todd, S., Zhao, J., & Bernhardt, M. (2010). Phonological awareness skills in the two languages of Mandarin-English bilingual children. *Clinical Linguistics & Phonetics, 4–5,* 387–400. https://doi.org/10.3109/02699200903532508.

Mascheretti, S., Facoetti, A., Giorda, R., Beri, S., Riva, V., Trezzi, V., et al. (2015). GRIN2B mediates susceptibility to intelligence quotient and cognitive impairments in developmental dyslexia. *Psychiatric Genetics, 25,* 9–20. https://doi.org/10.1097/YPG.0000000000000068.

McBride-Chang, C., Liu, P. D., Wong, T., Wong, A., & Shu, H. (2012). Specific reading difficulties in Chinese, English, or both: Longitudinal markers of phonological aware-ness, morphological awareness, and RAN in Hong Kong Chinese children. *Journal of Learning Disabilities, 45*(6), 503–514. https://doi.org/10.1177/0022219411400748.

Nagy, W. E., García, G. E., Durgunoğlu, A. Y., & Hancin-Bhatt, B. (1993). Spanish-English bilingual students' use of cognates in English reading. *Journal of Reading Behavior, 25,* 241–259. https://doi.org/10.1080/10862969009547816.

Nakamoto, J., Lindsey, K., & Manis, F. (2007). A longitudinal analysis of English language learners word decoding and reading comprehension. *Reading and Writing, 20,* 691–719. https://doi.org/10.1007/s11145-006-9045-7.

Nakamoto, J., Lindsey, K., & Manis, F. (2008). A cross-linguistic investigation of English language learners' reading comprehension in English and Spanish. *Scientific Studies of Reading, 12,* 351–371. https://doi.org/10.1080/10888430802378526.

Nakamura, P., Koda, K., & Joshi, M. (2014). Biliteracy acquisition in Kannada and English: A developmental study. *Writing System Research, 6,* 132–147. https://doi.org/10.1080/17586801.2013.855620.

Oakhill, J. V., & Cain, K. (2012). The precursors of reading ability in young readers: Evidence from a four-year longitudinal study. *Scientific Studies of Reading, 16,* 91–121. https://doi.org/10.1080/10888438.2010.529219.

Organisation for Economic Co-operation and Development. (2010). *Closing the gap for immigrant students: Policies, practice and performance.* Paris, France: OECD.

Pacton, S., & Deacon, S. H. (2008). The timing and mechanisms of children's use of morphological information in spelling: A review of evidence from French and English. *Cognitive Development, 23,* 339–359. https://doi.org/10.1016/j.cogdev.2007.09.004.

Pasquarella, A., Chen, X., Lam, K., Luo, Y., & Ramírez, G. (2011). Cross-language transfer of morphological awareness in Chinese-English bilinguals. *Journal of Research in Reading, 34,* 23–42. https://doi.org/10.1111/j.1467-9817.2010.01484.x.

Pasquarella, A., Grant, A., & Gottardo, A. (2012). Comparing factors related to reading comprehension in adolescents who speak English as a first (L1) or second (L2) language. *Scientific Studies of Reading, 16,* 475–500. https://doi.org/10.1080/10888438.2011.593066.

Perfetti, C. (1985). *Reading ability.* New York: Oxford University Press. https://doi.org/10.1080/10888430701530730.

Phakiti, A., Hirsh, D., & Woodrow, L. (2013). It's not only English: Effects of other individual factors on English language learning and academic learning of ESL international students in Australia. *Journal of Research in International Education, 12,* 239–258. https://doi.org/10.1177/1475240913513520.

Prior, A., Goldina, A., Shany, M., Geva, E., & Katzir, T..(2014). Lexical inference in L2: Predictive roles of vocabulary knowledge and reading skill beyond reading comprehension. *Reading and Writing.* https://doi.org/10.1007/s11145-014-9501-8.

Proctor, C. P., & Mo, E. (2009). The relationship between cognate awareness and English com-prehension among Spanish-English bilingual fourth grade students. *TESOL Quarterly, 43*(1), 126–136. https://doi.org/10.1002/j.1545-7249.2009.tb00232.x.

Proctor, C. P., Carlo, M., August, D., & Snow, C. (2005). Native Spanish-speaking children reading in English: Toward a model of comprehension. *Journal of Educational Psychology, 97,* 246–256. https://doi.org/10.1037/0022-0663.97.2.246.

Quiroga, T., Lemos-Britton, Z., Mostafapour, E., Abbott, R. D., & Berninger, V. W. (2002). Phonological awareness and beginning reading in Spanish-speaking ESL first graders: Research into practice. *Journal of School Psychology, 41,* 85–111. https://doi.org/10.1016/S0022-4405(01)00095-4.

Rack, J. P., Snowling, M. J., & Olson, R. K. (1992). The nonword reading deficit in developmental dyslexia: A review. *Reading Research Quarterly, 27,* 29–53. https://doi.org/10.2307/747832.

Ramírez, G., Chen, X., Geva, E., & Kiefer, H. (2010). Morphological awareness in Spanish-English bilingual children: Within and cross-language effects on word reading. *Reading and Writing: An Interdisciplinary Journal, 23,* 337–358. https://doi.org/10.1007/s11145-009-9203-9.

Ramírez, G., Chen, X., Geva, E., & Luo, Y. (2011). Morphological awareness and word reading in English language learners: Evidence from Spanish- and Chinese-speaking children. *Applied Psycholinguistics, 32,* 601–618. https://doi.org/10.1017/S0142716411000233.

Reed, J. C. (1970). The deficits of retarded readers: Fact or artifact? *The Reading Teacher, 23*(4), 347–352.

Roessingh, H., & Kover, P. (2003). Variability of ESL learners' acquisition of cognitive academic language proficiency: What can we learn from achievement measures? *TESL Canada Journal, 21,* 1–21. http://doi.org/10.18806/tesl.v21i1.271.

Roman, A. A., Kirby, J. R., Parrila, R. K., Wade-Woolley, L., & Deacon, S. H. (2009). Toward a comprehensive view of the skills involved in word reading in Grades 4, 6, and 8. *Journal of Experimental Child Psychology, 102,* 96–113. https://doi.org/10.1016/j.jecp.2008.01.004.

Royer, J. M., & Carlo, M. S. (1991). Transfer of comprehension skills from native to second language. *Journal of Reading, 3,* 450–455.

Saiegh-Haddad, E., & Geva, E. (2008). Morphological awareness, phonological awareness, and reading in English-Arabic bilingual children. *Reading and Writing: An Interdisciplinary Journal, 21*(5), 481–504. https://doi.org/10.1007/s11145-007-9074-x.

Saiegh-Haddad, E., & Geva, E. (2010). Acquiring reading in two languages: An introduction to the special issue. *Reading and Writing, 23,* 263–267. https://doi.org/10.1007/s11145-009-9208-4.

Schiff, R., & Calif, S. (2007). Role of phonological and morphological awareness in L2 oral word reading. *Language Learning, 57,* 271–298. https://doi.org/10.1111/j.1467-9922.2007.00409.x.

Schoonen, R., Hulstijn, J., & Bossers, B. (1998). Metacognitive and language-specific knowledge in native and foreign language reading comprehension: An empirical study among Dutch students in grades 6, 8 and 10. *Language Learning, 48,* 71–106. https://doi.org/10.1111/1467-9922.00033.

Schwartz, M., & Shaul, Y. (2013). Narrative development among language-minority children: The role of bilingual versus monolingual preschool education. *Language, Culture and Curriculum, 26,* 36–51. https://doi.org/10.1080/07908318.2012.760568.

Seymour, P. H., Aro, M., & Erskine, J. M. (2003). Foundation literacy acquisition in Euro-pean orthographies. *British Journal of Psychology, 94,* 143–174. https://doi.org/10.1348/000712603321661859.

Shanahan, T., & Beck, I. (2006). Effective literacy teaching for English-language learners. In D. August & T. Shanahan (Eds.), *Developing literacy in second-language learners: A report of the National Literacy Panel on language-minority children and youth* (pp. 415–488). Mahwah, NJ: Erlbaum.

Shaywitz, S. E., & Shaywitz, B. A. (2005). Dyslexia (specific reading disability). *Biological Psy-chiatry, 57*(11), 1301–1309. https://doi.org/10.1016/j.biopsych.2005.01.043.

Siegel, L. S. (1992). An evaluation of the discrepancy definition of dyslexia. *Journal of Learning Disabilities, 25*(10), 618–629. https://doi.org/10.1177/002221949202501001.

Snow, C. E., Burns, M. S., & Griffin, P. (Eds.). (1998). *Preventing reading difficulties in young children*. Washington, DC: National Academies Press.

Snow, C. E., & Dickinson, D. K. (1990). Social sources of narrative skills at home and at school. *First Language, 10*, 87–103. https://doi.org/10.1177/014272379001002901

Solari, E. J., Aceves, T. C., Higareda, I., Richards-Tutor, C., Filippini, A. L., Gerber, M. M., et al. (2014). Longitudinal prediction of 1st and 2nd grade English oral reading fluency in English language learners: Which early reading and language skills are better predictors? *Psychology in the Schools, 51*, 126–142. https://doi.org/10.1002/pits.21743.

Stahl, S. A., & Nagy, W. E. (2006). *Teaching word meanings*. Mahwah, NJ: Erlbaum.

Stanovich, K. E., & West, R. F. (1989). Exposure to print and orthographic processing. *Reading Research Quarterly, 21*, 360–407. https://doi.org/10.2307/747605.

Storch, S. A., & Whitehurst, G. J. (2002). Oral language and code-related precursors to reading: Evidence from a longitudinal structural model. *Developmental Psychology, 38*(6), 934. https://doi.org/10.1037/0012-1649.38.6.934.

Stuebing, K. K., Barth, A. E., Cirino, P. T., Francis, D. J., & Fletcher, J. M. (2008). A response to recent re-analyses of the National Reading Panel report: Effects of systematic phonics instruction are practically significant. *Journal of Educational Psychology, 100*, 123–134. https://doi.org/10.1037/0022-0663.100.1.123.

Sun-Alperin, M. K., & Wang, M. (2011). Cross-language transfer of phonological and orthographic processing skills from Spanish L1 to English L2. *Reading and Writing: An Interdisciplinary Journal, 24*, 591–614. https://doi.org/10.1007/s11145-009-9221-7.

Swanson, H. L., & Lussier, C. M. (2001). A selective synthesis of the experimental literature on dynamic assessment. *Review of Educational Research, 71*(2), 321–363. https://doi.org/10.3102/00346543071002321.

Swanson, H. L., Rosston, K., Gerber, M., & Solari, E. (2008). Influence of oral language and phonological awareness on children's bilingual reading. *Journal of School Psychology, 46*(4), 413–429. https://doi.org/10.1016/j.jsp.2007.07.002.

Tannock, R. (2013). Rethinking ADHD and LD in *DSM-5*: Proposed changes in diagnostic criteria. *Journal of Learning Disabilities, 46*, 5–25. https://doi.org/10.1177/0022219412464341.

Thomas, W. P., & Collier, V. (1997). *School effectiveness for language minority students* (NCBE Resource Collection Series, No. 9). Washington, DC: National Clearinghouse for Bilingual Education.

U.S. Department of Education. (2006). *Effective literacy and English language instruction for English learners in the elementary grades*. Retrieved from http://ies.ed.gov/ncee/wwc/Docs/PracticeGuide/20074011.pdf.

United Nations Educational, Scientific and Cultural Organization (UNESCO). (2005). *Guidelines for inclusion: Ensuring access to education for all*. Paris, France: United Nations Educational, Scientific and Cultural Organization. Retrieved from http://unesdoc.unesco.org/images/0014/001402/140224e.pdf.

Vellutino, F. R., Fletcher, J. M., Snowling, M. J., & Scanlon, D. M. (2004). Specific reading disability (dyslexia): What have we learned in the past four decades? *Journal of Child Psychology and Psychiatry, 45*(1), 2–40. https://doi.org/10.1046/j.0021-9630.2003.00305.x.

Verhoeven, L. (2000). Components in early second language reading and spelling. *Scientific Studies of Reading, 4*, 313–330. https://doi.org/10.1207/S1532799XSSR0404_4.

Verhoeven, L., & van Leeuwe, J. (2012). The simple view of second language reading throughout the primary grades. *Reading and Writing, 25*, 1805–1818. https://doi.org/10.1007/s11145-011-9346-3.

Wade-Woolley, L., & Geva, E. (2000). Processing novel phonemic contrasts in the acquisition of L2 word reading. *Scientific Studies of Reading, 4*, 295–311. https://doi.org/10.1207/S1532799XSSR0404_3.

Wagner, R. K., & Torgesen, J. K. (1987). The nature of phonological processing and its causal role in the acquisition of reading skills. *Psychological Bulletin, 101*(2), 192–212. https://doi.org/10.1037/0033-2909.101.2.192.

Wagner, R., Torgesen, J., & Rashotte, C. (1994). Development of reading-related phonological processing abilities: New evidence of bidirectional causality from a latent variable longitudinal study. *Developmental Psychology, 30*(1), 73–87. https://doi.org/10.1037/0012-1649.30.1.73.

Wang, M., & Geva, E. (2003). Spelling acquisition of novel English phonemes in Chinese children. *Reading and Writing, 16,* 325–348. https://doi.org/10.1023/A:1023661927929.

Wang, M., Park, Y., & Lee, K. R. (2006). Korean-English biliteracy acquisition: Cross-language phonological and orthographic transfer. *Journal of Educational Psychology, 98,* 148–158. https://doi.org/10.1037/0022-0663.98.1.148.

Wang, M., Perfetti, C. A., & Liu, Y. (2005). Chinese-English biliteracy acquisition: Cross-language and writing system transfer. *Cognition, 97,* 67–88. https://doi.org/10.1016/j.cognition.2004.10.001.

Wechsler Intelligence Scale for Children (WISC)

Wise, N., & Chen, X. (2010). At-risk readers in French immersion: Early identification and early intervention. *Canadian Journal of Applied Linguistics, 13,* 128–149.

Wolf, M., & Bowers, P. (1999). The double-deficit hypothesis for the developmental dyslexias. *Journal of Educational Psychology, 91*(3), 415–438. https://doi.org/10.1037/0022-0663.91.3.415.

Wolf, M., & Katzir-Cohen, T. (2001). Reading fluency and its intervention. *Scientific Studies of Reading, 5*(3), 211–239. https://doi.org/10.1207/S1532799XSSR0503_2.

Yaghoub-Zadeh, Z., Farnia, F., & Geva, E. (2012). Toward modeling reading development in young English as second language learners. *Reading and Writing: An Interdisciplinary Journal, 25,* 163–187. https://doi.org/10.1007/s11145-010-9252-0.

Yopp, H. K. (1992). Developing phonemic awareness in young children. *The Reading Teacher, 45*(9), 696–703.

Zehler, A. M., Fleischman, H. L., Hopstock, P. J., Pendzick, M. L., & Stephenson, T. G. (2003). *Descriptive study of services to LEP students and LEP students with disabilities* (Special Topic Report #4). Minnesota: National Center on Educational Outcomes.

Zhang, D., Koda, K., & Sun, X. (2014). Morphological awareness in biliteracy acquisition: A study of young Chinese EFL readers. *International Journal of Bilingualism, 18*(6), 570–585. https://doi.org/10.1177/1367006912450953.

Ziegler, J. C., & Goswami, U. (2005). Reading acquisition, developmental dyslexia, and skilled reading across languages: A psycholinguistic grain size theory. *Psychological Bulletin, 131*(1), 3–29. https://doi.org/10.1037/0033-2909.131.1.3.

Part II
Assessment and Intervention

Chapter 7
The Identification of Reading Disabilities

Jeremy Miciak and Jack M. Fletcher

Abstract The criteria for identification of a specific learning disability (SLD) as outlined by a consensus group convened by the Office of Special Education Programs in the US Department of Education are discussed. Next, a hybrid approach to assessment is explained that puts a focus on assessments that inform instruction within a multi-tiered system of support. Measurement issues and challenges are described, as are methods for identifying SLD which, despite their common use in practice, lack validity. Finally, a set of operating principles designed to improve the reliability of diagnostic decisions are recommended.

All struggling readers require explicit and comprehensive interventions that are differentiated according to their relative strengths and weaknesses in component skills and delivered with sufficient intensity, regardless of whether they have been formally identified with a reading disability (RD). Thus, the RD special education identification process should not be utilized as a gateway for remedial instruction only for students who qualify, or as a process of sorting struggling readers into groups based on historic approaches based on outmoded concepts of aptitude and discrepancy. Instead, the RD identification process has two goals: (1) to inform instruction and (2) to determine if curriculum and assessment adaptations and legal protections are necessary. Among these objectives, the pre-eminence of instructional planning is illustrated through an example: No combination of assessment and curriculum adaptations and modifications in isolation will help a child struggling with reading learn to read—the student will require *instruction*; differentiated, explicit instruction in reading and reading-related skills is the only evidence-based treatment for RD.

J. Miciak (✉) · J. M. Fletcher
University of Houston, Houston, TX, USA
e-mail: Jeremy.Miciak@times.uh.edu

J. M. Fletcher
e-mail: jmfletch@Central.uh.edu

© Springer Nature Switzerland AG 2019   159
D. A. Kilpatrick et al. (eds.), *Reading Development and Difficulties*,
https://doi.org/10.1007/978-3-030-26550-2_7

7.1 Assessment for Instruction

To ensure a valid RD identification process, we must consider aspects of the identification process beyond test selection and decision making. Modern validity theory posits that validity is not an inherent attribute of a test or procedure. Instead, validity must be considered holistically as an evaluation of the information, procedures, and decisions we make, as well as the consequences of those decisions (Messick, 1987). With this in mind, the discussion surrounding the identification of RD must move beyond issues of classification and eligibility and toward processes that help children become better readers. Recommendations of this type are often associated with the implementation of multi-tier systems of support (MTSS) service delivery systems and with evaluations of instructional response. However, the fundamental importance of explicit instruction must be recognized regardless of the specific criteria and process a school or district wishes to employ. This is because the primary goal of identification is not simply eligibility. The primary goal is improved treatment of persistent reading difficulties. Funds spent on eligibility subtract from funds available for intervention (Glutting, Watkins, & Youngstrom, 2003; MacMillian & Siperstein, 2002). Therefore, formal testing implemented as part of the identification process should be limited to only those tests that will inform future intervention (i.e., the formulation of an effective *individualized education program* [IEP]). This approach to RD identification results in a comprehensive evaluation that is less time consuming and informs intervention because it focuses on the direct assessment of academic skills and instructional response (Fletcher, Lyons, Fuchs, & Barnes, 2018).

A consensus group convened by the Office of Special Education Programs in the Department of Education recommended three essential criteria for the identification of specific learning disabilities (SLD), among which RD would be the most common domain (Bradley, Danielson, & Hallahan, 2002). The comprehensive evaluation to identify SLD must document three criteria:

(1) the student demonstrates low achievement in at least one of the eight domains for SLD eligibility;
(2) the student has demonstrated an inadequate instructional response to generally effective, evidence-based instruction that was implemented with appropriate fidelity and dosage;
(3) the team considered and ruled out exclusionary factors specified in federal law, including that low achievement is primarily due to intellectual disabilities, sensory deficits, serious emotional disturbances, a lack of opportunity to learn, or language minority status where low achievement is due to lack of proficiency in English. Perhaps more important as part of a comprehensive evaluation, contextual factors and other disorders that co-occur with SLD need to be addressed in a treatment plan and must be evaluated a case-by-case basis.

These essential criteria for SLD identification apply to all methods of identification, including methods premised on the identification of a cognitive discrepancy or methods that rely on data generated within an MTSS service delivery system. In the sections that follow, we provide recommendations for the documentation of each of these criteria as part of an RD identification process with special attention to how the data collected as part of the RD identification process can inform future instruction. We call this *assessment for instruction* and present it as a hybrid approach for RD identification, as it incorporates data from standardized assessments, measures of instructional response, and a consideration of contextual factors that impact learning. This approach represents the foundation of a valid and fair RD identification process (Fletcher et al., 2018).

7.1.1   Criterion 1: Low Achievement

It is a common misconception that standardized assessments have no role in RD identification processes that rely, in part, on data generated within an MTSS framework. We recommend assessment of current academic functioning in all areas of suspected difficulties with a norm-referenced assessment because it provides valuable information for instruction and eligibility. A short assessment of current achievement levels and individual strengths and weaknesses in reading, math, and writing provides valuable data for the development of an IEP, particularly in achievement areas and grades for which curriculum-based measures (CBM) are not well established (Ardoin, Christ, Morena, Cormier, & Klingbeil, 2013). Some argue that the administration of norm-referenced achievement tests is not necessary because there exist sufficient school-based data on referred students' academic achievement to document low achievement (Kovaleski, VanDerHeyden, & Shapiro, 2013). However, the comprehensive evaluation for special education eligibility is often the first formal evaluation of achievement for the student across all domains and subdomains of academic achievement. Proponents of methods based on intervention response often argue that CBM data are sufficient to demonstrate low achievement and inadequate response to intervention. In fact, CBMs may be slightly less reliable than many norm-referenced tests and do not provide a comprehensive picture of the student's skills within a specific domain (e.g., basic reading, reading fluency, and comprehension; Barth et al., 2008; Fletcher et al., 2014). Further, important educational decisions such as special education eligibility should never be based on a single test or criterion; multiple data are always required. Thus, even when employing a method based on the identification of inadequate response to intervention, we recommend that the IEP team use data from both CBM and norm-referenced assessments because it will result in a more reliable identification process and because the use of multiple data is required in many states.

The use of norm-referenced achievement tests allows for an efficient assessment of individual performance across the six academic domains of potential SLDs identified in IDEA. Even if a student is referred due to specific concerns about difficulties in reading, it is critical to comprehensively assess performance across all achievement domains and rule out co-occurring difficulties in math or writing, as students with RD are at elevated risk for difficulties in other domains (Kovas et al., 2007;

Landerl & Moll, 2010). The assessment process should always address both foundational and higher-order skills. In each domain (e.g., reading, math, writing), the goal
is to provide accurate data on students' strengths and weaknesses so that their subsequent instruction and interventions can leverage strengths and target weaknesses.
Additionally, it is important to consider automaticity in foundational skills since the
inability to work quickly may require adaptations in classroom instruction and provide directions for future intervention (Geary & Hoard, 2002; Kuhn, Schwanenflugel,
& Meisinger, 2010). All of these data can be collected quickly and efficiently through
a single, well-designed achievement battery (see Table 7.1 for common examples) or
some combination of subtests from different standardized achievement tests. However, we would suggest caution in the construction of extensive assessment batteries
that rely on different subtests from different tests. First, the different normative bases
for different standardized tests are a significant source of unreliability (Fletcher et al.,
2014). Second, one goal of any assessment process should be to minimize the time
spent testing. Instructional time is a finite resource and should be valued.

Table 7.1 Overview of common achievement tests by achievement construct

Construct	Woodcock—Johnson IV	Wechsler individual achievement test III	Kaufman test of educational achievement III
Reading			
Word recognition	Word identification	Word reading	Letter and word recognition
	Word attack	Pseudoword decoding	Nonsense word decoding
Reading fluency	Word reading fluency	Oral reading fluency	Silent reading fluency
	Sentence reading fluency		Word recognition fluency
			Decoding fluency
Reading comprehension	Passage comprehension	Reading comprehension	Reading comprehension
Math			
Math computations	Calculation	Numerical operations	Computation
Math problem solving	Applied problems	Problem solving	Concepts and applications
Writing			
Written expression	Spelling	Spelling	Spelling
Supplemental tests			
Math fluency	Math facts fluency	Math fluency	Math fluency
Writing fluency	Sentence writing fluency	Alphabet writing fluency	Writing fluency
Written expression	Writing samples	Writing composition	Written expression

Reading. Under IDEA 2004, students can be identified with SLD in reading in three domains: basic reading, reading fluency, and reading comprehension. Problems in basic reading are indicated by trouble with reading words accurately and fluently. Students with problems in basic reading are also likely to demonstrate difficulties in spelling. Students with specific problems with reading fluency may read accurately, but slowly. In most cases, this dysfluency also impacts reading comprehension. However, some students may not demonstrate problems with reading words or text accurately and fluently but still may struggle to understand what they read. These students may have specific reading comprehension difficulties. Although it is tempting to identify and treat a single domain of reading difficulty, it is important to recognize that most students with reading difficulties demonstrate deficits in all three domains and will require comprehensive interventions across domains.

Word recognition accuracy. Most normative assessments include subtests that require the untimed oral reading of isolated real words and pseudowords (phonetically regular non-words). These tests assess students' sight-word knowledge and the ability to decode print. Tests of word reading accuracy are often the best single predictor of overall academic achievement and are vital for the identification of dyslexia (Vellutino, Fletcher, Snowling, & Scanlon, 2004), which is defined by problems reading and spelling words accurately and fluently in isolation (International Dyslexia Association, 2002).

Reading fluency. There are many quick, efficient assessments of reading fluency and most norm-referenced assessments of academic achievement now include a reading fluency subtest. These subtests may vary in format, for example, some require the students to read single words aloud accurately and fluently, while others may require the student to read the connected text (i.e., sentences and/or paragraphs) aloud. Each of these assessment formats is acceptable and provides an important indicator of how efficiently the student is able to read the text. The key to each of these formats is that the student reads text aloud quickly and accurately so that fluency can be measured in terms of words read correctly per minute. Some fluency assessments are hybrid fluency and comprehension tasks, in which the student must silently read text and process it, for example, by telling whether the sentence read is true or false. These assessments also measure fluency, but combine comprehension skills and should not be understood as pure measures of either reading fluency or reading comprehension.

Reading comprehension. Reading comprehension represents a complex higher-order skill (see Oakhill, Cain, and Elbro, Chap. 5, this volume). Its complexity creates difficulties for assessment and no single measure should be viewed as a perfect indicator of the student's ability to read and understand the text; different reading comprehension tests will give slightly different scores because of differences in how they assess reading comprehension (Keenan, Betjemann, & Olson, 2008). To account for this variability in tasks, it is important to note the nature of the material the students are asked to read as well as the response format. For example, reading comprehension performance is affected by numerous factors, including: (1) the characteristics of the text read (sentences, short passages, and different genres [narrative, expository]); (2) how the child responds to demonstrate that she understands what she read (cloze, open-ended questions, multiple choice, think aloud); (3) how much she must remember (answering questions with and without the text available); and (4) the complexity of the text and the ideas within (vocabulary elaboration vs. knowledge, inferencing, and activation of background knowledge). If a test contains considerable text that the student cannot read accurately and with fluency, the test is unlikely to isolate comprehension skill and a different test better matched to the student's current reading levels may be necessary. This is one concern about using only state-mandated assessments of reading. Many state-mandated assessments of reading contain grade-level text that is inaccessible to many students with basic reading problems. While these data are valuable in understanding the extent to which a student can do grade-level work, they may not provide as much information about the students' relative strengths across reading domains.

Planning for reading interventions. To the extent possible, data from the comprehensive assessment related to individual skills in word recognition, fluency, and reading comprehension should be used to differentiate instruction in reading. Students with severe reading difficulties across all of these domains will need a comprehensive reading program that includes systematic instruction in foundational reading skills, while students with specific deficits in comprehension may require more text and language-focused interventions. These determinations can be made by planning an assessment that incorporates tests listed in Table 7.1.

Mathematics. There are two eligibility domains in IDEA 2004: calculation (dyscalculia) and problem solving. We recommend that both domains be assessed, even if the primary concern for the referral was related to reading difficulties. This is because reading and reading-related skills (i.e., language, working memory) have a significant influence on mathematics and many students have problems in both reading and math. Measures of math calculation typically include items that range from basic arithmetic to algebra and geometry. Because math computations typically rely on a relatively language-free paper-and-pencil format, it is particularly useful for isolating potential math difficulties in the presence of potential reading and language problems for students with RD. In contrast, problem-solving tests typically involve solving real-life math problems, often in the form of linguistically complex questions that must be read to solve. For students with RD, these sorts of problems are frequently difficult both because of the reading task and the language skills to solve the problems. Basic math computation and fact retrieval difficulties are best addressed through comprehensive math programs that teach procedural knowledge through word problems that build math reasoning and math vocabulary skills (Fuchs et al., 2009). A comprehensive assessment can assist in intervention planning by providing data to guide the amount of time devoted to practicing fact retrieval and basic arithmetic during the problem-solving intervention.

Written Expression. IDEA 2004 specifies a broad category involving written expression, which includes both transcription (handwriting and handwriting fluency) and composition (essay or story writing). Most students with RD also experience difficulties in writing, so it is important for a comprehensive assessment to include an evaluation of individual performance in this domain. Composition and transcription are closely linked; difficulties with handwriting and spelling can affect essay composition (Connelly, Campbell, MacLean, & Barnes, 2006), highlighting the complex and interrelated nature of the writing task. Most norm-referenced tests also include a measure of spelling, which may represent the primary source of difficulty in written expression for many children with word reading difficulties. An analysis of spelling errors may help identify whether the spelling problem is related to underdeveloped phonological awareness or with the student's knowledge of English orthography. Spelling tests, like any writing task, can also be utilized as an informal assessment of handwriting.

Data from these assessments can be utilized to assist in treatment planning. For example, there are well-established methods for teaching transcription (handwriting and spelling). The strongest evidence for programs involving composition is Self-Regulated Strategy Development, which teaches strategies for compositing and editing, along with organizational components (Graham, McKeown, Kiuhara, & Harris, 2012).

7.1.2   Criterion 2: Instructional Response

Prior to IDEA 2004, the documentation of adequate instruction was considered an exclusionary criterion for identification with SLD. That is, the comprehensive assessment was required to specify that the student's academic difficulties were not primarily the result of inadequate instructional opportunity. IDEA 2004 strengthened this requirement by making an inadequate response to instruction an inclusionary criterion necessary for the identification SLD. As a result of this shift, the IDEA 2004 statutes indicate that a student cannot be identified with SLD without documentation that he has received appropriate evidence-based instruction and has responded inadequately to this intervention. These data are required regardless of the identification method employed and do not require the full implementation of a school-wide MTSS. First, data must be presented to document that the student has received evidence-based instruction. These data might include intervention descriptions, data on fidelity of implementation, and dosage (attendance). Inadequate intervention response is most frequently documented through CBMs, which may show limited progress and low achievement following interventions. However, other forms of assessment can also be utilized to document inadequate instructional response, such as grades, high-stakes assessments that are completed in each year, or progress monitoring data that are not collected as part of an MTSS. Although it is possible to collect these data outside a well-articulated MTSS framework, data related to both the adequacy of instruction and instructional response are most efficiently collected in a school-wide MTSS framework that includes universal screening, targeted interventions with attendance and fidelity data, as well as routine progress monitoring. Although identification with SLD is not the primary goal of a school-wide MTSS—improved instruction and student outcomes are always the goals—data routinely collected as part of MTSS can be easily used to satisfy this criterion.

For documenting inadequate instructional response, data from CBMs in reading, math, and spelling are most frequently utilized. CBMs are typically short, timed probes of important academic proficiency indicators. In reading, these indicators may be reading fluency with word lists or connected text, or maze tasks that are thought to relate more closely to reading comprehension. The critical insight of CBM assessment is that the CBM probe does not assess the sum of all reading-related skills a student is expected to master, but instead represents an efficient, easily assessed, general outcome that correlates strongly with more complex reading skills (Deno, 2003). In math, computation fluency CBM may assess fluency with different grade-appropriate calculations on a short, timed assessment. In written expression, timed spelling tests, alphabet writing tests, and other procedures may be employed. As noted above, norm-referenced assessments can also be used to assess skills or age ranges for which there are few or no validated CBM. Whether one uses CBM or a norm-referenced assessment, the critical component for RD identification is the student's level following the intervention (often called a final status model; Fuchs & Deshler, 2007). This is because the information on growth is contained in the end point following intervention—different end points are achieved only by observing differential growth during intervention for students with similar reading difficulties (Schatschneider, Wagner, & Crawford, 2008). For modifying instruction, the slope is very important because it allows for timely adjustments (Fletcher et al., 2018).

7.1.3   Criterion 3: Contextual Factors

Academic difficulties have many potential causes; some of these potential causes are explicitly listed as exclusionary criteria for SLD identification in IDEA 2004. For example, it is critical to consider whether another disability may be the primary cause of academic difficulties, such as a sensory problem, intellectual disability, or another pervasive disturbance of cognition, like autism spectrum disorder. These disorders each have specific identification criteria and will require interventions that address a much broader range of skills than the narrow impairment in adaptive skills that typically characterize SLD. Additionally, the IEP team should consider whether contextual factors that may interfere with achievement, such as limited English proficiency, co-morbid behavioral problems, and/or economic disadvantage may be the primary cause of low achievement. The goal of this part of the comprehensive assessment is to determine, to the extent possible, whether these contextual factors may represent the primary cause of low achievement or a co-morbid condition. Such questions are not easily answered, but addressing them may assist in planning for interventions that are maximally effective. For example, if the team determined that inadequate instructional opportunity due to persistent absences is the most likely cause of academic difficulties, an appropriate intervention plan would directly address school attendance *in addition to* academic interventions. For children with ADHD, it is important that the intervention plan addresses both attention and academic difficulties (Tamm et al., 2017). Anxiety might also limit the effectiveness of stand-alone academic interventions, with Grills-Taquechel et al. (2013) reporting that many Grade 1 students who are inadequate responders have elevated anxiety levels on self-report anxiety measures. If a child is struggling to read and exhibits high levels of anxiety, a treatment program that addresses both reading and anxiety is critical. The critical consideration in assessing all of these contextual factors is how to improve the effectiveness of the intervention program.

Limited English proficiency is another issue that must be considered when identifying SLD and particularly RD as many students with RD demonstrate language deficits (Geva, Xi, Massey-Garrison, & Mak, Chap. 6, this volume). Children who grow up in households in which the home language is different from the language of instruction are at greater risk for academic difficulties, primarily due to the difficulties associated with mastering academic content while learning a second language. Yet, there are no clear criteria or assessments that would differentiate a child with achievement difficulties due to RD from a child who demonstrates limited English proficiency and has trouble reading. Depending on resources and instructional context, it may be helpful to include assessments of oral language proficiency and achievement in both English and the student's home language. However, these results must be interpreted with caution and careful attention to the individual's language exposure. For example, many English learners attend English-only classrooms and have not received academic instruction in their first language. Parsing the interconnected issues of academic difficulties and language proficiency takes careful consideration, to ensure that a student is not identified as RD simply because she lacks the English proficiency to perform well on achievement tests in English (see Geva et al., Chap. 6, this volume).

To address all potential exclusionary factors and better plan for intervention, the comprehensive assessment process should routinely include parent and teacher rating scales of behavior and academic adjustment, along with parent-completed developmental and medical history forms. These scales may identify co-occurring behavior problems and historical factors (e.g., history of brain trauma) that are important to screen. If there is evidence for behavioral co-morbidity, the guidelines for identifying these disorders in the Diagnostic and Statistical Manual of the American Psychiatric Association, Fifth Edition (DSM-5), should be followed. Simply referring a child for educational interventions without identifying and treating these factors will increase the probability of a poor intervention response.

7.2 Evidence for a Hybrid Approach Prioritizing Instruction

7.2.1 Differentiated Instruction Improves Outcomes

There is accumulating evidence that using academic assessment data to differentiate instruction by intensity, group size, dosage, and content can improve student outcomes in reading (Gersten et al., 2008; Roberts, Vaughn, Fletcher, Stuebing, & Barth, 2013). This is particularly true when considering MTSS frameworks that include targeted Tier 2 and Tier 3 interventions addressing student difficulties in increasing levels of intensity. Further, there is evidence that tailoring instruction to match a student's skill profile within reading can improve outcomes in Tier 1 and in targeted Tier 2 and Tier 3 interventions (Connor et al., 2009, 2013). Although evidence for improved student outcomes is not typically offered in support of specific assessments, assessment systems, or approaches to assessment, such evidence is critically important for evaluating the utility and validity of a proposed comprehensive assessment process.

7.2.2   Classifications Based on Instructional Response Are Valid

An additional way to evaluate the utility and validity of a proposed assessment and identification process is to evaluate the underlying classification hypotheses. All classifications are hypotheses about the fundamental attributes of a group. Like any scientific hypothesis, classification hypotheses should be evaluated through empirical research. One critical test for any proposed classification hypothesis is whether the resulting subgroups differ in a meaningful way on external dimensions—that is attributes that are not used to form the groups (Morris & Fletcher, 1988). For example, to evaluate a proposed RD classification, a study should apply the proposed identification criteria and create two subgroups of students: those who meet the criteria and those who do not. To the extent possible, the study should evaluate the most stringent test of the classification hypothesis. For example, when testing the validity of a method premised on the identification of an IQ-achievement discrepancy, the study should compare groups of students with similar reading scores who do and who do not demonstrate an IQ-achievement discrepancy. By controlling for reading level, this contrast directly tests the validity of an IQ-achievement discrepancy as an inclusionary criterion. If the resulting subgroups differ in meaningful ways (e.g., behavior, cognitive attributes, intervention outcomes), we could consider this evidence for the validity of classifications based on an IQ-achievement discrepancy.

There is considerable evidence that RD classifications based on a hybrid approach that prioritizes instruction will identify subgroups of students who differ on meaningful external dimensions. For example, empirical studies suggest that classifications based on differential intervention response result in subgroups of inadequate responders who differ in educationally important ways, including: academic level (Al Otaiba & Fuchs, 2006; Nelson, Benner, & Gonzalez, 2003; Vellutino, Scanlon, Small, & Fanuele, 2006), cognitive characteristics (Fletcher et al., 2011; Miciak, Stuebing et al., 2014), behavior (Al Otaiba & Fuchs, 2006; Nelson et al., 2003), and even brain activation patterns (Molfese, Fletcher, & Denton, 2013; Rezaie et al., 2011).

7.3   Measurement Issues and Challenges to Reliable Identification

7.3.1   The Attributes of RD Are Dimensional

Broadly speaking, there are two types of psychological or health disorders: categorical and dimensional. Categorical disorders represent binary conditions: Either the individual has the disorder, or not. For example, most viral infections are binary conditions. You either have the flu or you do not. However, not all disorders in psychology and health are categorical. Some disorders are dimensional, meaning the disorder is defined through a division of a continuous distribution with no natural demarcation. Obesity is one example of a dimensional disorder. There is no natural threshold that separates individuals who are obese from those who are merely overweight. Instead, clinicians and researchers create thresholds to identify individuals who are obese based on empirical evidence of health outcomes for individuals with similar scores on important metrics, such as weight, height, Body Mass Index (BMI), or direct measurement of body fat. In considering interventions for obesity, a skilled clinician would take into account other factors, such as family history, dietary factors that increase the risk for cardiovascular events, and the individual's performance on other key indicators of health.

Assessing the attributes of RD should be similar. Although researchers once thought that there was a bimodal distribution indicative of a categorical disorder (Rutter & Yule, 1975), more rigorous evaluations of the distribution of attributes of LD find that these attributes are continuously distributed with no natural demarcations. For example, in reading there is no natural line that differentiates students with RD from students without RD who experience reading difficulties (Jorm, Share, Matthews, & Matthews, 1986; Shaywitz, Escobar, Shaywitz, Fletcher, & Makuch, 1992). As in the obesity example, adherence to rigid cut points is inherently problematic. An individual with a BMI of 29.1 is highly similar to an individual with a BMI of 30.1, despite the fact that these individuals fall on opposite sides of the cut point for obesity. Similarly, a student who scores in the 15th percentile in reading comprehension and a student who scores in the 10th percentile are likely very similar, and the difference in their scores may be the result of nothing more than measurement error (Francis et al., 2005). It is likely that the educational needs of these students will be highly similar. As a result, it is important that the IEP team reject the application of strict cut points for decision making and instead think in terms of confidence intervals and a likely range of potential scores.

7.3.2   The Attributes of RD Are Latent Constructs

A latent construct is a theoretical trait that cannot be directly observed or measured. Reading proficiency is a latent construct. It cannot be directly observed, and we can learn nothing about an individual's reading proficiency outside of our attempts to measure behaviors that we believe are theoretically related to the latent construct. In reading, these behaviors include the ability to summarize, answer questions about, or coherently discuss the read text. These behaviors are strong indicators of reading proficiency, but no indicator (test) perfectly measures the latent construct of interest because no reading test measures all aspects of reading proficiency. Some tests will evaluate a subset of skill-related reading proficiency and not assess other skills; others will measure reading proficiency differently. Thus, it is important to remember that all test scores, observations, or rating scales include uncertainty and error. This fact has important implications for the reliability of RD identification decisions at the individual level, as we will see below.

7.3.3   All Methods for Identification Are Unreliable at the Individual Level

All RD identification methods demonstrate limited reliability at the individual level (Fletcher et al., 2014; Francis et al, 2005; Macmann, Barnett, Lombard, Belton-Kocher, & Sharpe, 1989). If formula or rigid cut point is used, a student identified by one method may not be identified with RD using another method, or even another set of tests (Macmann & Barnett, 1985; Taylor, Miciak, Fletcher, & Francis, 2017). This issue of low agreement in who demonstrates RD and who does not is a universal concern when using imperfect tests with fixed cut points. This is true whether the cut point is a score on a reading comprehension test (e.g., a standard score less than 85) or if a cut point on the difference of two scores is utilized (e.g., a discrepancy between IQ and achievement greater than 15). This is because we cannot know where the student's "true score" falls relative to the cut point due to measurement error. Even when testing the same student, different tests or the same tests on different measurement occasions will generate a range of scores. Thus, the IEP team should express the unreliability of the test as the standard error of measurement and specify a confidence interval so that a range of scores could indicate the potential presence of RD. Additionally, the team should incorporate other data that might inform the decision, such as previous academic and classroom performance, grades, observations of the child, and the parent's and teacher's perceptions of the student's performance.

7.4 Alternative Approaches to RD Identification Lack Validity

7.4.1 Aptitude-Achievement Discrepancy

Methods for SLD and RD identification premised on the identification of a discrepancy between the student's ability and her actual achievement have a long history in special education in the USA. In 1977, federal regulations accompanying the Education for All Handicapped Children Act (subsequently renamed the Individuals with Disabilities Education Act) specified that a discrepancy between a student's IQ and achievement must be documented for identification with SLD in any achievement domain, including reading. These methods are premised on the notion that a cognitive discrepancy between aptitude and achievement is a definitional attribute of SLDs, capturing "unexpected underachievement" and differentiating students with SLDs from slow learners and students with expected low achievement (Kavale, Kauffman, Bachmeier, & LeFever, 2008).

Although these methods are technically still allowed under federal law and are permitted in many states, there is little to recommend their adoption. In the decades since their codification in federal regulation, considerable research emerged questioning the basis for classifications based on an IQ-achievement discrepancy (for a review, see Hallahan & Mercer, 2002). Like all methods that rely on the application of strict cut points to psychometric data, numerous studies have illustrated that IQ-achievement discrepancy methods are unreliable for individual identification decisions (Francis et al., 2005; Macmann & Barnett, 1985). However, in contrast to a hybrid method that identifies low achievement and inadequate instructional response, there is little evidence for the validity of classifications based on an IQ-achievement discrepancy. This is because students with low achievement who demonstrate an IQ-achievement discrepancy and students with low achievement who do not demonstrate a discrepancy do not differ in educationally meaningful ways. For example, poor readers with and without a discrepancy demonstrate similar cognitive and behavioral profiles that tend to reflect the severity of their reading impairment and the relation between the cognitive and achievement skills (Hoskyn & Swanson, 2000; Stuebing et al., 2002). Further, long-term outcomes are very similar for students with and without an IQ-achievement discrepancy because they develop reading skills very similarly. This is true even when considering how students will respond to targeted interventions. In a meta-analysis evaluating how well IQ predicts intervention response, Stuebing, Barth, Molfese, Weiss, and Fletcher (2009) found that IQ accounted for almost no unique variance in intervention outcomes. This means that IQ (and therefore IQ-achievement discrepancy) could not be used to predict who would respond and who would not—it contributed no unique information. Finally, in functional neuroimaging studies, Tanaka et al. (2011) and Simos et al. (2014) found no differences in the activation patterns associated with word reading in groups of poor readers divided by the presence or absence of an IQ-achievement discrepancy.

7.4.2   Patterns of Strengths and Weaknesses

In recent years, as dissatisfaction with IQ achievement discrepancy methods has grown, proponents for cognitive discrepancy methods for SLD and RD identification have begun to call for more complex methods premised on the identification of an intra-individual pattern of cognitive processing strengths and weaknesses (PSW methods) as an inclusionary criterion for SLD identification. These methods, often referred to as PSW methods, "Third Way Methods," Cross-Battery Assessment Methods, or by other names, are conceptually consistent, but have been operationally defined in numerous ways. For example, some methods rely on purely ipsative intra-individual comparisons that rely on difference scores between different cognitive and academic skills, while others seek to identify normative strengths and deficits within an individual's cognitive and achievement test results (Flanagan, Ortiz, & Alfonso, 2013; Hale & Fiorello, 2004; Naglieri, 1999). As discussed in previous sections, none of the proposed PSW methods overcomes challenges to reliability at the individual level. Different methods to operationalize PSW criteria will identify different students, with agreement levels between the methods approaching chance agreement (Fletcher, et al., 2014; Miciak et al., 2016). Further, small changes in the tests administered have significant negative effects on the reliability of individual decisions because PSW methods rely on complex comparisons across multiple measures and domains (Taylor et al., 2017).

In addition to universal concerns about the reliability of decisions emerging from PSW methods, there is very little empirical evidence that supports the validity and utility of decisions based on the application of these methods. Research on these methods is just beginning to emerge and even proponents of the methods acknowledge that at this time, there is not sufficient evidence to recommend the adoption of PSW methods (Schneider & Kaufman, 2017). Recent empirical research has also raised significant questions about whether such evidence is likely to emerge. For example, in one notable study, we compared the response to an intensive reading intervention of students who met PSW criteria in reading and students who did not. We found no educationally meaningful differences in how students responded to the intervention, suggesting that students with reading difficulties with and without an intra-individual pattern of strengths and weaknesses are very similar (Miciak et al., 2016). Additionally, the assertions by many PSW proponents that an assessment of cognitive processes is necessary to individually tailor interventions should be weighed against the resounding lack of evidence for the effectiveness of cognitively tailored interventions. Recent literature reviews and meta-analyses conclude that the evidence for aptitude by treatment interactions and cognitively tailored interventions is preliminary at best and does not support widespread adoption (Burns et al., 2016; Kearns & Fuchs, 2013). Moreover, the evidence that cognitive assessments contribute value-added information to the identification or predictive information for intervention response is limited, except in the case of young children with little exposure to instruction (Fletcher & Miciak, 2017).

7.4.3   Recommendations to Improve Reliability for RD Identification

1. *Avoid rigid cut points:* All thresholds and cut points that divide continuous, normally distributed test scores are arbitrary and problematic. There is no natural threshold that would differentiate struggling readers with RD from struggling readers without RD. Students whose scores are similar and who may span an arbitrary cut point for eligibility are likely to be very similar and demonstrate the same educational needs. Thus, IEP teams should avoid making decisions based on the strict application of arbitrary cut points. The educational needs of the student should guide decision making, not formulae or strict numeric criteria.

2. *Utilize multiple data.* The identification of a student with RD should not be based on a single data point. A single test score or criteria is likely to demonstrate significant unreliability. Further, basing decisions on a single data point would not meet statutory requirements that require that a comprehensive assessment includes multiple data.

3. *Utilize confidence intervals:* Confidence intervals are an acknowledgment that all test scores include uncertainty and are reported as a range of plausible values. Instead of applying firm cut points, confidence intervals generate a range of value in which there is a high probability the true score will reside. Identification criteria for other disabilities have moved toward processes that incorporate confidence intervals and clinical judgment. For example, determining levels of IQ for an intellectual disability typically requires the application of the standard error of measurement to create a 95% confidence interval. Since IQ scores two standard deviations below the average of 100 are usually required (i.e., 70 or below), this is expressed as a score between 65 and 75.

4. *Error in provision of intervention:* Although all assessment processes include error and unreliability, the negative effects of this unreliability to students can be mitigated when teams prioritize instructional need in deciding intervention plans. Academic interventions are relatively low cost and can have significant, positive effects on educational trajectories, particularly when provided early.

5. *Use tests with the same normative basis:* One significant source of unreliability in decision making and test interpretation is the use of different norming populations for the calculation of normed standard scores. Because different tests have different norming populations, a specific score will vary according to its relative standing in the norming population. This source of error can be mitigated by using tests that feature the same norming population.

Acknowledgements   This research was supported by Award Number P50 HD052117, Texas Center for Learning Disabilities, from the Eunice Kennedy Shriver National Institute of Child Health and Human Development to the University of Houston. The content is solely the responsibility of the authors and does not necessarily represent the official views of the Eunice Kennedy Shriver National Institute of Child Health and Human Development or the National Institutes of Health.

Additional Resources

Fletcher, J. M., Lyons, G. R., Fuchs, L. S., & Barnes, M. A. (2010). Learning disabilities: From identification to intervention. (2nd ed,). New York, NY: The Guilford Press.
Fletcher, J. M., & Miciak, J. (2017). Comprehensive cognitive assessments are not necessary for the identification and treatment of learning disabilities. *Archives of Clinical Neuropsychology, 32*(1), 2–17.
www.texasldcenter.org.

References

Al Otaiba, S., & Fuchs, D. (2006). Who are the young children for whom best practices in reading are ineffective? An experimental and longitudinal study. *Journal of Learning Disabilities, 39*(5), 414–431.
Ardoin, S. P., Christ, T. J., Morena, L. S., Cormier, D. C., & Klingbeil, D. A. (2013). A systematic review and summarization of the recommendations and research surrounding curriculum-based measurement of oral reading fluency (CBM-R) decision rules. *Journal of School Psychology, 51*(1), 1–18.
Barth, A. E., Stuebing, K. K., Anthony, J. L., Denton, C. A., Mathes, P. G., Fletcher, J. M., et al. (2008). Agreement among response to intervention criteria for identifying responder status. *Learning and Individual Differences, 18*(3), 296–307.
Bradley, R., Danielson, L., & Hallahan, D. P. (Eds.). (2002). *Identification of learning disabilities: Research to practice.* Mahwah, NJ: Erlbaum.
Burns, M. K., Petersen-Brown, S., Haegele, K., Rodriguez, M., Schmitt, B., Cooper, M., et al. (2016). Meta-analysis of academic interventions derived from neuropsychological data. *School Psychology Quarterly, 31*(1), 28–42.
Connelly, V., Campbell, S., MacLean, M., & Barnes, J. (2006). Contribution of lower order skills to the written composition of college students with and without dyslexia. *Developmental Neuropsychology, 29*(1), 175–196.
Connor, C. M., Morrison, F. J., Fishman, B., Crowe, E. C., Al Otaiba, S., & Schatschneider, C. (2013). A longitudinal cluster-randomized controlled study on the accumulating effects of individualized literacy instruction on students' reading from first through third grade. *Psychological Science, 24*(8), 1408–1419.
Connor, C. M., Piasta, S. B., Fishman, B., Glassney, S., Schatschnedier, C., Crowe, E., …& Morrison, F. J. (2009). Individualizing student instruction precisely: Effects of child by instruction interactions on first graders' literacy development. *Child Development, 80*(1), 77–100.
Deno, S. L. (2003). Developments in curriculum-based measurement. *The Journal of Special Education, 37*(3), 184–192.
Flanagan, D. P., Ortiz, S. O., & Alphonso, V. C. (Eds.). (2013). *Essentials of cross-battery assessment* (3rd ed.). Hoboken, NJ: Wiley.
Fletcher, J. M., Lyons, G. R., Fuchs, L. S., & Barnes, M. A. (2018). *Learning disabilities: From identification to intervention.* (2nd ed.). New York, NY: The Guilford Press.
Fletcher, J. M., & Miciak, J. (2017). Comprehensive cognitive assessments are not necessary for the identification and treatment of learning disabilities. *Archives of Clinical Neuropsychology, 32*(1), 2–7.
Fletcher, J. M., Stuebing, K. K., Barth, A. E., Denton, C. A., Cirino, P. T., Francis, D. J., et al. (2011). Cognitive correlates of inadequate response to reading intervention. *School Psychology Review, 40*(1), 3–22.

Fletcher, J. M., Stuebing, K. K., Barth, A. E., Miciak, J., Francis, D. J., & Denton, C. A. (2014). Agreement and coverage of indicators of response to intervention: A multi-method comparison and simulation. *Topics in Language Disorders, 34*(1), 74–89.

Francis, D. J., Fletcher, J. M., Stuebing, K. K., Lyon, G. R., Shaywitz, B. A., & Shaywitz, S. E. (2005). Psychometric approaches to the identification of learning disabilities: IQ and achievement scores are not sufficient. *Journal of Learning Disabilities, 38*, 98–110.

Fuchs, D., & Deshler, D. D. (2007). What we need to know about responsiveness to intervention (and shouldn't be afraid to ask). *Learning Disabilities Research & Practice, 22*(2), 129–136.

Fuchs, L. S., Powell, S. R., Seethaler, P. M., Cirino, P. T., Fletcher, J. M., & Zumeta, R. O. (2009). Remediating number combination and word-problem deficits among students with mathematics difficulties: A randomized control trial. *Journal of Educational Psychology, 101*, 561–576.

Geary, D. C., & Hoard, M. K. (2002). Learning disabilities in basic mathematics. In J. M. Royer (Ed.), *Mathematical cognition* (pp. 93–115). Greenwich, CT: Information Age Publishing.

Gersten, R., Compton, D., Connor, C. M., Dimino, J., Santoro, L., Linan-Thompson, S., & Tilly, W. D. (2008). Assisting students struggling with reading: Response to Intervention and multi-tier intervention for reading in the primary grades. In *A practice guide. (NCEE 2009–4045)*. Washington, DC: National Center for Education Evaluation and Regional Assistance, Institute of Education Sciences, US Department of Education. National Center for Education Evaluation and Regional Assistance, Institute of Education Sciences. Retrieved from http://ies.ed.gov/ncee/wwc/publications/practiceguides.

Graham, S., McKeown, D., Kiuhara, S., & Harris, K. R. (2012). A meta-analysis of writing instruction for students in the elementary grades. *Journal of Educational Psychology, 104*(4), 879–896.

Grills-Taquechel, A. E., Fletcher, J. M., Vaughn, S. R., Denton, C. A., & Taylor, P. (2013). Anxiety and inattention as predictors of achievement in early elementary school children. *Anxiety Stress and Coping, 26*(4), 391–410.

Glutting, J. J., Watkins, M. W., & Youngstrom, E. A. (2003). Multifactored and cross-battery ability assessments: Are they worth the effort? In C. R. Reynolds & R. W. Kamphaus (Eds.), *Handbook of psychological and educational assessment of children: Intelligence, aptitude, and achievement* (pp. 343–374). New York: Guilford Press.

Hale, J. B., & Fiorello, C. A. (2004). *School neuropsychology: A practitioner's handbook*. New York, NY: The Guilford Press.

Hallahan, D. P., & Mercer, C. D. (2002). Learning disabilities: Historical perspectives. In R. Bradley, L. Danielson, & D. P. Hallahan (Eds.), *Identification of learning disabilities: Research to practice* (pp. 1–65). Mahwah, NJ: Lawrence Erlbaum Associates.

Hoskyn, M., & Swanson, H. L. (2000). Cognitive processing of low achievers and children with reading disabilities: A selective meta-analytic review of the published literature. *School Psychology Review, 29*(1), 102–119.

International Dyslexia Association. (2002). *Dyslexia definition consensus project*. Accessed May 10, 2018 at https://dyslexiaida.org/definition-consensus-project/.

Jorm, A. F., Share, D. L., Matthews, M., & Matthews, R. (1986). Cognitive factors at school entry predictive of specific reading retardation and general reading backwardness: A research note. *Journal of Child Psychology, 27*, 45–54.

Kavale, K. A., Kauffman, J. M., Bachmeier, R. J., & LeFever, G. B. (2008). Response-to-intervention: Separating the rhetoric of self-congratulation from the reality of specific learning disability identification. *Learning Disability Quarterly, 31*(3), 135–150.

Kearns, D. M., & Fuchs, D. (2013). Does cognitively focused instruction improve the academic performance of low-achieving students? *Exceptional Children, 79*(3), 263–290.

Keenan, J. M., Betjemann, R. S., & Olson, R. K. (2008). Reading comprehension tests vary in the skills they assess: Differential dependence on decoding and oral comprehension. *Scientific Studies of Reading, 12*(3), 281–300.

Kovaleski, J. F., VanDerHeyden, A. M., & Shapiro, E. S. (2013). *The RTI approach to evaluating learning disabilities*. New York, NY: The Guilford Press.

Kovas, Y., Haworth, C. M., Harlaar, N., Petrill, S. A., Dale, P. S., & Plomin, R. (2007). Overlap and specificity of genetic and environmental influences on mathematics and reading disability in 10-year-old twins. *Journal of Child Psychology and Psychiatry, 48,* 914–922.

Kuhn, M. R., Schwanenflugel, P. J., & Meisinger, E. B. (2010). Aligning theory and assessment of reading fluency: Automaticity, prosody, and definitions of fluency. *Reading Research Quarterly, 45*(2), 230–251.

Landerl, K., & Moll, K. (2010). Comorbidity of learning disorders: Prevalence and familial transmission. *Journal of Child Psychology and Psychiatry, 51*(3), 287–294.

Macmann, G. M., & Barnett, D. W. (1985). Discrepancy score analysis: A computer simulation of classification stability. *Journal of Psychoeducational Assessment, 4,* 363–375.

Macmann, G. M., Barnett, D. W., Lombard, T. J., Belton-Kocher, E., & Sharpe, M. N. (1989). On the actuarial classification of children: Fundamental studies of classification agreement. *The Journal of Special Education, 23*(2), 127–149.

MacMillan, D. L., & Siperstein, G. N. (2002). Learning disabilities as operationally defined by schools. In R. Bradley, L. Danielson, & D. Hallahan (Eds.), *Identification of learning disabilities: Research to practice* (pp. 287–333). Mahwah NJ: Erlbaum.

Messick, S. (1987). Validity. *ETS Research Report Series, 1987*(2). Princeton, NJ: ETS.

Miciak, J., Fletcher, J. M., Stuebing, K. K., Vaughn, S., & Tolar, T. D. (2014). Patterns of cognitive strengths and weaknesses: Identification rates, agreement, and validity for learning disabilities identification. *School Psychology Quarterly, 29,* 21–37.

Miciak, J., Stuebing, K. K., Vaughn, S., Roberts, G., Barth, A. E., & Fletcher, J. M. (2014). Cognitive attributes of adequate and inadequate responders to reading intervention in middle school. *School Psychology Review, 43*(4), 407–427.

Miciak, J., Williams, J. L., Taylor, W. P., Cirino, P. T., Fletcher, J. M., & Vaughn, S. (2016). Do processing patterns of strengths and weaknesses predict differential treatment response? *Journal of Educational Psychology, 108,* 898–909.

Molfese, P. J., Fletcher, J. M., & Denton, C. A. (2013). Adequate versus inadequate response to reading intervention: An event-related potentials assessment. *Developmental Neuropsychology, 38*(8), 534–549.

Morris, R. D., & Fletcher, J. M. (1988). Classification in neuropsychology: A theoretical framework and research paradigm. *Journal of Clinical and Experimental Neuropsychology, 10*(5), 640–658.

Naglieri, J. A. (1999). *Essentials of CAS Assessment.* Hoboken, NJ: Wiley.

Nelson, R. J., Benner, G. J., & Gonzalez, J. (2003). Learner characteristics that influence the treatment effectiveness of early literacy interventions: A meta-analytic review. *Learning Disabilities Research & Practice, 18*(4), 255–267.

Rezaie, R., Simos, P. G., Fletcher, J. M., Cirino, P. T., Vaughn, S., & Papanicolaou, A. C. (2011). Temporo-parietal brain activity as a longitudinal predictor of response to educational interventions among middle school struggling readers. *Journal of the International Neuropsychological Society, 17*(5), 875–885.

Roberts, G., Vaughn, S., Fletcher, J., Stuebing, K., & Barth, A. (2013). Effects of a response-based, tiered framework for intervening with struggling readers in middle school. *Reading Research Quarterly, 48*(3), 237–254.

Rutter, M., & Yule, W. (1975). The concept of specific reading retardation. *Journal of Child Psychology and Psychiatry, 16*(3), 181–197.

Schatschneider, C., Wagner, R. K., & Crawford, E. C. (2008). The importance of measuring growth in response to intervention models: Testing a core assumption. *Learning and Individual Differences, 18*(3), 308–315.

Schneider, W. J., & Kaufman, A. S. (2017). Let's not do away with comprehensive cognitive assessments just yet. *Archives of Clinical Neuropsychology, 32*(1), 8–20.

Shaywitz, S. E., Escobar, M. D., Shaywitz, B. A., Fletcher, J. M., & Makuch, R. (1992). Evidence that dyslexia may represent the lower tail of a normal distribution of reading ability. *New England Journal of Medicine, 326,* 145–150.

Simos, P. G., Fletcher, J. M., Rezaie, R., & Papanicolaou, A. C. (2014). Does IQ affect the functional brain network involved in pseudoword reading in students with reading disability? A magnetoencephalography study. *Frontiers in Human Neuroscience, 7*, 932–941.

Stuebing, K. K., Barth, A. E., Molfese, P. J., Weiss, B., & Fletcher, J. M. (2009). IQ is not strongly related to response to reading instruction: A meta-analytic interpretation. *Exceptional Children, 76*(1), 31–51.

Stuebing, K. K., Fletcher, J. M., LeDoux, J. M., Lyon, G. R., Shaywitz, S. E., & Shaywitz, B. A. (2002). Validity of IQ-discrepancy classifications of reading disabilities: A meta-analysis. *American Educational Research Journal, 39*(2), 469–518.

Tamm, L., Denton, C. A., Epstein, J. N., Schatschneider, C., Taylor, H., Arnold, L. E., et al. (2017). Comparing treatments for children with ADHD and word reading difficulties: A randomized clinical trial. *Journal of Consulting and Clinical Psychology, 85*(5), 434–446.

Tanaka, H., Black, J. M., Hulme, C., Stanley, L. M., Kesler, S. R., Whitfield-Gabrieli, S., et al. (2011). The brain basis of the phonological deficit in dyslexia is independent of IQ. *Psychological Science, 22*(11), 1442–1451.

Taylor, W. P., Miciak, J., Fletcher, J. M., & Francis, D. J. (2017). Cognitive discrepancy models for specific learning disabilities identification: Simulations of psychometric limitations. *Psychological Assessment, 29*(4), 446–457.

Vellutino, F. R., Fletcher, J. M., Snowling, M. J., & Scanlon, D. M. (2004). Specific reading disability (dyslexia): What have we learned in the past four decades? *Journal of Child Psychology and Psychiatry, 45*(1), 2–40.

Vellutino, F. R., Scanlon, D. M., Small, S., & Fanuele, D. P. (2006). Response to intervention as a vehicle for distinguishing between children with and without reading disabilities: Evidence for the role of kindergarten and first-grade interventions. *Journal of Learning Disabilities, 39*(2), 157–169.

Chapter 8
Effective Prevention and Intervention for Word-Level Reading Difficulties

David A. Kilpatrick and Shawn O'Brien

Abstract The research on the prevention and intervention for word reading problems is reviewed in two parts. First, several key issues are addressed that bear on understanding the findings from the vast reading intervention literature. These include (1) interpreting intervention research in light of the findings from studies of orthographic learning, (2) examining assumptions inherent in current intervention approaches, (3) understanding why some students require intervention in the first place, (4) distinguishing research-based principles from research-based programs, and (5) examining the best ways to determine the effectiveness of interventions for word reading problems. Second, key intervention research findings are examined through the lens of the preliminary issues discussed in the first section. These findings reveal very positive prospects for preventing a large portion of reading difficulties based on modifications to general education classroom instruction. They also show that very substantial reading improvements can be made by struggling readers if the most effective principles are applied to our intervention efforts.

A substantial number of students struggle in learning to read (Fletcher, Lyons, Fuchs, & Barnes, 2018), with 30% or more of fourth graders reading below a basic level (NAEP 2015, 2017). A recent assessment of Tier 2 reading remediation indicated that children experience minimal benefit from such help (Balu et al., 2015). This is consistent with decades of research showing that even with reading intervention, weak readers typically remain weak readers (Jacobson, 1999; Maughan, Hagell, Rutter, & Yule, 1994; Protopapas, Sideridis, Mouzaki, & Simos, 2011; Short, Feagans, McKinney, & Appelbaum, 1986).

Despite these discouraging findings, research indicates that effective prevention and intervention efforts can reduce the percentage of at-risk readers who develop reading problems (Foorman, Francis, Fletcher, Schatschneider, & Mehta, 1998;

D. A. Kilpatrick (✉)
State University of New York College at Cortland, Cortland, NY, USA
e-mail: kilpatrickd@cortland.edu

S. O'Brien
School Psychologist (retired), Iron River, WI, USA
e-mail: drshawnobrien@me.com

© Springer Nature Switzerland AG 2019
D. A. Kilpatrick et al. (eds.), *Reading Development and Difficulties*,
https://doi.org/10.1007/978-3-030-26550-2_8

NICHD, 2000; Shapiro, & Solity, 2008; Vellutino et al., 1996). There is evidence that struggling readers may be able to gain and maintain approximately one standard deviation of improvement on normed reading assessments (McGuinness, McGuinness, & McGuinness, 1996; Torgesen et al., 2001; Torgesen, Wagner, Rashotte, Herron, & Lindamood, 2010; Truch, 1994, 2003, 2004). It was strong research outcomes like this (Foorman et al., 1998; NICHD 2000; Torgesen et al., 2001; Vellutino et al., 1996) that prompted the development of response to intervention and multi-tiered systems of support (RTI/MTSS). There is little evidence, however, that the actual instructional and intervention techniques that yielded the highly effective research results have been incorporated into RTI/MTSS implementation efforts (Balu et al., 2015).

This chapter will examine the most effective prevention and intervention approaches for difficulties with *word-level* reading. Oakhill, Cain, and Elbro (Chap. 5, this volume) discuss interventions for reading comprehension difficulties not attributable to word reading problems. The goal of this chapter is to present and integrate findings from multiple relevant niche areas within the scientific literature on reading. This is intended to build a deeper understanding of how reading development unfolds and why some remedial approaches might work better than others.

8.1   Word Learning Research Versus Intervention Research

Empirical reading research is a vast global enterprise conducted by scientists in various branches of psychology, speech pathology, linguistics, education, special education, literacy, medicine, and neuroscience. In the USA, tens of millions of federal dollars are spent each year on such research, with millions more funded by other governments and private foundations. Reading research is reported in scientific journals and is largely unknown outside the community of researchers themselves. Studies of educational professionals consistently demonstrate that there is little familiarity with the findings from the scientific study of reading (Moats, Chap. 3, this volume). This includes K-3 general education teachers (Cunningham, Perry, Stanovich, & Stanovich, 2004), special education teachers (Boardman, Argüelles, Vaughn, Tejero Hughes, & Klingner, 2005), literacy specialists (Moats, 1994, 2009), and school psychologists (Nelson & Machek, 2007).

Every year, several hundred empirical research reports and reviews on reading appear in English-language scientific journals. The field is so vast that it is impossible for researchers to remain current with the entire enterprise. Reading scientists must specialize in one or more of the many niche areas within the field. This may explain a curious observation: The research on word-level reading intervention and the research on word learning (i.e., how we learn and remember written words for later recall) do not overlap in any substantive way. It is extremely rare for either of these specialized areas to cite research from the other area. Miles and Ehri (Chap. 4, this volume) review word learning, more properly referred to as orthographic learning. The present chapter is intended to provide an overview of the word reading intervention literature, but also integrates these two literatures. The goal of this chapter is to leverage the findings from both of these areas to inform best practice in prevention and intervention with reading difficulties and disabilities.

8.2   Prerequisite Issues

There are many different reading philosophies from which different (and even contradictory) remedial suggestions have arisen. How should one navigate through these possibilities in a manner that will inform best practices? To assist with this, we will examine some prerequisite issues critical to identifying the most effective interventions.

(1) How to best measure/estimate intervention effectiveness.
(2) Distinguish between effective instructional *principles* and effective *programs*.
(3) The assumptions behind current approaches to teaching and remediating reading.
(4) How research on orthographic learning can help interpret the findings from the intervention literature.
(5) Why some children struggle and thus require intervention in the first place.

8.3   Determining Instructional or Intervention Effectiveness

There are multiple ways to measure progress in word reading skills. The four most common will be examined below.

8.3.1   Raw Score Improvements

Raw score improvements demonstrate progress, but they cannot tell us if a student is catching up. A weak second grader may go from 12 words correct per minute (wcpm) on a paragraph reading test to 36 wcpm. However, this tripling of raw scores does not necessarily mean this intervention is effective. During that same time frame, typically developing readers, on average, progressed from 50 to 95 wcpm. The 38-wcpm gap has grown to 59 wcpm. Thus, raw score improvements do not necessarily mean "catching up."

8.3.2 Statistical Significance

Statistical significance is used to judge the likelihood that two statistical outcomes are due to chance rather than the factor under study (e.g., the type of reading intervention). Statistical significance *cannot* tell us if an intervention is effective. Perhaps, both approaches under study are inferior to all other approaches. In that case, statistical significance only means that one intervention *was less ineffective* than the other. An experimental group may show statistically significant gains compared to a control group while not closing the gap with typical peers. This is not a hypothetical concern. Numerous studies have demonstrated statistically significant differences compared to control groups, despite normative reading assessment gains of only 0 to 4 standard score points (e.g., Christodoulou et al., 2017; Mitchell & Begeny, 2014; Vaughn et al., 2010, 2012).

8.3.3 Effect Size

Effect size is a common statistic in intervention research. It indicates the *magnitude* of the difference between an experimental and control group, or between pretest and posttest scores. An effect size of +1.0 means one group made one standard deviation of improvement relative to the comparison group (or relative to the pretest scores). Despite its common use in intervention research, effect size cannot be consistently relied upon to determine intervention effectiveness. The authors of the intervention study that prompted Tier 3 of RTI stated that effect sizes are "misleading in that they do not provide information about the rate of normalization of reading skills. Instead, they describe the advantage in reading growth for children in an experimental condition relative to a control condition" (Torgesen et al., 2001, p. 34). Consider the following examples.

Vaughn et al. (2012) found a +.49 effect size, which represents the equivalent of about a 7.5 standard score point difference. However, the normative standard score gain for the experimental group was 0. This discrepancy resulted from the fact that the control group's normative performance declined during the intervention period. The +.49 effect size was based on a comparison with the control group, not a normative group.

Christodoulou et al. (2017) reported an impressive +.96 effect size for a summer tutoring program for poor word readers. Yet, a normed word identification posttest yielded a gain of less than one standard score point (.61) by the experimental group. This discrepancy occurred because the experimental group was compared to an untreated control group of poor word readers during the summer break. The control group's normative performance declined, resulting in the experimental group scoring much higher than the no-treatment control group on the post-intervention word identification test.

These examples illustrate how effect size can potentially make ineffective approaches seem effective. The reverse can be true as well. Torgesen et al. (2010) studied two intervention groups and a control group. The two intervention groups had similar results with a combined average effect size of +.53. Yet, the standard score point outcomes of the intervention groups were 21 and 23 points, gains that rank among the strongest in the intervention literature. The moderate +.53 effect size resulted from the fact the control group displayed a strong outcome of 14 standard score points. This significantly minimized the differences between experimental and control groups, yielding a moderate effect size.

All three of the studies used the same test to measure word reading improvement, the word identification subtest from the Woodcock Reading Mastery Test-Revised (WRMT-R). Despite using the same outcome yardstick, they obtained discrepant measurements between effect sizes and standard scores. This is because effect sizes involve comparing an experimental group to a control group. Control groups do not represent a stable baseline across studies. To determine intervention efficacy, it thus seems judicious to supplement effect sizes with normative score progress.

8.3.4 Normative Standard Score Point Gains

Keenan, Betjemann, and Olson (2008) noted that the inter-correlations among word identification subtests tend to be high (unlike reading comprehension subtests). This suggests that such normed subtests do a suitable job of reflecting and stratifying the skill levels of students in the general population. If that is the case, then nationally normed word identification subtests provide a useful supplement to effect sizes when determining the effectiveness of instructional or intervention approaches. Normative scores can suggest whether an experimental group's progress allowed them to close the gap relative to a national norm group. "Standard scores are an excellent metric for determining the 'success' or 'failure' of interventions for children with reading disabilities, because they describe the child's relative position within the distribution of reading skills in a large standardization sample" (Torgesen, 2005, p. 524).

Despite this strength, normative comparisons have difficulties as well. They do not represent an equal interval scale, and a few items on a subtest can make a larger or smaller impact on the standard score depending on the age of the student. Also, norms represent a slice in time and participants in research studies are typically being compared to an earlier cohort. Furthermore, if normative gains are not accompanied by an effect size comparison with a control group, it is difficult to know whether normative improvements were related to factors going on in that local situation independent of the intervention under study. As a result of these concerns, it appears that effect sizes and standard scores both appear to be needed to best determine the efficacy of a given intervention approach or program.

8.4   Distinguishing Between Principles and Programs

Although commercially available programs have been included within various studies, researchers typically select such programs to illustrate a particular underlying
concept, principle, or general approach, not to do a study on that particular program.
For example, if researchers want to compare a three-cueing system reading approach
with a phonic approach, they typically select a commercially available example of
each to address their research questions. This is more efficient than creating an
experimenter-designed program in order to study a given principle or practice.

Though some programs, or parts of programs, have been used in research, there
exists no Consumer Reports-style body of research evidence that allows educators to
compare among existing reading programs. The majority of reading programs on the
market have no direct research support reported in scientific journals. This means that
educational professionals need to become familiar with the concepts and principles
that research has shown to be effective or ineffective. With that knowledge, educators
can make more informed decisions when considering various reading programs and
intervention approaches.

The What Works Clearinghouse (WWC), bestevidence.org, and similar outlets
seem to approximate that Consumer Reports-type of service for educational professionals. But those well-intentioned efforts have been problematic for at least two
reasons. First, they rely primarily on effect size to judge program effectiveness, not
standard score gains. Second, there is not a substantial pool of program-specific
research from which these outlets can draw. Thus, the WWC and similar outlets
are no substitute for educational professionals who are well-informed regarding the
findings from reading research.

There is a more useful outlet for educators that avoids the inherent difficulties with
the WWC, bestevidence.org, and similar sources. The U S Department of Education's
Institute of Education Sciences (IES) has developed IES Practice Guides that are
useful sources of research information. They focus on findings related to concepts,
principles, and approaches rather than on specific programs. Two useful examples,
which can be easily accessed via an Internet search, are Foorman et al. (2016) and
Gersten et al. (2008).

8.5   The Assumptions Behind Reading Instruction
and Intervention

All of the traditional approaches to teaching reading can be classified into one of
four general categories based on their *unit of focus*. For phonics instruction (Chall
& Popp, 1996), the unit of focus is the letter and digraph (e.g., *ch, sh, oa, ee*). For
the linguistic approach (Bloomfield & Barnhart, 1961), the focus is on the rime unit
(cl*ip*, d*ip*, l*ip*, s*ip*). For the whole word/look–say approach, the focus is the word as a

unit (Adams, 1990). For the whole language/balanced literacy/three-cueing approach (Goodman, 1996), the unit of focus is the sentence or paragraph.

Within these approaches, there are variations and teachers generally draw techniques from multiple approaches. Nonetheless, it is useful to be aware of the underlying assumptions of each approach because they drive instruction and intervention. An examination of the assumptions behind them may provide a window into our current intervention efforts and may help us understand why these classic approaches provide limited benefits for struggling readers (Balu et al., 2015; Jacobson, 1999; Maughan et al., 1994; Protopapas et al., 2011; Short et al., 1986).

The Phonics Approach. The goal of phonics instruction is for students to independently read newly encountered words using letter-sound knowledge and phonological blending (Chall & Popp, 1996; Beck & Beck, 2013). Although the phonics approach supports the identification of unfamiliar words, it seems that phonics authorities assume that after multiple successful opportunities of phonetically decoding words, those words eventually are remembered as visual wholes (Chall & Popp, 1996; Beck & Beck, 2013), presumably based on the visual memory hypothesis, described below. This visual memorization is also called upon to address irregular or exception words (Chall & Popp, 1996; Beck & Beck, 2013). Despite these concerns, there is a large and long-standing history of research findings showing that phonics instruction in K-2 yields superior results to the linguistic, whole word, and balanced instruction approaches (Adams, 1990, Anderson, Hiebert, Scott, & Wilkinson 1985; Bond & Dykstra, 1967; Brady, 2011; NICHD, 2000).

The Linguistic Approach. The linguistic approach (Bloomfield & Barnhart, 1961) is intended to support beginning readers by focusing instruction on onsets and rimes, which generally is easier than phoneme-level processing (Adams, 1990). The assumption seems to be that rimes are learned as visual wholes. Thus, like phonics, this approach presumes that some form of visual memory supports learning to read.

Whole Word Approach. The whole word approach appears to be squarely founded upon the visual memory hypothesis. The visual memory hypothesis assumes that visual memory underpins skilled reading, as readers quickly access familiar words from a visual memory bank of some sort. This has very strong intuitive appeal. When we look at a chair and say "chair," or we see the printed word *chair* and say "chair," it feels like the same process—visual input and verbal output. But this strong intuition does not align with numerous research findings.

The Inadequacy of the Visual Memory Hypothesis. Because the visual memory hypothesis appears to play an essential role in the whole word, phonics, and linguistic approaches, it is important to consider its validity. Multiple findings from independent lines of research have clearly demonstrated that, despite its intuitive appeal, the visual memory hypothesis does not accurately describe how skilled readers store or retrieve printed words. This evidence is briefly summarized below (see Kilpatrick, 2015 for citations).

Some of the reasons we know that reading is not based in any substantial way on visual memory include: (1) There is a very weak correlation between visual memory skills and word-level reading; (2) there are moderate to strong correlations between various phonemic tasks and word-level reading; (3) individuals who are deaf have great difficulty with word-level reading despite their typical visual memory skills; (4) studies using different fonts, cases, and personal handwriting, including mixed case studies (e.g., wOrDs LiKe tHiS), show that it is the *sequence of letters* that is stored and instantly activated, not the visual appearance of the word; (5) brain imaging studies show differing activation patterns between naming written words that are familiar to us, naming nonsense words, naming faces, and naming visually presented objects (Dehaene & Cohen, 2011; Sand & Bolger, Chap. 10, this volume); (6) anecdotally, we sometimes "block" on people's names when we see them or even the names of visually presented objects ("hand me that thingy over there"), yet we never fail to recall familiar written words, suggesting that word reading involves more than a simple visual–phonological retrieval process. None of these six factors are explicable based on the intuitive notion that visual memory plays a major role in remembering written words.

Rather than visual memory, readers store words in long-term memory based on *orthographic memory* (Ehri 2005, 2014; Ehri & Saltmarsh, 1995; Kilpatrick, 2015, Miles & Ehri, this volume; Rack, Hulme, Snowling, & Wightman, 1994; Share, 1995, 2011). This refers to a memory for a particular letter order, regardless of the visual characteristics of the word (i.e., uppercase, lowercase, varying fonts, or personal handwriting in cursive or script). For example, in the word *bear,* none of the four uppercase letters looks the same as its lowercase counterpart (*BEAR, bear*). Yet once a child learns a word in one case, they typically have instant retrieval of that word in the other case, or another font, despite the visual dissimilarities. It is thus the letter order that comprises orthographic memory.

Whole Language/Balanced Literacy. The assumption inherent in this approach is that the sentence or paragraph context is a significant contributor to word-level reading (Goodman, 1996, 2005). The idea is that three systems simultaneously cue the reader to gain meaning from print: context, linguistic information (grammar and syntax), and letter-sound knowledge (often only the first letter is needed to help the previous two cueing systems to correctly determine the word). A key assumption is that context plays a large role in identifying written words. This theory cannot account for the fact that skilled readers can quickly and accurately read words in isolation, while struggling readers cannot. Although context is essential for meaning, it is rarely necessary for instant and accurate word recognition (except for homographs like *wind/wind, dove/dove, present/present*).

8.5.1 A Note on Reading Approaches

All four of the classic approaches have origins in the 1800s or earlier (Adams, 1990; Smith, 1965), predating the scientific revolution in reading. Our current reading instruction and remediation continue to be based on the same assumptions, even though research in the last 40–50 years has invalidated many of these assumptions. The visual memory hypothesis, which plays a central role in the whole word approach and a supporting role in the phonics and linguistic approaches, is inconsistent with a vast amount of research findings (Kilpatrick, 2015). The fourth approach, whole language/balanced literacy, promotes strategies that are inconsistent with research findings about how we remember written words. Perhaps, it is not surprising, then, that we have had a long history of discouraging results when addressing reading difficulties (Balu et al., 2015; Jacobson, 1999; Maughan et al., 1994; Protopapas et al., 2011; Short et al., 1986).

8.6 Contributions from the Orthographic Learning Research

Recall that orthographic learning involves remembering a word such that it is instantly, effortlessly, and accurately recalled and requires no phonic decoding or guessing. Miles and Ehri (Chap. 4, this volume) detail how this works, so it is recommended that the reader becomes familiar with that chapter in order to fully understand what follows. Yet, it may be useful to highlight some key points that will guide our understanding as we seek to interpret why different interventions yield widely differing outcomes.

First, orthographic learning research indicates that word reading is not based on visual memory (Ehri, 2005; Kilpatrick, 2015; Share, 1995). It should thus not be surprising that remedial approaches that focus primarily on visual exposure yield limited results. Visual memory-based intervention methods include expecting children to memorize words as unanalyzed wholes and reading practice approaches that assume visual exposure/repetitions will develop visual memories of those words.

Second, the two major cognitive theories of orthographic learning, Ehri's *orthographic mapping theory* and Share's *self-teaching hypothesis,* both affirm the centrality of letter-sound knowledge and phonemic skills for storing words in long-term memory. Although this may seem counterintuitive, it is strongly supported in the research literature (Cardoso-Martins, Mamede Resende, & Assunção Rodrigues, 2002; Dixon, Stuart, & Masterson, 2002; Ehri, 2005, 2014; Kilpatrick, 2015; Laing & Hulme, 1999; Miles & Ehri, this volume; Rack et al., 1994; Share, 1999; Stuart, Masterson, & Dixon, 2000). The implication is that instructional approaches that do not focus on letter-sound skills and phonemic skills should not be expected to yield optimal results.

Third, studies examining Share's self-teaching hypothesis have shown that for typically developing readers from second grade on, only one to four exposures are needed before a newly encountered word becomes permanently stored for later, effortless retrieval (Cunningham, Perry, Stanovich, & Share, 2002; Share, 1999, 2004). If a student routinely requires many more exposures than that, the student's orthographic learning ability is presumably impaired. Because orthographic learning is based on letter-sound skills and phonemic skills, it is the acquisition of those skills that will allow students to improve their ability to remember written words, not simply providing multiple exposures.

Fourth, orthographic learning theory and the self-teaching hypothesis both propose that the process of remembering words is implicit. This tenet is easily confirmed. Consider the fact that adult skilled readers have an instantaneously accessible word reading vocabulary (called an *orthographic lexicon* or *sight word vocabulary*) ranging from 30,000 to 80,000 words (Crowder & Wagner, 1992; Rayner & Polletsek, 1989), depending on reading experience. It seems fair to say that we do not remember putting conscious effort into storing tens of thousands of words (with occasional exceptions for very difficult or unusual words). The vast majority of words in our very large orthographic lexicons were added incidentally after encountering and sounding out new words (Share, 1995, 1999, 2011).

Research supporting Share's self-teaching hypothesis indicates that students add new words to their sight vocabularies/orthographic lexicons after successful encounters—via phonic decoding—with previously unfamiliar words in the context of silent reading of real text (Cunningham et al., 2002; Share, 1999, 2004). If an unfamiliar word is not phonically decoded, the prospects for remembering the word diminish greatly (Share, 1999). Ehri's orthographic mapping theory explains the cognitive mechanism underlying this memory process (Ehri, 2005; Kilpatrick, 2015; Miles & Ehri, Chap. 4, this volume). A word's pronunciation is parsed into its segmented phonemes, which in turn is mapped onto the letters in the written word. What is already known and established in long-term memory is the oral form of the word. This known pronunciation is used to encode/remember the word's written form (Ehri, 2005), which only happens if students have skilled access to the phonemes within the oral pronunciations. Lacking such proficient phonemic skills disrupts this connection-forming process.

As mentioned, the connection-forming process behind orthographic mapping appears to be implicit, that is, automatic and largely unconscious. If the process of storing words in long-term memory is largely unconscious in nature, it necessarily follows that the letter-sound and phonemic skills required to support that process must also be at a level of proficiency such that they are automatic and unconscious.

8.7   Determining Why Students Struggle in Word-Level Reading

When making decisions about remediation for students with poor word reading skills, we should consider the large research literature which investigates why some students struggle in learning to read words. Most popular notions about poor word-level reading, particularly when using the term *dyslexia*, focus on presumed visual–spatial–perceptual deficits. Such notions are inconsistent with the scientific findings (Ahmed, Wagner, & Kantor, 2012; Fletcher et al., 2018; Vellutino, Fletcher, Snowling, & Scanlon, 2004). Reading researchers operationally define word reading difficulties/dyslexia as poor performance in word identification tests despite adequate effort and opportunity, and not due to blindness, deafness, or severe intellectual disability (Fletcher et al., 2018; Hulme & Snowling, 2009; Vellutino et al., 2004). Poor word-level reading combined with typical language skills is referred to as dyslexia, while poor word-level reading combined with weak language skills is referred to as mixed reading difficulty or garden-variety poor readers (Gough & Tunmer, 1986; Joshi, Chap. 1, this volume). Regardless, in either case the poor word-level reading appears to be the result of the same causal factors.

What causes poor word-level reading/dyslexia? Elsewhere in this volume, the genetic and neurodevelopmental factors are discussed (Byrne, Olson, & Samuelsson, Chap. 9; Sand & Bolger, Chap. 10). For our purposes, dyslexia is the result of the phonological-core deficit (Fletcher et al., 2018; Hulme & Snowling, 2009; Morris et al., 1998; Stanovich & Siegel, 1994; Vellutino et al., 2004). There is a consensus that individuals with the phonological-core deficit display one or more of the following:

- Poor phonemic awareness/analysis
- Poor phonemic blending/synthesis
- Poor rapid automatized naming
- Poor phonological working memory
- Poor letter-sound knowledge/nonsense word reading.

For years, researchers have referred to the phonological-core deficit as the most common cause of dyslexia, which seems to leave the door open to other possible causes. It is worth noting, however, that a recent review of dyslexia research referred to the phonological-core deficit multiple times as the "universal cause" of dyslexia (Ahmed et al., 2012). The authors did not explain this important shift in terminology. However, their reasoning can be inferred from the dyslexia research literature in that (1) we fail to find students who are struggling word-level readers who receive a "clean bill of health" on all five phonological-core characteristics listed above (Morris et al., 1998), and (2) four decades of scientific research into dyslexia have yet to reveal a compelling case for alternative causal explanations. There may be correlational features that occur among students with dyslexia, but there is no evidence for causality (Vellutino et al., 2004). The conclusion drawn from this is that with the caveats mentioned above, poor word-level reading is caused by poor phonological processing at some level or another. This conclusion is not surprising given the nature of alphabetic writing.

The Alphabetic Principle. Alphabetic writing systems are designed to capture the speech stream. Characters (letters) within alphabetic writing represent the individual sounds (phonemes) produced when people speak. Letters and letter combinations (e.g., *ch, th; ee, oa*) represent phonemes, not words. In any alphabetic writing system, we write phoneme-based characters that we string together to form words. These letter strings represent the sequences of sounds in the pronunciations of oral words. English is more inconsistent in phoneme-to-letter representation than "regular" written languages such as Italian or Spanish (Seymour, Aro, & Erskine, 2003; Ziegler & Goswami, 2005). Nonetheless, English writing is designed to transcribe oral speech at the level of individual phonemes within oral language. The insight that the characters on the page represent the segmented phonemes within spoken words is called the *alphabetic principle*. Poor word-level readers have poor awareness of the phonemic structure of spoken language and thus struggle with developing and applying the alphabetic principle. Because phoneme-level skills are necessary for both phonic decoding and remembering words, poor conscious or unconscious access to the phonemic structure of spoken language makes it very difficult to acquire these central aspects of reading.

We can conclude from the research on dyslexia that students' word-level reading difficulties are primarily the result of the phonological-core deficit (Ahmed et al., 2012; Morris et al., 1998; Vellutino et al., 2004). Their poor access to the phonemic structure of the spoken language makes reading difficult for them. Reading interventions that successfully address this underlying problem would be expected to have better results than interventions that do not address the source of their reading difficulty.

8.7.1 Summary of Prerequisite Issues

We have examined the five prerequisite issues that help to establish the groundwork for making sense of the reading intervention research literature. First, we will rely on the assumption that for word-level reading, normative standard score outcomes are a useful supplement to effect size for determining intervention effectiveness. Second, we acknowledge that instruction and intervention research focuses primarily on principles and approaches, rather than on validating specific reading programs. Thus, we will seek to abstract from that research the best practices in terms of principles and approaches. Third, all of the four classic ways of approaching reading instruction and intervention (phonics, linguistics, whole word, whole language/balanced literacy) were developed long before the scientific study of reading and are insufficiently consistent with the findings from that research. Although the phonics approach yields superior results compared to the other three, it lacks a reliable mechanism for helping students remember the words they read.

Fourth, the orthographic learning literature has generated findings that can be used to guide our understanding of reading intervention. These include (1) word storage and retrieval are not based on visual memory; (2) letter-sound skills and phonemic skills are central to remembering words; (3) from second grade on, new words are remembered after only 1–4 exposures in typically developing readers; and (4) memory for words is largely an implicit, unconscious process, so the letter-sound and phonemic skills that support that process must also be proficient enough to operate unconsciously. Fifth, the nature of alphabetic writing combined with the last 40 years of research into dyslexia suggests that the phonological-core deficit is centrally responsible for word-level reading difficulties. These five prerequisite considerations provide important organizing principles and generate predictions that will bring clarity to the large and growing word-level reading intervention research.

8.8 Orthographic Learning Findings "Predict" Prevention and Intervention Outcomes

As mentioned previously, the orthographic learning and the word-level intervention literatures function independently. There appear to be no prospective studies designed to examine prevention or intervention from the perspective of Ehri's and Share's orthographic learning theories. However, we can do a "thought experiment" that involves applying findings from the orthographic learning research to the existing prevention and intervention research. This can yield valuable insights into those existing literatures.

The general findings from the orthographic learning research yield three predictions, or more specifically, expectations (i.e., because they interpret preexisting data). First, attempts at teaching struggling readers using visual memory strategies would not be expected to produce strong results, whether via visual memorization of whole words or reading practice using sentences and paragraphs. For students not skilled at remembering the words they read, multiple exposures would have limited benefit.

A second expectation would be that instruction and intervention efforts that do not include both letter-sound instruction and instruction in phonemic awareness skills would not have results as strong as interventions that include both of those elements.

The third expectation would be that intervention efforts that promote letter-sound skills and phonemic skills to the point of automaticity would yield better results than those that only result in simple accuracy on such tasks, but which lack automaticity. It is presumed that automaticity in letter-sound skills and oral phoneme analysis skills would facilitate the implicit and unconscious orthographic mapping process (Ehri 2005, 2014; Kilpatrick, 2015, 2018; Miles & Ehri, Chap. 4, this volume).

As mentioned, these expectations or predictions represent a thought experiment. It is nonetheless useful because it allows us to conceptually apply the orthographic learning research findings to understanding the instructional differences found among various intervention studies. The next sections provide an overview of the prevention and intervention research and will illustrate how orthographic learning research explains the widely varying standard score point outcomes we find within the intervention literature.

8.9 Prevention of Reading Difficulties

There is extensive evidence showing that a large proportion of reading difficulties can be prevented. The National Reading Panel (NRP) reviewed a large body of K-1 studies showing dramatic reductions in the number of struggling readers when students were explicitly taught phonological awareness and letter-sound relationships (NICHD, 2000).

The NRP found that students trained in kindergarten and/or first grade in phonological awareness performed at the level equivalent to 7 standard score points higher in reading than those who did not receive such training. This dropped off to 4–5 standard score points at follow-up which is expected given that most students eventually learn basic phonological awareness skills without being taught (Kilpatrick, 2015). The picture was quite different with at-risk students. The Panel found an impressive 13 standard score point difference in reading between trained and untrained at-risk students. This difference increased to 20 points at follow-up indicating the enduring benefit to at-risk readers. Such students do not appear to develop these skills on their own, so if these skill deficits are not addressed, most at-risk students continue to struggle in reading.

The NRP found similar results for teaching letter-sound skills in K-1. Those trained explicitly and systematically in letter-sound relationships averaged the equivalent of 6 or 7 standard score points higher on word reading tests than those without such instruction. At-risk students showed an even greater benefit. They performed at a level equivalent to 11 points higher than their untrained at-risk counterparts on tests of word reading.

Application of Orthographic Learning Research. Empirical studies that support Ehri's orthographic mapping theory and Share's self-teaching hypothesis affirm that words are remembered based on their letter sequence (i.e., orthographic memory), irrespective of the appearance of the word (uppercase, lowercase, differing fonts, and handwriting). They also affirm that letter-sound knowledge and phonemic awareness skills are both central to the word memory process. It is well established that letter-sound knowledge and phonological skills are important for phonic decoding (called *phonological recoding* by researchers; e.g., Share, 1995), yet their centrality for *remembering* newly encountered words (Cardoso-Martins et al., 2002; Dixon et al., 2002; Ehri, 2005, 2014; Kilpatrick, 2015, 2018; Laing & Hulme, 1999; Stuart et al., 2000) seems less well known.

The research on preventing reading difficulties, though conducted independently of the orthographic learning research, is consistent with their findings. The successful prevention studies routinely used control groups with instruction based on assumptions from the classic visual memory-based whole word approach and/or the traditional three-cueing system approach (the basis of whole language and balanced instruction). As suggested above, the orthographic learning research would predict that visual memory-based instruction and three-cueing-oriented instruction would not promote learning to read as well as instruction that directly focuses on letter-sound relationships and on the oral phonemic structure of spoken words, which is what the prevention research indicates. Thus, the orthographic learning research and the prevention research closely align to build a strong foundation for understanding the nature of reading development, as well as the specific K-1 curricular elements needed for helping to prevent reading difficulties.

8.10   Interventions for Students with Reading Difficulties

8.10.1   Previous Reviews of Research

Since 1999, there have been over three dozen reviews and meta-analyses of the reading intervention research (e.g., Bus & van IJzendoorn, 1999; Edmonds et al., 2009; Ehri, Nunes, Stahl, & Willows, 2001; Flynn, Zheng, & Swanson, 2012; NICHD, 2000; Suggate, 2016; Torgesen, 2004, 2005; Wanzek & Vaughn, 2007; Wanzek et al., 2013). It is not the purpose here to catalog those reviews, nor to independently review the hundreds of intervention studies that have been conducted over the last 40 years. Rather, the goal is to identify important trends in those reviews, and the intervention research more generally, which highlight a significant and encouraging pattern in the research results.

Factors Affecting Intervention Outcomes. The various reviews and meta-analyses have examined numerous mediating factors that may influence the outcomes of intervention efforts. Five of the most commonly researched mediating factors are (1) socioeconomic status (SES); (2) age/grade of the student; (3) instructor-to-student ratio; (4) severity of the reading problem; and (5) length of intervention.

The findings across these reviews do not necessarily align with intuition. The first two factors appear to have a small overall impact on intervention outcome. Although SES is highly correlated with reading scores in nonintervention research, its impact on intervention outcomes appears to be much more modest (e.g., Suggate, 2016). Also, younger students generally seem to benefit more from intervention than older students, although this is only a modest trend in the literature (e.g., Flynn et al., 2012). The other three factors do not show a consistent pattern across studies. For example, contrary to popular assumption, 1:1 instruction resulted in no better results than 1:2 or 1:3 (e.g., Elbaum, Vaughn, Hughes, & Moody, 2000).

Although perhaps counterintuitive, these findings are nonetheless encouraging, since we cannot change a student's SES, nor his or her age. Also, 1:1 instruction and lengthy interventions are impractical and expensive. It is also encouraging that the most severe cases can make significant progress. In studies with the strongest outcomes, students gained approximately a standard deviation in reading regardless of their starting point. For example, 87 students in the McGuinness et al. (1996) study began about one standard deviation below the mean and finished at the mean. In the Torgesen et al. (2001) study, 60 students started, on average, two standard deviations below the mean and finished at about one standard deviation below the mean.

There are three common features found in the traditional reviews and meta-analyses of the reading intervention literature that are of interest here. First, they have all yielded generally modest results across reviews, presenting a rather non-optimistic picture for the prospects for struggling readers to normalize their reading performance.[1] Second, most of the reviews focused on mediating factors like those mentioned above (age, intervention length, instructor/student ratio, SES, etc.). Surprisingly, few (e.g., Flynn et al., 2012) examined the nature of the remedial instruction as a mediating factor.

Third, most reviews and all meta-analyses used effect size as their primary or lone metric for determining the impact of the mediating factors, as well as their estimates of efficacy in general. For reasons previously discussed, reliance on effect size alone could yield results that obscure an underlying pattern, since this metric may overestimate or underestimate the impact of any given intervention, relative to normative gains. In two reviews (Flynn et al., 2012; Torgesen, 2005), the authors indicated that perhaps normative scores should also be considered when seeking to determine efficacy:

> Standard scores are an excellent metric for determining the "success" or "failure" of interventions for children with reading disabilities. (Torgesen, 2005, p. 524)

> Finally, researchers need to use norm-referenced measures of reading ability to ensure that intervention learning transfers to general skill application, as well as provides a reference with which one can compare performance. (Flynn et al., 2012, pp. 30–31)

Torgesen's (2005) review was rare in that it focused on normative scores, but it was not a systematic review. It was a selective presentation of intervention findings based on a combination of case studies, an in-depth presentation of an earlier published study (Torgesen et al., 2001), and a listing and brief overview of 14 studies. However, Torgesen (2005) did not distinguish between some of the finer differences among the studies he reviewed in terms of the precise content of the phonics and phonological awareness instruction, nor did he explore the possible factors as to why some studies yielded moderate standard score gains (5–9 points) and others had stronger results (12–19 points).

Following the lead of Torgesen (2005), Kilpatrick (2015) focused on normative score gains when reviewing some of the more commonly cited and reviewed intervention studies. This synthesis revealed a pattern in which instructional approaches directly aligned with the magnitude of the standard score point gains. It appears that this pattern had not been previously identified. One speculation is that the reliance upon effect sizes, which have the potential of underestimating or overestimating the impact of particular interventions, may have obscured this pattern. Another possibility is that, as mentioned previously, few reviews examined the nature of the remedial instruction as a mediating factor. A summary of that non-meta-analytic research synthesis is presented below.

---

[1]The term "normalize" is typically used by researchers to refer to when weak readers raise their reading performance above the 30th or 40th percentiles, depending on how "normalize" is defined in any given study.

8.10.2 The Phonemic Proficiency Intervention Continuum

When one examines intervention studies using standard score gains on nationally normed word identification subtests, an interesting pattern emerges. Consistent with the orthographic learning research literature, instruction that focuses on visual memorization and visual exposure through reading practice results in minimal standard score gains among struggling readers. By contrast, much greater improvements have been found on normed word identification tests when reading interventions directly address and train the skills that the orthographic learning literature indicates are needed for remembering words (i.e., phonemic awareness and letter-sound skills). When examining actual instructional practices found in the intervention studies and using standard score gains as an index of intervention efficacy, three general levels of standard score point outcomes emerge. These levels align closely with three different levels of intensity of the phonemic awareness instruction across the various studies.

- Minimal: 0–5.8 standard score point gains
- Moderate: 6–9 standard score point gains
- Highly effective: 10–25 standard score point gains.

Minimal: 0–5.8 Standard Score Point Gains. In this category are interventions that involve visual memorization, reading practice (including repeated readings), and phonics instruction not supplemented with oral-only phonemic awareness training. Most studies in this group of instructional approaches yielded 2–4 standard score points.

An example in this category is READ 180, which relies on practice and exposure and does not teach phonics or phonemic awareness. Most studies and reviews of this program only report effect sizes with no standard scores (e.g., Slavin, Cheung, Groff, & Lake, 2008). However, Papalewis reported two standard score point gains after a year in the program (from the 20th percentile to the 24th percentile, i.e., 87.5–89.5). Failure Free Reading is marketed as a "nonphonic" approach for making large reading gains through extensive reading practice during a 100-hour intervention program. The standard score results range from 1 to 5 points on normed word reading tests (Algozzine & Lockavith, 1998; Keller & Just, 2009; Torgesen et al., 2007).

Repeated Reading. Repeated reading appears to be a popular intervention for struggling readers, but its efficacy is often assumed rather than demonstrated. A 2009 review of research on repeated readings did not find sufficient efficacy for the method (Chard, Ketterlin-Geller, Baker, Doabler, & Apichatabutra, 2009). Two recent reviews of repeated reading appear to present it in a somewhat positive light (Lee & Yoon, 2017; Stevens, Walker, & Vaughn, 2017). Yet, the authors said that they found support for improvement in reading rate "only by using nontransfer practiced passages for students with RD [reading disabilities]" (Lee & Yoon, 2017, p. 221). The review by Stevens et al. (2017) found very little evidence for transfer to unpracticed passages. Additionally, both reviews relied on effect size and neither review addressed the issue of standard score gains on normative assessments. In studies of repeated reading that report normative scores, gains tend to range from 1 to 5 standard score points (e.g., O'Connor, White, & Swanson, 2007; Wexler, Vaughn, Roberts, & Denton, 2010).

The orthographic learning literature provides a lens for interpreting these findings. For students not skilled in orthographic mapping (i.e., remembering written words), simple exposure and repetition do not improve their ability to retain newly encountered words in any substantial way. The theoretical basis for repeated readings (see Chard et al., 2009) does not adequately address why some students struggle in remembering words. Since repeated reading interventions do not teach the skills required for efficient orthographic mapping, they would not be expected to yield strong, sustained normative results with struggling readers. Likewise, interventions involving large amounts of reading practice (not repeated reading) have similar, limited results (O'Connor et al., 2007; Wexler et al., 2008; see comments above on Failure Free Reading and READ 180). Ultimately, there is no research evidence to suggest that repeated reading, or similar practice-based interventions, substantially closes the gap between struggling readers and their typical peers.

Phonics Instruction Without Additional Oral Phonemic Awareness. Letter-sound skills are essential for learning to read an alphabet-based writing system. They are also a necessary but not sufficient ingredient in orthographic learning (Ehri, 2005, Share, 1995). Phonological blending, which is the skill needed to blend phonemes into words, is a central element in phonic decoding (NICHD, 2000; Share, 1995). Thus, if a student can successfully sound out real or nonsense words, phoneme-level blending skills have been established. A beginning reader apparently does not require phoneme analysis skills to do phonic decoding. Thus, letter-sound knowledge + phoneme-level blending = phonic decoding.

However, according to Ehri's theory of orthographic learning, memory for written words requires the additional phonological skill of phoneme analysis. As mentioned, there is ample empirical support for the notion that phonemic analysis skills are central to creating orthographic memories of written words. It appears that phoneme-level blending to contributes to reading via its role in phonic decoding while phonemic analysis appears to assist in establishing a memory of the letter order of a written word via attaching pronunciations of words to their written forms (Ehri, 2005; Kilpatrick, 2015). Note that the flow of information in this memory process goes from (1) stored oral pronunciations to (2) pronunciations segmented at the phoneme level to (3) the letters that represent those oral pronunciations. This represents the opposite flow of information from what we find in phonic decoding, which goes from (1) letters to (2) phonemes to (3) oral pronunciations. Skilled readers display proficiency in both directions.

This apparent division of duty between two phonological skills, blending and analysis, helps explain a common pattern in the research literature. When students are given explicit and systematic phonics instruction, but no additional oral-only phonemic awareness/analysis instruction, their normed nonsense word reading scores grow substantially, often 10, 15, or 20 standard score points. However, their gains on normative tests of real-word identification tend to be in the 2–5 standard score point range (Blachman et al., 2004; Kuder, 1990; Ritchey & Goeke, 2006; Stebbins et al., 2012; Torgesen et al., 2007; Vaughn et al., 2012). This can be accounted for from the orthographic learning literature. As mentioned, memory for words is implicit and thus the letter-sound and phonemic analysis skills that underlie this memory process must also be implicit. Below it will be argued that simple segmentation and blending accuracy, without automaticity, are not enough to efficiently add words to the orthographic lexicon. However, that degree of phonemic skills appears to be sufficient for phonic decoding, allowing them to make gains on tests of nonsense word reading.

Whether using a practice-based/visual memory approach or even an explicit and systematic phonic approach lacking oral phonemic awareness training, reading interventions that do not address the underlying phonemic inefficiencies of students with the phonological-core deficit do not display strong normative gains on real-word reading tests.

Other Approaches with Limited Outcomes. Other approaches display limited reading improvements, such as the use of color overlays or lenses, visual tracking training or other visual training, the use of a special font, and catering to students' learning styles.

Visual color overlays and lenses might possibly address optical sensitivity but do not directly relate to reading difficulties (Wilkins, Lewis, Smith, Rowland, & Tweedie, 2001). Presumably, overlays or lenses make reading more comfortable for such individuals. There is no evidence, however, that such an optical condition causes dyslexia or that overlays can turn struggling readers into average readers.

Studies of visual tracking and other visual trainings have not resulted in improved reading scores. There are hundreds of studies showing that poor readers struggle with reading words in isolation, even though visual tracking is not required for single word reading. There appears to be no evidence that there are students who are competent readers of words in isolation but who, due to visual tracking problems, struggle in reading sentences and paragraphs. There may well be a correlation between visual tracking and dyslexia, but correlation is not the same as causation. Indeed, the evidence seems to suggest that poor reading causes poor visual tracking (Ahmed et al., 2012). The eyes of students who are poor readers dart back and forth to use context to understand what they read, because many words are not familiar to them, and they cannot reliably sound out those words. Research shows that when typical students are given text above their reading level, their visual tracking deteriorates as their eyes dart about the text in an effort to determine the meaning of many unfamiliar words (Ahmed et al., 2012; Hyönä & Olson, 1995). Also, students with alleged poor visual tracking display no such tracking issues when reading text that is easy for them. If such students had an inherent visual tracking problem, we would expect poor tracking at all levels of readability.

Some have observed that poor visual tracking in struggling readers may also apply to nonword stimuli. To understand a possible reason for this, consider the fact that aside from reading, there is no other activity during which humans use refined ocular-motor skills in which eyes sweep in a very smooth, precise, and consistent horizontal manner for long periods of time. Since students with dyslexia do very little reading, and from the outset their reading is characterized by eyes darting around for clues, it is difficult to know how they would develop the precise and untiring horizontal ocular-motor scanning abilities similar to their typically developing peers. Such speculation aside, the American Academy of Pediatrics (2009) teamed up with professional optometric and ophthalmological associations to publish a joint statement, asserting that visual training practices do not benefit children in their reading skills.

The *Dyslexie* font was developed to help those with dyslexia to read. On the developer's Web site, they say, "The most common reading errors of dyslexia are swapping, mirroring, changing, turning and melting letters together" (www.dyslexiefont.com/en/typeface/ retrieved August 6, 2018). It is not clear what research they were referring to, given that the most common reading errors in dyslexia have to do with simple accuracy and fluency, typically independently of the characteristics they mention. The transpositions of letters among struggling readers (e.g., reading *form* as *from* or *spilt* as *split*) are only one of several issues related to accuracy that such readers display. Orthographic learning research demonstrates that there is no need to appeal to confusions based on the visual characteristics of a given font, as long as it is legible to the reader. Rather, this letter transposition phenomenon is best understood as the student not having a precise memory for that specific letter sequence combined with inaccurate phonic decoding skills. A word that a student has not orthographically mapped does not have a stable existence in his or her long-term memory for the precise letter order. The Dyslexie font appears to thus be based on a misconception about dyslexia that dyslexia is characterized by visual confusion. A recent study of the Dyslexie font bears this out. Kuster, van Weerdenburg, Gompel, and Bosman (2018) did two studies of the Dyslexie font. One study included 170 children with dyslexia, and the second studied 147 students, some with dyslexia ($n = 102$) and some without ($n = 45$). They found in both studies that neither the students with dyslexia nor the typical readers showed any benefit from the Dyslexie font with either reading speed or accuracy compared to Ariel or Times New Roman, nor did they prefer the Dyslexie font over the others.

Teaching to a student's learning style (visual learner vs. auditory learner vs. kinesthetic learner; global learner vs. analytic learner; and left-brain learner vs. right-brain learner) is a highly intuitive concept that has been a mainstay in education. The popularity of instruction based on learning styles continues, despite four decades of research showing that it is not effective (for reviews, see Kavale & Forness, 1987; Pashler et al. 2008; Stahl, 1995; Stahl & Kuhn, 1999). Any time and effort devoted to a learning style approach would have the disadvantage that it directs time and effort away from approaches that work.

Moderate: 6–9 Standard Score Point Gains. In this category are interventions that involve systematic phonics instruction and basic phonemic awareness instruction (segmentation and blending), combined with reading practice. It is notable that all the intervention studies with this level of results or higher (next category) included explicit and systematic phonics instruction. It appears there are no studies that have yielded and maintained normative standard score gains above 5 points on word-level reading tests that excluded explicit letter-sound instruction. This reinforces the notion that phonics skills are necessary but not sufficient for struggling readers to demonstrate substantial improvements.

Lovett and colleagues (e.g., Frijters, Lovett, Sevcik, & Morris, 2013; Lovett et al., 1994; Lovett, Lacerenza, Borden, Frijters, Steinbach, & De Palma, 2000; Lovett, Lacerenza, De Palma, & Frijters, 2012) have published numerous intervention studies, often with struggling readers from the late elementary level to the high school level. Across various studies, students were trained in letter-sound skills and other code-based reading strategies (e.g., looking for familiar letter sequences within unfamiliar words). From their descriptions of their interventions, it appears that basic phonological awareness is trained via segmentation and blending activities. Their studies tend to produce outcomes in the range of about 7–8 standard score point gains on normed tests of word identification (Frijters et al., 2013; Lovett et al., 2012).

Similar results were obtained by Rashotte, MacPhee, and Torgesen (2001). They studied first through sixth graders who received an intervention that consisted of phonemic segmentation and blending training, phonics, and "reading and writing for meaning" (p. 123). The students in first through fourth grades gained 8 standard score points on a normed word identification subtest, while the fifth- and sixth-grade participants gained 7 points. The intervention group gained 19 points on a normed nonsense word reading test. As mentioned previously, phonemic blending along with letter-sound skills appears to be all that is needed to develop phonic decoding skills, but is not sufficient for skilled orthographic learning. This may explain the large gains in the normative nonsense word reading test, while real-word reading demonstrated more moderate gains. Some of the literature reviews acknowledge this pattern of stronger gains with nonsense words relative to real words (e.g., Bus & IJzendoorn, 1999; Torgesen, 2005). Most studies in this outcome category taught phoneme segmentation. It is argued below that simple segmentation training and assessment are not able to assure that segmentation skills are automatic, which appears to be necessary to become efficient at orthographic learning.

Highly Effective: 10–25 Standard Score Point Gains. In this category of studies are interventions using more challenging phonemic manipulation activities along with systematic phonics instruction and reading practice. One of the earliest such studies was that of Alexander, Andersen, Heilman, Voeller, and Torgesen (1991). They demonstrated an average of 12.5 standard score point gains on the WRMT-R Word Identification subtest among 7–12-year-olds. Their WRMT-R Word Attack (nonsense word reading) improved by 20 points. Their study was limited because there were only ten participants. Yet, it inspired other studies with similar, strong results.

The most influential study in this category is that of Torgesen and colleagues (2001), which played a role in prompting Tier 3 of RTI. These researchers intervened with 60 severely reading disabled third- through fifth-grade students. Their initial average score on the WRMT-R Word Identification subtest was at the second percentile. Half of the students were provided a commercially available intervention program consisting of phonemic manipulation activities, phonics instruction, and reading practice. Only about 5% of the instructional time was allotted to reading practice. The other half of the participants were provided an experimenter-designed program consisting of the same three elements, but 50% of the instructional time was allotted to reading practice.

Both groups of students gained an average of 14 standard score points on the WRMT-R Word Identification subtest and 20–27 points on the Word Attack subtest. At a two-year follow-up, additional testing showed the word identification score for both groups averaged 18 points above their pretest scores, suggesting additional improvement and no regression. The researchers indicated that 39.5% of these students did well enough that they no longer required special educational help in reading.

Simos et al. (2002) replicated the Torgesen et al. (2001) study while examining the impact of reading improvements on the brain. They did pre-intervention and post-intervention MSI brain scans with students with reading disabilities and age-matched peers who had typical reading skills. Due to the limits imposed by the cost of MSI scans, only eight students with reading disabilities participated. Their ages ranged from 7 to 17. They used two commercially available intervention programs that contained all three of the same key elements of phoneme manipulation training, explicit phonics instruction, and reading practice. Three students used one program, and five used the other. Six of the eight poor readers had initial normed word identification scores below the 3rd percentile, while the other two had scores at the 13th and 18th percentiles. After the intervention, the percentiles ranged from the 38th to 60th percentiles. When translated into standard scores, and the individual performances tallied, these students made an average of 25 standard score point gains on the word identification test. Additionally, the clear pre-intervention differences in brain activation patterns between the reading disabled and typical readers on the MSI scan disappeared in the post-intervention scans.

Truch (1994) presented clinical data on 281 clients with dyslexia who ranged in age from 5 to 55. At that time, his clinic used the Lindamood Auditory Discrimination in Depth (ADD) program. The ADD program used intensive phoneme manipulation activities, letter-sound instruction, and reading practice. On average, clients gained 17 standard score points on the word reading subtest from the Wide Range Achievement Test-Revised (WRAT-R) and 17 points on the WRAT-R spelling subtest. Gains were equivalent across all age groups.

A noteworthy element of the Truch (1994) study was that only one single client out of 281 did not improve his or her phonemic awareness in response to direct training. That represents less than one half of one percent of the study sample. Also, 75% of the clients reached the ceiling on the Lindamood Auditory Conceptualization Test after the training, which assesses phonemic manipulation skills. For those individuals to reach ceiling suggests that they achieved a functionally average level of phonemic awareness as a result of this training. Given the large number of participants (compared to 10 in Alexander et al., 1991 and 8 in Simos et al., 2002), this suggests that nearly all individuals of any age (24 clients were between the ages of 18 and 55) can improve their phonemic awareness skills with appropriate training, and a large majority (75% in Truch's study) can develop virtually normal phonemic awareness skills.

This finding deserves careful consideration. Most intervention studies either provide no oral phonemic training or only provide the more basic segmentation and/or blending training. In such circumstances, normed standard score gains ranged from 0 to 9 points. But when more advanced phonemic skills are trained, using phoneme manipulation activities, word reading score gains range from 10 points (Wise, Ring, & Olson, 1999) to 25 points (Simos et al., 2002). If there is a causal connection between these more advanced phonemic skills and reading, it is encouraging to note that the key skill that weak readers lack is indeed malleable and correctable. And when corrected, alongside explicit phonics instruction and reading practice, we see the largest intervention gains in all of the intervention literature. *Treatment resistors*, the name given to students who do not respond well to explicit phonics interventions and reading practice interventions, typically lack sufficient phonemic awareness skills and letter-sound skills (Torgesen, 2000). The Truch (1994) study, and other studies reviewed from this "highly effective" category, shows that the underlying deficits hindering the progress of dyslexic readers can be successfully remediated.

McGuinness et al. (1996) demonstrated an average of nearly 14 standard point gains in real-word identification and 19.5 points in nonsense word reading using the Phono-Graphix program. That program includes the three key elements that produce the highest results in the research literature, phonemic manipulation training, phonics instruction, and reading practice. Their clinical study involved 87 students ranging in age from 6 to 16.

The 12-Hour Effect. An interesting finding with the McGuinness et al. (1996) study was that their results were achieved following only 12 hours of instruction. Since these results seemed overly positive, Truch (2003) sought to replicate them using the Phono-Graphix program. He had a larger clinical sample of 203 participants and achieved similar sized standard score point gains, but it took an average of 80 hours of instruction to achieve this rather than 12. Being aware of the findings from McGuinness et al., (1996), Truch examined data on the tutored clients after the first 12 hours of instruction. He found an average of 7 standard score point gains in word reading after that brief period. By 80 hours, it had grown to 13.7. Truch (2003) accounted for the difference in the timing of the similar outcomes as being due to the fact that his clients initially had more severe reading difficulties than those in the McGuinness et al. (1996) study.

Truch (2003) identified what he called the "12-hour effect." After reporting results with hundreds of individuals tutored in the ADD and Phono-Graphix programs (Truch, 1994, 2003), Truch (2004) developed his own intervention program called Discover Reading. It contained the same three key elements as the other two. He gathered data on 146 clients tutored in this program after the first 12 hours of intervention. He found they made an average of 6.5 standard score point gains in word reading after that short period, and by 80 hours reached an average of 14.4 standard score point gains. In each of these three studies (McGuinness et al. 1996; Truch, 2003, 2004), the phonemic awareness skills reached ceiling by 12 hours of instruction. After that, the students continued to grow in their word reading skills, presumably because they now had the cognitive architecture to more efficiently remember the words they were reading. With no intervention studies directly informed by the orthographic learning research, this interpretation remains speculative.

One interesting finding across the three studies just described (McGuinness et al., 1996; Truch 2003, 2004) is that phonemic awareness skills were developed in struggling readers in a short period of time. Another study that demonstrated this was

Bhat, Griffin, and Sindelar (2003). They provided phonemic manipulation training with 40 students in sixth to eighth grade whose average initial phonemic awareness skills were in the first to second percentile as assessed on the Comprehensive Test of Phonological Processing (CTOPP). After 18 sessions across four weeks, the researchers saw a 29 standard score point improvement on the CTOPP Phonological Composite. However, there was no improvement in word reading, likely due to the fact that the study lacked any phonics instruction or reading practice, which the authors acknowledged. Despite this, Bhat et al. (2003) reinforced the studies by McGuinness et al. (1996) and Truch (2003, 2004), showing that deficient phonemic awareness skills can be remediated quickly using phonemic manipulation activities. It is also notable that nearly all of the studies discussed in this section required less than half of a school year. The rapid nature of these gains was acknowledged in a federal report (Torgesen et al., 2007). Citing studies reviewed in this and the previous section, the report stated, "Several studies have recently shown that intensive, skillfully delivered instruction can accelerate the development of reading skills in children with very severe reading disabilities, and do so at a much higher pace than is typically observed in special education programs" (Torgesen et al., 2007, p. 1).

Across various studies, several intervention programs were used to generate very strong results, some were experimenter designed while other are commercially available. Each of these programs had the same three elements: phonemic manipulation training, explicit and systematic phonics instruction, and reading practice. This illustrates one of the prerequisite considerations mentioned earlier in the chapter. One may argue that the ADD, Phono-Graphix, and Discover Reading programs are research-based, yet each has only a few studies that examined them directly. However, when we examine the common instructional elements across studies, we develop a picture of a more well-established research-based *approach* to addressing reading difficulties.

There are other studies that meet the criteria for the highly effective category (Torgesen et al., 1999, 2010; Torgesen, Rashotte, Alexander, Alexander, & MacPhee, 2003; Wise et al., 1999), which all share the same fundamental instructional characteristics. The success of these characteristics can be understood when we consider them in light of research on orthographic learning and on dyslexia (see below).

8.10.3 Summary of the Three Levels of Intervention Outcomes

The varying pattern of outcomes described above, based on differing instructional protocols, represents a phonemic proficiency intervention continuum. When no (or minimal) phonemic awareness is incorporated into an intervention, the gains are limited. When some phonemic skills are taught, but they represent primarily accuracy in the basic tasks of blending and segmentation, the results are stronger. However, when the phonemic awareness training includes the more challenging phonemic manipulation activities, the results represent the strongest outcomes in the word reading intervention literature. This pattern is consistent with the orthographic learning literature and was anticipated two decades ago. One of the studies with highly successful outcomes compared three intervention groups, each varying in the explicitness or nature of the phonemic awareness intervention. The authors noted, "The most phonemically explicit condition produced the strongest growth in word level reading skills" (Torgesen et al., 1999, p. 579).

Recall that phonemic skills are essential for efficient orthographic mapping to occur, that is, efficient storage of words for later retrieval. For this to happen, phonemic skills must be automatic and largely unconscious. Thus, when phonemic skills are trained to the level of accuracy, but not to automaticity, there may be improvements in phonic decoding skills, but limited improvements in the ability to efficiently add words to the orthographic lexicon (i.e., sight vocabulary). Yet when students receive more challenging phonemic awareness training, particularly using phoneme manipulation activities (phoneme deletion and substitution of phonemes within various positions within words), a greater degree of phonemic proficiency develops (see below). This presumably allows students to more easily remember the words they read, resulting in the largest standard score point gains found in the intervention literature (e.g., Alexander et al., 1991; McGuinness et al., 1996; Simos et al., 2002; Torgesen et al., 1999, 2001, 2010; Truch, 1994).

Kilpatrick (2015, 2018) offers an explanation for why phonemic manipulation activities likely provide a greater degree of phonemic proficiency than phonemic segmentation and blending training. Consider what is required to accomplish a phoneme deletion or substitution task. To delete or substitute a phoneme from a blend (e.g., to delete the /l/ from *slip* to get *sip* or change /l/ in *fly* to /r/ to get *fry*), one must (1) segment the word, (2) isolate the location of the target sound in that word, (3) delete or substitute the sound, and (4) blend the remaining sounds. Thus, skills associated with four conventional phonological awareness tasks (segmentation, isolation, manipulation, and blending) are all performed as part of a single task. If a student is able to respond to such items instantly, as typically developing readers can, then the amount of time devoted to any one of those four tasks is minimal, suggesting a substantial degree of proficiency.

The key skill needed for orthographic mapping is phoneme-level analysis/segmentation (Ehri, 2005). But when a response to a task requires *only* segmentation, there is no way to know for certain if an immediate response involves automaticity and unconscious access to the phonemes, or if a student quickly deconstructed the word to correctly respond to that segmentation task. However, if a student responds instantly to a phoneme manipulation task, where four conventional phonemic tasks occur in rapid succession, then one's confidence is increased that the analysis/segmentation skill is automatic and unconscious.

The integration of the orthographic learning literature and the word reading intervention literature presented in this chapter currently lacks direct, empirical demonstration. As previously mentioned, there exist no studies in the intervention literature that were explicitly based on the orthographic learning theories of Ehri or Share. However, the practice of using the combination of phoneme manipulation activities, explicit phonics instruction, and reading practice yields the largest standard score point gains in all of the intervention literature, supported by moderate to strong effect sizes. This suggests that regardless of the theoretical reasons why this instructional formula is so successful, it appears to represent best practice with struggling word-level readers.

8.11 Summary and Conclusions

It was mentioned earlier that the existing reviews and meta-analyses of intervention research present a fairly non-optimistic picture of the prospects of students with reading difficulties making large and sustained improvements in their reading skills. In this chapter, it has been argued that after addressing key, prerequisite issues, a more optimistic picture comes into focus.

The use of standard score gains to determine intervention efficacy and the examination of the instructional components of intervention studies in light of the orthographic learning literature results in the emergence of a pattern of results not identified in previous intervention reviews and meta-analyses. This pattern should provide encouragement to educators because it indicates that when instructional and intervention efforts are aligned with a scientific understanding of word learning, struggling readers make far greater gains than we have seen with approaches based on older assumptions about reading.

Skilled word reading requires letter-sound skills and phonemic skills to the level that they allow students not only to sound out new words, but to efficiently remember words via orthographic mapping (Ehri, 2005, 2014). Prevention studies show that students trained in these skills in K-1 have fewer reading problems than those without such training. Struggling readers whose remedial interventions include these central elements outperform those whose interventions do not. Also, the more extensive phonemic training using phonemic manipulation activities fares even better.

The intervention research seems to be best understood in light of the orthographic learning research. When viewed from that perspective, we see a phonemic proficiency continuum emerges. Given the phonemic nature of our alphabetic writing system, this should not come as a surprise. The degree of progress in real-word reading appears to be related to the level of proficiency in phonemic skills trained in the intervention. When no phonemic awareness is directly trained, there are limited results. When basic accuracy in phonemic segmentation and/or blending is trained, there are measurably better results. With more in-depth instruction in phonemic awareness using phonemic manipulation training, which presumably fosters phonemic proficiency, students gain, on average, a full standard deviation in word reading. Although this pattern of outcomes does not spring from intuitive or traditional assumptions about reading, it is consistent with the orthographic learning literature. At present, it appears that incorporating these three elements into instruction and intervention represents best practice.

References

Adams, M. J. (1990). *Beginning to read: Thinking and learning about print.* Cambridge, MA: MIT Press.

Ahmed, Y., Wagner, R. K., & Kantor, P. T. (2012). How visual word recognition is affected by developmental dyslexia. In J. S. Adelman (Ed.), *Visual word recognition* (Vol. 2, pp. 196–215)., Meaning and context, individuals and development New York: Psychology Press.

Alexander, A. W., Andersen, H. G., Heilman, P. C., Voeller, K. K. S., & Torgesen, J. K. (1991). Phonological awareness training and remediation of analytic decoding deficits in a group of severe dyslexics. *Annals of Dyslexia, 41,* 193–206.

Algozzine, B., & Lockavith, J. F. (1998). Effects of the failure free reading program on students at-risk for reading failure. *Special Services in the Schools, 13*(1–2), 95–105.

American Academy of Pediatrics. (2009). Learning disabilities, dyslexia, and vision. *Pediatrics, 124,* 837–844. https://doi.org/10.1542/peds.2009-1445.

Anderson, R. C., Hiebert, E. H., Scott, J. A., & Wilkinson, I. A. G. (1985). *Becoming a nation of readers: Report of the commission on reading.* Washington, D.C.: National Academy of Education.

Balu, R., Zhu, P., Doolittle, F., Schiller, E., Jenkins, J., & Gersten, R. (2015). *Evaluation of response to intervention practices for elementary school reading* (NCEE 2016-4000). Washington, DC: National Center for Education Evaluation and Regional Assistance, Institute of Education Sciences, U.S. Department of Education.

Beck, I. L., & Beck, M. E. (2013). *Making sense of phonics, second edition: The hows and whys.* New York: Guilford.

Bhat, P., Griffin, C. C., & Sindelar, P. T. (2003). Phonological awareness instruction for middle school students with learning disabilities. *Learning Disabilities Quarterly, 26,* 73–87.

Blachman, B. A., Schatschneider, C., Fletcher, J. M., Francis, D. J., Clonan, S. M., Shaywitz, B. A., et al. (2004). Effects of intensive reading remediation for second and third graders and a 1-year follow-up. *Journal of Educational Psychology, 96,* 444–461.

Bloomfield, L., & Barnhart, C. L. (1961). *Let's read: A linguistic approach.* Detroit, MI: Wayne State University Press.

Boardman, A. G., Argüelles, M. E., Vaughn, S., Hughes, M. T., & Klingner, J. (2005). Special education teachers' views of research-based practices. *Journal of Special Education, 39*(3), 168–180.

Bond, G. L., & Dykstra, R. (1967). The cooperative research program in first-grade reading instruction. *Reading Research Quarterly, 2*(4), 5–142.

Brady, S. A. (2011). Efficacy of phonics teaching for reading outcomes: Indications from post-NRP research. In S. A. Brady, D. Braze, & C. A. Fowler (Eds.), *Explaining individual differences in reading: Theory and evidence* (pp. 69–96). New York: Psychology Press.

Bus, A. G., & van IJzendoorn, M. H. (1999). Phonological awareness and early reading: A meta-analysis of experimental training studies. *Journal of Educational Psychology, 91*(3), 403–414.

Cardoso-Martins, C., Resende, S. Mamede, & Rodrigues, L. Assunção. (2002). Letter name knowledge and the ability to learn to read by processing letter-phoneme relations in words: Evidence from Brazilian Portuguese-speaking children. *Reading and Writing: An Interdisciplinary Journal, 15*(3–4), 409–432.

Chall, J. S., & Popp, H. M. (1996). *Teaching and assessing phonics: Why, what, when, how.* Cambridge, MA: Educators Publishing Service.

Chard, D. J., Ketterlin-Geller, L. R., Baker, S. K., Doabler, C., & Apichatabutra, C. (2009). Repeated reading interventions for students with learning disabilities: Status of the evidence. *Exceptional Children, 75*(3), 263–281.

Christodoulou, J. A., Cyr, A., Murtagh, J., Chang, P., Lin, J., Guarino, A. J., et al. (2017). Impact of intensive summer reading intervention for children with reading disabilities and difficulties in early elementary school. *Journal of Learning Disabilities, 50*(2), 115–127.

Crowder, R. G., & Wagner, R. K. (1992). *The psychology of reading: An introduction.* New York: Oxford University Press.

Cunningham, A. E., Perry, K. E., Stanovich, K. E., & Share, D. L. (2002). Orthographic learning during reading: Examining the role of self-teaching. *Journal of Experimental Child Psychology, 82,* 185–199.

Cunningham, A. E., Perry, K. E., Stanovich, K. E., & Stanovich, P. J. (2004). Knowledge of K-3 teachers and their knowledge calibration in the domain of early literacy. *Annals of Dyslexia, 54,* 139–167.

Dehaene, S., & Cohen, L. (2011). The unique role of the visual word form area in reading. *Trends in Cognitive Sciences, 15*(6), 254–262.

Dixon, M., Stuart, M., & Masterson, J. (2002). The relationship between phonological awareness and the development of orthographic representations. *Reading and Writing: An Interdisciplinary Journal, 15*(3–4), 295–316.

Edmonds, M. S., Vaughn, S., Wexler, J., Reutebuch, C. K., Cable, A., & Tackett, K. K. (2009). A synthesis of reading interventions and effects on reading outcomes for older struggling readers. *Review of Educational Research, 79,* 262–300.

Ehri, L. C. (2005). Learning to read words: Theory, findings, and issues. *Scientific Studies of Reading, 9*(2), 167–188.

Ehri, L. C. (2014). Orthographic mapping in the acquisition of sight word reading, spelling memory, and vocabulary learning. *Scientific Studies of Reading, 18*(1), 5–21.

Ehri, L. C., Nunes, S. R., Stahl, S. A., & Willows, D. M. (2001). Systematic phonics instruction helps students learn to read: Evidence from the National Reading Panel's meta-analysis. *Review of Educational Research, 71*(3), 393–447.

Ehri, L. C., & Saltmarsh, J. (1995). Beginning readers outperform older disabled readers in learning to read words by sight. *Reading and Writing: An Interdisciplinary Journal, 7,* 295–326.

Elbaum, B., Vaughn, S., Hughes, M. T., & Moody, S. W. (2000). How effective are one-to-one tutoring programs in reading for elementary students at risk for reading failure? A meta-analysis of the intervention research. *Journal of Educational Psychology, 92*(4), 605–619.

Flynn, L. J., Zheng, X., & Swanson, H. L. (2012). Instructing struggling older readers: A selective meta-analysis of intervention research. *Learning Disabilities Research & Practice, 27*(1), 21–32.

Fletcher, J. M., Lyon, G. R., Fuchs, L. S., & Barnes, M. A. (2018). *Learning disabilities: From identification to intervention* (2nd ed.). New York: Guilford.

Foorman, B., et al. (2016). *Foundational skills to support reading for understanding in kindergarten through 3rd grade* (NCEE 2016-4008). Washington, DC: National Center for Education Evaluation and Regional Assistance (NCEE), Institute of Education Sciences, U.S. Department of Education.

Foorman, B. R., Francis, D. J., Fletcher, J. M., Schatschneider, C., & Mehta, P. (1998). The role of instruction in learning to read: Preventing reading failure in at-risk children. *Journal of Educational Psychology, 90*(1), 37–55.

Frijters, J. C., Lovett, M. W., Sevcik, R. A., & Morris, R. D. (2013). Four methods of identifying change in the context of a multiple component reading intervention for struggling middle school readers. *Reading and Writing: An Interdisciplinary Journal, 26,* 539–563.

Gersten, R., Compton, D., Connor, C. M., Dimino, J., Santoro, L., Linan-Thompson, S., & Tilly, W. D. (2008). *Assisting students struggling with reading: Response to Intervention and multi-tier intervention for reading in the primary grades. A practice guide.* (NCEE 2009-4045). Washington, DC: National Center for Education Evaluation and Regional Assistance, Institute of Education Sciences, U.S. Department of Education.

Goodman, K. S. (1996). *On reading.* Portsmouth, NH: Heinemann.

Goodman, K. S. (2005). Making sense of written language: A lifelong journey. *Journal of Literacy Research, 37,* 1–24.

Gough, P. B., & Tunmer, W. E. (1986). Decoding, reading, and reading disability. *Remedial and Special Education, 7,* 6–10.

Hulme, C., & Snowling, M. J. (2009). *Developmental disorders of language learning and cognition.* Malden, MA: Wiley-Blackwell.

Hyönä, J., & Olson, R. K. (1995). Eye fixation patterns among dyslexic and normal readers: effects of word length and word frequency. *Journal of Experimental Psychology. Learning, Memory, and Cognition, 21*(6), 1430–1440.

Jacobson, C. (1999). How persistent is reading disability? Individual growth curves in reading. *Dyslexia, 5,* 78–93.

Kavale, K. A., & Forness, S. R. (1987). Substance over style: Assessing the efficacy of modality testing and teaching. *Exceptional Children, 54*(3), 228–239.

Keenan, J. M., Betjemann, R. S., & Olson, R. K. (2008). Reading comprehension tests vary in the skills they assess: Differential dependence on decoding and oral comprehension. *Scientific Studies of Reading, 12*(3), 281–300.

Keller, T. A., & Just, M. A. (2009). Altering cortical connectivity: Remediation-induced changes in the white matter of poor readers. *Neuron, 64,* 624–631.

Kilpatrick, D. A. (2015). *Essentials of assessing, preventing, and overcoming reading difficulties.* Hoboken, NJ: Wiley.

Kilpatrick, D. A. (2018). Incorporating recent advances in understanding word-reading skills into specific learning disability diagnoses: The case of orthographic mapping. In D. P. Flanagan & E. M. McDonough (Eds.), *Contemporary intellectual assessment: Theories, tests, and issues* (4th ed.). New York: Guilford.

Kuder, S. J. (1990). Effectiveness of DISTAR reading program for children with learning disabilities. *Journal of Learning Disabilities, 23*(1), 69–71.

Kuster, S. M., van Weerdenburg, M., Gompel, M., & Bosman, A. M. T. (2018). Dyslexie font does not benefit reading in children with or without dyslexia. *Annals of Dyslexia, 68,* 25–42.

Laing, E., & Hulme, C. (1999). Phonological and semantic processes influence beginning readers' ability to learn to read words. *Journal of Experimental Child Psychology, 73,* 183–207.

Lee, J., & Yoon, S. Y. (2017). The effects of repeated reading on reading fluency for students with reading disabilities: A meta-analysis. *Journal of Learning Disabilities, 50*(2), 213–224.

Lovett, M. W., Borden, S. L., DeLuca, T., Lacerenza, L., Benson, N. J., & Brackstone, D. (1994). Treating the core deficits of developmental dyslexia: Evidence of transfer of learning after phonologically- and strategy-based reading training programs. *Developmental Psychology, 30*(6), 805–822.

Lovett, M. W., Lacerenza, L., Borden, S. L., Frijters, J. C., Steinbach, K. A., & De Palma, M. (2000). Components of effective remediation for developmental reading disabilities: Combining phonological and strategy-based instruction to improve outcomes. *Journal of Educational Psychology, 92*(2), 263–283.

Lovett, M. W., Lacerenza, L., De Palma, M., & Frijters, J. C. (2012). Evaluating the efficacy of remediation for struggling readers in high school. *Journal of Learning Disabilities, 45*(2), 151–169.

Maughan, B., Hagell, H., Rutter, M., & Yule, W. (1994). Poor readers in secondary school. *Reading and Writing: An Interdisciplinary Journal, 6,* 125–150.

McGuinness, C., McGuinness, D., & McGuinness, G. (1996). Phono-Graphix: A new method for remediating reading difficulties. *Annals of Dyslexia, 46,* 73–96.

Mitchell, C., & Begeny, J. C. (2014). Improving student reading through parents' implementation of a structured reading program. *School Psychology Review, 43*(1), 41–58.

Moats, L. C. (1994). Missing foundation in teacher education: Knowledge of the structure of spoken and written language. *Annals of Dyslexia, 44,* 81–102.

Moats, L. (2009). Still wanted: Teachers with knowledge of language. Introduction to special issue. *Journal of Learning Disabilities, 42*(5), 387–391.

Morris, R. D., Steubing, K. K., Fletcher, J. M., Shaywitz, S. E., Lyon, G. R., Shankweiler, D. P., et al. (1998). Subtypes of reading disability: Variability around a phonological core. *Journal of Educational Psychology, 90,* 347–373.

NAEP. (2015). National assessment of educational progress: Nation's report card. Washington, D. C.: Institute for Educational Sciences, U.S. Department of Education. https://nces.ed.gov/nationsreportcard/.

NAEP. (2017). National assessment of educational progress: Nation's report card. Washington, D. C.: Institute for Educational Sciences, U.S. Department of Education.

National Institute of Child Health and Human Development. (2000). Report of the national reading panel. Teaching children to read: An evidence-based assessment of the scientific research literature on reading and its implications for reading instruction: Reports of the subgroups (NIH Publication No. 00-4754). Washington, DC: U.S. Government Printing Office.

Nelson, J. M., & Machek, G. R. (2007). A survey of training, practice, and competence in reading assessment and intervention. *School Psychology Review, 36*(2), 311–327.

O'Connor, R. E., White, A., & Swanson, H. L. (2007). Repeated reading versus continuous reading: Influences on reading fluency and comprehension. *Exceptional Children, 74*(1), 31–46.

Pashler, H., McDaniel, M., Rohrer, D., & Bjork, R. (2008). Learning styles: Concepts and evidence. *Psychological Science in the Public Interest, 9*(3), 105–119.

Protopapas, A., Sideridis, G. D., Mouzaki, A., & Simos, P. G. (2011). Matthew effects in read- ing comprehension: Myth or reality? *Journal of Learning Disabilities, 44*(5), 402–420.

Rack, J., Hulme, C., Snowling, M., & Wightman, J. (1994). The role of phonology in young children's learning of sight words: The direct mapping hypothesis. *Journal of Experimental Child Psychology, 57,* 42–71.

Rashotte, C. A., MacPhee, K., & Torgesen, J. K. (2001). Effectiveness of a group reading instruction program with poor readers in multiple grades. *Learning Disabilities Quarterly, 24,* 119–134.

Rayner, K., & Pollatsek, A. (1989). *The psychology of reading.* Hillsdale, NJ: Erlbaum.

Ritchey, K. D., & Goeke, J. L. (2006). Orton-Gillingham and Orton-Gillingham—Based reading instruction: A review of the literature. *Journal of Special Education, 40*(3), 171–183.

Seymour, P. K., Aro, M., & Erskine, J. M. (2003). Foundation literacy acquisition in European orthographies. *British Journal of Psychology, 94,* 143–174.

Shapiro, L. R., & Solity, J. (2008). Delivering phonological and phonics training within whole-class teaching. *British Journal of Educational Psychology, 78,* 597–620.

Share, D. L. (1995). Phonological recoding and self-teaching: Sine qua non of reading acquisition. *Cognition, 55,* 151–218.

Share, D. L. (1999). Phonological recoding and orthographic learning: A direct test of the Self-Teaching Hypothesis. *Journal of Experimental Child Psychology, 72,* 95–129.

Share, D. L. (2004). Orthographic learning at a glance: On the time course and developmental onset of self-teaching. *Journal of Experimental Child Psychology, 87,* 267–298.

Share, D. (2011). On the role of phonology in reading acquisition: The self-teaching hypothesis. In S. A. Brady, D. Braze, & C. A. Fowler (Eds.), *Explaining individual differences in reading: Theory and evidence* (pp. 45–68). New York: Psychology Press.

Short, E. J., Feagans, L., McKinney, J. D., & Appelbaum, M. I. (1986). Longitudinaly stability of LD subtypes based on age- and IQ-achievement discrepancies. *Learning Disability Quarterly, 9,* 214–225.

Simos, P. G., Fletcher, J. M., Bergman, E., Breier, J. I., Foorman, B. R., Castillo, E. M., et al. (2002). Dyslexia-specific brain activation profile becomes normal following successful remedial training. *Neurology, 58,* 1203–1213.

Slavin, R. E., Cheung, A., Groff, C., & Lake, C. (2008). Effective reading programs for middle and high schools: A best-evidence synthesis. *Reading Research Quarterly, 43*(3), 290–322.

Smith, N. B. (1965). *American reading instruction.* Newark, DE: International Reading Association.

Stahl, S. A. (1999). Different strokes for different folks: A critique of learning styles. American Educator, Fall, 1–5.

Stahl, S. A., & Kuhn, M. R. (1995). Does whole language or instruction matched to learning styles help children learn to read? *School Psychology Review, 24*(3), 393–404.

Stanovich, K. E., & Siegel, L. S. (1994). Phenotypic performance profile of children with reading disabilities: A regression-based test of the phonological-core variable-difference model. *Journal of Educational Psychology, 86*(1), 24–53.

Stebbins, M. S., Stormont, M., Lembke, E. S., Wilson, D. J., & Clippard, D. (2012). Monitoring the effectiveness of the Wilson reading system for students with disabilities: One district's example. *Exceptionality: A Special Education Journal, 20*(1), 58–70.

Stevens, E. A., Walker, M. A., & Vaughn, S. (2017). The effects of reading fluency interventions on the reading fluency and reading comprehension performance of elementary students with learning disabilities: A synthesis of the research from 2001 to 2014. *Journal of Learning Disabilities, 50*(5), 576–590.

Stuart, M., Masterson, J., & Dixon, M. (2000). Spongelike acquisition of sight vocabulary in beginning readers? *Journal of Research in Reading, 23*(1), 12–27.

Suggate, S. P. (2016). A meta-analysis of the long-term effects of phonemic awareness, phonics, fluency, and reading comprehension interventions. *Journal of Learning Disabilities, 49*(1), 77–96.

Torgesen, J. K. (2000). Individual differences in response to early interventions in reading: The lingering problem of treatment registers. *Learning Disabilities Research and Practice, 15,* 55–64.

Torgesen, J. K. (2004). Lessons learned from the last 20 years of research on interventions for students who experience difficulty learning to read. In P. McCardle & V. Chhabra (Eds.), *The voice of evidence in reading research* (pp. 355–382). Baltimore, MD: Brookes.

Torgesen, J. K. (2005). Recent discoveries on remedial interventions for children with dyslexia. In M. J. Snowling & C. Hulme (Eds.), *The science of reading: A handbook* (pp. 521–537). Malden, MA: Wiley-Blackwell.

Torgesen, J. K., Alexander, A. W., Wagner, R. K., Rashotte, C. A., Voeller, K. K. S., & Conway, T. (2001). Intensive remedial instruction for children with severe reading, disabilities: Immediate and long-term outcomes from two instructional approaches. Journal of Learning Disabilities, 34(1), 33–58, 78.

Torgesen, J. K., Rashotte, C. A., Alexander, A., Alexander, J., & MacPhee, K. (2003). Progress toward understanding the instructional conditions necessary for remediating reading difficulties in older children. In B. R. Foorman (Ed.), *Preventing and remediating reading difficulties: Bringing science to scale* (pp. 275–297). Baltimore, MD: York Press.

Torgesen, J., Schirm, A., Castner, L., Vartivarian, S., Mansfield, W., Myers, D. Stancavage, F. Durno, D., Javorsky, R., & Haan, C. (2007). National assessment of title I final report volume II: Closing the reading gap: Findings from a randomized trial of four reading interventions for striving readers (NCEE 2008-4013). Washington, DC: National Center for Education Evaluation and Regional Assistance, Institute of Education Sciences, U.S. Department of Education.

Torgesen, J. K., Wagner, R. K., Rashotte, C. A., Herron, J., & Lindamood, P. (2010). Computer-assisted instruction to prevent early reading difficulties in students at risk for dyslexia: Outcomes from two instructional approaches. *Annals of Dyslexia, 60,* 40–56.

Torgesen, J. K., Wagner, R. K., Rashotte, C. A., Rose, E., Lindamood, P., Conway, T., et al. (1999). Preventing reading failure in young children with phonological processing disabilities: Group and individual responses to instruction. *Journal of Educational Psychology, 91,* 579–593.

Truch, S. (1994). Stimulating basic reading processes using auditory discrimination in depth. *Annals of Dyslexia, 44,* 60–80.

Truch, S. (2003). Comparing remedial outcomes using LIPS and Phono-Graphix: An in-depth look from a clinical perspective. Unpublished manuscript. Reading Foundation, Calgary, Alberta, Canada. Available at http://readingfoundation.com/articles/.

Truch, S. (2004). Remedial outcomes with different reading programs. Paper presented at the International Dyslexia Association Conference, San Diego, CA. Available at http://readingfoundation.com/articles/.

Vaughn, S., Cirino, P. T., Wanzek, J., Fletcher, J. M., … Francis, D. J. (2010). Response to intervention for middle school students with reading difficulties: Effects of a primary and secondary intervention. School Psychology Review, 39(1), 3–21.

Vaughn, S., Wexler, J., Leroux, A., Roberts, G., Denton, C., Barth, A., et al. (2012). Effects of intensive reading intervention for eighth-grade students with persistently inadequate response to intervention. *Journal of Learning Disabilities, 45*(6), 515–525.

Vellutino, F. R., Fletcher, J. M., Snowling, M. J., & Scanlon, D. M. (2004). Specific reading disability (dyslexia): What have we learned in the past four decades? *Journal of Child Psychology and Psychiatry, 45*(1), 2–40.

Vellutino, F. R., Scanlon, D. M., Sipay, E. R., Small, S. G., Pratt, A., Chen, R., et al. (1996). Cognitive profiles of difficult-to-remediate and readily remediated poor readers: Early intervention as a vehicle for distinguishing between cognitive and experiential deficits as basic causes of specific reading disability. *Journal of Educational Psychology, 88*, 601–638.

Wanzek, J., & Vaughn, S. (2007). Research-based implications from extensive early reading interventions. *School Psychology Review, 36*, 541–561.

Wanzek, J., Vaughn, S., Scammacca, N. K., Metz, K., Murray, C. S., Roberts, G., et al. (2013). Extensive reading interventions for students with reading difficulties after grade 3. *Review of Educational Research, 83*(2), 163–195.

Wexler, J., Vaughn, S., Edmonds, M., & Reutebuch, C. K. (2008). A synthesis of fluency interventions for secondary struggling readers. *Reading and Writing: An Interdisciplinary Journal, 21*, 317–347.

Wexler, J., Vaughn, S., Roberts, G., & Denton, C. A. (2010). The efficacy of repeated reading and wide reading practice for high school students with severe reading disabilities. *Learning Disabilities Research & Practice, 25*(1), 2–10.

Wilkins, A. J., Lewis, E., Smith, F., Rowland, E., & Tweedie, W. (2001). Coloured overlays and their benefit for reading. *Journal of Research in Reading, 24*(1), 41–64.

Wise, B. W., Ring, J., & Olson, R. K. (1999). Training phonological awareness with and without explicit attention to articulation. *Journal of Experimental Child Psychology, 72*, 271–304.

Ziegler, J. C., & Goswami, U. (2005). Reading acquisition, developmental dyslexia, and skilled reading across languages: A psycholinguistic grain size theory. *Psychological Bulletin, 131*(1), 3–29.

Part III
Biological Perspectives

Chapter 9
Behavior-Genetic Studies of Academic Performance in School Students: A Commentary for Professionals in Psychology and Education

Brian Byrne, Richard K. Olson and Stefan Samuelsson

Abstract Available behavior-genetic research indicates that the single largest factor influencing individual differences in literacy development is genetic endowment. We briefly review some typical evidence and methodology used in studying the behavior-genetics of reading. We then outline three hypothetical educational scenarios and demonstrate how behavior-genetic studies might play out in them, with the aim of enhancing the critical capacity of school psychologists and other educational professionals to evaluate research findings in this area. We show that heritability estimates will tend to be higher in educational environments in which the instruction and other factors are more uniform, that the way subsamples are combined can affect estimates, and that population-level estimates cannot be used to determine the etiology of any individual child's performance. We address and dismiss genetic determinism, and review evidence to suggest that genetic accounts of reading disability may reduce blame and stigma yet increase pessimism about successful intervention. However, we argue that continued research into optimal ways to design and deliver curricula is quite compatible with the substantial heritability of individual differences in literacy and has already provided grounds for optimism. We also suggest that genetically derived constraints on academic progress bring into sharp focus questions about the goals of education.

Differences among students in reading and spelling are matters of great interest to educators and are the subjects of substantial amounts of research. Prominent among the factors that affect these differential aspects of achievement is the student's genetic endowment. The goal of this essay is to help psychologists and educators to enhance their understanding of what this fact means, and does not mean, for policy and

B. Byrne (✉)
University of New England, Armidale, Australia
e-mail: bbyrne@une.edu.au

R. K. Olson
University of Colorado, Boulder, USA

S. Samuelsson
Linköping University, Linköping, Sweden

© Springer Nature Switzerland AG 2019   213
D. A. Kilpatrick et al. (eds.), *Reading Development and Difficulties*,
https://doi.org/10.1007/978-3-030-26550-2_9

practice. We try to achieve this goal in part by considering how genetically sensitive research methods may play out in a range of educational scenarios. We link these hypothetical situations to real data where these exist.

It is not our aim to provide a systematic review of findings about the relative influence of genes and the environment on literacy. Such reviews are available (e.g., Asbury & Plomin, 2013; Kovas, Haworth, Dale, & Plomin, 2007; Little, Haughbrook, & Hart, 2017; Olson, Keenan, Byrne, & Samuelsson, 2014). Nevertheless, we offer some examples of these kinds of studies to (a) justify the claim that genes play a substantial role in literacy development, (b) lay a foundation for further appreciation of the methods employed in this area of research, and (c) consider the consequences for policy and practice of acknowledging the reality of the substantial genetic influence on literacy development.

9.1 Methods

Most *behavior-genetic* research, as it is typically termed, uses twins. Research of this sort takes advantage of the fact that there exist monozygotic (*MZ*, or "identical") and dizygotic (*DZ*, or "fraternal") twin types. Members of a monozygotic pair share all of their genes and members of a dizygotic pair share, on average, half of their segregating genes (i.e., genes that make individuals different from each other). When twins are raised together, as is overwhelmingly the case, *heritability* can be estimated as twice the difference between the within-pair monozygotic and dizygotic correlations. For example, if the correlation between monozygotic twins' performance on a reading test is X, and the correlation between dizygotic twins' performance on that same test is Y, then heritability is estimated at the difference between X and Y times two. *Variance* is a statistical way to measure the spread of the variation or variability (e.g., high-reading skills to low-reading skills) within a group. Heritability refers to the proportion of the variance on the trait that can be attributed to additive genetic variance. The proportion of the trait's variance that is not heritable is attributable to environmental factors that affect values on the trait (e.g., scores on reading tests). Twin studies allow for those factors to be partitioned into (1) ones that similarly influence both twins in a pair (i.e., *shared environment* such as family socioeconomic status, schools attended, and common teachers when both twins share schools and teachers), and (2) ones that twins do not share (i.e., *non-shared environment* such as individual illnesses, accidents, and separate teachers and friends). These values are generally calculated using a version of a statistical methodology called structural equation modeling that has been specially designed for twin data. This allows for computation of confidence intervals and tests of the statistical significance of values (Neale, Bokor, Xie, & Maes, 2002).

The validity of conclusions from classic twin design relies on several assumptions. One assumption is the *equal environments assumption* under which it is assumed that monozygotic twins are not treated more similarly than dizygotic twins. A second assumption is that there is no *assortative mating* for the trait under investigation;

for example, that adults do not select their mate based on similar levels of a trait. Violations of these assumptions can affect the accuracy of estimates of heritability and environmental influence unless the violations can be accommodated within the statistical modeling. There is a substantial literature on these and other assumptions, and we recommend a recent review by Barnes et al. (2014), which shows that twin research is generally robust in the face of possible violations of these assumptions (see also Plomin, DeFries, Knopik, & Neiderhiser, 2013).

9.2 Some Results

In Table 9.1, we document results from a range of studies using twin methodology. Just the heritability (A) and shared environment components (C) of variance are included in the table. The unique environment (E) is the remainder in each case (i.e., elements of the environment are not shared within a twin pair). Thus, $E = 1 - (A + C)$. The values are for individual differences except when identified as member of the lower end of the skill distribution (lowest 10%). When *latent variables,* such as reading comprehension, are indicated in the table, such variables are created by using multiple similar measures (e.g., different reading comprehension tests) and modeled as latent variables (i.e., the performance overlap across multiple reading comprehension tests provides a better estimate of reading comprehension than a single test, reducing measurement error).

It should be clear from Table 9.1 that the consistent finding is that genetic endowment accounts for a substantial proportion of the variability we see among children in their reading and spelling skills. This also includes whether or not a student performs at the bottom end of the distribution for reading and spelling, often referred to as *dyslexia* (Snowling & Hulme, 2005). The minimum heritability value is .39 and the maximum is .87. The studies vary somewhat in the contribution of shared environment to variance, and possible reasons for this are discussed later in the chapter.

We want to focus in particular on data from the *International Longitudinal Twin Study*, which is a longitudinal study of literacy development across four countries and three languages. We have selected this study not primarily because it is one that we (the authors) initiated but because its international component allows us to illustrate some interesting features of twin research.

Twin children in Australia, Norway, Sweden, and the USA were enrolled and assessed in their final preschool year (aged 4–5) and followed in literacy development for at least three further years near the end of kindergarten first grade and second grade. The total number of twin pairs was approximately 1000, with around half from the USA and a quarter each from Australia and Scandinavia (Norway and Sweden). They were assessed on a wide variety of literacy, cognitive, behavioral, and familial characteristics, but the focus here is on literacy and its known precursors. Some of these findings were presented in Table 9.1. Across several school grades, the results show: (1) a high level of heritability for multiple early literacy skills, (2) minimal shared environmental effects, and 3) modest unique environmental effects. It must

Table 9.1 Example results from twin studies of literacy

Sample	Measure	A	C	Reference
ILTS Kindergarten	Word identification	.70	.22	Byrne et al. (2010)
ILTS Kindergarten	Spelling	.39	.40	Byrne et al., (2010)
ILTS Grade 1	Word identification	.83	.01	Byrne et al., (2010)
ILTS Grade 1	Reading comprehension	.76	.03	Byrne et al., (2010)
ILTS Grade 1	Spelling	.72	.06	Byrne et al., (2010)
ILTS Grade 4	Word identification	.77	.14	Olson et al., (2011)
ILTS Grade 4	Reading comprehension	.86	.09	Olson et al., (2011)
NAPLAN Grade 3	Reading comprehension	.71	.05	Grasby et al., (2016)
NAPLAN Grade 9	Reading comprehension	.61	.13	Grasby et al., (2016)
CLDRC Multiple grades	Word identification LV	.87	.10	Christopher et al., (2016)
CLDRC Multiple grades	Reading comprehension LV	.82	.18	Christopher et al., (2016)
CLDRC Multiple grades, group membership, lowest 10%	Reading and spelling	.61	.30	Olson et al., (2014)
Florida Grade 1	Reading fluency	.62	.22	Taylor & Schatschneider, (2010)
TEDS Male 7-year-olds, group membership, lowest 10%,	Word identification	.67	.21	Harlaar et al., (2005)
TEDS Female 7-year-olds, group membership, lowest 10%,	Word identification	.50	.40	Harlaar et al., (2005)
WRRP Kindergarten + Grade 1	Word identification	.55	.34	Petrill et al., (2007)

Note: *A* Additive genetic influence; *C* Shared environment influence; *ILTS* International Longitudinal Twin Study; *CLDRC* Colorado Learning Disabilities Research Center; *NAPLAN* National Assessment Program: Literacy and Numeracy (Australia); *WRRP* Western Reserve Reading Project; *TEDS* Twins Early Development Study; *LV* Latent Variable

be noted that any measurement error is included in the figure representing the unique environmental effects.

9.3 The Story Becomes More Complex

As a way of introducing the contrasting scenarios we wish to employ, consider results from Samuelsson et al. (2008). They reported on reading test scores at the end of the first school year, kindergarten, separately for each country (combining Norway and Sweden in a single "country," Scandinavia). The scores were based on a combination of word and nonword reading efficiency from the *Test of Word Reading Efficiency* (Torgesen, Wagner & Rashotte, 1999). In Australia, the estimates of genetic, shared environment, and nonshared environmental influences were .84, .09, and .08, respectively. In the USA, they were .68, .25, and .07, and in Scandinavia, they were .33, .52, and .15. The contrast between Australia and Scandinavia is particularly marked, with the Australian heritability estimates being over two-and-a-half times higher and the estimates of shared environment being over five times lower than in Scandinavia. The U.S. estimates sit between these extremes.

It is unlikely that genetic differences between the nations account for these differing patterns of heritability because at the end of the second school year, the three countries fall into line, with almost identical heritability estimates of .80, .83, and .79 for Australia, the USA, and Scandinavia, respectively. Instead, it is likely that differing educational environments explain the contrasting results. In New South Wales, Australia (NSW., the site of the sample), kindergarten children attend a full school week (9 a.m. to 3 p.m.) and are subject to a state-wide curriculum that mandates that 35% of the time is spent on literacy instruction with agreed benchmarks as achievement targets throughout the year. In Colorado, the site of the U.S. sample, attendance is limited to half days (3–4 hours), and there is no state-mandated curriculum for kindergarten literacy, likely implying less uniformity in quantity and quality of instruction. In Scandinavia (at least at the time of the research), kindergarten attendance is not compulsory, although almost all children do attend, and the emphasis is on social and emotional development, with any literacy instruction being given informally and mostly at home. Thus, it appears that across the three sites, there is a continuum of intensity and extent of literacy instruction that corresponds to a continuum of heritability, which in turn is traded off with shared environmental influence.

A second result with similar implications arose during the course of the International Longitudinal Twin Study when about halfway through the multiyear recruitment process, Norway introduced formal literacy instruction into kindergarten, with a dedicated 6.2 hours per week. The educational change occurred in 2007. If the idea that the differences in heritability between Scandinavia and Australia just outlined were due to instructional differences, one would expect to see a change in the heritability estimates (and in average literacy scores) in the Norwegian sample exposed to the new, literacy-focused curriculum in comparison with those twins exposed to the previous curriculum. This is indeed what appears to have happened (Samuelsson, Byrne, Hulslander, & Olson, 2009). Word and nonword reading scores more than doubled, and spelling scores increased by almost 50%. The heritability of reading changed from .32 to .40, with a corresponding drop in the shared environmental effect. The spelling results were clearer with heritability increasing from .44 to .72, and shared environment dropping to .05. The twin numbers were (unavoidably) too small at 102 and 61 pairs, respectively for the old and new curricula, for significance testing, but the direction of the changes is exactly what would be expected on the hypothesis that increasing the intensity and uniformity of literacy instruction will lead to increased heritability estimates. These results are, by the way, particularly compelling evidence against the idea that genetic differences among the countries studied are behind the changes in heritability that are generated by changes in curricula.

The broad lesson from this set of results is that it is not appropriate to speak of *the* heritability of some variable. It is better to speak of the heritability of a variable *under X circumstances* (of sample, environmental particularities, period in history, and so on). And continuing the lesson is the greater the environmental range (as in Scandinavia for kindergarten literacy instruction), and the greater the size of the environmental influence. Heritability will tend to be highest in relatively uniform educational environments in which all children receive similar literacy opportunities (see also Asbury and Plomin, 2013, on this important point).

Armed with these concepts, let us now consider how behavior-genetic research might play out in some hypothetical educational systems with a view to refining our understanding of the implications of such research.

9.4   Scenarios

9.4.1   Scenario 1

The situation we consider here is: *Universal free education with mandatory attendance, a centralized curriculum, and a teaching workforce that delivers the curriculum in a uniform way within uniform school structures.*

This scenario incorporates minimal school environmental variability. In comparison with the situation for literacy instruction in kindergarten in Scandinavia and the USA., the NSW, educational jurisdiction in Australia appears to come closer to this scenario. Here, heritability was higher than in the other sites in the International Longitudinal Twin Study, and at .84, quite high indeed. Environmental influences that stem from school factors, such as the influence of individual teachers and class size, will decline to a negligible level.

Note that there is no information about how *well* students are performing. The curriculum may be suboptimal or teacher preparation might be flawed with all teachers trained to teach to the same (low) standard. That is, high heritability under these circumstances could go hand in hand with a low-jurisdiction-wide performance in comparison with other jurisdictions.

Individual children in Scenario 1: Even if heritability is high in the sampled population, this cannot be taken to mean that in any individual case of low-academic achievement, genes are the cause. The roughly 20–50% of population variance that is not attributable to genes leaves ample room for environmental factors to affect achievement in individual cases. Further, in the current state of (lack of) knowledge about actual genetic markers for low-level performance (discussed later), we have no way of identifying which children's problems are primarily genetic in origin and which are not. But even in the cases of (those unknown) children whose difficulties are primarily genetic in origin, well-designed and well-delivered intervention is likely to foster their literacy development (again, more later). Thus, the search for how individual environments affect literacy and its development remains a fully justified research endeavor even in the face of substantial group heritability in particular educational jurisdictions.

Groups of children under Scenario 1: Importantly, there may still be *groups* within the jurisdiction whose poor group performance is not attributable to genes. In Australia, for example, school attendance by indigenous students lags up to 20% behind nonindigenous students and (probably not coincidentally) their literacy performance lags as well (Purdie & Buckley, 2010). However indigenous Australians comprise only about 2.5% of the population, and so even if a behavior-genetic study was thoroughly representative of the population, which is in any case unlikely, the environmental circumstances of this small but important group is likely to have an undetectable influence on the estimate of the shared (or nonshared) environmental effect derived from twin studies.

As a second example, it has been reported that literacy (and numeracy) achievement across several grades assessed in nation-wide tests in Australia is adversely affected by arsenic, cadmium, and lead contamination in soil, dust, and aerosols in three cities with long histories of mining and metals processing (Dong, Taylor, Kristensen, & Zahran, 2015). The effect was magnified after controlling for school SES levels.

The general point emerging from these two examples is that high heritability should not inhibit the search for environmental causes of variance that apply to groups of students. Population subgroups, particularly relatively small ones, subject to deleterious environmental influences can remain below the radar in behavior-genetic studies using national samples.

Trends toward educational uniformity: Insofar as a nation, a state, or a school district may move toward a common curriculum for some or all school subjects, it can be expected that genes will become more prominent as a determinant of individual differences in academic achievement at the national (or state or school district) level. The same holds for moves toward uniform training standards for teachers and for aspects of school organization, such as class sizes. As a consequence, educational authorities who support these trends will need to accept an increasing role for genes in the variability of student achievement.

9.4.2   Scenario 2

As opposed to Scenario 1, here, we consider: *Elective education, no state financial support, with minimal guidelines for curriculum and its delivery in schools that vary in organizational structure.*

The picture here is education only for families that can afford to send their children to school, with few constraints on design and delivery of instruction. By the way of example, some of these characteristics are largely true of education in the African country of Swaziland. In Swaziland, the costs of education are prohibitive for many families. According to a World Bank report (Marope, 2010), 16% of Swaziland children were not enrolled in primary school, 74% were not enrolled in junior high school, and 88% were not enrolled in senior high school. The report also indicates that "school curricula do not clearly stipulate the skills and competencies that learners should acquire at each level" (p. 68) and states that teacher quality is subject to only scant checks. We are not saying that Swaziland is unique in its educational profile or that it should be criticized for it—after all, the country is burdened with very high financial and social costs of HIV/AIDS and has few natural resources other than agriculture and forestry. We simply wish to show that Scenario 2 is realistic.

A twin study of school achievement in the kind of environment is that Scenario 2 entails would, we hypothesize, show minimal genetic influence and substantial environmental effects, assuming that little in the way of informal education is offered in the home. These effects would be large of the shared environment kind if both twins in a family either attended school or did not attend school, and with increasing non-shared environmental effects if families could only afford to send one twin of a pair to school. The environmental effects would stem from the fact that zygosity would matter less for the degree to which twins are alike (the engine of etiological estimates in twin research) compared to the contrast between schooled and unschooled children. In other words, the contrast between monozygotic and dizygotic twin similarity would be dwarfed by the contrast between schooled and unschooled twin similarity.

This example illustrates that it would be a mistake to extrapolate to the world stage that the consistent findings of substantial heritability of literacy development derived from research in western societies. Access to education remains the major concern in many nations, and researchers who are working to bring to these countries affordable literacy lessons using scientifically validated methods deserve continuing support. For an account of one such project with a focus on African nations, initiated by Lyttinen and colleagues in Finland, see Ojanen et al. (2015). It is encouraging that UNESCO is supporting efforts like this (see https://www.jyu.fi/en/news/archive/2015/01/tiedote-2015-01-29-11-23-14-298438).

9.4.3   Scenario 3

Here, we consider: *Hybrid systems*.

Educational systems are in reality complex structures and may be getting more complex with a push, seen in some nations, to devolve more responsibility to individual schools for matters such as finance, staffing, curriculum and textbook choice, and management of special-needs students. In North America, giving states and provinces more control over educational decision making has a history going back to the 1970s in Florida and Alberta (Australian Education Union, 2012), and for a considerable number of years, legal and other issues surrounding this practice have been on the agenda (e.g., Florestal & Cooper, 1997; though a push for greater national common-core standards has characterized the last several years in the USA). So imagine, hypothetically, that within an educational jurisdiction that maintained overall responsibility for education, say NSW in Australia, there was considerable variety in curricula across individual subdistricts. Imagine further that some curricula were of high quality and some were quite suboptimal and that this difference influenced student performance. What would be the consequences for estimates of genetic and environmental influences?

The answer depends on the question being asked and on how it is answered. If the question is, "How heritable is literacy in Grade 2 in (say) N.S.W.?" then district-by-district variability in performance as a function of curriculum quality would increase the shared environmental effect, trading off with heritability. This is because, as a genuine factor affecting performance in children in general, the effect of the curriculum would be to raise or lower twins' scores irrespective of zygosity, thereby reducing the contrast between monozygotic and dizygotic twin correlations compared to a situation when there were uniformly effective curricula, or just one. In contrast, if the question is, "How heritable is literacy in District A, B, and so on," curriculum disappears as a factor, meaning that the shared environment influence will be limited to other things, such as the home and peers.

To the issue of how the question is answered and returning to our first one—heritability in NSW—it is common practice in behavior-genetic research to standardize within variables of no or minimal interest to the question in focus. For example, differences in age within a group of second-grade children may affect the scores on a literacy test. But if interest is in heritability in second grade irrespective of age, for example, when comparing with heritability in fourth grade, age will be controlled for statistically. The same would be true for, say, gender if it were not the focus of a particular study. Now, if in the hypothetical study of heritability in NSW researchers standardized literacy scores *within sub-districts*, the curriculum effect would disappear as an influence because all subdistricts would have means of zero (and *SDs* of unity) and heritability would be estimated as higher than when they did not do so. It is easy to scale-up this issue, say to the entire USA. If there was state-based effective environmental variability, for example, in teacher qualification standards (Darling-Hammond, 2000), standardizing within states would obscure this fact and simultaneously increase heritability estimates above those that would be obtained had standardization not been implemented.

Some data are available on this contrast (Byrne, Olson, & Samuelsson, 2013). As mentioned, the heritability of reading at the end of Grade 1 was almost identical in Scandinavia and Australia, at .80 and .79, respectively (with the USA at .83). But the Australian twins were reading at higher levels than their Scandinavian counterparts, with respective means of 43.8 ($SD = 16.3$, $N = 502$) and 25.6 (14.6, 576) on the identical (translated) test of word reading that was used. Similarly, mean reading comprehension scores were very different in the two samples, 26.1 ($SD = 7.4$) and 13.5 (8.3). It can be presumed that the inequalities come about because the Australian twins had just completed two years of formal reading instruction in comparison with the one year in Scandinavia, a clear environmentally driven difference. For word reading, the genetic and shared environmental influences when the two datasets are combined *after* within-country standardization are .83 and .00. In contrast, when the datasets are combined *without* within-country standardization, heritability drops to .59 and shared environment rises to .29. The same shift happens when reading comprehension is the literacy variable employed: following within-country standardization, .62 and .16; lacking within-country standardization, .38 and .49.

Earlier, we cautioned against referring to *the* heritability of a variable, instead referring to its heritability under X circumstances. To this, we can add, and *using Y analytic choices*.

9.5 Interim Summary and Looking Ahead

We have presented a variety of issues that educational professionals should be aware of in interpreting research that quantifies the relative influence of genes and various aspects of the environment on literacy development. They mostly boil down to being cognizant of the research settings and methodologies and realizing that if these change, so may the estimates. In particular, the trade-off between heritability and environmentality according to the environmental circumstances needs to be acknowledged. The more restricted and uniform the environmental range, the higher the heritability is likely to be. The more varied this environmental range, the greater is the potential for environmental influence. In some circumstances, subgroups in a population subject to the special effects of the environment may be invisible in national samples (e.g., an indigenous population in Australia, mentioned above). Finally, computational choices may affect the quantitative estimates, with our example being the choice to standardize or not standardize subsamples within a country or region. Such standardization within subsamples may obscure environmental effects that are real.

Despite these caveats, the weight of evidence is for a substantial effect of genes on literacy development, at least within those individual educational environments that have been studied so far. In the remainder of the chapter, we will discuss some of the implications of this conclusion. We first discuss the pitfalls of "genetic determinism," and then illustrate (a) how evidence for substantial heritability can be something of a mixed blessing, (b) how further research within the behavioral genetic framework may be able to guide instruction and intervention for children who struggle with reading, and (c) how the findings fit into the broader issue of the goals of education.

9.6   Genes Matter, But …

For professionals dealing with children and (and adults) struggling with literacy, and for the families of these children (and adult sufferers themselves), an understanding of how genes influence behavior is important. Here are some observations:

- There is no single gene responsible for reading (dis)ability. Despite media headlines that sometimes declare that *the* gene for X has been discovered, monogenetic disorders are extremely rare (Chabris, Lee, Cesarini, Benjamin, & Laibson, 2015). Behavioral traits are usually affected by thousands of individual mutations, each of tiny effect; for example, it has been estimated that schizophrenia, which is substantially heritable, is associated with 8300 "SNPs," *single-nucleotide polymorphisms*. It is likely that academic achievement skills are affected by even more (Chabris et al., 2015).
- The environment has, or can have, a substantial role in whether and how genes influence traits. A good example of the "can have" part is successful dietary manipulation and supplementation in cases of the metabolic disorder phenylketonuria. In the cases of marked reading disability, there is evidence that preventive efforts and well-designed and timely intervention can have long-lasting positive effects on literacy development in children showing signs of risk for reading disability (e.g., Blachman, Schatschneider, Fletcher, Murray, & Munger, 2014; Elbro & Petersen, 2004; Kilpatrick & O'Brien, Chap. 8, this volume).
- The environment can amplify the influence of genes through gene environment correlation (Plomin et al., 2013). In the case of literacy, children whose genes support reading skills tend to read more, thereby accruing the benefits of further reading practice. In contrast, children whose genes lead them to struggle with reading will in all likelihood read less, missing out on the benefits of extensive reading experience (for a summary of evidence supporting these expectations, see Olson et al., 2014). But although this may appear to be unalloyed bad news for those less well endowed genetically for reading, it also means that if these children *can* be encouraged to read, then what is essentially an environmental effect (reading experience) can minimize the amplification effect, particularly when accompanied by effective intervention opportunities (see Chap. 8). We return to the role of reading experience later.
- Epigenetics further complicates any simple picture of genetic influence. These are biochemical processes that leave DNA sequences intact but alter the expression of genes for good or ill (see Carey, 2012 for an accessible introduction). The environment, in the form of such factors as toxins, dietary abnormalities, and stress,

can modify gene expression through methylation and acetylation of nucleotides and histones. Among other things, this can mean that children with the same alleles at the sites of genes that are candidates for reading difficulties may be differentially affected.

Thus, genes cannot be conceptualized as deterministic (for an extended discussion, see Dar-Nimrod and Heine, 2011). Their possible effects are subject to opportunistic and deliberate environmental influences, and there is ample room for complex interactions among the many genes that affect a trait. The environmental influences in the case of literacy include, of course, preventative and remedial interventions. In Chap. 8, studies are reviewed that document improvements and, importantly, the maintenance of these improvements, even among students with the most significant word-level reading problems. Not all interventions produce large improvements or ones that last when followed up across months and/or years, but in Chap. 8, the principles that distinguish more from less impressive treatments are proposed. This should encourage practitioners to implement the quality interventions described in Chap. 8, despite the well-established findings that genes play a substantial role in accounting for variation in reading acquisition

The fact that many genes and their interactions are involved in reading development should discourage practitioners from looking forward to the day when a simple "genetic test" will accurately identify children at risk for reading disability. There is no realistic prospect of that happening.

9.7 Mixed Blessings

It is important for professionals and others to appreciate those "biogenetic" accounts of behavioral disorders are, in the words of Haslam and Kvaale (2015), a mixed blessing. Kvaale, Haslam, and Gottdeiner (2013) conducted a meta-analysis of what they refer to as the "medicalization" of psychological problems. Although reading disability was not among the disorders included in the research they summarized, and although we know of no research that has systematically studied literacy problems or other learning difficulties in this context, it is reasonable and prudent to assume that the conclusions that they draw would apply to these school-based disabilities.

The conclusions of Kvaale et al. (2013) were that providing people with biogenetic explanations (a) reduced stigma and blame associated with the disorders, but (b) increased pessimism about prognosis. In the authors' words, and in the context of mental health, "[m]edicalization of these problems may reduce blame, but at a cost. For example, pessimism about change could take hold of the affected individual, family members, mental health professionals, and the society at large, setting the stage for self-fulfilling prophesies that could seriously impede the recovery process" (p. 790). If these conclusions do indeed transfer to underachievement in reading, we could envisage relief from blame accompanied by a kind of fatalism on the part of parents, classroom teachers, and remediation specialists about prospects for recovery.

It is indeed possible that apprehension about a developing fatalism in part motivates the documented reluctance of many individuals working in education to acknowledge genetic influences on school achievement (Grigorenko, 2007).

Kvaale et al. (2013) underline the importance of not misinforming the public about biogenetic explanations, but urge caution in doing so to avoid negative side effects. The educational community needs to develop a narrative that reflects the scientific findings of reading disability but that at the same time discourages pessimism in affected individuals, their families, and relevant professionals. The International Dyslexia Association (IDA) is one organization that has faced the dilemma squarely. Its website (http://www.interdys.org) declares that dyslexia has neurobiological and genetic roots and at the same time encourages optimism that the difficulties can be overcome with proper diagnosis, appropriate phonologically based and multisensory training, "hard work," and the support of family, friends, and teachers. They identify successful figures in the arts, science, entertainment, and other fields who are classed as "dyslexic."

As helpful as the IDA's stance may be to those who engage with it, we are not aware of similar messages circulating in mainstream educational circles. With the growth of state- and nation-wide assessment in the basic school subjects of literacy and numeracy, and with scores made available in ways that families can compare their children with others and against criteria of achievement for each grade, many families will now discover low levels of performance in their children for the first time. If simultaneously public awareness of biogenetic accounts of school achievement increases, the unfortunate side effects that Kvaale et al. (2013) document may also become pervasive. The alternative of suppressing the biogenetic "story" is clearly unacceptable, and so the development of a compensating narrative becomes urgent in our view. Some of the highly encouraging results regarding the prevention and intervention with reading disabilities described in Chap. 8 can provide a basis for such a narrative.

9.8   Using Behavior-Genetic Studies to Inform Instruction and Intervention

It is one thing to quantify the relative influences of genes and the environment on a trait such as literacy. It is quite another thing to identify *how* these factors separately and together determine levels of the trait. We should note at the start that we are still unable to say much about the molecular biology responsible for variability even though there has been some progress at that level of explanation for severe forms of reading disability, with a handful of genes associated with the disorder being identified in replicated studies (Poelmans, Buitelaar, Pauls, & Franke, 2011). The main problem with gene identification for complex human characteristics is that a vast gap remains between the genetic variability that known genes can account for and the genetic variability itself based on behavioral studies such as those with twins. In medicine and other domains, this has been called the *missing heritability problem*, where typically liability for a disease that can be derived from identified genetic variants is just a few percent of the actual genetic liability (Maher, 2008). It is in fact this gap that forms the basis, mentioned earlier, for believing that complex traits are the product of very many genes, each of very small average effect in the population (Chabris et al., 2015).

Nevertheless, even though we know little about the actual genes affecting literacy, well-designed research can get closer to underlying cognitive processes than studies that simply analyze literacy itself. Measures of these cognitive processes need to be included alongside measures of literacy, and then, through multivariate genetic analyses, researchers can determine whether the processes underlying these measures are genetically correlated with the literacy phenotype. A common-sense analysis of learning to read words (one backed by a substantial research literature—see chapters in the volume edited by Snowling and Hulme [2005]) would implicate as a minimum (a) learning processes that can bind graphic symbols with morphophonological elements (initially, letters and phonemes, and later, letter strings and whole words), and (b) processes that support left-to-right decoding of letter strings, where a child needs to recover the phoneme that the first letter represents, hold it in mind while recovering the next letter's phoneme, continue this process, and finally, amalgamate the phoneme string into a word. The first of these is generally referred to as associative learning, the second as working memory.

In the International Longitudinal Twin Study, the researchers included several tasks that tap associative learning for graphic symbols and working memory for linguistic material. They indeed discovered that they are genetically correlated with (i.e., are *pleiotropic* with) early letter knowledge and later word reading efficiency (Byrne, Wadsworth, et al., 2013).

These findings immediately suggest diagnostics to predict whether a child will struggle with learning to read and remedial steps for those who subsequently do. Early difficulties learning letters relative to opportunity would be a warning sign, as would information, perhaps from standardized tests, of working memory deficiencies. Constraints on associative learning are best addressed, it is reasonable to assume, by more abundant exposure to letters and words. This advice is confirmed by purely behavioral data, for example from Reitsma (1983), who showed that children identified as reading disabled required more exposures to novel words to fix them in memory than other children did. While the suggestion of extended practice is hardly revolutionary, it does contrast to a degree with the dominant approach to reading difficulties, namely an emphasis on phonological awareness and explicit teaching of letter–sound relations.

We can draw other lessons from findings of genetically influenced variation in foundational processes supporting reading. Working memory will be a pivotal process at many points other than left-to-right decoding of words early in reading development. Assembling meaning from continuous text will also call upon working memory. The research implicating poor working memory as a factor affecting reading development is quite substantial (Fletcher, Lyon, Fuchs, & Barnes, 2018; Hulme & Snowling, 2009). Indeed, a variety of executive functions, working memory, inhibition, processing speed, and naming speed, is substantially related to reading skills, and most of that covariation is driven by genetic influence (Christopher et al., 2016). This in turn suggests that instructional practices that load executive functions like working memory unnecessarily will be detrimental to reading-disabled children; such practices could range from asking them to decode overly long words to text construction that delivers information in sentences with unnecessarily complex syntactic structures such as deep embedding. Educators designing material, from elementary readers to standard textbooks, would do well to keep this type of genetically influenced constraint in mind as they do their work. Otherwise, children who labor under these constraints will not only miss out on needed successful encounters with print and information from texts, but run the risk of declining motivation to read as they become dispirited by their attempts to do so (Byrne, 2005).

These, then, are examples of how genetically informative research can help guide practice, and why educational professionals are likely to benefit from its continuation and dissemination. Researchers, too, have a role to play here, namely in ensuring that the products of their efforts are made readily available to the communities that can turn them into good practice.

9.9 Goals of Education

The available evidence tells us that in educational environments that are relatively uniform in terms of child attendance, curriculum, teacher quality, and so on, genetic endowment will be a restraining factor for some children (and of course an enhancing one for others). But the evidence also tells us that well-designed instructional interventions and continued support can help moderate individual risk (see Chap. 8), and in fact produce encouraging results at the whole-of-district level (Sadoski & Wilson, 2006). So an important question becomes, how much academic equality among students should an educational jurisdiction strive for with the use of strenuous instructional strategies to compensate individuals and groups?

The question is a real one because there are only so many hours in the school day and an intensive focus on one school subject, literacy say, must come at the expense of another. The problem is compounded by the fact that multivariate behavior-genetic analyses have shown that there is a considerable amount of pleiotropy among school subjects; children who are genetically challenged in literacy, for example, are often challenged for at least some of the same (genetic) reasons in mathematics (Willcutt et al., 2013). Students who are burdened with genes that act in this pleiotropic fashion, that is across both domains, will need extra remedial help in both, placing that much more time pressure on them and on the school system to provide such remediation.

Realistically, again, schools probably need to differentially value academic subjects in terms of where the extraordinary efforts are directed. Literacy would normally appear high on that list because of its importance for educational progress (and life) in general, with mathematics close behind because of the grounding it furnishes for the physical and social sciences, and of course for everyday life in a technological society. These are not easy choices, but at least recognition of genetic limitations does force educators to make them. In contrast, clinging to the view that (almost) everything is down to the environment and that, therefore, there is a wide range of resources to intervene (improving teacher quality, reducing class sizes, ensuring greater involvement of families in the educational process, controlling time spent on social networking sites, ridding the environment of toxins, improving sleep habits and diet, and so on) may give rise to false hopes. Indeed, meta-analyses of reading interventions show that environmental factors (e.g., group size, number of intervention hours, SES), play a smaller role in intervention outcomes than we would intuitively expect (see Chap. 8 for a brief review). It is not that these factors are unimportant, but it is too optimistic by far to believe that these measures or a combination of them will level the playing field for students.

Thus, genetic endowment will remain an influence on achievement in actual educational systems, though educators committed to the notion that very high achievement is within the grasp of any child in one domain or another can take comfort in the fact that the environment can remain a substantial player in achievement. They can also take comfort in the long tradition of evidence that sustained practice over substantial periods of time can produce high-level skills in music, sporting activities, specialist academic pursuits, and other domains (Ericsson & Ward, 2007).

9.10 A Reiteration: Behavior-Genetic Studies Are About Variances, Not Means

In a thought experiment, imagine that a novel way of teaching reading was discovered that when introduced to schools raised the average skill level of all children to the degree that none now read at the low levels that previously would classify them as "dyslexic." None would now be hampered in the other parts of their education. It is a reasonable assumption that differences in, say, speed of reading, would remain and that they would be in part driven by genetic differences, but in practical terms, these would be of no more consequence than differences in speed of normal walking are now. Drawing out the implications of these observations, research should continue into the best way to teach literacy even though genes might continue to drive student differences. Findings of even high heritability for a trait do not imply that population averages cannot change, as indeed they have over time for the highly heritable variable of human height or, closer to home for the concerns of this article, for the almost equally heritable variable of intelligence (Dickens & Flynn, 2001).

9.11 Conclusions

- Genetic variability among students impacts individual differences in literacy. In most research conducted within a genetically informative framework to this point, genes account for half or more of the variance. But the quantitative estimates derived from each study need to be conditioned by important considerations, most notably the educational context in which it was undertaken. Environments that are both intensive and uniform will generate higher estimates of heritability than those that are less intensive and more variable. It would be quite inappropriate to import estimates from contexts like those in Scenario 1 to Scenario 2 situations. Doing so could weaken any motivation to change the educational circumstances that could be threatening the academic progress of Scenario 2 students.
- Quantitative estimates of heritability and environmentality can be affected by the way the calculations are done, as in our example of how results from multisite environments are standardized and combined.
- Heritability is about variability, not average levels of achievement. Comparisons across school districts, states, and countries are appropriate measures of averages. Further, even high levels of genetic influence should not inhibit the search for better ways of building and delivering the curriculum, nor of attending to any adverse academic circumstances of subgroups within a population.
- High heritability is not a recipe for inaction. Genes are never the full story. It is impossible to determine for any individual the degree to which genes versus environmental factors are at play. Given evidence that prevention and intervention efforts can ameliorate the adverse effects of genetic endowment, sustained efforts to remediate remain appropriate when children or groups are falling behind.
- Quantitative estimates do not, of themselves, tell us anything about how genes and aspects of the environment influence student achievement. Well-designed studies will build in measures other than literacy itself in an attempt to identify those factors. This is where hypotheses gained in other research can be of high value, such as when processes identified in purely phenotypic studies of reading development and dyslexia are incorporated into the research. The days of simply quantifying heritability and environmentality of literacy are, or ought to be, over.
- Despite the qualifications and cautions we have outlined, genetic endowment is a real player in relative levels of academic achievement, and will continue to be. Recognizing that fact can provide some relief for parents and teachers who may have been called on to bear more than their fair share of responsibility for children who struggle with one subject or another. But the same relief may be accompanied by greater pessimism about remediation, and the educational community needs to be proactive by developing ways to forestall unnecessarily gloomy attitudes about prognosis.
- The data we have surveyed also pose questions for educational systems about the extent they wish to compensate, at the individual or system level, for constraints imposed by genes. These are not easy questions to answer, but facing them squarely is a start.

Acknowledgements This research was supported by the Australian Research Council (DP0663498, DP0770805), the National Institute for Child Health and Human Development (HD27802, HD38526), the Swedish Research Council (2011–1905), and the Swedish Council for Working Life and Social Research (2011 0177).

References

Asbury, K., & Plomin, R. (2013). *G is for genes: The impact of genes on education and achievement*. Oxford, UK: Wiley-Blackwell.

Australian Education Union. (2012). *Devolution and education: A research report prepared by the Australian Education Union.* Retrieved from http://www.aeufederal.org.au/Publications/2012/Devandeducation.pdf.

Barnes, J. C., Wright, J. P., Boutwell, B. B., Schwartz, J. A., Connolly, E. J., Nedelec, J. L., et al. (2014). Demonstrating the validity of twin research in criminology. *Criminology, 52*, 588–626.

Blachman, B. A., Schatschneider, C., Fletcher, J. M., Murray, M. S., & Munger, K. (2014). Intensive reading remediation in grade 2 or 3: Are there effects a decade later? *Journal of Educational Psychology, 106*, 46–57.

Byrne, B. (2005). Theories of learning to read. In M. Snowling & C. Hulme (Eds.), *The science of reading: A handbook* (pp. 104–119). Oxford: Blackwell.

Byrne, B., Khlentzos, D., Olson, R. K., & Samuelsson, S. (2010). Evolutionary and genetic perspectives on educational attainment. In K. Littleton, C. Wood, & J. K. Staarman (Eds.), *International handbook of psychology in education* (pp. 3–33). Bingley, UK: Emerald Press.

Byrne, B., Olson, R. K., & Samuelsson, S. (2013). Subsample standardization in twin studies of academic achievement. In *Annual conference of the behavior genetics association*, July, Marseilles, France.

Byrne, B., Wadsworth, S., Boehme, K., Talk, A. C., Coventry, W. L., Olson, R. K., … Corley, R. (2013). Multivariate genetic analysis of learning and early reading development. *Scientific Studies of Reading, 17*, 224–242.

Carey, N. (2012). *The epigenetics revolution*. London, UK: Icon Books.

Chabris, C. F., Lee, J. J., Cesarini, D., Benjamin, D. J., & Laibson, D. I. (2015). The fourth law of behavior genetics. *Current Directions in Psychological Science, 24*, 304–312.

Christopher, M. E., Keenan, J. M., Hulslander, J., DeFries, J. C., Miyake, A., Wadsworth, S. J., et al. (2016). The genetic and environmental etiologies of the relations between cognitive skills and components of reading ability. *Journal of Experimental Psychology: General, 145*, 451–466.

Dar-Nimrod, I., & Heine, S. J. (2011). Genetic essentialism: On the deceptive determinism of DNA. *Psychological Bulletin, 137*, 800–818.

Darling-Hammond, L. (2000). Teacher quality and student achievement: A review of state policy evidence. *Educational Policy Analysis Archives, 8*. Retrieved from http://epaa.asu.edu/epaa/v8n1/.

Dickens, W. T., & Flynn, (2001). Heritability estimates versus large environmental effects: The IQ paradox resolved. *Psychological Review, 108*, 346–369.

Dong, C., Taylor, M. P., Kristensen, L. J., & Zahran, S. (2015). Environmental contamination in an Australian mining community and potential influences on early childhood health and behavioural outcomes. *Environmental Pollution, 207*, 345–356.

Elbro, C., & Peterson, D. K. (2004). Long-term effects of phoneme awareness and letter sound training: An intervention study with children at risk for dyslexia. *Journal of Educational Psychology, 96*, 660–670.

Ericsson, K. A., & Ward, P. (2007). Capturing the naturally occurring superior performance of experts in the laboratory: Toward a science of expert and exceptional performance. *Current Directions in Psychological Science, 16*, 346–350.

Fletcher, J. M., Lyon, G. R., Fuchs, L. S., & Barnes, M. A. (2018). *Learning disabilities: From identification to intervention* (2nd ed.). New York: Guilford.

Florestal, K., & Cooper, R. (1997). Decentralization of education: Legal issues, *Directions in Development Series*. Washington, DC: The World Bank. Retrieved from http://siteresources.worldbank.org/EDUCATION/Resources/278200-1099079877269/547664-1099080000281/Decent_ed_legal_issues_EN97.pdf.

Grasby, K. L., Coventry, W. L., Byrne, B., Olson, R. K., & Medland, S. E. (2016). Genetic and environmental influences on literacy and numeracy performance in Australian school children in grades 3, 5. 7, and 9. *Behavior Genetics, 46,* 627–648.

Grigorenko, E. L. (2007). How can genomics inform education? *Mind, Brain, and Education, 1,* 20–27.

Harlaar, N., Spinath, F. M., Dale, P. S., & Plomin, R. (2005). Genetic influences on early word recognition abilities and disabilities: A study of 7-year-old twins. *Journal of Child Psychology and Psychiatry, 46,* 373–384.

Haslam, N., & Kvaale, E. P. (2015). Biogenetic explanations of mental disorder: The mixed-blessings model. *Current Directions in Psychological Science, 24,* 399–404.

Hulme, C., & Snowling, M. J. (2009). *Developmental disorders of language and cognition*. Malden, MA: Wiley-Blackwell.

Kovas, Y., Haworth, C. M. A., Dale, P. S., & Plomin, R. (2007). The genetic and environmental origins of learning abilities and disabilities in the early school years. *Monographs of the Society for Research in Child Development, 72,* 1–160.

Kvaale, E. P., Haslam, N., & Gottdeiner, W. H. (2013). The "side effects" of medicalization: A meta-analytic review of how biogenetic explanations affect stigma. *Clinical Psychology Review, 33,* 782–794.

Little, C. W., Haughbrook, R., & Hart, S. A. (2017). Cross-study differences in the etiology of reading comprehension: A meta-analytical review of twin studies. *Behavior Genetics, 47,* 52–76.

Maher, B. (2008). Personal genomes: The case of the missing heritability. *Nature, 456,* 16–21.

Marope, M. (2010). The education system in Swaziland: Training and skills development for shared growth and competitiveness. *World Bank Working Paper No 188, Africa Region Human Development Department*, Washington, DC. Retrieved from http://siteresources.worldbank.org/EDUCATION/Resources/278200-1099079877269/education_system_in_Swaziland.pdf.

Neale, M. C., Boker, S. M., Xie, G., & Maes, H. H. (2002). *Mx: Statistical modeling* (6th ed.). VCU Box 900126, Richmond, VA 23298: Department of Psychiatry.

Ojanen, E., Ronimus, M., Ahonen, T., Chansa-Kabali, T., February, P., Jere-Folotiya, J., et al. (2015). GraphoGame—A catalyst for multi-level promotion of literacy in diverse contexts. *Frontiers in Psychology., 6,* 671.

Olson, R. K., Keenan, J. M., Byrne, B., & Samuelsson, S. (2014). Why do children differ in their reading and related skills? *Scientific Studies of Reading, 18,* 38–54.

Olson, R. K., Keenan, J. M., Byrne, B., Samuelsson, S., Coventry, W. L., Corley, R., … Hulslander, J. (2011). Genetic and environmental influences on vocabulary and reading development. *Scientific Studies of Reading, 15,* 26–46. https://doi.org/10.1080/10888438.2011.536128.

Petrill, S. A., Deater-Deckard, K., Thompson, L. A., Schatschneider, C., DeThorne, L. S., & Vandenbergh, D. J. (2007). Longitudinal genetic analysis of early reading: The western reserve reading project. *Reading and Writing, 20,* 127–146.

Poelmans, G., Buitelaar, J. K., Pauls, D. K., & Franke, B. (2011). A theoretical molecular network for dyslexia: Integrating available genetic findings. *Molecular Psychiatry, 16,* 365–382.

Plomin, R., DeFries, J. C., Knopik, V. S., & Neiderhiser, J. M. (2013). *Behavioral genetics* (6th ed.). New York, NY: Worth Publishers.

Purdie, N., & Buckley, S. (2010). School attendance and retention of Indigenous Australian students. *Issues paper No 1, Closing the Gap Clearinghouse*. Australian Institute of Health and Welfare, and Australian Institute of Family Studies. Retrieved from http://www.aihw.gov.au/closingthegap/documents/issues_papers/ctg-ip01.pdf.

Reitsma, P. (1983). Printed word learning in beginning readers. *Journal of Experimental Child Psychology, 75*, 321–339.

Sadoski, M., & Wilson, V. L. (2006). Effects of a theoretically based large-scale reading intervention in a multicultural urban school district. *American Educational Research Journal, 13*, 137 161.

Samuelsson, S., Byrne, B., Hulslander, J., & Olson, R. (2009). Behavior-genetic analyses of literacy development in more and less transparent orthographies: A comparison of Scandinavian and U.S./Australian children. In *Annual conference of the society for the scientific study of reading,* July: Boston, MA, USA.

Samuelsson, S., Byrne, B., Olson, R. K., Hulslander, J., Wadsworth, S., Corley, R, … DeFries, J. C. (2008). Response to early literacy instruction in the United States, Australia, and Scandinavia: A behavioral-genetic analysis. *Learning and Individual Differences, 18*, 289–295 (PMID: 19122888).

Snowling, M. J., & Hulme, C. (2005). *The science of reading: A handbook.* Oxford, UK: Blackwell.

Taylor, J., & Schatschneider, C. (2010). Genetic influence on literacy constructs in kindergarten and first grade: Evidence from a diverse twin sample. *Behavior Genetics, 40*, 591–602.

Torgesen, J. K., Wagner, R. K., & Rashotte, C. A. (1999). *Test of word reading efficiency.* Austin, TX: Pro-ed.

Willcutt, E. G., Petrill, S. A., Wu, S., Boada, R., DeFries, J. C., Olson, R. K., et al. (2013). Comorbidity between reading disability and math disability: concurrent psychopathology, functional impairment, and neuropsychological functioning. *Journal of Learning Disabilities, 46*, 500–516.

Chapter 10
The Neurobiological Strands of Developmental Dyslexia: What We Know and What We Don't Know

Lesley A. Sand and Donald J. Bolger

Abstract This chapter focuses on the definition of dyslexia as "neurobiological in origin" as prescribed by the International Dyslexia Association and National Institute of Child Health and Human Development. The chapter examines the notion of dyslexia as a specific learning disability and challenges the presumption that impairments are specific or limited to reading behavior based on behavioral and neurobiological evidence. The authors argue that the convergence of evidence from neuroimaging studies leading up to the adoption of the definition of dyslexia in 2003 is belied by a larger set of more divergent findings suggesting a variety of etiologies of the disorder. Moreover, the argument for a central phonological deficit behaviorally with neurobiological impairments in regions associated with receptive language processing (roughly surrounding Wernicke's area) may be just as much an outcome determined by multiple sources of lower-level impairments as it is a cause of dyslexia. Familial risk factors of the disorder are reflected in brain development, and behavior and evidence of genetic markers suggest a certain degree of heritability. However, clear evidence for environmental mediators and successful interventions yields a complex dynamic of how nature and nurture interact in the emergence of the disorder. Thus, this likely equifinality of the disorder requires that large datasets of neurobiological and behavioral data be culled to uncover endophenotypic subtypes or biotypes of dyslexia that may reflect differential responses to intervention.

> Dyslexia is a specific learning disability that is neurobiological in origin. It is characterized by difficulties with accurate and/or fluent word recognition and by poor spelling and decoding abilities. These difficulties typically result from a deficit in the phonological component of language that is often unexpected in relation to other cognitive abilities and the provision of effective classroom instruction. Secondary consequences may include problems in reading comprehension and reduced reading experience that can impede growth of vocabulary and background knowledge (Lyon, Shaywitz, & Shaywitz, 2003).

L. A. Sand · D. J. Bolger (✉)
University of Maryland, College Park, USA
e-mail: djbolger@umd.edu

L. A. Sand
e-mail: lesleyannsand@gmail.com; lsand@umd.edu

© Springer Nature Switzerland AG 2019
D. A. Kilpatrick et al. (eds.), *Reading Development and Difficulties*,
https://doi.org/10.1007/978-3-030-26550-2_10

Our primary aim in this chapter is to address the nature of developmental dyslexia[1] and our evolving understanding of it as "neurobiological in origin." Our hope is that the overview provided of the neurobiological research on dyslexia in this chapter may provide insight into the nature of the disorder, challenges in assessment and diagnosis, and the impact of interventions on the brain itself. The preceding definition of dyslexia was adopted in 2002 by the International Dyslexia Association (IDA) and subsequently by the National Institutes for Child Health and Development (NICHD) along with federal, state, and local educational systems.

While it may seem innocuous at first, the identification of dyslexia as a "specific learning disability" and one that is "neurobiological in origin" is laden with theoretical and pragmatic disputes that have a dramatic impact on the way that practitioners, parents, and individuals with dyslexia approach this disorder. For one, the term "specific learning disability" comes from the medical model or psychiatric notion that a disorder is discreet and unique from other impairments. As such, a specific learning disability in reading suggests that a person is impaired in reading to the exclusion of other intellectual or cognitive impairments that impact the potential to learn and achieve. The implication of this definition has historically been what is known as the *discrepancy criterion*. Consider the definition of a severe learning disability in Public Law 94–142, *The Education of All Handicapped Children Act* of 1975: "A severe discrepancy between [academic] achievement and intellectual ability." There has been great scrutiny with respect to the validity of the use of IQ measures (see Hampshire, Highfield, Parkin, and Owen, 2012) and the validity of the discrepancy criterion (Lyon et al., 2001; Stanovich & Siegel, 1994). Moreover, the lack of a reliable and theoretically substantive definition of dyslexia, and specific learning disabilities in general, has been a concern raised for over 40 years (Fletcher & Morris, 1986; Rutter and Yule, 1975; Lyon et al., 2001, 2003). This appears to be largely due to the heterogeneity of the disorder(s). In general, the model of neurodevelopmental or psychological disorders in which syndromes are considered to be qualitatively discrete entities identified by dissociations across behavioral indexes is argued to be outdated and potentially invalid (Lilienfeld & Treadway, 2016).

Whereas the genetics of reading (dis)ability are discussed further in this chapter and in this volume (Byrne, Olson, & Samuelsson, Chap. 9, this volume), reading is too recent in our evolutionary history to have occurred from genetic mutation— rather literacy emerges from the integration of visual and auditory object processing constrained by learned linguistic structures (e.g., phonology and morphology) and facilitated by our propensities for cognitive control. The inability to identify and decode words, the behavioral characteristic most indicative of reading ability, necessarily stems from deficits in the processing and integration of auditory/phonological, visual, linguistic, and/or motoric information. Thus, a deficit in reading is expected if a deficit exists in some linguistic or lower-level sensorimotor or attentional process. Furthermore, the acquisition of literacy skills is strongly related to working memory (Gathercole, Alloway, Willis, & Adams, 2006) and reading disability is highly

---

[1] Despite nominal disputes in the literature, we use the terms developmental dyslexia, dyslexia, reading impairment, reading disorder, and reading disability interchangeably in this chapter.

comorbid with attentional deficits (approximately 40–60%; Willcutt & Pennington, 2000) and other learning disabilities such as dyscalculia or math disability (approximately 56 89%; Fletcher, 2005; Fuchs & Fuchs, 2002). In short, failures in reading acquisition arise from a myriad of underlying cognitive, language, or sensorimotor deficits that have impacts that are generally not limited to reading behaviors alone. These different etiologies of the disorder have led to efforts to identify subtypes of dyslexia characterized by differential deficits (Eckert et al., 2018; Morris et al., 1998).

One might ask why understanding the etiology of dyslexia matters at all, except for purposes of scientific curiosity (e.g., Elliott & Gibbs, 2008). Supporters of this sentiment argue that the most important thing is that children learn to read and that interventions are necessary whether reading difficulties arise due to children's innate predisposition or result from inexperience. The answer is simple: Early intervention is the best medicine for ameliorating reading disabilities (Kilpatrick & O'Brien, Chap. 8, this volume). However, under a discrepancy criterion, reading difficulties are generally not revealed until a child is about eight or nine years old, when he or she should be reading independently. Thus, the discrepancy approach typically bypasses the early years when remedial support has the most impact (Torgesen, 2000). This "wait-to-fail" model results in students with reading disabilities spending years trying to catch up with their peers academically (Heibert & Taylor, 2000) and suffering low self-esteem and other negative psychosocial effects, many of which have lifelong negative consequences (Alexander-Passe, 2006; Terras, Thompson, & Minnis, 2009; Valås, 1999). Ideally, by understanding the neurobiological precursors to dyslexia as revealed by brain imaging, and combining this knowledge with the behavioral markers of reading failure, we can intervene before children begin formal schooling, using interventions specifically targeted to their individual deficits (Gabrieli, 2009; Ozernov-Palchik & Gaab, 2016). We believe this is a worthwhile goal.

10.1 What Does It Mean to Be Neurobiological in Origin?

The characterization of dyslexia as being rooted in brain-based processing deficiencies emerged in the 1990s amid the early period of functional brain imaging. However, it was in the early 1890s that French anatomist Dejerine first localized deficits in reading and writing to particular lesions in the brain (Dejerine & Symes, 1893; Geschwind, 1974). Specifically, Dejerine had come across a patient who suffered from both *alexia* with *agraphia*—the inability to read and write—who was found to have damage to the left temporal–parietal region during a postmortem examination. This region, located roughly above and behind the left ear, is also known as "Wernicke's area" after Carl Wernicke, a German neurologist who hypothesized a link between lesions in this area and the inability of patients to understand speech (Geschwind, 1970). More than 100 years later, this same region would become the central focus in the debate on the neural basis of reading disability.

The big question in this debate has not been *if* there are brain differences between individuals with dyslexia and normal readers. Brain imaging reveals that variations in both structure and function exist. However, to understand dyslexia one must go beyond the notion that something is amiss in the brain and recognize that different developmental trajectories in the neurobiological architecture and corresponding cognitive processes may lead to the outcome of reading failure. This is a concept known in systems theory as *equifinality*, wherein final states or objectives may be reached from disparate starting points (Skyttner, 2006). Literacy is an emergent process built upon a neurocognitive system of visual and auditory sensory processing, spoken language, attention, working memory, and multiple general cognitive functions. Thus, there is no singular brain structure or corresponding gene that would predispose homo sapiens to the visual word. It is therefore important that we adapt our understanding of dyslexia, at least in the context of a specific learning disability in reading, to a more *neuroconstructivist* model. By adopting this framework, we account for the multiple trajectories in underlying processes that may lead to this fundamental deficit. That is, reading acquisition is not comprised of "plug-and-play" modules that are either intact or disabled. Instead, learning to read is a dynamic process, resulting from multidirectional interactions between genes, brain, cognition, behavior, and environment (Karmiloff-Smith, 2009). Like many other neurocognitive impairments, dyslexia is not a singular trait, but rather a construct, with organic and situational elements that influence its manifestation in each individual. And like anorexia or autism—disorders with neurobiological roots—symptoms vary in severity, and the effectiveness of conventional interventions may or may not depend on the individual's processing deficits. As such, identifying disabled reading in the absence of other cognitive deficits or environmental influences would be much like looking for rainbows in the absence of water.

The search for answers has given rise to several theories and interpretations, each one exerting differential forces on the tug of war between the putative neurobiological origins and environmental influences associated with dyslexia. One of the earliest and most enduring supports the notion of a *phonological-core deficit* (Morris et al., 1998), referring to a difficulty in processing the sounds of language, and assigning those sounds to graphemes (i.e., one or more letters that represent a single phoneme, like *s*, *th*, or *oa*). The phonological-core deficit forms the basis of the very definition of dyslexia that was adopted in 2002 and remains in effect today. Specifically, this model posits that dyslexia is neurobiological in origin and stems from deficits in language processing. Further, it is from this theory that the connection to Wernicke's area—implicated by Dejerine—is made. Early studies (Shaywitz et al., 1998, 2002; Temple et al., 2000) found that dyslexic readers had significantly less brain activity in Wernicke's areas than normal readers during phonological and lexical tasks. These neurophysiological findings supported the notion of a phonological impairment underlying dyslexia and that underactivation specifically in Wernicke's region could provide a neural signature for this disability (Lyon et al., 2003).

The simple, classic understanding of a phonological deficit in reading appears to require further elaboration and refinement to account for additional factors that appear to influence reading development and dyslexia. Whereas phonological deficits may prove to be a common pathway leading to disabled reading, it may be an epiphe-nomenological account rather than a neurobiological mechanism. That is, the inabil-ity to parse the speech stream into effective phonological categories necessary for phonological awareness may be as much a product of the underlying processing diffi-culties of the individual as it is a cause of reading failure. As such, these phonological awareness deficits themselves arise from weaknesses in attentional/executive func-tioning (Facoetti et al., 2006, 2010), processing speed (Ahissar, 2007), the auditory system (Tallal, 1980), and/or some interactivity among these. Evidence from recent studies show lower-level auditory deficits in dyslexia early in childhood (Gaab, Gabrieli, Deutsch, Tallal, & Temple, 2007; Hämäläinen, Salminen, & Leppänen, 2013). These brain responses are not, however, necessarily diagnostic of the dis-order. Another concern with adhering strictly to a simple phonological-core deficit model localized to Wernicke's area is that studies published more recently show a more complex picture of dyslexia neurobiologically. For example, in addition to deficits in Wernicke's area, activation differences have also been revealed in other brain regions (see Fig. 10.1). These include (1) a location in the left occipital–tempo-ral area, coined the "visual word form area" (VWFA) located in the visual processing stream roughly behind the left ear, and (2) a region behind the left temple in the left inferior frontal gyrus, also known as "Broca's area" after French physician Paul

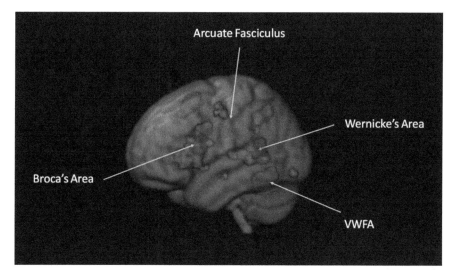

Fig. 10.1 Left hemisphere brain regions associated with dyslexia as described in this chapter. Broca's area (inferior frontal gyrus), Wernicke's area (temporal–parietal region), and the "visual word form area" or VWFA (occipital–temporal region). The arcuate fasciculus, one of the white matter tracts that connects these regions, is indicated by the purple band. Activation maps show regions preferentially related to dyslexia from an automated meta-analysis of 63 neuroimaging studies (http://neurosynth.org/), FDR corrected <0.01. Image created using MRIcroGL (http://mccauslandcenter.sc.edu/mricrogl)

Broca who associated lesions in this area with aphasia (Geschwind, 1970).[2] Other brain differences have been revealed in a variety of white matter fiber tracts, the connective tissue that links areas of the brain. The fiber tract most frequently implicated with reading is the arcuate fasciculus, connecting Broca's area in the frontal lobe with Wernicke's in the temporal–parietal junction (Peterson & Pennington, 2015).

An alternative theory—supporting environmental influences on brain development—posits that dyslexia is more akin to a *developmental delay* (Francis, Stuebing, Shaywitz, Shaywitz, & Fletcher, 1996). This proposal has been made to explain the gross neurobiological differences (structural) between children with dyslexia relative to their *age-matched* peers. For example, Krafnick and colleagues (2014) showed that when compared to *reading-matched* controls (younger children who are normal readers), the brain deficits in dyslexia are reduced, or generally not found, leading the authors to suggest that differences may be due to (a) delayed reading ability or (b) individual choices that lead to a lack of reading experience. That is, poor readers have fewer positive experiences with accurate word identification, and as a result, they may self-select away from literacy activities. Without reading experience, they fail to establish the neurobiological pathways for reading. This fuels what Keith Stanovich calls.

Matthew effects in reading: Good readers read more and thus improve, while poor readers read less and thus not only fail to improve, but get farther and farther behind their typically reading peers (Stanovich, 1986). If this is the case, structural brain differences may be a product or outcome of behaviors, rather than the behaviors being an outcome of structural impairments. While this argument is compelling, it is difficult to reconcile with functional MRI studies, showing that dyslexic children have less brain activity in Wernicke's area compared to *both* age-matched and reading-matched controls during a rhyming task (Hoeft et al., 2006).

Another important phenomenon supporting the notion of developmental delay is that reading failure is much more prevalent among individuals of low socioeconomic status (SES; Reardon, Robinson-Cimpian, & Weathers, 2014), and minority-language individuals (Hus, 2001). This is true, despite many English language learners not being identified as reading disabled due to challenges in teasing apart difficulties learning to read in a second language from authentic warning signs of reading impairments/dyslexia (Geva, Xi, Massey-Garrison, & Mak, Chap. 6, this volume). Nonetheless, possible explanations and contributing factors for the higher prevalence of reading impairment in low-SES and minority-language children include parental beliefs and behaviors (Phillips & Lonigan, 2005), lack of reading experience (Vellutino et al., 1996), and poor reading instruction (Connor et al., 2009; Vellutino, Fletcher, Snowling, & Scanlon, 2004). IQ also correlates highly with SES, especially in impoverished homes (Turkheimer, Haley, Waldron, D'Onofrio, & Gottesman, 2003) and school environments (Hart, Soden, Johnson, Schatschneider, & Tay-

---

[2]For the purposes of this chapter, and to avoid the potential confusion of anatomical labels, we will use more commonly recognized terminology, including *Wernicke's area*, and *Broca's area*, as well as *VWFA*. However, it should be noted that these labels which refer to a region's function are sources of debate as the putative structure–function relationships have become less well defined.

lor, 2013). Essentially, poverty suppresses positive influences, genetic or otherwise, whereas having resources often mitigates the impact of heritable risks' factors. It is also notable that impoverished environments lead to differential trajectories in the development of brain structures involved in memory (hippocampus) and language (prefrontal cortex) and are associated with behavioral deficits in these domains and additional executive functions (Noble, McCandliss, & Farah, 2007). Together, the strong influence of home and school, especially for children from low SES environments (Taylor & Schatschneider, 2010), as well as those at-familial risk (Powers et al., 2016), argues for a model in which the environment plays a more significant role than might be presumed for a disability that is "biologically based" (see for instance Schultz, 2008; reported in Reading Rockets [www.readingrockets.org/article/dyslexia-hereditary]). Such arguments for a biological basis for reading difficulties imply a strong distinction between nature and nurture, a distinction that can no longer be easily maintained given recent findings. That is, the environment can shape early brain development particularly for, but not limited to, those with genetic risk factors. Those neurobiological changes lay the foundation for the processing deficits that form the foundation of learning difficulties.

Another argument against a strict biological deficit model is that the presentation of dyslexia or reading disability is different across orthographies (Smythe & Everatt, 2000; Wimmer & Goswami, 1994). A language's orthography can be classified as *shallow* when the letter-sound correspondence is high, where each letter represents only one sound. In contrast, in languages with *deep* orthographies such as English, letters and graphemes can represent more than one sound, and sounds can be represented by more than one grapheme. Perhaps the most extreme example is the six different vowel sounds associated with the letter sequence—*ough*: *though*, *drought*, *ought*, *bough*, *rough*, and *through*.

Behaviorally, dyslexia is expressed in shallow orthographies such as Italian as slow but accurate reading, whereas, in deep orthographies, dyslexia is revealed earlier, and through decoding problems as children struggle to match letters to sounds (Ziegler & Goswami, 2005; Wimmer & Goswami, 1994). In the brain, different writing systems tend to utilize a similar network of cortical regions with some level of language-specific uniqueness likely reflecting the varying ties between orthography (e.g., letters/characters), phonology (e.g., phonemes or syllables), and meaning (Bolger, Perfetti, & Schneider, 2005). Moreover, while many studies of dyslexia in English show deficits in Wernicke's area, disabled readers across languages such as Italian and French show deficits in the VWFA (Paulesu, 2001). Also, the neural correlates of dyslexia vary across alphabetic and logographic languages. Dyslexics in Chinese display impairments in the prefrontal cortex in the right hemisphere (Siok, Niu, Jin, Perfetti, & Tan, 2008). Thus, despite some similarities in the manifestations of reading impairments across writing systems (Wagner et al., Chap. 2, this volume), the important differences suggest that there is likely not one unique singular neurobiological mechanism associated with dyslexia.

To summarize, the current definition of dyslexia as a specific learning disorder that is "neurobiological in origin" often leads to the notion of a discrete deficit with a well-established neural signature, which in 2001 appeared to be the consensus across the limited number of neuroimaging studies that had occurred by that time (review, Temple, 2002). However, this assumption requires a great deal of qualification, particularly considering the past 17 years of research on the cortical underpinnings of reading development and disability. In the next sections, we provide a brief historical look at some of the findings that led to the theoretical models above, describing how cognitive neuroscientists formed and reformed their concepts and beliefs through advancements in imaging technologies.

10.2   A Brief History of Brain Imaging in Dyslexia

10.2.1   Brain Structure

Dejerine was among the first to use postmortem studies to identify brain regions associated with speech and reading impairments (Dejerine & Symes, 1893). In postmortem studies in the mid-1970s, Galaburda and Kemper (1979) revealed abnormalities, mainly in left hemisphere reading-related brain regions, in a case study of an individual with a history of impaired reading. They also learned that this individual displayed symmetry in the temporal lobes (above the ears) in both hemispheres, which was contrary to findings from non-impaired readers, who consistently demonstrate left-dominant asymmetry patterns in and around Wernicke's area (Wada, Clarke, & Hamm, 1975) and Broca's area (Galaburda, Sanides, & Geschwind, 1978). Later, Galaburda, Sherman, Rosen, Aboitiz, and Geschwind (1985) described similar abnormalities in postmortem exams of four adult males with dyslexia. They also identified cortical neurons in unexpected areas, leading them to believe that they resulted from disruptions in neuronal migration patterns during fetal development. This suggested to them that a genetic link precipitated their appearance.

The advent of brain imaging technologies enabled scientists to study the brain in vivo, allowing for greater flexibility in the age and number of individuals they could study. Many early investigators focused their efforts on structural differences in the neural anatomy of dyslexic readers, following up, so to speak, on their predecessor's postmortem discoveries. New technologies also afforded the opportunity to measure both gray and white matter separately. Among the most prominent findings from these investigations included reduced gray matter volumes in the left hemisphere language and reading areas, chiefly Wernicke's area, the right hemisphere homologue to Wernicke's, Broca's area, and the VWFA (Brambati et al., 2004; Brown et al., 2001; Kronbichler et al., 2006, 2008; Silani et al., 2005). More recently, several research groups have conducted meta-analyses, two of which converge on a consistent pattern of gray matter reductions in both Wernicke's areas along with its right hemisphere homologue for individuals with dyslexia (Linkersdörfer, Lonnemann, Lindberg, Hasselhorn, & Fiebach, 2012; Richlan, Kronbichler, & Wimmer, 2013). Additionally, by using a slightly different analysis technique, Linkersdörfer et al.

(2012) also revealed overall less gray matter in the VWFA for dyslexic individuals compared to typical readers.

Structural studies also measure the anatomy of white matter fiber tracts, which are essentially long bands of myelinated axons that form connections between areas of gray matter. One of the most important for reading is the arcuate fasciculus, which connects Wernicke's and posterior reading-related regions with Broca's and other frontal reading-related structures. In good readers, the arcuate fasciculus is a thick, robust bundle of fibers with bidirectional connections (Catani & Mesulam, 2008). In individuals with dyslexia, however, the arcuate fasciculus, along with other white matter tracts in both hemispheres, have fewer fibers, and less myelination in those present (Beaulieu et al., 2005; Deutsch et al., 2005; Rimrodt, Peterson, Denckla, Kaufmann, & Cutting, 2010). Further, results from a meta-analysis show that the most consistent findings for white matter reductions are in Wernicke's area (Vandermosten, Boets, Wouters, & Ghesquière, 2012), which is remarkably consistent with Dejerine's findings in the late nineteenth century.

10.2.2   Brain Function

The technological advancements in brain imaging over the course of the past 50 years have allowed for more than just a look at structure, but also to look at cortical activity through the measurement of electrical current arising from synapses using electroen-cephalography (EEG) or magnetoencephalography (MEG), gauging cerebral blood flow and the consumption of glucose with positron emission tomography (PET), or detecting changes in the blood oxygen level through the use of functional magnetic resonance imaging (fMRI). Each of these techniques makes different assumptions about "neural activity" and how those signals are elicited while participants are engaged in some cognitive function via a behavioral task. Each has drawbacks with respect to their level of resolution (i.e., precision) of their measurement of either temporal (*when* neural processes are happening) or spatial (*where* specifically these processes are occurring) information. Yet, when taken together, these techniques have painted a picture of a cortical reading network with specific processes that unfold over time (Marinković, 2004; Marinković et al., 2003; McDonald et al., 2010; Thesen et al., 2012) across regions associated with vision, audition, and semantics. These pro-cesses interact in a manner suggesting that spelling, phonology, and meaning occur as a function of integration among the network of regions (Bolger, Hornickel, Cone, Burman, & Booth, 2008; Graves, Desai, Humphries, Seidenberg, & Binder, 2010). Studies investigating the neural correlates of reading described a "biological signa-ture for reading," asserting that Wernicke's area was integral to both phonological and semantic judgments (Shaywitz, 1996). At first glance, this may suggest a physical impairment in this brain region, especially in light of early postmortem studies reveal-ing left hemisphere lesions (Dejerine & Symes, 1893). However, Rumsey and col-leagues (1992) showed that during attentional tasks, brain activations in individuals with dyslexia appeared normal, and that reduced activity in Wernicke's area seemed to be confined to phonological tasks. This led investigators to believe that there was nothing fundamentally amiss in Wernicke's region, except when affected individuals performed lexical tasks. This profile of reduced leftward activity for language processes was also observed in dyslexic individuals across orthographies, specifically Italian, English, and French (Paulesu, 2001). Other studies suggested a failure of coordination, or connections, between reading-related brain regions. For example, during a rhyming and memory task, Paulesu and colleagues (1996) showed that men with dyslexia had similar brain activity as control participants in both Broca's and Wernicke's areas. However, in contrast to controls, these regions did not activate *together* in the dyslexic group, leading the authors to propose that dyslexia could result from a disconnection between anterior and posterior regions used for reading. This idea was bolstered by findings using functional connectivity (the correlated activity between two or more regions of the brain). Specifically, the suggestion that impaired reading resulted from the failure of Broca's and Wernicke's areas to activate together, because Broca's area seemed to function normally (Rumsey, Horwitz, et al., 1997; Rumsey, Nace, et al., 1997). Over the next few years, however, functional activation studies consistently revealed a pattern of underactivation in Wernicke's area and the VWFA, along with *typical* or *greater* activity in prefrontal regions of cortex when reading in English (Brunswick, McCrory, Price, Frith, & Frith, 1999; Milne & Grafman, 2001; Shaywitz et al., 1998) and German (Kronbichler et al., 2006). Some investigations also revealed activity increases in the right hemisphere homologue to Wernicke's area in dyslexia (Milne & Grafman, 2001; Milne, Syngeniotis, Jackson, & Corballis, 2002). Researchers suggested that perhaps increases in Broca's area and the posterior right hemisphere were compensatory, to make up for weak phonological and orthographic processes in left posterior regions. More recently, meta-analyses summarize and support the structural and functional brain findings from the last couple of decades. A meta-analysis by Maisog and colleagues (2008) looking at 9 studies of dyslexia in children confirms the pattern of hypo-activation in the VWFA region and regions surrounding Wernicke's area (bilaterally), as well as hyper-activation in the right hemisphere homologue or Broca's area. Richlan and colleagues (2009) similarly looked at studies of both children and adults and also found consistently weaker activation for dyslexics compared to typical readers in the VWFA region as well as Wernicke's region bilaterally with mixed results in Broca's area. Separately, a meta-analysis by Paulesu, Danelli, and Berlingeri (2014) points to a lack of activation chiefly in and around the VWFA, along with the suggestion that altered brain activity in Broca's region relates more to attentional and motor-related impairments. In an effort to identify the overlap between studies of structural deficits and functional activation, Linkersdörfer and colleagues (2012) converged on a region within Wernicke's area being most commonly associated with reduced gray matter volume and reduced activity during lexical processing in dyslexia, but also found the largest overlap of deficiencies in gray matter volume and function in the VWFA.

As studies in adults converged on a neurological profile of dyslexia with disruptions in Wernicke's area and the VWFA, researchers turned to children. Once again provoking the tug of war between genes and environment, the big question was if, when, and how the brains of dyslexic children reveal the "neurobiological signature" that was becoming increasingly accepted among neurocognitive researchers. Early on, studies uncovered signs that children with dyslexia in fact shared a similar neurobiological framework as adults (Georgiewa et al., 1999; Shaywitz et al., 2002). They also showed that activations in Broca's area bilaterally were higher in older than younger children with dyslexia, presumably due to greater compensatory behaviors, and that activity in the VWFA corresponded to reading scores (Shaywitz et al., 2002). Other studies with young participants showed how left hemisphere impairments only presented themselves when sound-grapheme mapping became difficult. Compared to their peers, children with dyslexia showed similar brain activity while making easy rhyming judgments (e.g., "hint-mint" or "jazz-razz"). However, when judgments were more difficult due to spelling irregularities (e.g., "pint-mint" or "jazz-has"), the dyslexic group had reduced brain activity in Wernicke's area, illustrating their struggle to connect the phonemic structure of spoken words with the spelling patterns used to represent those words (Cao, Bitan, Chou, Burman, & Booth, 2006). However, the reductions in activation to irregular words (i.e., words that do not represent consistent spelling–sound patterns in English) are due to the fact that typical readers show greater activity to these words across the entire network (compared to regular-spelled or consistently spelled words), whereas as children with dyslexia do not show such sensitivity (Bolger, Minas, Burman & Booth, 2008). This pattern of activation was found even when the words were presented auditorily (Desroches et al., 2009). The lack of activation for individuals with dyslexia is attributed to the lack of interactivity across the network to integrate spelling–sound patterns, particularly between the VWFA and Wernicke's area (Cao, Bitan & Booth, 2008).

Other accounts of the roots of dyslexia addressed the hypothesis that disabled reading was due to the inability to quickly and accurately process lower-level sensory information. Several theories account for the phonological deficits in dyslexia as stemming from lower-level impairments in the auditory processing stream (Ahissar, 2007; Tallal & Gaab, 2006). For example, Temple and colleagues (2000) tested Tallal's (1980) auditory temporal processing deficit theory and showed that in individuals with dyslexia, Broca's area was less sensitive to rapid acoustic information mirroring human speech sounds. More recently, evidence has suggested that the roots of dyslexia—and disordered phonological processing of the speech stream— may lie in the earliest stages of the auditory system, where the brain stem receives input directly from the cochlea (Banai et al., 2009; Chandrasekaran, Hornickel, Skoe, Nicol, & Kraus, 2009; Hornickel & Kraus, 2013).

In a related argument, researchers have pointed to deficits in rapid visual processing, known as "magnocellular deficits," as the mechanism underlying disrupted reading in dyslexia (Demb, Boynton, Best, & Heeger, 1998; Galaburda & Livingstone, 1993; Stein, 2001, 2014). The magnocellular cells of the visual system are prevalent in the region of the brainstem that receives direct input from the retina. These neurons are sensitive to rapid changes in the visual stream that enable motion tracking and rapid changes in visual–spatial processing (Livingstone & Hubel, 1988). A series of studies by Facoetti and colleagues have shown that individuals with dyslexia are impaired in attention shifting (Facoetti & Molteni, 2001; Facoetti, Pagnoni, Turatto, Marzola, & Mascetti, 2000) using both visual and auditory spatial tasks (Facoetti,

Trussardi, et al., 2010; Facoetti, Corradi, Ruffino, Gori, & Zorzi, 2010). Interestingly, these impairments tended to impact disabled readers who had deficits in reading non-words, an indicator of phonological decoding (Facoetti et al., 2006; Facoetti, Trussardi, et al., 2010). There has, however, been much debate about the magnocellular deficits, as many studies failed to show predicted impairments (Johannes, Kussmaul, Münte, & Mangun, 1996; Ramus et al., 2003). These equivocal findings in the literature may be due to task selection. Specifically, individuals with reading impairments show deficits with stimuli presented sequentially rather than simultaneously (Ben-Yehudah & Ahissar, 2004). While many theorists have dismissed the magnocellular theory (Hutzler, Kronbichler, Jacobs, & Wimmer, 2006; Skottun, 2005), it is interesting to note that both the auditory and visual system accounts point to bundles of cells that neighbor each other along the brainstem (the medial and lateral geniculate nuclei, respectively), at the earliest stages of sensory processing. In short, sensory deficits early in the processing pathway such as the brainstem provide a compelling account for how variations in the manifestations of dyslexia may be rooted in the differential development in the neurobiology of sensory/perceptual systems.

The dominant accounts of dyslexia discount the notion that these early sensory processing deficits fundamentally underlie the phonological impairments, pointing instead to differential activity in right and left frontal regions (Heim et al., 2010; Schulz et al., 2008). Other investigations focused on difficulties in associating sounds with words. For example, using MEG measurements in the VWFA, Salmelin, Kiesilä, Uutela, Service, & Salonen (1996) showed that good readers were able to recognize a word 180 milliseconds after seeing it, whereas dyslexic individuals either had no response in this component or had a slower, weaker response. Using MEG, Simos and colleagues (2005) localized this deficit to Wernicke's area. Additionally, McCrory and colleagues (2005) showed that dyslexic readers had reduced brain activity in the VWFA when naming objects in pictures as well as naming words, but their behavioral performance was unimpaired.

Even while acknowledging the pervasive phonological and orthographic difficulties in learning to decode words, Shaywitz and Shaywitz (2008) propose that disruptions in attentional mechanisms are a barrier to reading fluency. This "bottleneck hypothesis" suggests that impairments to attention and speed of activating verbal representations from visual input throttle the identification of words and thus reading speed and comprehension. This notion of a single underlying mechanism between ADHD and RD has been repeatedly examined (see Pennington, 2006; Wilcutt & Pennington, 2000) with recent evidence from behavioral genetics suggesting independent mechanisms underlying the two disorders. But those who are comorbid (between 25 and 40%) for both disorders have a common genetic influence on processing speed (Willcutt et al., 2010). Thus, it is important to look at the genetic mechanisms that may lead to differential development.

10.3   Genetic Roots of Dyslexia

10.3.1   Behavioral Genetics

While seeking the etiology of dyslexia, many have turned to behavioral genetics, a field of study that investigates the influence of genes and environment on human behavior. Such studies have shown that, like most cognitive traits (Plomin, Haworth, Meaburn, Price, & Davis, 2013), individual differences in reading ability have moderate-to-strong heritability factors (Byrne, Olson, & Samuelsson, Chap. 9, this volume). For example, familial studies from around the globe show dyslexia occurring in 68% of identical twins, and 40–60% of dyslexic individuals have an affected first-degree relative (Grigorenko, 2004). As discussed at length in Chap. 9, these studies converge on a profile of genetic factors exerting more influence on early reading skills than environmental causes.

The fact that dyslexia has a genetic component is only part of the story, however, as individuals' expressed behaviors (their *phenotype*) depends on the interplay between one's genetic make-up (their *genotype*) and their environment. In other words, the expression of one's genes depends on their personal experiences. It is perhaps not surprising that the most extreme conditions have the most impact on children. That is, heritability is sensitive to both high-risk (e.g., family chaos) and low-risk environments (e.g., positive parent–child communication; Harlaar et al., 2005). For example, lower verbal scores were found in over 2000 four-year-old twin pairs who lived in high-risk environments (e.g., SES, family chaos, maternal depression) compared with low-risk environments, despite similar genetic factors (Asbury, Wachs, & Plomin, 2005). For reading development, important environmental factors including the home literacy environment (HLE), teachers, and schools can have a "protective" influence and mitigate other risks. For instance, Logan and colleagues (2014) found that early HLE and the quality of very early reading curriculum were important, but that over time this effect was diminished, largely because children spend relatively more time in school than at home between the ages of 6 and 12. The potential impact of protective factors was also illustrated in a recent meta-analysis including 95 studies reviewing the behavioral characteristics of children with family risk of developmental dyslexia (Snowling & Melby-Lervåg, 2016). The authors conclude that atypical phonological processing may be construed as an endophenotype of dyslexia, but that its impact may be moderated by protective home literacy factors. Date from studies by Byrne and colleagues (Chap. 9, this volume) suggests that as environmental conditions become more uniform, heritability then accounts for a lion's share of the variance.

10.3.2   Molecular Genetics

The fact that heredity plays a strong role leads us to ask, "Which gene, or genes, are implicated?" Byrne and colleagues (Chap. 9, this volume) state: "there is no single gene responsible for reading (dis)ability." Individual candidate gene mutations generally have minute implications for complex behaviors. It is often the multiplicative effect of dozens to hundreds of alleles that impact the structural development of neural systems or neurochemical signaling pathways. Currently, six main gene polymorphisms are consistently linked to developing reading difficulties and diagnosis of dyslexia across several languages and cultures and directly impact brain development including C2Orf3, MRPL19, DYX1C1, DCDC2d, KIAA0319, and ROBO1 (Gialluisi, Newbury, Wilcutt, Consortium, & Luciano, 2014; Grigorenko, 2005; Grigorenko et al., 2007; Peterson & Pennington, 2015).

Focusing on the most prominent genetic marker, a "deletion"[3] in DCDC2d is implicated in 10–17% of cases of dyslexia. In a sample of over 500 individuals from families in the Colorado Learning Disabilities Research Center (Meng et al., 2005), a disruption to the DCDC2 gene was localized in the brain's reading-related areas (Wernicke's, Broca's, VWFA, and arcuate fasciculus). When a deletion is imposed on the DCDC2d gene in a rodent model, disrupted neuronal migration patterns resulted in disordered white matter fiber tracts (Meng et al., 2011). Moreover, DCDC2d is associated with the inability to parse individual speech sounds from a stream of speech in rodents, even though trained rats are able to detect speech sounds when they are presented individually (Centanni et al., 2016). Interestingly, behavioral therapy with speech training in these rats eliminated auditory processing impairments (Centanni et al., 2014), consistent with the research showing that humans are malleable in these auditory/phonological skills (see Chap. 8, this volume). Interestingly, deletion of the DCDC2 gene has also been linked to weaker visual–spatial processing consistent with the magnocellular theory (Cicchinni et al., 2015).

In general, genetic models in rodents have mimicked the findings in human neuroimaging of impaired readers. A deletion of the KIAA0319 gene in rats precipitates anatomical alterations that mimic those seen in Broca's and Wernicke's areas in dyslexic children (Platt et al., 2013). Moreover, the DYX1C1, DCDC2d, and KIAA0319 genes have also been associated with abnormal white matter volume in the arcuate fasciculus, the white matter tract connecting frontal and posterior areas and linked to fluent reading (Darki, Peyrard-Janvid, Matsson, Kere, & Klingberg, 2012). Other genetic markers have been associated with specific behavioral markers of dyslexia. Specifically, a KIAA0319 variation or "haplotype" is associated with deficits in rapid auditory processing (Szalkowski et al., 2012) and phoneme processing (Centanni et al., 2014). Like the other candidates, it is associated with reading abilities in the general population and further to dyslexia (Paracchini et al., 2006).

These studies demonstrate that certain genes, or combinations of genes, are associated with the neurobiological traits associated with dyslexia, and investigators

---

[3] A gene deletion or mutation is when DNA or part of a chromosome does not replicate when the gene is passed on.

continue to make strides to integrate genetic information with existing knowledge of the brain mechanisms and behaviors, with the goal of bridging the subcellular pathways to the expression of reading problems (for reviews, see Galaburda, LoTurco, Ramus, Fitch, & Rosen, 2006; Peterson & Pennington, 2015). However, when viewed together with the evidence from behavioral genetics, these candidate genes may serve as biomarkers for risk for reading disorder, but clear evidence of risk pathway has not yet been established. A critical component of this approach is to identify and track particular populations who are at risk in early childhood or even infancy.

10.4 Neurobiological Markers and Early Detection of Dyslexia

As described above, poor behavioral performance on reading measures in both children and adults with dyslexia is accompanied by deviant brain structure and function during reading-related tasks, especially in Wernicke's area, Broca's area, the VWFA, and the arcuate fasciculus (Richlan et al., 2013). For language researchers and educators, the question remains: Do brain differences predate formal reading instruction? In other words, are they contingent upon one's phenotype, or are they shaped by experience, either through reading experience, or the lack thereof? Neurological investigations have undertaken to evaluate the *predictive capacity* of familial risk in pre-reading children. *At risk* refers to children who have at least one first-degree relative with dyslexia, and *not at risk* indicates no family history.

10.4.1 Markers Revealed in Brain Anatomy Differences

Earlier, we described structural brain abnormalities in dyslexic readers, which include reduced gray matter in left hemisphere brain areas important for reading and language (for a review, see Richlan, Kronbichler, & Wimmer, 2013). Recent evidence has extended these findings to children with a family history of dyslexia, and in fact reveals gray matter reductions in children even *before* they are exposed to reading instruction (Raschle, Chang, & Gaab, 2011). This is consistent with the heritability factors that influence brain development. Another study linked the maternal history of reading disability with less gray matter volume in their children before they were taught to read (Black et al., 2012). Further, there is evidence indicating that reading skills at the end of second grade were positively related to more gray matter in left hemisphere reading areas at the start of first grade (Linkersdörfer et al., 2014). Interestingly, Linkersdörfer and colleagues (2014) also showed that better readers had *less* gray matter volume in other left hemisphere language areas, perhaps due to experience-dependent neural pruning as readers become increasingly skilled.

In addition to reduced gray matter in reading regions, atypical integrity and connectivity in white matter tracts are also associated with behavioral predictors of dyslexia in children. For example, white matter volume in left hemisphere reading regions at age five predicted reading skills in Grade 3, even beyond the effects of family risk (Myers et al., 2014). Another example comes from a group of kindergarten students with little to no formal reading instruction, where lower phonological awareness scores were consistent with smaller volume in the left arcuate fasciculus, which, as previously mentioned, is the white matter tract connecting the anterior and posterior language regions in the brain (Saygin et al., 2013). Significantly lower density in the arcuate fasciculus has even been shown in at-risk infants as young as 5–18 months old (Langer et al., 2015), as well as in preliterate children (Vandermosten et al., 2015). Together, these findings strongly suggest that atypical white matter integrity in language regions—recruited later as reading regions—is precursors to reading difficulties during the literacy period in which dyslexia emerges, rather than a result of poor reading experience.

A notable exception to the results above, however, is evidence from a longitudinal investigation of 27 Norwegian children who were randomly recruited prior to formal reading instruction and scanned annually until they were 11 years old, which was after they had learned to read and dyslexia diagnoses had been made (Clark et al., 2014). In this sample, atypical connection patterns within the language/reading areas were not observed until 11 years, suggesting that changes in these children likely resulted following the onset of reading experience, not prior to it. Clark and colleagues (2014) thus propose that the neuroanatomical precursors for dyslexia lie in lower-level areas responsible for auditory and visual processing, as well as in core executive functions, rather than the "reading-related network" per se. On the other hand, a more recent study scanned children at five and eight years of age, or before and after children learned to read, and found evidence that allowed them to predict the location of each child's left hemisphere VWFA at eight years by examining the connectivity patterns in this area at 5 years of age *before* it was influenced by general reading instruction (Saygin et al., 2016). These findings generally uphold the notion that brain connections used to support reading acquisition are in place prior to the start of formal reading instruction.

Other structural measurements of interest to cognitive neuroscientists include the thickness and surface area of the cerebral cortex, the outer covering of the brain. For example, when they compared at-risk to not-at-risk beginning readers, Hosseini and colleagues (2013) revealed differences in both Broca's and Wernicke's areas, as well as in other subcortical regions in the at-risk children when compared to the not at-risk group. More detailed investigations of anatomy have studied the sulcal patterns (the grooves that surround the gyri, or humps, of the cerebral cortex covering the brain) of Wernicke's and the VWFA in the left hemisphere in at-risk and not-at-risk pre-readers (Im et al., 2016). Abnormal sulcal patterns were evident in the at-risk pre-reading groups, again suggesting that atypical cortical development predates reading instruction. Im and colleagues (2016) also showed that in reading impaired elementary students who had learned to read, poor performance in word and non-word reading scores was positively associated with atypical sulcal patterns. Although there have been some equivocal findings, the evidence appears to generally support the notion that abnormalities in structural brain development predate school-based literacy instruction. However, as noted, home literacy environment does have a differential, likely protective effect, on brain development for those who are both at risk and not at risk for dyslexia. Recent work by Powers and colleagues (2016) examined the effect of high- and low-risk home literacy environments on brain development in 5 year olds at risk for dyslexia ($n = 29$) and controls ($n = 21$). Their findings revealed high- and low-risk home literacy environments had differential influence on brain development both in children at risk for dyslexia and those without family risk factors, highlighting the interplay of genes and environment.

10.4.2   Markers Revealed by Functional Activation Differences

Beyond the structural variations evident in those with a familial risk of dyslexia, the disrupted activation patterns have similarly been investigated to determine whether the neural signatures (reduced activity in posterior regions like Wernicke's and the VWFA) are present before reading onset. Raschle and colleagues (2014) measured brain activity in at-risk and not at-risk pre-reading children while they listened to real words. They found that the at-risk children had reduced activation in Wernicke's area, along with the VWFA and its right homologue, and that activation in these areas bore significant correlations with pre-reading skills in both groups. It is notable, however, that the investigators failed to show increases in Broca's region, which has been shown for school-aged children diagnosed with dyslexia, for the at-risk children suggesting that these compensatory mechanisms come into play after reading onset. A similar paradigm tested brain responses in at-risk and no-risk pre-readers to "rapid auditory processing" of non-linguistic sounds. As mentioned above, this skill is hypothesized to underlie deficient phonological processing in dyslexic individuals (Raschle, Stering, Meissner, & Gaab, 2014). Brain responses in both groups correlated positively with the behavioral measures of phonological processing, and in the at-risk children, Broca's area revealed atypical responses (underactivation) to the sounds. In a similar experiment with Polish-speaking kindergarten and first graders, Debska and colleagues (2016) showed that a rhyming task elicited less brain activity in at-risk compared to no-risk children in left hemisphere language regions for both kindergarten and first graders. However, while no behavioral differences on a range of tasks from letter knowledge and phonemic awareness to word identification were shown between the groups during kindergarten, in first grade, the at-risk children had slower reaction times and scored lower on a reading task. These results provide additional evidence that functional abnormalities from familial risk are also present *prior* to reading instruction and that the behavioral manifestations of risk increase as formal schooling progresses.

While it is relatively easy to measure children's processing signature related to auditory stimuli, relatively few studies have attempted to trace the neural circuitry for reading in at-risk and no-risk children, as reading ability poses an obvious confound. One of the first studies to examine the neural signature of readers at risk for dyslexia used a non-word rhyme-matching task (Simos et al., 2000). Participants were asked to decide whether two pronounceable non-words (e.g., "kume" and "nool") rhymed, a task that tapped phonological decoding skills. At-risk children displayed reduced task-related activity in the left Broca's and Wernicke's areas, along with *increases* in activity in their right hemisphere homologues. Others have investigated the mechanisms underlying visual systems related to reading, specifically alphabetic and orthographic knowledge (i.e., single letters and letters in a string). Findings show reduced activation in Broca's and Wernicke's areas for children with family risk factors for dyslexia (Specht et al., 2009). Together, these studies argue in support of genetic factors predisposing people to reading failure, as they show both altered structure and disrupted activation patterns before children are taught to read.

10.4.3 Neurophysiological Markers of Processing Deficits

Studying neural activity in vivo with younger children is especially challenging particularly with MRI technology, because the environment can be noisy and intimidating and it requires that the child remain still and compliant for extended periods of time. Because they are relatively inexpensive and less intimidating, techniques like EEG/ERPs have long been used by researchers to study near-instantaneous neural responses in young children and infants. Furthermore, having been in use for decades, a large body of research shows that ERPs—and the indices described below—are reliable predictors for language and reading outcomes (Dawson, Finley, Phillips, & Galpert, 1986; Guttorm, Leppanen, Richardson, & Lyytinen, 2001; Molfese & Molfese, 1985, 1997; Molfese, 2000; Neville, Coffey, Holcomb, & Tallal, 1993; Tallal, Stark, & Mellits, 1985). In auditory and language literature, researchers are interested in neural responses that occur extremely quickly, typically between 100 and 500 milliseconds after a stimulus is presented (i.e., between one-tenth of a second and half a second). The most commonly studied brain responses are referred to as "N1" (a negative deflection at 80–120 milliseconds after stimulus onset), "P3" (a positive deflection at about 300 milliseconds), and "MMN" (mismatch negativity), which refers to negative deflection starting at about 100 milliseconds after stimulus onset, and lasting 50–200 milliseconds. The MMN is so named because it is sensitive to deviant auditory stimuli, for example, an aberrant sound presented during a stream of like tones or syllables (Molfese, Molfese, & Kelly, 2001). Information recorded from ERPs is generally compared to different conditions of experimental stimuli, allowing scientists to compare the brain's response to different events. Consequently, they have been instrumental in investigations examining differences in auditory responses in both timing and intensity for children who are at risk for dyslexia and those without genetic risk factors.

Due to the relationship between auditory processing sensitivity and pre-reading phonological processing and speech perception, investigators have utilized varied auditory stimuli, from consonant–vowel syllables (e.g., "ba," "da," "ga") to non-words (e.g., "ret," "lud") to evaluate early sound processing in young children. The consensus from these studies is that infants who grow up and acquire reading easily process speech in the prototypical left hemisphere language regions (for a review, see Lyytinen et al., 2005). In contrast, infants who are later diagnosed with dyslexia show the opposite effect, processing speech sounds predominantly in the right hemisphere. Remarkably, these patterns for speech processing that are already present at the first 36 hours of life seem to reliably predict (92%) the children who are identified as dyslexic at 8 years of age (Molfese, 2000). In babies at risk for dyslexia, only about *half* show the aberrant right hemisphere dominance for speech (Leppänen et al., 2010; Lyytinen et al., 2005). Additionally, differences in auditory response patterns are not exclusively associated with familial risk children. For example, in *both* at-risk and not at-risk children, right hemisphere dominance was associated with poorer receptive language skills at 2½ years, and deviant left hemisphere patterns were associated with poorer verbal memory at age five (Guttorm et al., 2005). When these same children started school at 6½ years of age, only the at-risk children who had atypical rightward responses as infants scored lower than the controls on phonological skills, rapid naming, and letter knowledge (Guttorm, Leppanen, Hamalainen, Eklund, & Lyytinen, 2010). These findings suggest that impairments in low-level auditory processing skills, together with abnormal speech processing, may be one of the developmental pathways to a reading disability, especially in children with family risk (Leppänen et al., 2012). Furthermore, when taken together with the results from the ERP investigations discussed above, they support the notion that atypical auditory processing mechanisms predate the onset of reading and language acquisition. One dilemma for researchers and practitioners is whether the clinical application of EEG/ERP technology would benefit or unnecessarily harm parents and children who are (or may be) at risk for reading failure. That is, does providing this knowledge to parents that their infant is likely at risk for reading disability (a disorder that may manifest almost 6 years later) create a realm of overwhelming anxiety long before the onset of literacy experience? In this regard, it is helpful to look at the effects of intervention on the brain.

10.5 Effects of Intervention and Plasticity in Dyslexia

Among the most important revelations of brain imaging studies in dyslexia is the understanding that the brain is indeed plastic and that prevention and intervention efforts have the power to alter the brain's anatomy and impact its capacity to function appropriately and efficiently. Few children with reading impairments feel confident about their academic abilities, as they watch their normal-reading peers easily access and unlock the code of written language. Adults who experienced reading failure as children can readily recall their feelings of inadequacy and low-esteem (Alexander-

Passe, 2006). In this section, we discuss how various interventions not only result in better performance in reading-related skills, but also that the brain has ability to change and become more "normalized" with intensive, targeted reading interventions. Specifically, as reading skills improve, through intervention, the networks of regions recruited effectively function more like those of typical readers. This is powerful information for a child who wants to give up and the parents and educators who are working tirelessly alongside them. Further, understanding the underlying brain mechanisms associated with such improvements provides valuable information regarding their success or failure.

10.5.1 Structural Changes Associated with Reading Interventions

We have previously detailed consistent evidence of structural abnormalities in both gray and white matter associated with dyslexia (Richlan et al., 2013, Linkersdorfer et al., 2012). The question in this section is whether these structures undergo measurable change as a result of reading interventions, and if so, how. Despite the focus on anatomical differences present in dyslexia, relatively few investigations have attempted to quantify and describe changes in gray matter resulting from reading interventions. Those that have, however, show promising results. For example, Krafnik and colleagues (2011) report on 11 dyslexic children who received training on mental imagery, articulation, and tracing of letters, groups of letter, and words. Brain scans were collected at three time points: (1) before training, (2) after training, and (3) eight weeks after the training period had ended. All children showed moderate improvements in their reading skills as a result of the intervention. Additionally, increases in gray matter volume were noted in reading- and memory-related regions between the first and second scans. However, there were no measurable changes in gray matter volume between the second and third scans, suggesting that volume changes were a direct consequence of training. Unfortunately, this study had no control participants, so it remains unclear whether this may be a general phenomenon, or if it is limited to children with dyslexia. On the other hand, Keller and Just (2009) compared children with reading difficulties who received 100 hours of intensive explicit word decoding intervention to a group of similar children who did not, as well as a group of typically achieving peers. Prior to intervention, children with reading difficulties showed deficient white matter fiber tracks connecting frontal and parietal regions (in this case the superior longitudinal fasciculus that runs adjacent to the arcuate fasciculus which was repeatedly identified previously), which subsequently strengthened for those readers who engaged in the 6-month intervention, but not for those who received no intervention. This change in white matter fiber density was correlated with modest changes in nonsense-word reading ability. However, there was no demonstrable impact on real-word reading, timed or untimed. Other investigations have also shown that brain structure can predict future reading outcomes. For example, increases in the volume of the arcuate fasciculus and related white matter tracts between kindergarten and Grade 3 were more indicative of reading outcomes than were family risk status, SES, and other pre-reading measures (Myers et al., 2014). And in dyslexic adolescents, the integrity of the right arcuate fasciculus was shown to relate to reading skills 2½ years later, regardless of the students schooling or reading experience during that time (Hoeft et al., 2011). Although they pale in number with respect to functional studies, evidence of structural changes associated with intervention and instruction provides the backdrop from which we can interpret the latter. That is, the changes in white matter fibers that are associated with improved reading performance depict a strengthening communication network between frontal (Broca's) and posterior (Wernicke's and the VWFA) regions.

10.6   Functional Changes Associated with Reading Interventions

Summarizing the effects of intervention studies is an imperfect science, both due to individual differences in participants and also due to methodological variables. Important variables include (1) skills that are the focus of the intervention, (2) duration, and (3) outcome measure. Examples of intervention strategies can include sound processing, letter-sound awareness, fluency, comprehension, letter/word writing, vocabulary, or any combination of these and other reading-related skills. Important factors related to duration include the overall quantity in terms of number of hours or days, frequency, and time between the two measurements. Outcome measures describe the skills tested after remediation. For example, are they tested on letter-sound awareness, single word reading, reading speed, comprehension, or other skills? In this section, we summarize representative findings first by intervention type, then performance task during the brain measurement.

Due to their strong association with reading ability, phonological processing skills are frequently the focus of interventions. For example, Simos et al. (2002) measured brain activation patterns in a small sample of dyslexic children (7–17 years old), all of whom had severe difficulties with phonological processing and single word reading (see more in Chap. 8, this volume). Participants along with age-matched controls were scanned before and after the dyslexia group received 80 hours of phonological processing and letter-sound training. Commercially available programs were used, based on demonstrated efficacy in improving core difficulties related to reading. Six participants received *Phono-Graphix* while two received the *Lindamood Phoneme Sequencing Program*. During the scan, participants read non-words like *yote* and *soat* and decided if the pair rhymed. Results from the initial scan showed that the control group displayed activation typical to such tasks, specifically in the left posterior Wernicke's area. The dyslexia group showed essentially the opposite. They displayed little or no activation in Wernicke's area, along with increases in activity in the same region of the right hemisphere. After two months of remedial instruction for phonological awareness and letter-sound skills, participants with dyslexia showed both improved word identification performance and more "normalized" brain activity, including dramatic increases in Wernicke's area in response to the non-word rhyme-detection task. When translating the reported percentile gains into standard scores, the students in the Simos et al. (2002) studies made, on average, a 25 standard score gain in word recognition, which represents one of the strongest results in the intervention literature.

Meyler, Keller, Cherkasskya, Gabrieli, and Just (2008) investigated the effect of multiple intervention approaches including Corrective Reading, Wilson Reading, Spell Read Phonological Auditory Training (PAT), and Failure Free Reading (see Torgesen et al., 2006) on higher-level tasks (reading text). The authors identified fifth graders qualifying as poor readers ($n = 23$) or good readers ($n = 12$) and scanned them three times: before training, after 100 hours of training, and again one year later. The task performed during the brain scan was sentence comprehension, wherein they determined whether or not sentences made sense (e.g., *The dog chased the cat* or *The man fed the dress*). Before training, the poor readers showed less activation in and around Wernicke's region and its right hemisphere homologue while reading sentences. However, after training, modest, but reliable gains in reading ability were accompanied by greater activation in Wernicke's area in these struggling readers. One year later, even fewer differences in brain activation were shown relative to skilled readers, which the authors proposed could be the result of increased practice and fluency.

Adults also have shown plasticity effects associated with phonological training. Eden and colleagues (2004) investigated adults ($M = 42.5$ years old) with and without dyslexia who underwent brain scans while listening to words. They were instructed to repeat either the whole word or the word without its initial sound (e.g., after hearing *chat* the response would be *at*). Compared to the control group, the dyslexic group displayed less activity in the left hemisphere along with increased response in right hemisphere regions in response to the task. Individuals with dyslexia then received eight weeks of phonological awareness training (using the Lindamood Phoneme Sequencing Program mentioned above) before the scanning task was repeated. In the post-training scan, the dyslexia group shifted to the leftward pattern of activation in frontal cortex along with increases in several right hemisphere areas. This shift corresponded with significant accuracy improvements in non-word decoding and phonemic processing and mixed results in word identification, but no effects in terms of overall reading speed or comprehension.

Apart from phonologically based interventions, research studies have also implemented programs providing more broad-based literacy skills. For example, Aylward and colleagues (2003) implemented a three-week literacy training program (28 hours total) with 11-year-old children. Interventions were consistent with the National Reading Panel's (2000) recommendations (these include linguistic awareness, alphabetic principle, fluency, and reading comprehension). Children performed two tasks during the brain scans collected both before and after training: (a) a phoneme-matching task (e.g., Do *ploat* and *drow* have the same vowel sound?) and (b) a morpheme-matching task (e.g., Does *corner* come from the word *corn*?).

The dyslexia group's neural responses were more like the control group's after the training for both tasks, and improvements were also shown in the group's word-level reading scores. Reading fluency or comprehension measures were not reported, so it is unknown if these higher-level skills were impacted.

Other investigations have tested the effects of significantly longer periods of remedial treatment. Examples include two studies in which children with dyslexia received over 100 hours of sound-, word-, and text-based instruction (Simos et al., 2007; Shaywitz et al., 2004). In the Shaywitz et al. (2004) intervention, children (6–9.5 years) received 50 minutes of individualized tutoring daily (an average of 105 hours) for 8 months using elements of best practices as outlined by the National Reading Panel (2000). During the pre- and post-treatment scans, children matched sounds to letters (e.g., child hears /b/ then see B-T or B-K). Post-training, the dyslexic children showed both normalized brain patterns and increased reading fluency. Simos and colleagues (2007) provided dyslexia children (7–9 years) with two interventions. The first included training in decoding skills for 2 hours per day over 8 weeks using the *Phono-Graphix* program (McGuinness, McGuinness, & McGuinness, 1996). Subsequently, children were trained in fluency for an hour per day for another 8 weeks using *Read Naturally* (Ihnot, Mastoff, Gavin & Hendrickson 2001). In the dyslexia group, training gains were exhibited neurally through faster brain reactivity as well as overall greater activations in leftward reading-related brain regions. Furthermore, this group showed behavioral improvements in both phonological decoding and word reading efficiency (text reading fluency was not reported). Together, these results—especially those suggesting a multipronged skills-based approach is better—are encouraging.

Unfortunately, however, there are a group of children who fail to respond even to intensive, prolonged remediation (Torgesen, 2000). Researchers have used imaging to try to determine the brain mechanisms associated with these so-called *nonresponders* (Davis et al., 2011; Odegard et al., 2008). Perhaps not surprisingly, not only do these children with dyslexia fail to show behavioral improvements, but their neural profiles also "resist" normalization. That is, they continue to exhibit more posterior right hemisphere activity than the prototypical left hemisphere reading network. A study of young adults who showed discrepant reading in elementary school but either remained *persistently poor readers* (continued to be discrepant) or *compensated readers* (scored in the average range) by high school found that the persistently poor readers had widespread underactivation in the reading network in both hemispheres, but that the compensated readers only showed underactivation in the left Wernicke region (Shaywitz et al., 2004), These findings underscore the strong relationship between behavioral expression of reading skill with the underlying neural mechanisms. In fact, some investigators show that long-term reading skills are tied to brain structures and inherent activation patterns, and not to experience. For example, Hoeft and colleagues (2011) showed that children with dyslexia who had more activity in the right frontal lobe (roughly homologous to Broca's area) during a rhyming task and greater white matter integrity along the superior longitudinal fasciculus from this region were better readers 2½ years later, regardless of their experience or participation in remedial programs during that time. Thus, despite the strong evidence of the plasticity of the brain and the effectiveness of intervention approaches, some neural deficits indicate larger impediments to remediation suggesting a variety of etiologies of the disorder.

10.7 Conclusions

Our fundamental goal in this chapter was to revisit the notion that dyslexia is neurobiological in origin, particularly within the framework of a specific learning disability. Culling the past 15–20 years of neurobiological and genetic research since the establishment of this most recent definition provides a picture of the situation that has not much changed from the debates of the early 1970s. That is, there are a modest number of children and adults (5–15%) who fail to acquire literacy despite instruction (the adequacy of which can be debated), but the field remains mystified by the neurocognitive etiology of the disorder. Moreover, because reading ability occurs along a continuum, the distinction between those who are "impaired" in learning and those who are just "poor readers" is argued to be somewhat arbitrary with cutoffs and decision points differing not only between states, but even between schools within the same local educational agencies (Shaywitz et al., 1992). The cognitive and behavioral profiles of these children as measured in psychoeducational assessments are often wide-ranging with the emergence of several subgroups, the broadest category being those afflicted with weaknesses in phonological processing (Fletcher et al., 2018). However, the nature of the phonological deficit itself, which is generally assumed to be a failure of the "language system" (Shaywitz, Mody, & Shaywitz, 2006), has also been argued as stemming from lower-level auditory processing (Tallal, 1980) or due to deficits in the attention, access, and retrieval of phonological information rather than a failure to formulate such knowledge in the first place (Ramus & Szenkovits, 2008).

A great promise of this new era of brain research has been that it would shine greater insight into the nature of developmental learning disorders and so many other psychological impairments. Clearly, the intent to characterize dyslexia in 2001 as neurobiological in origin was a product of this great hope and seemingly converging evidence from the early years of this nascent science. However, the study of cognitive neuroscience is a microcosm of the broader field of psychological science insomuch as we are limited by the established decision points, behavioral diagnostics, and measures of psychological function developed in the clinical domain. Thus, investigations into the neurobiology of dyslexia are less likely to provide insight into a common etiology of impaired reading; rather they are likely to elucidate the variety of subtypes that are evident from clinical practice. So does this mean that neuroscientific studies of dyslexia add little to our understanding of the disorder? Not necessarily. What can generally be argued from the common deficits in those early neuroimaging is that neurobiologically, dyslexia is a multiply determined outcome. These structural and functional deficits in the core regions involved in the computations of representing the orthographic, phonological, and semantic features of written words are likely the products of the underlying causes. Just as genetic differences indicate biological variations that serve as biomarkers for potential risk of disease given particular environmental conditions, shining a light on particular deficits in brain activity or structure may soon highlight, in conjunction with behavioral data, a need for intervention in one or more cognitive or perceptual abilities. The conundrum of bringing more data points to the understanding of dyslexia is that we introduce more degrees of freedom and with an exponential number of interactions. As the era of "big data" moves forward, the likelihood that patterns will emerge in the biological data that will enable us to not only identify subtypes of the disorders, but also reveal which interventions are likely to be effective based on those profiles. Such evidence of "biotypes" has recently been elucidated in depression (Drysdale, Grosenick, Downar, Dunlop et al., 2017) where particular patterns of connectivity in brain activation not only predict behavioral measures, but also responsiveness to intervention approaches using neural stimulation.

For over 130 years, we have looked to the brain to understand our deficits in language and reading, and over the course of time, we have found a more complex picture of not only the biological mechanisms, but also the behavioral manifestations of the disorder. The multitude of data suggests that reading (dis)ability emerges from an intricate set of cognitive skills and capacities each of which has a set of neural signatures that are proscribed by both molecular mechanisms inherent to the genome and a fertile environment of input available to the child at the appropriate period of development. Simply stating that "the origin of the disorder is neurobiological in nature" is neither theoretically satisfying—it has no explanatory power—nor has it been to this point diagnostically significant. However, there is far more cause for optimism. Big data projects such as the Dyslexia Data Consortium (www.dyslexiadata.org) led by Mark Eckert at the Medical University of South Carolina may soon reveal biotypes of dyslexia with indicators for intervention, and the growing database of genetic information threaded into the Research Domain of Criterion (RDOC) database at NIMH may yield endophenotypic markers to follow.

10.8 A Primer on the Methods of Cognitive Neuroscience

Neuroimaging techniques provide a window into a living brain. As with any discipline, cognitive neuroscience includes jargon and vocabulary unfamiliar to many. To facilitate the reader's general understanding of this chapter, we include a brief overview of imaging techniques as well as aspects of the brain and its activity that are measured.

10.8.1 Structural Imaging

Researchers who are concerned with the size, shape, and density of specific structures use structural brain scans. The main components of interest are two types of tissues that comprise the central nervous system: gray matter (GM) and white matter (WM). *Gray matter,* which processes information in the brain, is mostly composed of neurons and unmyelinated axons. Unmyelinated means that they lack the whitish-colored coating (a fatty protein) called myelin. Axons are the protrusions that extend from the neuronal cell bodies and carry signals between them. In contrast, *white matter* is mainly composed of long-range myelinated axons that transmit signals to gray matter. White matter has very few neuronal cell bodies. Myelin coats these axons, which both protect them and improve their transmission signal. Therefore, this tissue looks whitish in color relative to the gray matter. Gray matter is mainly on the surface of the brain, while white matter lies deep within the inner layer of cortex. Because many of the complex brain functions occur in the outermost part of the brain (in the cerebrum, including 1–2 mm of gray matter and also the white matter axons that connect this surface to the rest of the brain), the surface of the human brain has a bumpy, convoluted appearance with *gyri* (ridges) and *sulci* (depressions or grooves). Some of the structural measurements of interest researcher's use are: (1) gray and white matter volume, (2) white matter connections and overall connectivity in the brain, (3) the appearance of the gyri and/or sulci, and (4) total surface area of the brain. The main tool used by cognitive neuroscientists today is magnetic resonance imaging.

- **Magnetic Resonance Imaging**. If you have ever had an MRI, you have experienced the same equipment used by cognitive neuroscientists. Magnetic resonance imaging (MRI) creates a powerful magnetic field that interacts with the body's magnetic tissues to create an image. Because the density of protons is so much greater in gray matter compared to white matter, a typical image will clearly reveal these differences.
- **Diffusion Tensor Imaging**. MRI scanners are also used to study the myelinated white matter tracts in the brain, using a technique called diffusion tensor imaging (DTI). DTI measures the density and motion of water in the axons, which is possible partly due to the fatty boundary created by the myelin sheath. In white matter, diffusion generally follows the axon and is mostly "anisotropic" which means that it is directionally dependent. In contrast, gray matter is less anisotropic, and cerebrospinal fluid is isotropic, or without directionality. DTI measurements of interest include (but are not limited to) the overall rate of diffusion [mean diffusivity (MD)] as well as principal directionality of the diffusion [fractional anisotropy (FA)].

10.8.2   Functional Imaging

Functional brain imaging techniques allow researchers to view the processes of the brain at work, through measuring either electrical or metabolic activity.

- **PET**. Positron emission tomography (PET) maps functional processes in the brain by using trace amounts of short-lived radioactive material. As the radioactive material decays, it releases a positron signal that can be measured. With the advent of newer noninvasive technologies, PET has fallen out of favor, but research articles using PET remain part of the literature.

- **fMRI**. Functional magnetic resonance imaging (fMRI) measures changes in the blood oxygenation level-dependent signal (BOLD signal) and flow that occur in response to neural activity. Areas of activity in the brain consume more oxygen, so blood flow is increased in these areas. fMRI can be used to produce activation maps of neural activity that relates to specific cognitive processes. fMRI has very high spatial ("where") resolution, but is relatively poor for measuring temporal ("when") events. Resting-state fMRI (RSfMRI) utilizes correlations of the BOLD signal across brain regions to uncover connectivity between areas.
- **EEG**. The electroencephalogram (EEG) is a recording of the brain's electrical activity in milliseconds. EEG signatures from healthy brains in different states are relatively predictable, so they provide a useful tool to detect abnormalities or deviations. Measurements of interest, called **event-related potentials** (**ERPs**), are extracted from this recording and provide time-sensitive information of the brain's activity during the cognitive processes. As ERPs have superior temporal resolution, but are poor in terms of spatial predictions, these studies generally focus on the magnitude (or "amplitude"), which is an index of the strength, and latency (duration and timing) of neural responses.
- **MEG**. Magnetoencephalography (MEG) is used to record the magnetic fields produced by the brain's electrical activity using magnetometers. Superconducting quantum interference devices (SQUIDs) are currently the most common magnetometer used. Like EEG, MEG has high temporal resolution but relatively low spatial resolution. The advantage that magnetic field measurements have over EEG is that they are less likely to become distorted due to surrounding tissue and scalp. In some instances, this technique is referred to as MSI, or magnetic source imaging.

References

Ahissar, M. (2007). Dyslexia and the anchoring-deficit hypothesis. *Trends in Cognitive Sciences, 11*(11), 458–465. https://doi.org/10.1016/j.tics.2007.08.015.

Alexander-Passe, N. (2006). How dyslexic teenagers cope: An investigation of self-esteem, coping and depression. *Dyslexia, 12*(4), 256–275. https://doi.org/10.1002/dys.318.

Asbury, K., Wachs, T. D., & Plomin, R. (2005). Environmental moderators of genetic influence on verbal and nonverbal abilities in early childhood. *Intelligence, 33*(6), 643–661. https://doi.org/10.1016/j.intell.2005.03.008.

Aylward, E. H., Richards, T. L., Berninger, V. W., Nagy, W. E., Field, K. M., Grimme, A. C., et al. (2003). Instructional treatment associated with changes in brain activation in children with dyslexia. *Neurology, 61*(2), 212–219.

Banai, K., Hornickel, J., Skoe, E., Nicol, T., Zecker, S., & Kraus, N. (2009). Reading and subcortical auditory function. *Cerebral Cortex, 19*(11), 2699–2707. https://doi.org/10.1093/cercor/bhp024.

Beaulieu, C., Plewes, C., Paulson, L. A., Roy, D., Snook, L., Concha, L., et al. (2005). Imaging brain connectivity in children with diverse reading ability. *NeuroImage, 25*(4), 1266–1271. https://doi.org/10.1016/j.neuroimage.2004.12.053.

Ben Tchudah, O., & Ahissar, M. (2004). Sequential spatial frequency discrimination is consistently impaired among adult dyslexics. *Vision Research, 44*(10), 1047–1063. https://doi.org/10.1016/j.visres.2003.12.001.

Black, J. M., Tanaka, H., Stanley, L., Nagamine, M., Zakerani, N., Thurston, A., … Hoeft, F. (2012). Maternal history of reading difficulty is associated with reduced language-related gray matter in beginning readers. *NeuroImage, 59*(3), 3021–3032. https://doi.org/10.1016/j.neuroimage.2011.10.024.

Bolger, D. J., Hornickel, J., Cone, N. E., Burman, D. D., & Booth, J. R. (2008a). Neural correlates of orthographic and phonological consistency effects in children. *Human Brain Mapping, 29*(12), 1416–1429.

Bolger, D. J., Minas, J., Burman, D. D., & Booth, J. R. (2008b). Differential effects of orthographic and phonological consistency in cortex for children with and without reading impairment. *Neuropsychologia, 46*(14), 3210–3224. https://doi.org/10.1016/j.neuropsychologia.2008.07.024.

Bolger, D. J., Perfetti, C. A., & Schneider, W. (2005). Cross-cultural effect on the brain revisited: Universal structures plus writing system variation. *Human Brain Mapping, 25,* 92–104. https://doi.org/10.1002/hbm.20124.

Brambati, S. M., Termine, C., Ruffino, M., Stella, G., Fazio, F., Cappa, S. F., et al. (2004). Regional reductions of gray matter volume in familial dyslexia. *Neurology, 63*(4), 742–745. https://doi.org/10.1212/01.WNL.0000134673.95020.EE.

Brown, W., Eliez, S., Menon, V., Rumsey, J., White, C., & Reiss, A. (2001). Preliminary evidence of widespread morphological variations of the brain in dyslexia. *Neurology, 56*(6), 781–783. https://doi.org/10.1212/wnl.56.6.781.

Brunswick, N., McCrory, E., Price, C. J., Frith, C. D., & Frith, U. (1999). Explicit and implicit processing of words and pseudowords by adult developmental dyslexics. A search for Wernicke's Wortschatz? *Brain, 122*(10), 1901–1917. https://doi.org/10.1093/brain/122.10.1901.

Cao, F., Bitan, T., & Booth, J. R. (2008). Effective brain connectivity in children with reading difficulties during phonological processing. *Brain and Language, 107*(2), 91–101.

Cao, F., Bitan, T., Chou, T. L., Burman, D. D., & Booth, J. R. (2006). Deficient orthographic and phonological representations in children with dyslexia revealed by brain activation patterns. *Journal of Child Psychology and Psychiatry and Allied Disciplines, 47*(10), 1041–1050. https://doi.org/10.1111/j.1469-7610.2006.01684.x

Catani, M., & Mesulam, M. (2008). The arcuate fasciculus and the disconnection theme in language and aphasia: History and current state. *Cortex, 44*(8), 953–961. https://doi.org/10.1016/j.cortex.2008.04.002.

Centanni, T., Booker, A. B., Chen, F., Sloan, A. M., Carraway, R. S., Rennaker, R. L., … Kilgard, M. P. (2016). Knockdown of dyslexia-gene DCDC2 interferes with speech sound discrimination in continuous streams. *Journal of Neuroscience, 36*(17), 4895–4906. https://doi.org/10.1523/jneurosci.4202-15.2016.

Centanni, T., Chen, F., Booker, A. M., Engineer, C. T., Sloan, A. M., Rennaker, R. L., … Kilgard, M. P. (2014). Speech sound processing deficits and training-induced neural plasticity in rats with dyslexia gene knockdown. *PLoS ONE, 9*(5). https://doi.org/10.1371/journal.pone.0098439.

Chandrasekaran, B., Hornickel, J., Skoe, E., Nicol, T., & Kraus, N. (2009). Context-dependent encoding in the human auditory brainstem relates to hearing speech in noise: Implications for developmental dyslexia. *Neuron, 64*(3), 311–319. https://doi.org/10.1016/j.neuron.2009.10.006.

Cicchini, G. M., Marino, C., Mascheretti, S., Perani, D., & Morrone, M. C. (2015). Strong motion deficits in dyslexia associated with DCDC2 gene alteration. *Journal of Neuroscience, 35*(21), 8059–8064.

Clark, K. A., Helland, T., Specht, K., Narr, K. L., Manis, F. R., Toga, A. W., et al. (2014). Neuroanatomical precursors of dyslexia identified from pre-reading through to age 11. *Brain, 137*(12), 3136–3141. https://doi.org/10.1093/brain/awu229.

Connor, C. M., Piasta, S. B., Fishman, B., Glasney, S., Schatschneider, C., Crowe, E., … Morrison, F. J. (2009). Individualizing student instruction precisely: Effects of child × instruction interactions on first graders' literacy development. *Child Development, 80*(1), 77–100. https://doi.org/10. 1111/j.1467-8624.2008.01247.x.

Darki, F., Peyrard-Janvid, M., Matsson, H., Kere, J., & Klingberg, T. (2012). Three dyslexia susceptibility genes, DYX1C1, DCDC2, and KIAA0319, affect temporo-parietal white matter structure. *Biological Psychiatry, 72*(8), 671–676. https://doi.org/10.1016/j.biopsych.2012.05.008.

Davis, N., Barquero, L., Compton, D. L., Fuchs, L. S., Fuchs, D., Gore, J. C., et al. (2011). Functional correlates of children's responsiveness to intervention. *Developmental Neuropsychology, 36*(3), 288–301.

Dawson, G., Finley, C., Phillips, S., & Galpert, L. (1986). Hemispheric specialization and the language abilities of autistic children. *Society for Research in Child Development, 57*(6), 1440–1453.

Debska, A., Łuniewska, M., Chyl, K., Banaszkiewicz, A., Zelechowska, A., Wypych, M., … Jednoróg, K. (2016). Neural basis of phonological awareness in beginning readers with familial risk of dyslexia-Results from shallow orthography. *NeuroImage, 132*, 406–416. https://doi.org/10. 1016/j.neuroimage.2016.02.063.

Dejerine, M., & Symes, W. L. (1893). Some recent papers on neurophysiology. *Brain, 16*(1–2), 318–320.

Demb, J. B., Boynton, G. M., Best, M., & Heeger, D. J. (1998). Psychophysical evidence for a magnocellular pathway deficit in dyslexia. *Vision Research, 38*(11), 1555–1559. https://doi.org/ 10.1016/s0042-6989(98)00073-3.

Desroches, A. S., Cone, N. E., Bolger, D. J., Bitan, T., Burman, D. D., & Booth, J. R. (2010). Children with reading difficulties show differences in brain regions associated with orthographic processing during spoken language processing. *Brain Research, 1356*, 73–84.

Deutsch, G. K., Dougherty, R. F., Bammer, R., Siok, W. T., Gabrieli, J. D. E., & Wandell, B. (2005). Children's reading performance is correlated with white matter structure measured by diffusion tensor imaging. *Cortex, 41*(3), 354–363. https://doi.org/10.1016/s0010-9452(08)70272-7.

Drysdale, A. T., Grosenick, L., Downar, J., Dunlop, K., Mansouri, F., Meng, Y., … & Schatzberg, A. F. (2017). Resting-state connectivity biomarkers define neurophysiological subtypes of depression. *Nature medicine, 23*(1), 28.

Eckert, M. A., Vaden, Jr., K. I., Gebregziabher, M., & Dyslexia Data Consortium. (2018). Reading profiles in multi-site data with missingness. *Frontiers in Psychology, 9*, 644.

Eden, G. F., Jones, K. M., Cappell, K., Gareau, L., Wood, F. B., Zeffiro, T. A., … & Flowers, D. L. (2004). Neural changes following remediation in adult developmental dyslexia. *Neuron, 44*(3), 411–422.

Eden, G. F., VanMeter, J. W., Rumsey, J. M., Maisog, J. M., Woods, R. P., & Zeffiro, T. A. (1996). Abnormal processing of visual motion in dyslexia revealed by functional brain imaging. *Nature, 382*, 66–69. https://doi.org/10.1038/382066a0.

Elliott, J. G., & Gibbs, S. (2008). Does dyslexia exist? *Journal of Philosophy of Education, 42*(3–4), 475–491. https://doi.org/10.1111/j.1467-9752.2008.00653.x.

Facoetti, A., Corradi, N., Ruffino, M., Gori, S., & Zorzi, M. (2010a). Visual spatial attention and speech segmentation are both impaired at familial risk for developmental dyslexia. *Dyslexia, 16*(3), 226–239. https://doi.org/10.1002/dys.413.

Facoetti, A., & Molteni, M. (2001). The gradient of visual attention in developmental dyslexia. *Neuropsychologia, 39*(4), 352–357. https://doi.org/10.1016/S0028-3932(00)00138-X.

Facoetti, A., Pagnoni, G., Turatto, M., Marzola, V., & Mascetti, G. (2000). Visual-spatial attention in developmental dyslexia. *Cortex, 36*(1), 109–123. https://doi.org/10.1016/s0010-9452(08)70840-2.

Facoetti, A., Trussardi, A. N., Ruffino, M., Lorusso, M. L., Cattaneo, C., Galli, R., … Zorzi, M. (2010). Multisensory spatial attention deficits are predictive of phonological decoding skills in developmental dyslexia. *Journal of Cognitive Neuroscience, 22*(5), 1011–1025. https://doi.org/ 10.1162/jocn.2009.21232.

Facoetti, A., Zorzi, M., Cestnick, L., Lorusso, M. L., Molteni, M., Paganoni, P., … Mascetti, G. G. (2006). The relationship between visuo-spatial attention and nonword reading in developmental dyslexia. *Cognitive Neuropsychology, 23*(6), 841–855. https://doi.org/10.1080/ 0LU4JLJ0J0040J0J0.

Fletcher, J. M. (2005). Predicting math outcomes: Reading predictors and comorbidity. *Journal of Learning Disabilities, 38*(4), 308–312.

Fletcher, J. M., Lyon, G. R., Fuchs, L. S., & Barnes, M. A. (2018). *Learning disabilities: From identification to intervention.* Guilford Publications.

Fletcher, J. M., & Morris, R. (1986). Classification of disabled learners: Beyond exclusionary definitions. *Handbook of cognitive, social, and neuropsychological aspects of learning disabilities, 1,* 55–80.

Francis, D. J., Stuebing, K. K., Shaywitz, S. E., Shaywitz, B. A., & Fletcher, J. M. (1996). Developmental lag versus deficit models of reading disability: A longitudinal individual growth curves analysis. *Journal of Educational Psychology, 88*(1), 3–17.

Fuchs, L. S., & Fuchs, D. (2002). Mathematical problem-solving profiles of students with mathematics disabilities with and without comorbid reading disabilities. *Journal of learning disabilities, 35*(6), 564–574.

Gaab, N., Gabrieli, J. D. E., Deutsch, G. K., Tallal, P., & Temple, E. (2007). Neural correlates of rapid auditory processing are disrupted in children with developmental dyslexia and ameliorated with training: An fMRI study. *Restorative Neurology and Neuroscience, 25*(3–4), 295–310.

Gabrieli, J. D. E. (2009). Dyslexia: A new synergy between education and cognitive neuroscience. *Science (New York, NY), 325*(5938), 280–283. https://doi.org/10.1126/science.1171999.

Galaburda, A. M., & Kemper, T. L. (1979). Cytoarchitectonic abnormalities in developmental dyslexia: A case study. *Annals of Neurology, 6*(2), 94–100. https://doi.org/10.1002/ana. 410060203.

Galaburda, A. M., & Livingstone, M. (1993). Evidence for a magnocellular defect in developmental dyslexia. *Annals of the New York Academy of Sciences, 682*(1), 70–82. https://doi.org/10.1111/j. 1749-6632.1993.tb22960.x.

Galaburda, A. M., LoTurco, J., Ramus, F., Fitch, R. H., & Rosen, G. D. (2006). From genes to behavior in developmental dyslexia. *Nature Neuroscience, 9*(10), 1213–1217. https://doi.org/10. 1038/nn1772.

Galaburda, A. M., Sanides, F., & Geschwind, N. (1978). Human brain. Cytoarchitectonic left-right asymmetries in the temporal speech region. *Archives of Neurology, 35*(12), 812–817.

Galaburda, A. M., Sherman, G. F., Rosen, G. D., Aboitiz, F., & Geschwind, N. (1985). Developmental dyslexia: Four consecutive patients with cortical anomalies. *Annals of Neurology, 18*(2), 222–233. https://doi.org/10.1002/ana.410180210.

Gathercole, S. E., Alloway, T. P., Willis, C., & Adams, A. M. (2006). Working memory in children with reading disabilities. *Journal of Experimental Child Psychology, 93*(3), 265–281.

Georgiewa, P., Rzanny, R., Hopf, J. M., Knab, R., Glauche, V., Kaiser, W. A., & Blanz, B. (1999). fMRI during word processing in dyslexic and normal reading children. *Neuroreport, 10*(16), 3459–65 (10599862).

Geschwind, N. (1970). The organization of language and the brain. *Science, 170*(961), 940–944. https://doi.org/10.1126/science.170.3961.940.

Geschwind, N. (1974). *Selected papers on language and the brain* (Vol. 16). Dordrecht: Springer, Netherlands. https://doi.org/10.1007/978-94-010-2093-0.

Gialluisi, A., Newbury, D. F., Wilcutt, E. G., Consortium, T. S. L. I., & Luciano, M. (2014). Genome-wide screening for DNA variants associated with reading and language traits. *Genes, Brain and Behavior, 13*(7), 686–701. https://doi.org/10.1111/gbb.12158.

Graves, W. W., Desai, R., Humphries, C., Seidenberg, M. S., & Binder, J. R. (2010). Neural systems for reading aloud: a multiparametric approach. *Cerebral Cortex, 20*(8), 1799–1815. https://doi. org/10.1093/cercor/bhp245.

Grigorenko, E. L. (2004). Genetic bases of developmental dyslexia: A capsule review of heritability estimates. *Enfance, 56*(3), 273–288. https://doi.org/10.3917/enf.563.0273.

Grigorenko, E. L. (2005). A conservative meta-analysis of linkage and linkage-association studies of developmental dyslexia. *Scientific Studies of Reading, 9*(3), 285–316. https://doi.org/10.1207/s1532799xssr0903.

Grigorenko, E. L., Naples, A., Chang, J., Romano, C., Ngorosho, D., Kungulilo, S., … Bundy, D. (2007). Back to Africa: Tracing dyslexia genes in East Africa. *Reading and Writing: An Interdisciplinary Journal, 20*(1–2), 27–49. https://doi.org/10.1007/s11145-006-9017-y.

Guttorm, T., Leppanen, P. H. T., Hamalainen, J. A., Eklund, K. M., & Lyytinen, H. J. (2010). Newborn event-related potentials predict poorer pre-reading skills in children at risk for dyslexia. *Journal of Learning Disabilities, 43*(5), 391–401. https://doi.org/10.1177/0022219409345005.

Guttorm, T., Leppanen, P., Poikkeus, A., Eklund, K., Lyytinen, P., & Lyytinen, H. (2005). Brain event-related potentials (ERPs) measured at birth predict later language development in children with and without familial risk for dyslexia. *Cortex, 41*(3), 291–303. https://doi.org/10.1016/S0010-9452(08)70267-3.

Guttorm, T., Leppanen, P. H. T., Richardson, U., & Lyytinen, H. (2001). Event-related potentials and consonant differentiation in newborns with familial risk for dyslexia. *Journal of Learning Disabilities, 34*(6), 534–544. https://doi.org/10.1177/002221940103400606.

Hämäläinen, J. A., Salminen, H. K., & Leppänen, P. H. T. (2013). Basic auditory processing deficits in dyslexia: Systematic review of the behavioral and event-related potential/ field evidence. *Journal of Learning Disabilities, 46*(5), 413–427. https://doi.org/10.1177/0022219411436213.

Hampshire, A., Highfield, R. R., Parkin, B. L., & Owen, A. M. (2012). Fractionating human intelligence. *Neuron, 76*(6), 1225–1237.

Harlaar, N., Butcher, L. M., Meaburn, E., Sham, P., Craig, I. W., & Plomin, R. (2005). A behavioural genomic analysis of DNA markers associated with general cognitive ability in 7-year-olds. *Journal of Child Psychology and Psychiatry and Allied Disciplines, 46*(10), 1097–1107. https://doi.org/10.1111/j.1469-7610.2005.01515.x.

Hart, S. A., Soden, B., Johnson, W., Schatschneider, C., & Taylor, J. (2013). Expanding the environment: Gene × school-level SES interaction on reading comprehension. *Journal of Child Psychology and Psychiatry, 54*(10), 1047–1055. https://doi.org/10.1111/jcpp.12083.

Heibert, E. H., & Taylor, B. M. (2000). Beginning reading instruction: Research on early interventions. In M. L. Kamil, P. B. Mosenthal, P. David Pearson, & R. Barr (Eds.), *Handbook of reading research, Vol. III* (pp. 455–482). Mahwah NJ: Lawrence Erlbaum.

Heim, S., Grande, M., Pape-Neumann, J., van Ermingen, M., Meffert, E., Grabowska, A., … Amunts, K. (2010). Interaction of phonological awareness and "magnocellular" processing during normal and dyslexic reading: behavioural and fMRI investigations. *Dyslexia, 16*(3), 258–282. https://doi.org/10.1002/dys.

Hoeft, F., Hernandez, A., McMillon, G., Taylor-Hill, H., Martindale, J. L., Meyler, A., … Gabrieli, J. D. E. (2006). Neural basis of dyslexia: A comparison between dyslexic and nondyslexic children equated for reading ability. *Journal of Neuroscience, 26*(42), 10700–10708. https://doi.org/10.1523/jneurosci.4931-05.2006.

Hoeft, F., McCandliss, B. D., Black, J. M., Gantman, A., Zakerani, N., Hulme, C., … & Gabrieli, J. D. (2011). Neural systems predicting long-term outcome in dyslexia. *Proceedings of the National Academy of Sciences, 108*(1), 361–366.

Hornickel, J., & Kraus, N. (2013). Unstable representation of sound: A biological marker of dyslexia. *Journal of Neuroscience, 33*(8), 3500–3504. https://doi.org/10.1523/JNEUROSCI.4205-12.2013.

Hosseini, S. M. H., Black, J. M., Soriano, T., Bugescu, N., Martinez, R., Raman, M. M., … Hoeft, F. (2013). Topological properties of large-scale structural brain networks in children with familial risk for reading difficulties. *NeuroImage, 71*, 260–274. https://doi.org/10.1016/j.neuroimage.2013.01.013.

Hus, Y. (2001). Early reading for low-ses minority language children: An attempt to "catch them before they fall". *Folia Phoniatrica et Logopaedica, 53*(3), 173–182.

Hutzler, F., Kronbichler, M., Jacobs, A. M., & Wimmer, H. (2006). Perhaps correlational but not causal: No effect of dyslexic readers' magnocellular system on their eye movements during reading. *Neuropsychologia, 44*(4), 637–648. https://doi.org/10.1016/j.neuropsychologia.2005. 06.006.

Im, K., Raschle, N. M., Smith, S. A., Ellen Grant, P., & Gaab, N. (2016). Atypical sulcal pattern in children with developmental dyslexia and at-risk kindergarteners. *Cerebral Cortex, 26*(3), 1138–1148. https://doi.org/10.1093/cercor/bhu305.

Johannes, S., Kussmaul, C. L., Münte, T. F., & Mangun, G. R. (1996). Developmental dyslexia: Passive visual stimulation provides no evidence for a magnocellular processing defect. *Neuropsychologia, 34*(11), 1123–1127. https://doi.org/10.1016/0028-3932(96)00026-7.

Karmiloff-Smith, A. (2009). Nativism versus neuroconstructivism: Rethinking the study of developmental disorders. *Developmental Psychology, 45*(1), 56–63. https://doi.org/10.1037/a0014506.

Keller, T. A., & Just, M. A. (2009). Altering cortical connectivity: Remediation-induced changes in the white matter of poor readers. *Neuron, 64*(5), 624–631.

Krafnick, A. J., Flowers, D. L., Luetje, M. M., Napoliello, E. M., & Eden, G. F. (2014). An investigation into the origin of anatomical differences in dyslexia. *The Journal of Neuroscience, 34*(3), 901–908. https://doi.org/10.1523/JNEUROSCI.2092-13.2013.

Kronbichler, M., Hutzler, F., Staffen, W., Mair, A., Ladurner, G., & Wimmer, H. (2006). Evidence for a dysfunction of left posterior reading areas in German dyslexic readers. *Neuropsychologia, 44*(10), 1822–1832. https://doi.org/10.1016/j.neuropsychologia.2006.03.010.

Kronbichler, M., Wimmer, H., Staffen, W., Hutzler, F., Mair, A., & Ladurner, G. (2008). Developmental dyslexia: Gray matter abnormalities in the occipitotemporal cortex. *Human Brain Mapping, 29*(5), 613–625. https://doi.org/10.1002/hbm.20425.

Langer, N., Peysakhovich, B., Zuk, J., Drottar, M., Sliva, D. D., Smith, S., … Gaab, N. (2015). White matter alterations in infants at risk for developmental dyslexia. *Cerebral Cortex, 27*(2):1027–1036. https://doi.org/10.1093/cercor/bhv281.

Leppänen, P. H. T., Hämäläinen, J. A., Guttorm, T., Eklund, K. M., Salminen, H. K., Tanskanen, A., … Lyytinen, H. J. (2012). Infant brain responses associated with reading-related skills before school and at school age. *Neurophysiologie Clinique/Clinical Neurophysiology, 42*(1–2), 35–41. https://doi.org/10.1016/j.neucli.2011.08.005.

Leppänen, P. H. T., Hämäläinen, J. A., Salminen, H. K., Eklund, K. M., Guttorm, T. K., Lohvansuu, K., … Lyytinen, H. (2010). Newborn brain event-related potentials revealing atypical processing of sound frequency and the subsequent association with later literacy skills in children with familial dyslexia. *Cortex, 46*(10), 1362–1376. https://doi.org/10.1016/j.cortex.2010.06.003.

Lilienfeld, S. O., & Treadway, M. T. (2016). Clashing diagnostic approaches: DSM-ICD versus RDoC. *Annual Review of Clinical Psychology, 12,* 435–463.

Linkersdörfer, J., Jurcoane, A., Lindberg, S., Kaiser, J., Hasslehorn, M., Fiebach, C. J., et al. (2014). The association between gray matter volume and reading proficiency: A longitudinal study of beginning readers. *Journal of Cognitive Neuroscience, 27*(2), 308–318. https://doi.org/10.1162/jocn.

Linkersdörfer, J., Lonnemann, J., Lindberg, S., Hasselhorn, M., & Fiebach, C. J. (2012). Grey matter alterations co-localize with functional abnormalities in developmental dyslexia: An ALE meta-analysis. *PLoS ONE, 7*(8). https://doi.org/10.1371/journal.pone.0043122.

Livingstone, M. S., & Hubel, D. (1988). Segregation of form, color, movement, and depth: Anatomy, physiology, and perception. *Science, 240*(4853), 740–749. https://doi.org/10.1126/science.3283936.

Logan, J. A., Hart, S. A., Cutting, L., Deater-Deckard, K., Schatschneider, C., & Petrill, S. (2014). Reading development in young children: Genetic and environmental influences. *Child Development, 84*(6), 2131–2144. https://doi.org/10.1111/cdev.12104.

Lyon, G. R., Fletcher, J. M., Shaywitz, S. E., Shaywitz, B. A., Torgesen, J. K., Wood, F. B., … & Olson, R. (2001). Rethinking learning disabilities. *Rethinking Special Education for a New Century,* 259–287.

Lyon, G. R., Shaywitz, S. E., & Shaywitz, B. A. (2003). A definition of dyslexia. *Annals of Dyslexia, 53*(1), 1–14. https://doi.org/10.1007/s11881-003-0001-9.

Lyytinen, H., Guttorm, T., Huttunen, T., Hamalainen, J., Leppanen, P., & Vesterinen, M. (2005). Psychophysiology of developmental dyslexia: a review of findings including studies of children at risk for dyslexia. *Journal of Neurolinguistics, 18*(2), 167–195. https://doi.org/10.1016/j.jneuroling.2004.11.001.

Maisog, J. M., Einbinder, E. R., Flowers, D. L., Turkeltaub, P. E., & Eden, G. F. (2008). A meta-analysis of functional neuroimaging studies of dyslexia. *Annals of the New York Academy of Sciences, 1145*(1), 237–259.

Marinković, K. (2004). Spatiotemporal dynamics of word processing in the human cortex. *The Neuroscientist, 10*(2), 142–152. https://doi.org/10.1177/1073858403261018.

Marinković, K., Dhond, R. P., Dale, A. M., Glessner, M., Carr, V., & Halgren, E. (2003). Spatiotemporal dynamics of modality-specific and supramodal word processing. *Neuron, 38*(3), 487–497.

McCrory, E. J., Mechelli, A., Frith, U., & Price, C. J. (2005). More than words: A common neural basis for reading and naming deficits in developmental dyslexia? *Brain, 128*(2), 261–267. https://doi.org/10.1093/brain/awh340.

McDonald, C. R., Thesen, T., Carlson, C., Blumberg, M., Girard, H. M., Trongnetrpunya, A., ... Halgren, E. (2010). Multimodal imaging of repetition priming: Using fMRI, MEG, and intracranial EEG to reveal spatiotemporal profiles of word processing. *NeuroImage, 53*(2), 707–717. https://doi.org/10.1016/j.neuroimage.2010.06.069.

McGuinness, C., McGuinness, D., & McGuinness, G. (1996). Phono-graphix TM: A new method for remediating reading difficulties. *Annals of Dyslexia, 46*(1), 73–96.

Meng, H., Powers, N. R., Tang, L., Cope, N. A., Zhang, P. X., Fuleihan, R., ... & Gruen, J. R. (2011). A dyslexia-associated variant in DCDC2 changes gene expression. *Behavior Genetics, 41*(1), 58–66.

Meng, H., Smith, S. D., Hager, K., Held, M., Liu, J., Olson, R. K., ... Gruen, J. R. (2005). DCDC2 is associated with reading disability and modulates neuronal development in the brain. *Proceedings of the National Academy of Sciences, 102*(47), 17053–8. https://doi.org/10.1073/pnas.0508591102.

Meyler, A., Keller, T. A., Cherkassky, V. L., Gabrieli, J. D. E., & Just, M. A. (2008). Modifying the brain activation of poor readers during sentence comprehension with extended remedial instruction: A longitudinal study of neuroplasticity. *Neuropsychologia, 46*(10), 2580–2592.

Milne, E., & Grafman, J. (2001). Ventromedial prefrontal cortex lesions in humans eliminate implicit gender stereotyping. *The Journal of Neuroscience, 21*(12), RC150.

Milne, R. D., Syngeniotis, A., Jackson, G., & Corballis, M. C. (2002). Mixed lateralization of phonological assembly in developmental dyslexia. *Neurocase, 8*(3), 205–209. https://doi.org/10.1093/neucas/8.3.205.

Molfese, D. L. (2000). Predicting dyslexia at 8 years of age using neonatal brain responses. *Brain and Language, 72*(3), 238–245. https://doi.org/10.1006/brln.2000.2287.

Molfese, D. L., & Molfese, V. J. (1985). Electrophysiological indices of auditory discrimination in newborn infants: The bases for predicting later language development? *Infant Behavior and Development, 9*(2), 197–211.

Molfese, D. L., & Molfese, V. J. (1997). Discrimination of language skills at five years of age using event-related potentials recorded at birth. *Developmental Neuropsychology, 13*(2), 135–156. https://doi.org/10.1080/87565649709540674.

Molfese, D. L., Molfese, V. J., & Kelly, S. (2001). The use of brain electrophysiology techniques to study language: A basic guide for the beginning consumer of electrophysiology information. *Learning Disability Quarterly, 24*(3), 177. https://doi.org/10.2307/1511242.

Morris, R. D., Stuebing, K. K., Fletcher, J. M., Shaywitz, S. E., Lyon, G. R., Shankweiler, D. P., ... Shaywitz, B. A. (1998). Subtypes of reading disability: Variability around a phonological core. *Journal of Educational Psychology, 90*(3), 347–373. https://doi.org/10.1037/0022-0663. 90 3 347

Myers, C., Vandermosten, M., Farris, R., Hancock, R., Gimenez, P., Black, J., ... Hoeft, F. (2014). White matter morphometric changes uniquely predict children's reading acquisition. *Psychological Science, 25*(10), 1870–1883. https://doi.org/10.1177/0956797614544511.

National Reading Panel (US), National Institute of Child Health, & Human Development (US). (2000). *Report of the national reading panel: Teaching children to read: An evidence-based assessment of the scientific research literature on reading and its implications for reading instruction: Reports of the subgroups.* National Institute of Child Health and Human Development, National Institutes of Health.

Neville, H. J., Coffey, S. A., Holcomb, P. J., & Tallal, P. (1993). The neurobiology of sensory and language processing in language-impaired children. *Journal of Cognitive Neuroscience, 5*(2), 235–253. https://doi.org/10.1162/jocn.1993.5.2.235.

Noble, K. G., McCandliss, B. D., & Farah, M. J. (2007). Socioeconomic gradients predict individual differences in neurocognitive abilities. *Developmental Science, 10*(4), 464–480. https://doi.org/10.1111/j.1467-7687.2007.00600.x.

Odegard, T. N., Ring, J., Smith, S., Biggan, J., & Black, J. (2008). Differentiating the neural response to intervention in children with developmental dyslexia. *Annals of dyslexia, 58*(1), 1.

Ozernov-Palchik, O., & Gaab, N. (2016). Tackling the "dyslexia paradox": Reading brain and behavior for early markers of developmental dyslexia. *Wiley Interdisciplinary Reviews: Cognitive Science, 7*(2), 156–176. https://doi.org/10.1002/wcs.1383.

Paracchini, S., Thomas, A., Castro, S., Lai, C., Paramasivam, M., Wang, Y., ... & Francks, C. (2006). The chromosome 6p22 haplotype associated with dyslexia reduces the expression of KIAA0319, a novel gene involved in neuronal migration. *Human Molecular Genetics, 15*(10), 1659–1666.

Paulesu, E. (2001). Dyslexia: Cultural diversity and biological unity. *Science, 291*(5511), 2165–2167. https://doi.org/10.1126/science.1057179.

Paulesu, E., Danelli, L., & Berlingeri, M. (2014). Reading the dyslexic brain: multiple dysfunctional routes revealed by a new meta-analysis of PET and fMRI activation studies. *Frontiers in Human Neuroscience, 8*(November), 830. https://doi.org/10.3389/fnhum.2014.00830.

Paulesu, E., Frith, U., Snowling, M., Gallagher, A., Morton, J., Frackowiak, R. S. J., et al. (1996). Is developmental dyslexia a disconnection syndrome? *Evidence from PET scanning. Brain, 119*(1), 143–157. https://doi.org/10.1093/brain/119.1.143.

Pennington, B. F. (2006). From single to multiple deficit models of developmental disorders. *Cognition, 101*(2), 385–413.

Peterson, R., & Pennington, B. (2015). Developmental dyslexia. *Annual Review of Clinical Psychology, 11,* 283–307. https://doi.org/10.1146/annurev-clinpsy-032814-112842.

Phillips, B. M., & Lonigan, C. J. (2005). Social correlates of emergent literacy. In M. J. Snowling & C. Hulme (Eds.), *The science of reading: A handbook* (pp. 173–187). Oxford, UK: Blackwell Publishing Ltd. https://doi.org/10.1002/9780470757642.ch10.

Platt, M. P., Adler, W. T., Mehlhorn, A. J., Johnson, G. C., Wright, K. A., Choi, R. T., ... Rosen, G. D. (2013). Embryonic disruption of the candidate dyslexia susceptibility gene homolog Kiaa0319-like results in neuronal migration disorders. *Neuroscience, 248,* 585–593. https://doi.org/10.1016/j.neuroscience.2013.06.056.

Plomin, R., Haworth, C. M. A., Meaburn, E. L., Price, T. S., & Davis, O. S. P. (2013). Common DNA markers can account for more than half of the genetic influence on cognitive abilities. *Psychological Science, 24*(4), 562–568. https://doi.org/10.1177/0956797612457952.

Powers, S. J., Wang, Y., Beach, S. D., Sideridis, G. D., & Gaab, N. (2016). Examining the relationship between home literacy environment and neural correlates of phonological processing in beginning readers with and without a familial risk for dyslexia: An fMRI study. *Annals of Dyslexia, 66*(3), 337–360.

Ramus, F., Rosen, S., Dakin, S. C., Day, B. L., Castellote, J. M., White, S., et al. (2003). Theories of developmental dyslexia: Insights from a multiple case study of dyslexic adults. *Brain, 126*(4), 841–865. https://doi.org/10.1093/brain/awg076.

Ramus, F., & Szenkovits, G. (2008) What phonological deficit? *The Quarterly Journal of Experimental Psychology, 61*(1),129–141. https://doi.org/10.1080/17470210701508822

Raschle, N. M., Chang, M., & Gaab, N. (2011). Structural brain alterations associated with dyslexia predate reading onset. *NeuroImage, 57*(3), 742–749. https://doi.org/10.1016/j.neuroimage.2010.09.055.

Raschle, N. M., Stering, P. L., Meissner, S. N., & Gaab, N. (2014). Altered neuronal response during rapid auditory processing and its relation to phonological processing in prereading children at familial risk for dyslexia. *Cerebral Cortex, 24*(9), 2489–2501. https://doi.org/10.1093/cercor/bht104.

Reardon, S. F., Robinson-Cimpian, J. P., & Weathers, E. S. (2014). Patterns and trends in racial/ethnic and socioeconomic academic achievement gaps. In H. A. Ladd & M. E. Goertz (Eds.), *Handbook of research in education finance and policy*. Mahwah, NJ: Lawrence Erlbaum.

Richlan, F., Kronbichler, M., & Wimmer, H. (2009). Functional abnormalities in the dyslexic brain: A quantitative meta-analysis of neuroimaging studies. *Human Brain Mapping, 30*(10), 3299–3308.

Richlan, F., Kronbichler, M., & Wimmer, H. (2013). Structural abnormalities in the dyslexic brain: A meta-analysis of voxel-based morphometry studies. *Human Brain Mapping, 34*(11), 3055–3065. https://doi.org/10.1002/hbm.22127.

Rimrodt, S. L., Peterson, D. J., Denckla, M. B., Kaufmann, W. E., & Cutting, L. E. (2010). White matter microstructural differences linked to left perisylvian language network in children with dyslexia. *Cortex, 46*(6), 739–749. https://doi.org/10.1016/j.cortex.2009.07.008.

Rumsey, J. M., Andreason, P., Zametkin, A. J., Aquino, T., King, A. C., Hamburger, S. D., … Cohen, R. M. (1992). Failure to activate the left temporoparietal cortex in dyslexia. An oxygen 15 positron emission tomographic study. *Archives of Neurology, 49*(5), 527–34.

Rumsey, J. M., Horwitz, B., Donohue, B. C., Nace, K., Maisog, J. M., & Andreason, P. (1997a). Phonological and orthographic components of word recognition. A PET-rCBF study. *Brain, 120*(5), 739–759. https://doi.org/10.1093/brain/120.5.739.

Rumsey, J. M., Nace, K., Donohue, B., Wise, D., Maisog, J. M., & Andreason, P. (1997b). A positron emission tomographic study of impaired word recognition and phonological processing in dyslexic men. *Archives of Neurology, 54*(5), 562–573.

Rutter, M., & Yule, W. (1975). The concept of specific reading retardation. *Journal of Child Psychology and Psychiatry, 16*(3), 181–197.

Salmelin, R., Kiesilä, P., Uutela, K., Service, E., & Salonen, O. (1996). Impaired visual word processing in dyslexia revealed with magnetoencephalography. *Annals of Neurology, 40*(2), 157–162. https://doi.org/10.1002/ana.410400206.

Saygin, Z. M., Osher, D. E., Norton, E. S., Youssoufian, D. A., Beach, S., Feather, J., Gaab, N., Gabrieli, J., K. N. (2016). Connectivity precedes function in the development of the visual word form area. *Nature Neuroscience, 19*(9). https://doi.org/10.1038/nn.4354.

Saygin, Z. M., Norton, E. S., Osher, D. E., Beach, S. D., Cyr, A. B., Ozernov-Palchik, O., … Gabrieli, J. D. E. (2013). Tracking the roots of reading ability: White matter volume and integrity correlate with phonological awareness in prereading and early-reading kindergarten children. *The Journal of Neuroscience, 33*(33), 13251–13258. https://doi.org/10.1523/jneurosci.4383-12.2013.

Schultz, J. J. (2008). Is dyslexia hereditary? family education network. https://www.school.familyeducation.com/learningdisabilities/ genetics/42788.html. Retrieved from Aug 25, 2008.

Schulz, E., Maurer, U., van der Mark, S., Bucher, K., Brem, S., Martin, E., et al. (2008). Impaired semantic processing during sentence reading in children with dyslexia: Combined fMRI and ERP evidence. *NeuroImage, 41*(1), 153–168. https://doi.org/10.1016/j.neuroimage.2008.02.012.

Shaywitz, B. E., Shaywitz, S. E., Blachman, B. A., Pugh, K. R., Fulbright, R. K., Skudlarski, P., Mencl, W. E., Constable, R. T., Holahan, J. M, Marchione, K. E. Fletcher, J. M., Lyon, G., R., &

Gore, J. C. (2004). Development of left occipitotemporal systems for skilled reading in children after a phonologically-based intervention. *Biological Psychiatry, 55*, 926–933.

Shaywitz, B. A., Shaywitz, S. E., Pugh, K. R., Mencl, W. E., Fulbright, R. K., Skudlarski, P., … Gore, J. C. (2002). Disruption of posterior brain systems for reading in children with developmental dyslexia. *Biological Psychiatry, 52*(2), 101–110. https://doi.org/10.1016/s0006-3223(02)01365-3.

Shaywitz, S. E. (1996). Dyslexia. *Scientific American*, 98–104.

Shaywitz, S. E., Escobar, M. D., Shaywitz, B. A., Fletcher, J. M., & Makuch, R. (1992). Evidence that dyslexia may represent the lower tail of a normal distribution of reading ability. *New England Journal of Medicine, 326,* 145–150.

Shaywitz, S. E., Mody, M., & Shaywitz, B. A. (2006). Neural mechanisms in dyslexia. *Current Directions in Psychological Science, 15*(6), 278–281.

Shaywitz, S. E., & Shaywitz, B. A. (2008). Paying attention to reading: The neurobiology of reading and dyslexia. *Development and Psychopathology, 20*(4), 1329–1349. https://doi.org/10.1017/S0954579408000631.

Shaywitz, S. E., Shaywitz, B. A., Pugh, K. R., Fulbright, R. K., Constable, R. T., Mencl, W. E., … Gore, J. C. (1998). Functional disruption in the organization of the brain for reading in dyslexia. *Proceedings of the National Academy of Sciences, 95*(5), 2636–2641. https://doi.org/10.1073/pnas.95.5.2636.

Silani, G., Frith, U., Demonet, J. F., Fazio, F., Perani, D., Price, C., … Paulesu, E. (2005). Brain abnormalities underlying altered activation in dyslexia: A voxel based morphometry study. *Brain, 128*(10), 2453–2461. https://doi.org/10.1093/brain/awh579.

Simos, P. G., Fletcher, J. M., Bergman, E., Breier, J. I., Foorman, B. R., Castillo, E. M., … & Papanicolaou, A. C. (2002). Dyslexia-specific brain activation profile becomes normal following successful remedial training. *Neurology, 58*(8), 1203–1213.

Simos, P. G., Fletcher, J. M., Sarkari, S., Billingsley-Marshall, R., Denton, C. A., & Papanicolaou, A. C. (2007). Intensive instruction affects brain magnetic activity associated with oral word reading in children with persistent reading disabilities. *Journal of Learning Disabilities, 40*(1), 37–48.

Simos, P. G., Sarkari, S., Castillo, E. M., Billingsley-Marshall, R. L., Pataraia, E., Clear, T., et al. (2005). Reproducibility of measures of neurophysiological activity in Wernicke's area: A magnetic source imaging study. *Clinical Neurophysiology, 116*(10), 2381–2391. https://doi.org/10.1016/j.clinph.2005.06.019.

Siok, W. T., Niu, Z., Jin, Z., Perfetti, C. A., & Tan, L. H. (2008). A structural-functional basis for dyslexia in the cortex of Chinese readers. *Proceedings of the National Academy of Sciences, 105*(14), 5561–5566. https://doi.org/10.1073/pnas.0801750105.

Skottun, B. C. (2005). Magnocellular reading and dyslexia. *Vision Research, 45*(1), 133–134. https://doi.org/10.1016/j.visres.2003.09.039.

Skyttner, L. (2006). *General systems theory: Problems, perspective, practice.* Singapore: World Scientific Publishing. https://doi.org/10.1142/5871.

Smythe, I., & Everatt, J. (2000). Dyslexia diagnosis in different languages. In L. Peer & G. Reid (Eds.), *Multilingualism, literacy and dyslexia.* London: David Fulton.

Snowling, M. J., & Melby-Lervåg, M. (2016). Oral language deficits in familial dyslexia: A meta-analysis and review. *Psychological Bulletin, 142*(5), 498–545.

Specht, K., Hugdahl, K., Ofte, S., Nygård, M., Bjørnerud, A., Plante, E., et al. (2009). Brain activation on pre-reading tasks reveals at-risk status for dyslexia in 6-year-old children. *Scandinavian Journal of Psychology, 50*(1), 79–91. https://doi.org/10.1111/j.1467-9450.2008.00688.x.

Stanovich, K. E. (1986). Matthew effects in reading: Some consequences of individual differences in the acquisition of literacy. *Reading Research Quarterly, 21*(4), 360–407. https://doi.org/10.1598/RRQ.21.4.1.

Stanovich, K. E., & Siegel, L. S. (1994). Phenotypic performance profile of children with reading disabilities: A regression-based test of the phonological-core variable-difference model. *Journal of Educational Psychology, 86*(1), 24.

Stein, J. (2001). The magnocellular theory of developmental dyslexia. *Dyslexia, 7*(1), 12–36. https://doi.org/10.1002/dys.186.

Stein, J. (2014). Dyslexia: The role of vision and visual attention. *Current Developmental Disorders Reports, 1*(4), 267–280. https://doi.org/10.1007/s40474-014-0030-6.

Szalkowski, C. E., Fiondella, C. G., Galaburda, A. M., Rosen, G. D., LoTurco, J. J., & Fitch, R. H. (2012). Neocortical disruption and behavioral impairments in rats following in utero RNAi of candidate dyslexia risk gene Kiaa0319. *International Journal of Developmental Neuroscience, 30*(4), 293–302. https://doi.org/10.1016/j.ijdevneu.2012.01.009.

Tallal, P. (1980). Auditory temporal perception, phonics, and reading disabilities in children. *Brain and Language, 9*(2), 182–198. https://doi.org/10.1016/0093-934X(80)90139-X.

Tallal, P., & Gaab, N. (2006). Dynamic auditory processing, musical experience and language development. *Trends in Neuroscience, 29*(7), 382–390. https://doi.org/10.1016/j.tins.2006.06.003.

Tallal, P., Stark, R., & Mellits, E. (1985). Identification of language-impaired children on the basis of rapid perception and production skills. *Brain and Language, 25*(2), 314–322.

Taylor, J., & Schatschneider, C. (2010). Genetic influence on literacy constructs in kindergarten and first grade: Evidence from a diverse twin sample. *Behavior Genetics, 40*(5), 591–602. https://doi.org/10.1007/s10519-010-9368-7.

Temple, E. (2002). Brain mechanisms in normal and dyslexic readers. *Current Opinion in Neurobiology, 12*(2), 178–183. https://doi.org/10.1016/S0959-4388(02)00303-3.

Temple, E., Poldrack, R. A., Protopapas, A., Nagarajan, S., Salz, T., Tallal, P., … Gabrieli, J. D. E. (2000). Disruption of the neural response to rapid acoustic stimuli in dyslexia: Evidence from functional MRI. *Proceedings of the National Academy of Sciences, 97*(25), 13907–13912. https://doi.org/10.1073/pnas.240461697.

Terras, M. M., Thompson, L. C., & Minnis, H. (2009). Dyslexia and psycho-social functioning: An exploratory study of the role of self-esteem and understanding. *Dyslexia, 15*(4), 304–327.

Thesen, T., McDonald, C. R., Carlson, C., Doyle, W., Cash, S., Sherfey, J., … Halgren, E. (2012). Sequential then interactive processing of letters and words in the left fusiform gyrus. *Nature Communications, 3*, 1284. https://doi.org/10.1038/ncomms2220.

Torgesen, J. K. (2000). Individual differences in response to early interventions in reading: The lingering problem of treatment resisters. *Learning Disabilities Research & Practice, 15*, 55–64.

Torgesen, J., Myers, D., Schirm, A., Stuart, E., Vartivarian, S., Mansfield, W., … & Haan, C. (2006). National assessment of title I: Interim report. Volume II: Closing the reading gap: First year findings from a randomized trial of four reading interventions for striving readers. *National Center for Education Evaluation and Regional Assistance*.

Turkheimer, E., Haley, A., Waldron, M., D'Onofrio, B., & Gottesman, I. I. (2003). Socioeconomic status modified heritability of IQ in young children. *Psychological Science, 14*(6), 623–628. https://doi.org/10.1046/j.0956-7976.2003.psci_1475.x.

Valås, H. (1999). Students with learning disabilities and low-achieving students: Peer acceptance, loneliness, self-esteem, and depression. *Social Psychology of Education, 3*(3), 173–192. https://doi.org/10.1023/A:1009626828789.

Vandermosten, M., Boets, B., Wouters, J., & Ghesquière, P. (2012). A qualitative and quantitative review of diffusion tensor imaging studies in reading and dyslexia. *Neuroscience and Biobehavioral Reviews, 36*(6), 1532–1552. https://doi.org/10.1016/j.neubiorev.2012.04.002.

Vandermosten, M., Vanderauwera, J., Theys, C., De Vos, A., Vanvooren, S., Sunaert, S., … Ghesquière, P. (2015). A DTI tractography study in pre-readers at risk for dyslexia. *Developmental Cognitive Neuroscience, 14*, 8–15. https://doi.org/10.1016/j.dcn.2015.05.006.

Vellutino, F. R., Fletcher, J. M., Snowling, M. J., & Scanlon, D. M. (2004). Specific reading disability (dyslexia): What have we learned in the past four decades? *Journal of Child Psychology and Psychiatry, 45*(1), 2–40.

Vellutino, F. R., Scanlon, D. M., Sipay, E. R., Small, S. G., Pratt, A., Chen, R., et al. (1996). Cognitive profiles of difficult-to-remediate and readily remediated poor readers: Early intervention as a vehicle for distinguishing between cognitive and experiential deficits as basic causes of specific reading disability. *Journal of Educational Psychology, 88,* 601–638.

Wada, J. A., Clarke, R., & Hamm, A. (1975). Cerebral hemispheric asymmetry in humans. Cortical speech zones in 100 adults and 100 infant brains. *Archives of Neurology, 32*(4), 239–246.

Willcutt, E. G., & Pennington, B. F. (2000). Comorbidity of reading disability and attention-deficit/hyperactivity disorder: Differences by gender and subtype. *Journal of Learning Disabilities, 33*(2), 179–191.

Willcutt, E. G., Pennington, B. F., Duncan, L., Smith, S. D., Keenan, J. M., Wadsworth, S., … & Olson, R. K. (2010). Understanding the complex etiologies of developmental disorders: behavioral and molecular genetic approaches. *Journal of Developmental and Behavioral Pediatrics: JDBP, 31*(7), 533.

Wimmer, H., & Goswami, U. (1994). The influence of orthographic consistency on reading development: Word recognition in English and German children. *Cognition, 51*(1), 91–103.

Ziegler, J. C., & Goswami, U. (2005). Reading acquisition, developmental dyslexia, and skilled reading across languages: A psycholinguistic grain size theory. *Psychological Bulletin, 131*(1), 3.